Java™ Web Services Programming

Java™ Web Services Programming

Rashim Mogha, V V Preetham

M&T Books
An imprint of Wiley Publishing, Inc.

Best-Selling Books • Digital Downloads • e-Books • Answer Networks
e-Newsletters • Branded Web Sites • e-Learning

Java™ Web Services Programming

Published by
Wiley Publishing, Inc.
909 Third Avenue
New York, NY 10022
www.wiley.com

Copyright © 2002 by Wiley Publishing, Inc., Indianapolis, Indiana

ISBN: 0-7645-4952-9

Manufactured in the United States of America

10 9 8 7 6 5 4 3 2 1

1O/RU/QY/QS/IN

Published by Wiley Publishing, Inc., Indianapolis, Indiana
Published simultaneously in Canada

For general information on our other products and services or to obtain technical support, please contact our Customer Care Department within the U.S. at 800-762-2974, outside the U.S. at 317-572-3993 or fax 317-572-4002.

Wiley also publishes its books in a variety of electronic formats. Some content that appears in print may not be available in electronic books.

Library of Congress Cataloging-in-Publication Data: 2002108113

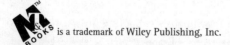

About the Authors

Rashim Mogha is a Microsoft Certified Solution Developer (MCSD). Rashim has had the opportunity to work on varied technical assignments, such as ACT! 2000, SQL Server, Goldmine, A+ certification, Cisco, and Forte for Java. Her work involves design, development, testing, and implementation of instructor-led training courses. Her primary responsibilities include training development executives, project management, instructional review, technical review, and ensuring ISO compliance. She enjoys writing.

V V Preetham provides consultancy services to organizations on J2EE specs and technologies, such as EJB on WebLogic, Java, Tomcat, and XML. V V has a wide experience in working with various Java APIs, Java 2 technologies, BEA WebLogic Server, and Core J2EE patterns.

Credits

EXECUTIVE EDITOR
Chris Webb

PROJECT EDITOR
Sharon Nash

TECHNICAL EDITOR
David Wall

COPY EDITOR
William A. Barton

EDITORIAL MANAGER
Mary Beth Wakefield

**VICE PRESIDENT AND
EXECUTIVE GROUP PUBLISHER**
Richard Swadley

**VICE PRESIDENT AND EXECUTIVE
PUBLISHER**
Bob Ipsen

EXECUTIVE EDITORIAL DIRECTOR
Mary Bednarek

PROJECT COORDINATOR
Nancee Reeves

**GRAPHICS AND PRODUCTION
SPECIALISTS**
Beth Brooks
Kristin McMullan
Shelley Norris
Laurie Petrone
Jeremey Unger

QUALITY CONTROL TECHNICIANS
John Greenough
Andy Hollandbeck
Carl Pierce

PROOFREADING AND INDEXING
TECHBOOKS Production Services

To my mother, Kamla
  — Rashim

Preface

IN TODAY'S BUSINESS SCENARIOS, mergers and acquisitions seem the order of the day. This situation has led to a need for distributed Web applications that can cater to the business needs of the industry. In the past, many in the distributed-technology arena attempted to provide an efficient framework for integrating disparate systems that consist of component-based applications. Such systems, however, were too brittle for change or were very expensive to integrate. They were huge, monolithic code bases, which were difficult to modify or change. The architecture was fixed and probably came from a single vendor. Examples of such systems include CORBA, Distributed Smalltalk, and Java RMI. The effectiveness of these systems was insufficient for use in dynamic e-business frameworks across the Internet. Solutions such as CORBA and RMI required strict adherence to proprietary standards or tight compliance to data structures and a shared context among disparate systems. Because of these constraints, the industry sought a better solution – one that offers a loosely coupled architecture, is reusable and adaptable to change, and is extensible. Web services emerged as the most likely answer to these requirements.

Web services are, in reality, a synergy of different services, consisting of loosely coupled, disparate systems that, in turn, consist of component-based, modular application frameworks. A Web service provides you with a collection of operations and makes them available by using standard interfaces, which the business offering the services thoroughly describes and publishes to a service registry. Distributed clients can then easily locate such services and remotely invoke them via the Web by using standardized messaging formats based on XML.

On a more specific level, Web services are a collection of several related technologies that make up a *technology stack*. Registering and announcing one's Web services involve the use of the following protocols:

- SOAP
- WSDL
- WSFL
- UDDI
- ebXML

The Java platform, with its flexibility, scalability, reliability, and write-once, run-anywhere features, is the de-facto standard that businesses use for developing extensible Web services. Registering more than five million downloads from the Sun site, Java has clearly established itself as the preferred programming language for Web developers. To further ease the task of developers, Sun Microsystems has introduced its Java Web Services Developer Pack.

This Web-services pack is a collection of Application Programming Interfaces (APIs) and architectures developed by Sun Microsystems and the other members of the Java community. These APIs and architectures provide Java support for important Web-services features. This book seeks to provide Web developers with an in-depth knowledge of how to create Web services. The book discusses the Web-services technology stack, which includes UDDI, SOAP, and WSDL. The book also discusses the Java Web-services architecture and the complete suite of Java APIs for XML. This book is meant for all who want to learn how to create Java Web services. It is also ideal for developers who have already created Web services and want to use the Web-services pack to improve their efficiency at their jobs.

Icons Used in This Book

This book uses two icons, Note and Cross-Reference. Here's what these icons mean:

Note icons provide supplemental information about the subject — but generally something that isn't quite the main idea.

This icon directs you to related information in another chapter or on a Web site.

How This Book Is Organized

The basic aim of this book is to equip developers with the knowledge necessary to create Java Web services. The book starts with the basics of Web services. After the reader is thoroughly briefed on the concept of Web services, the book moves on to discuss the Web-services technology stack and the Java Web-services architecture.

The book is divided into the following three parts:

Part 1: Introduction to Web Services

Part 1 provides an overview of Web services. It discusses the need for Web services, goes into detail about the service-oriented architecture (SOA), and describes how SOA fits into the current e-business model. This part also discusses the advantages of the Web-services model over other existing models in the industry.

Part 2: Web Services Technology Stack

This part discusses various components of the Web-services technology stack, such as XML, WSDL, SOAP, and UDDI. The chapters in this part discuss how to implement these Web-services technology-stack components in detail, with the help of numerous examples.

Part 3: The Java Web Services Architecture

Part 3 begins with an introduction to Java Server Pages (JSPs) and servlets. It then discusses J2EE's role in Web services. After thoroughly covering the basics of the Java Web-services architecture, the chapters in this part discuss the following APIs that you use to access Web services:

- ◆ Java API for XML Processing (JAXP)

- ◆ Java API for XML Binding (JAXB)

- ◆ Java API for XML Messaging (JAXM)

- ◆ Java API for XML-based RPC (JAX-RPC)

- ◆ Java API for XML Registries (JAXR)

Part 4: Appendixes

This part includes appendixes that act as a quick reference for readers. This part also contains an appendix on the Java WSDP. This appendix illustrates how to use the WSDP to create Web applications.

Companion Web Site

This book provides a companion Web site from which you can download the code from various chapters. All the code listings reside in zip files at www.wiley.com/ extras under the Java Web Services Programming link. If you don't currently have WinZip, you can download an evaluation version from www.winzip.com.

Acknowledgments

I would like to acknowledge the contribution of all involved in making this book a reality, both at NIIT and Wiley Publishing, Inc. My special thanks go to the project manager at NIIT, Anita Sastry. Without her constant support, this book wouldn't be possible. A very special thanks, as well, goes to Simanta for his timely help. And a BIG *Thanks* to Shweta, Shilpa, and all my dear friends for giving me the support of solid friendship when I needed it the most. I would also like to thank my co-author V V Preetham for his coordination.

Also, I give my special thanks to Acquisitions Editor Christopher K. Webb and Project Editor Sharon Nash for giving me an opportunity to write this book. A very special thanks, too, goes to Technical Editor David Wall and Senior Copy Editor Bill Barton for their valuable inputs and constant support.

— Rashim Mogha

I would like to take the opportunity to thank everybody who was involved in creating this book: At NIIT, project manager Anita Sastry, the graphics team, and the technical editors. At Wiley Publishing, Inc., Acquisitions Editor Christopher K. Webb and Project Editor Sharon Nash, along with Technical Editor David Wall and Senior Copy Editor Bill Barton, for their support and encouragement. I also take this opportunity to thank all who have directly or indirectly contributed in writing this book.

— V V Preetham

Contents at a Glance

Contents

Part III   The Java Web Services Architecture

Part I

Introduction to Web Services

CHAPTER 1
Web Services Architecture

Chapter 1

Web Services Architecture

IN THIS CHAPTER

Web Services – an overview

◆ Service-oriented architecture

◆ Service roles

◆ The technology stack

◆ Architectural processes

◆ The value chain

IN THE PRESENT BUSINESS SCENARIO, *e-business* is the buzzword. The concept of e-business is facilitated by Web services. *Web services* are self-contained, modular applications that are defined, published, and accessed across the Web. This chapter provides an overview of the concept of Web services. It discusses the service-oriented architecture (SOA) and describes how SOA fits in the current e-business model. The chapter also discusses the advantages of the Web-services model over other existing models in the industry.

Web Services – An Overview

In today's competitive era, a global presence seems to be the recipe for success. Almost all businesses are converging toward e-business as the means to make a mark in the global market. With the increasing complexity of the business needs, however, the IT industry quickly realized that providing e-business solutions to the businesses was not easy. Although many technologies, such as Remote Method Invocation (RMI) and Common Object Request Broker Architecture (CORBA) were available, none seemed appropriate for use in dynamic e-business solutions. These technologies required a tight compliance with the back-end data structures and were vulnerable to change. A need existed, therefore, for a technology that enabled the integration of loosely coupled, disparate systems. *Web services* answered this need in the industry.

Web services themselves are made of loosely coupled, disparate systems. These disparate systems, in turn, consist of component-based applications and use standardized messaging formats based on the eXtensible Markup Language (XML).

To understand the applicability of the Web-services model, you need to understand its architecture. Following are the basic components of the Web-services model:

◆ Service-oriented architecture

◆ Service roles

◆ Technology stack

◆ Architectural processes

◆ Value chain

The remainder of this chapter describes each of these components in detail.

Service-Oriented Architecture

Service-oriented architecture (SOA) forms the basis of the Web-services model. SOA has evolved from the *object-oriented model,* in which you treat all entities as *objects.* Similarly, in SOA you treat all entities as *services.* You create services by using objects, which are merely reusable software components. SOA provides a programming model that enables services residing on any network to be published, located, and invoked by other services.

SOA defines the *service model,* which derives from the object model. The service model has the following features:

◆ Service-abstraction

◆ Service-encapsulation

◆ Service-modularity

◆ Service-polymorphism

The following sections go into further detail about each of these features.

Service-abstraction

In the object model, abstraction defines the characteristics of an object. Similarly, in the service model, *service-abstraction* defines the characteristics of a service.

Consider an example: You have an e-shopping application that includes a checkout task. This task consists of two subtasks, one that accesses a credit card verification service and a shipping service for the delivery of goods. The credit card verification service displays a message indicating whether the card is verified successfully. This service is divided into subprocesses, which can include any of the following:

- Authorizing the accessing client system

- Validating the arguments

- Database query and lookup

- Authenticating the credit

- Generating application exceptions

- Returning a logical output

These subprocesses take the following input arguments:

- Cardholder name

- Cardholder address

- Credit card number

- Card expiration date

- Amount to verify

As you may notice, this example can be represented by a *use case,* as shown in Figure 1-1. You use a use case in developing application to model the application and provide a structure for it.

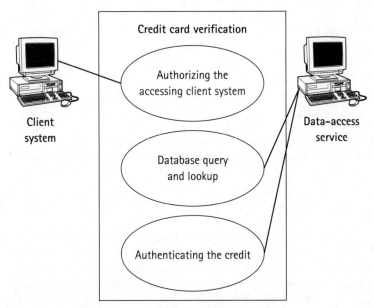

Figure 1-1: Use cases for a credit card verification service

A system boundary defines what the system does to fulfill the objective of the program. The system boundary for the credit card verification service contains the following use cases:

- **Authorizing the accessing client system:** The purpose of this use case is to enables clients to log on to the service after verifying their client IDs. The primary actor is the client system. In this use case, a client system logs in to the service, which authenticates the client ID. The service then sets the context for the client ID to permit access to specific resources. This permission may be based on a policy file.

- **Database query and lookup:** The purpose of this use case is to verify a client's profile. The primary actor is the data-access service. In this use case, the service obtains the client-related information based on the client ID from the database. The service also checks the status of the client ID and verifies the client's profile. The validating the argument subprocess is also performed in this use case.

- **Authenticating the credit:** This use case verifies the credit details of the client. The primary actor is the data-access service. In this use case, the service verifies the input details for the credit card. To do so, the service accesses an external credit database to verify the credit card. After verification, the service authorizes the transaction. After the transaction is complete, the service records the transaction to a database. The service may also record the pattern of service usage.

After the authenticating the credit use case, the more generalized subprocesses, such as generating application exception and returning a logical output subprocess occur.

Notice that this description defines the characteristics of the credit card verification service. This characterizing of a service, based on its rationale, is known as *service-abstraction*.

After defining the characteristics of the credit card verification service, you can uniquely identify this service among other services. You can define service-abstraction, therefore, as the capability to define and characterize the operations of a service.

Service-encapsulation

After defining the characteristics of a service, hiding the rationale processes of the service from the user is essential. Hiding the process from the user of the service is known as *service-encapsulation*. Just as abstraction and encapsulation are complementary to each other in the object model, service-abstraction and service-encapsulation are similarly complementary in the service model.

Service-encapsulation benefits both the user and the implementer. The user benefits from the simplicity of using such services. Users needn't worry about the internal processes of service-abstraction. Neither does a user need to bother about the structural details and can, instead, just provide a plug-and-play logic for service-abstraction. The implementer benefits from the extensibility of such a model. The implementer can replace the existing version of the implementation with an enhanced version without affecting the users.

Service-modularity

Service-modularity partitions the service into loosely coupled modules of service-abstractions that you can combine with each other to create a reusable service library. You may recall from the preceding sections that any application that you place as a service on the Web consists of multiple service-abstractions, which are encapsulated. These service-abstractions can use other service-abstractions within their workflow. For example, a shopping cart service-abstraction might use a credit card verification service-abstraction in its workflow. This interdependency of service-abstractions calls for a library of services. Such a library is beneficial in the following ways:

- ◆ The service library can catalog the service-abstractions based on the rationale of the service.

- ◆ The service library provides a common mechanism for reusing service-abstractions.

- ◆ The service library categorizes the use of service-abstractions.

- ◆ The service library acts as a container for all service-abstractions.

The benefits of modularity lie in placing the application into packages, modules, or libraries, which already exist in the Object Oriented (OO) world.

The basic idea behind service-modularity is to provide service-abstractions modules that, in turn, are made up of other service-abstractions. Although these service-abstractions are bundled in a given module, they have no tight semantic binding with each other. These service-abstractions in a module, however, are cohesive, as they relate with other service-abstractions in the module.

To understand service-modularity, consider the checkout task module example that I discuss in the section "Service-abstraction," a little earlier in this chapter. The checkout module consists of the credit verification service and the shipping service, which are both service-abstractions. They are loosely coupled, yet they are related to each other.

Service-polymorphism

Polymorphism is not a new concept in the current industry. It is widely used in the object model to achieve extensibility. *Service-polymorphism* provides the capability to invoke different service behaviors by using a single, generically defined service interface of a service-abstraction. The service interface exposes various service methods of a Web service. Service-polymorphism enables the dynamic runtime binding of services. This feature enables a service to use another service dynamically at runtime.

To understand service-polymorphism, consider an example of a publishing service. If you assume a particular service-abstraction, the Web services for publishing framework, you can use this service-abstraction in the following polymorphic manner.

Consider that this service-abstraction defines a generic service interface, which takes a common set of data as input so that it can publish that data in the appropriate manner. Given this generic service interface, a service provider can define a specific service module to convert the data into, say, an Adobe PDF representation. As a client, suppose that you need to use a service to publish data in the Adobe format. In such a situation, you can add the appropriate code in your client application to use a specific implementation of a generic service interface to publish the data as a PDF file. Later, however, your needs may change from the existing PDF publishing standard to a more industry-applicable Wireless Markup Language (WML) (or similar) format. In such a situation, you do not need to break the client code, because the code is built around a generic service interface. You just need to add the appropriate code in your application that enables you to use this generic service interface for a specific implementation to publish the data as WML.

All the service provider needs to do is to provide a different implementation for the same service interface. A well-encapsulated service-abstraction provides the extensibility that you require in this situation.

This process of providing a loosely coupled service-abstraction of a generic service interface is known as service-polymorphism.

The difference between the object-polymorphism and service-polymorphism is that the concept of inheritance is absent in service-polymorphism. In the object model, you achieve polymorphism by inheriting an already existing class. In the service model, however, service hierarchy is not required because service-encapsulation encompasses the necessary steps to arrive at polymorphic behavior.

Service Roles

A Web-service application can play different roles in SOA. To understand the architectural processes, you need to know about these roles. Following are the roles that Web-service applications can play in the SOA:

- ◆ **Service provider:** A *service provider* supplies a Web-service application or a Web-service module in the SOA. The service provider must conform to the principles of the service model before publishing the Web service on the Web. Publishing is a process in which the service provider registers the service interface of the service-abstraction to a centralized registry.

◆ **Service broker:** You can consider a *service broker* as a centralized directory that you can use to provide directory services, such as registering and discovery. The service broker is responsible for making the Web service available to any potential requestor. A service broker is also known as a *service registry.*

◆ **Service requestor:** A *service requestor* is a potential client of the Web-services module. It is the consumer of a service that the service provider makes available through the service broker. The service requestor looks up or discovers the services that are available in the service registry. After finding the desired service, the requestor can use the respective provider to invoke the available service.

Figure 1-2 depicts the generalized interactions between these roles.

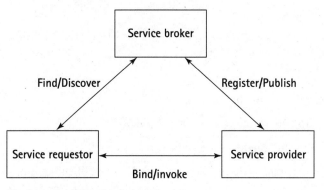

Figure 1-2: Interaction between roles

The following sections discuss these roles in terms of their behavior.

Service provider

Service provider is a generic role, applicable to either a Web-services module or a business entity. More specifically, this role comprises the following phases:

◆ Creation (roles that people play)

■ Analysis and design

■ Development and testing of the service framework

■ Documentation

■ Deployment of the services on the processing nodes

◆ Publishing (role that businesses play)

◆ Perseverance (roles that Web-service processing nodes play)

■ Waiting for a requestor to bind to the provider nodes

■ Management of a dormant state through some activation logic

■ Lease management

The service provision provided by a service provider includes the application-level services, such as transaction service and messaging service that apply to the industry-specific business context. No limitations exist in the availability of application-level services in the current industry. The biggest problem, however, is to make services that the existing application service providers (ASPs) already provide interoperable. SOA solves this problem, because loose coupling, interoperability, and dynamic service usage are the focal points of SOA.

Service broker

A *service broker* is a centralized registry that contains an index of all the published services of the service providers. You can consider the following as some of the phases in the service-broker role:

◆ Startup and registration of the broker to a centralized URL

◆ Providing a portal for the registration of Web services

◆ Making the services available to the consumers

◆ Managing request-response activities at the time of both publishing and subscription

A service broker, as a part of the Web services architecture, simplifies the process of publishing and subscribing. It also handles the following life-cycle tasks:

◆ Connection management: A service broker manages the connection of the service requestor and the service provider to it.

◆ Transaction monitoring: Service broker monitors the business transaction between the service requestor and the service provider.

◆ Event services

◆ Security mapping: Service broker handles security-related issues in a service transaction.

◆ Profile exchange between the processing nodes on the service-provider architecture

◆ Component registry on the service broker

- ◆ Connector discovery: Service brokers assists in the discovery of service endpoints.

- ◆ Content-based routing: Service brokers provide routing of messages based on the content of the message.

The respective components in the service broker architecture manage these tasks. Unless specified, these components default to a centralized registry for publishing the Web services. Technically, you can consider a service broker as a combination of an application server and such Web-services standards as WSDL, UDDI, SOAP, and WSFL.

Refer to Chapters 3, 4, and 5 to know more about WSDL, SOAP, and UDDI.

The service-broker role is the most interesting and most vexed role, because the lines between the provider-registry contract and the registry-requestor contract fade as for this role takes on more functionality. You must, therefore, understand the specifics of service provision that the service broker provides. You should also analyze the need to use the functionalities of the service broker.

Service requestor

A *service requestor* is a distributed client on the Internet who is interested in availing of the service that the provider offers. A service requestor can be a person who is browsing the Internet, a business organization, or simply another Web-services application that uses published services.

The following stages are associated with the service-requestor role:

- ◆ Preliminary
  - ■ Prepare a requirement list
  - ■ Classify the requirements based on services
  - ■ Draft a plan of action
- ◆ Discovery
  - ■ Look for a central registry for services that can satisfy the current needs
  - ■ Discover those services
  - ■ Obtain the proxy for the service-abstraction from the provider

- ◆ Invocation

  - ■ Bind to the service-abstraction on the processing nodes of the provider

  - ■ Invoke the service by using the service interface that the provider publishes

The service requestor can participate in the Web-services architecture by using the service-abstractions that it obtains from the registry. The service broker can mediate for a content-based exchange of messages at the time of invocation. The service broker can also become available on the processing nodes at the provider's end to handles all the application-level testing.

The requestor usually binds to the provider's framework at runtime, which is why such a framework is called *dynamic*. After binding to the provider framework, the requestor can hold such binds persistently through out the lifetime of the application architecture, or the requestor can participate in a lease contract. If a requestor binds persistently, the requestor is not constrained to a particular time span to use the service. If a requestor participates in a lease contract, the requestor can use the service only for the time specified in the contract.

After the lease time ends, the service-broker architecture generates appropriate events that either renews or terminates the lease.

Technology Stack

The *technology stack* is the component of the Web-services model that provides a high-level view of the layered architecture of SOA. The technology stack consists of open industry *standards*. The following standards constitute the technology stack of the Web-services model:

- ◆ Simple Object Access Protocol (SOAP)

- ◆ Web Services Description Language (WSDL)

- ◆ Web Services Flow Language (WSFL)

- ◆ Universal Description, Discovery and Integration (UDDI)

- ◆ Electronic Business Extensible Markup Language (ebXML)

These standards in the technology stack help derive the relationships between the service roles. In addition to these standards, some SOA standards and protocols also make the technology stack. A partial list of these protocols and standards is as follows:

- ◆ Hypertext Transfer Protocol (HTTP)

- ◆ Simple Mail Transfer Protocol (SMTP)

- ◆ File Transfer Protocol (FTP)

- ◆ Message broker

- ◆ Internet Inter-ORB Protocol (IIOP)

These so-called layers of standards make up the current technology stack of the SOA. Some additional evolving standards can also be introduced in the technology stack of the SOA later. For now, however, I consider only these rudimentary elements as the building blocks in the SOA stack.

Figure 1-3 gives a conceptual overview of the SOA stack. The diagram provides the basic idea of how UDDI, SOAP, WSDL, ebXML, and WSFL fit as layers into the Web-services model.

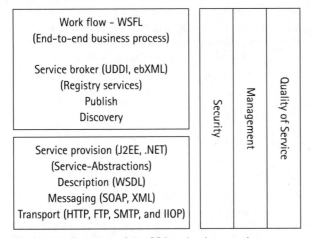

Figure 1-3: Overview of the SOA technology stack

Notice that the standards appear in the appropriate layers of the Web-services model. The right-hand columns provide the operational aspects of the SOA stack, which are common for all the layers and span the entire Web-services model.

Figure 1-4 explains the relationship between the SOA roles, based on the standards that they use to relate with each other.

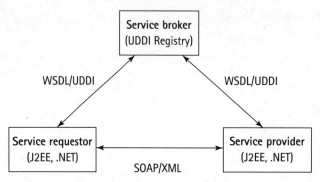

Figure 1-4: Relationship between the SOA roles

Notice that the service-abstractions are marked as either J2EE (SunONE) or .NET. Although these are the most prominent service-abstraction implementations available in the industry, service-abstractions are not limited to only these specific implementations. You can choose any existing legacy code and provide a Web-services wrapper, which exposes those services to the Internet. In addition, service-provision frameworks from different vendors also provide various benefits.

Some of the layers present in the SOA stack are still considered as evolving. Figure 1-5 illustrates the core and the emergent standards of the SOA stack.

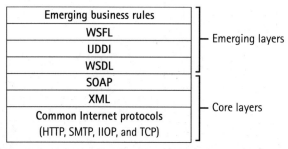

Figure 1-5: Core and emergent standards of the SOA stack

Web services are vendor driven and, therefore, need standards for interoperability. These standards are actually driven by a group of vendors forming organizations such as RosettaNet, OASIS, or ebXML, are all initiatives for interoperability standards among different vendors.

Given an emergent layer such as UDDI, the interoperability standard is proposed by the bodies that initiate the standard in an appropriate stack of its own to justify its emergence. Figure 1-6 shows the proposed interoperability stack for UDDI and how it fits with other standards.

Universal Service Interop Protocols (These layers are not yet defined)	
UDDI	Interop Stack
UDDI	
SOAP	
XML	
Common Internet protocols	

Figure 1-6: The interoperability stack for UDDI

The interoperability stack runs alongside all the derived standards, which suggests that interoperability among the layers of standards is also a primary concern in the SOA stack.

Architectural Processes

This section provides an elaborate view of the processes involved in the working framework of the Web-services model. Following are the primary processes involved in the Web-services model:

- ◆ Description
- ◆ Discovery
- ◆ Invocation

You can relate with these processes with the SOA roles that provide a high-level view of the interaction among the roles. In any given Web-services implementation is a particular order in which you manage the execution of the processes. To begin, you create a service-abstraction that you encapsulate. You then compartmentalize service-abstractions into their respective modules. You describe such modules by using a service interface and publish the information about the service to a registry. The clients who are interested in availing these services need to locate them in the centralized registry on the Internet. After finding an appropriate service framework, the clients need to bind to the processing nodes or the application server of the service provider. Then, the clients need to invoke the service by using a standard protocol from the SOA stack.

Figure 1-7 depicts a sequential flow among the SOA roles on the UDDI framework and the use of the standards presented in the SOA stack. It also provides the flow for executing these standards from the perspective of various description, discovery, and invocation scenarios.

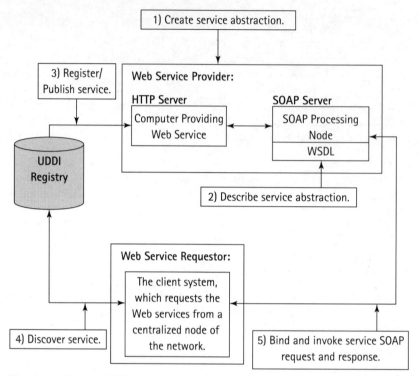

Figure 1-7: Sequential flow based on the UDDI framework

The preceding figure shows the following sequence of execution:

1. **Creation of service-abstraction:** In this step, you create an elaborate framework of an application module, conforming to the specifications of the service model. You create this framework by using the available programming models, such as J2EE or .NET.

2. **Description of service-abstraction:** You provide a service interface to the service module. You describe the service interface by using the Web Services Description Language (WSDL).

3. **Register/publish the service:** You publish or register the service interface to a centralized registry. The standards involved in registration are WSDL and UDDI.

4. **Discovery of service:** A client or a service requestor who is interested in the service looks up the service in the central registry, based on the service functionality that the service provides. The standards used are WSDL and UDDI.

5. **Binding and invocation:** The service requestor, after discovering the service, binds to the appropriate SOAP processing node of the service

provider. After the binding succeeds, the service requestor can use the service that the application server on the service provider's end makes available. The invocation semantics are generally termed as a method-based request and response model. This request and response uses the SOAP and XML messaging standards.

The following sections further discuss the primary processes in the Web-services model.

Description

Conceptually, *description* is the first distinguishable primary process of the Web-services model. Description is a process where the service provider describes the service-abstraction for a service. This description involves the following general semantics of the application:

- Structural description: Description of the service structure.

- Service interface description: Description of the interface that exposes the service methods.

- Description of types: Description of the data types involved in the service.

- Description of messages that the service module can accept: Description of the types of message that the service accepts.

- Description of the operation semantics: Description of the operation semantics that the service follows.

- Description of the ports: Description of the address for binding.

- Description of the port types: Description of the operations that can be performed on the service.

- Description of the bindings involved: Description of how the client needs to bind with the service.

- Description of services: Description of the service such as the parameters that the service accepts.

- Resource description: Description of the resources that the service uses.

- Process-flow description: Description of the process flow of the service application.

The description process contains a stack of its own. Figure 1-8 provides the architecture of the description stack.

| Work flow and end-to-end process description (WSFL) |
| Resource Description Framework (RDF) |
| Service-Interface (WSDL) |
| Structure (XML Schemas) |

Figure 1–8: Architecture of the description stack

As you may notice, the description stack starts by describing the structure that's using the XML schemas. The next step in the description stack is to describe the service-abstraction, which it does by using WSDL. The syntax of the WSDL enables you to describe the message types, ports, port types, service, and binding. At the core, a WSDL file is a XML file that describes the service-abstractions in a platform-neutral, programming-neutral, and architecture-neutral manner. The Resource Description Framework (RDF) is actually an emerging standard that provides the description of the Web-services model in a software-independent manner. WSFL is one of the initiatives in the process flow and pattern descriptions. The WSFL standard describes the end-to-end flow of the business processes involved in smoothly executing the application service logic.

 The WSDL standard is primarily based on other XML technologies, such as schemas and namespaces.

Discovery

The process of *discovery* is the next sequence in executing the Web-services model. In this process, a client or service requestor looks for services in a standard registry. The client then discovers the service on the registry. The following two steps are involved in finding a Web service.

1. Lookup

2. Discovery

Figure 1-9 gives a generalized picture of the discovery stack of a standard service registry.

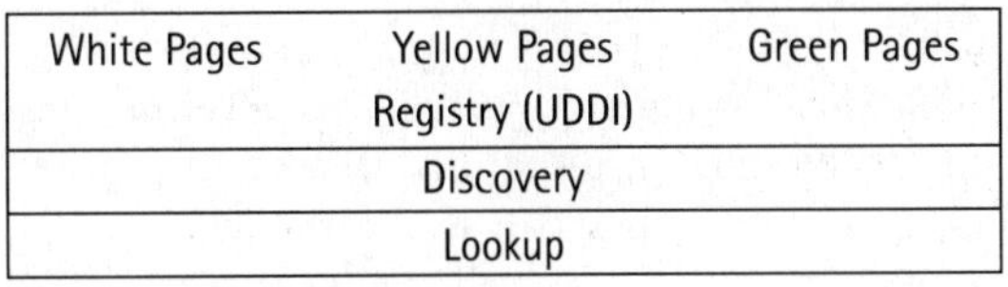

White Pages	Yellow Pages	Green Pages
	Registry (UDDI)	
	Discovery	
	Lookup	

Figure 1-9: The discovery stack

The main component in the discovery stack is the *registry*. The registry is also referred to as a *directory*. The registry doesn't always need to involve UDDI. It can also be a standards-based repository such as ebXML or a service broker that complies with the Web-services standards.

UDDI, which is generally used, provides a centralized registry for Web services so that they gain *location transparency*, a concept with roots in the distributed-computing arena. Consider a service-abstraction that is available on a SOAP processing node called "A" in an implementation. A certain client may be interested in obtaining this service. If the client is manually informed of location "A" of the service module, that client needs to write the necessary logic to statically bind to location A. This approach works fine as long as the service module remains available through location "A." If you relocate the service to a faster processing node, available in location "B," however, the existing code of the client, which statically binds to location "A," breaks.

To counter such a scenario, the distributed-computing model provides directory services in the form of registries so that the service requestor doesn't need to write code to statically bind to the service-abstraction. Instead, the requestor can look up a centralized UDDI registry for the service (by its functionality, as opposed to its name) and dynamically bind to such a service. If the service is available at location "A," the client can dynamically bind to such a service through the UDDI framework. If the service is relocated, the client doesn't need to change the client-side plug-in logic for the service, provided the service uses the same UDDI framework because the client can still dynamically bind to such a service through the UDDI framework even if it moves to some other location.

The UDDI registry is actually categorized into different directory services. Following are the available directories under the UDDI registry:

♦ White Pages

♦ Yellow Pages

♦ Green Pages

The following sections describe each of these directories.

WHITE PAGES

White Pages provides a directory mechanism for registering the Web services specific to the name of the business entity, contact information, IDs, or any other description. If clients have any of this information, they can search the white pages of the UDDI to look up an appropriate service.

YELLOW PAGES

Yellow Pages provides a directory mechanism for registering the Web services specific to the services themselves. They also register the product index of the service. The provider can categorize the service under geographic location or under a specific industry code for the business entity.

GREEN PAGES

Green Pages provides a directory mechanism for registering the Web services specific to the functionality of the service. A service provider publishes a service-abstraction based on e-business rules, operational descriptions, invocation descriptions, and data-binding aspects of the service-abstraction. Service requestors or clients can look up the service, depending on the required functionality.

Figure 1-10 shows the relationship between the specifications, the XML schema, and the UDDI business-registry that provides "register once, published everywhere" access to information about Web services.

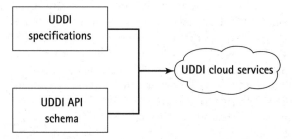

Figure 1-10: Relationship between UDDI specifications and XML schema to provide UDDI service

The UDDI specifications and schema are used by service brokers that provide registry service to build discovery services on the Internet. These discovery services provide a consistent publishing interface and enable the discovery of services through programs.

Invocation

After you create a module and define the necessary interface for it, you publish that module to a registry. This publishing is then categorized based on the functionality, business ID, or geographic location of the service and placed under the appropriate directory.

Eventually, the service requestor looks for the service. After discovering the service, the requestor binds to the relative processing server of the service provider and then invokes the service.

In this section, I explain the *invocation* process by considering the SOAP standards and the XML messaging standards that support the smooth execution of the services involved.

The invocation process is based on the following activities:

◆ Bind

◆ Remote Procedure Call

The preceding activities are performed on top of a standards-based protocol, such as SOAP and XML.

Figure 1-11 provides a representation of the invocation stack.

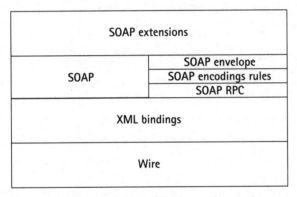

Figure 1-11: Representation of the invocation stack

As you can see, the invocation stack has the *wire protocol* as its base. A wire protocol is a protocol that the underlying transport layer supports. This layer provides the message bindings to the underlying Internet layers, such as HTTP, SMTP, FTP, and Message. The next layer is the XML layer, which provides the standard XML binding for the wire protocols. On top of the XML layer is the SOAP protocol (as of SOAP specification 1.2). The SOAP protocol provides a software-neutral, wire-protocol-neutral, and architecture-neutral execution. SOAP is the core protocol on which the invocation semantics is based. The design goals of SOAP are simplicity and extensibility.

Value Chain

Web services seem to be a very promising proposition for leveraging investments for a better ROI (Return On Investments). Value chain of a Web service is a combination of the service supplier and other suppliers that work together to add value to the service to satisfy market demands.

This section discusses the Web-services infrastructure necessary to provide a value proposition in the *value chain* of the Web-services model. Following is a partial list of the components of the Web-services infrastructure:

- ◆ Web-services standards

  - SOAP: SOAP is a standard protocol for information exchange.

  - UDDI/ebXML: UDDI and ebXML are standards for providing business registries.

  - WSDL: WSDL is a standard for describing Web services in a registry.

  - WSFL: WSFL is a standard XML language to describe Web services composition.

  - XML: XML is the standard data format used in Web services.

- ◆ Service roles

  - Provider: A provider is one who provides a service.

  - Registry: A registry publishes the service provided by a service provider.

  - Requestor: A requestor is one who consumes the service.

- ◆ Modules of disparate systems

- ◆ Wire protocol

  - Internet: Internet is a collection of computer networks that are interconnected.

  - TCP/IP, UDP, HTTP/HTTPS/HTTPR, SMTP: These are transporting protocols of the Web service framework.

  - Messaging (synchronous, asynchronous): Messaging is the process of transmission of SOAP messages in the Web service framework.

  - Network OS

- ◆ Implicit services

  - Clustering: Clustering is the integration of workstations, storage devices and interconnection to form a single system.

  - Fault tolerance: Fault tolerance is the design of computer systems that do not get affected in the case of failure of a component. At such situation a back up component provides the service.

  - Parallel processing: Parallel processing means the processing of instructions by multiple processors to reduce processing time.

- Load balancing: Load balancing is the division of work between computers to provide faster service.

- Failover: Failover is a design to encounter service failures.

◆ Distributed services

- Distributed garbage collection: Distributed garbage collection is the process of recycling of unused memory.

- Activation: Activation is the process of transferring a persistent component to memory.

- Object-by-reference: Object-by-reference allows a reference to a object to be passed to a remote system over the wire.

- Distributed file system: Distributed file system allows a client to work with data stored in a server effortlessly.

- Distributed transactions: Distributed transaction enables client to easily begin, commit, and rollback service transactions in a distributed environment.

You need to take all these components into consideration before designing a Web-services application module.

Based on the preceding components, you can derive a value chain for the Web-services model. You can consider the following the major players in the Web-services value chain:

◆ Standards body

◆ Framework providers

◆ Tool and product vendors

◆ Web Services Developers (WSD)

◆ Web Services Marketers (WSM)

◆ Web Services Providers (WSP)

◆ Web Services Consumers (WSC)

The following sections describe the roles of various components in the Web-services value chain.

Standards body

A *standards body* is a group of organizations that ponder over the benefits of a particular Web-services standard such as SOAP or WSDL. A standards body guards the openness and interoperability of the Web-services technology. Some examples of these bodies are W3C, IETF, and RosettaNet.

Framework providers

Framework providers are those entities that develop the rules of engagement for standards and the architectural perspectives on how to integrate the existing services and evolve. A very noticeable line exists between the standards body and the framework providers. The providers play an active role in the standards body, but their respective frameworks concentrate on using the standards to provide brand positioning for their own products and services. Some examples of frameworks are SunONE, .NET, and Hewlett Packard's (HP) eSpeak.

Tool and product vendors

These entities form a category of large and small business vendors who provide the tools that automate some or most of the development pragmatics of e-business. They provide Web-services-compliant tools, such as application servers and databases, appropriately segmented for business-to-business integration (B2Bi), business-to-consumer (B2C), peer-to-peer (P2P), supply chain, electronic customer relationship management (eCRM), and enterprise resource planning (ERP). Examples of such product vendors include IBM, Ariba, Sun, Microsoft, Hewlett Packard, and BowStreet.

Web Services Developers (WSD)

Web Services Developers are those engineers who provide the manpower services to create and maintain the Web-services infrastructure. These are the software architects, programmers, and managers who are well qualified in the software-engineering principles specific to Web-services technology.

Web Services Marketers (WSM)

Web Services Marketers make up the business- or the selling-side representation of Web services. They promote the adoption of emerging Web-services. They aim for the advancement of the technology in the business community. Without the WSMs creating the necessary demand in selling such services, the industry would crumble.

Web Services Providers (WSP)

Web Services Providers are like the application service providers (ASPs) of the current era. They are a combination of WSD and WSM. They provide the application-service modules to provide such utility services as leasing, metering, and accessing application-specific interfaces.

Web Services Consumers (WSC)

Web Services Consumers are on the receiving end of the Web services spectrum and on the giving end of the economy. They are the mass community that provides the much-needed impetus for generating the economy. These are the requestors and consumers who use Web services to solve their business needs.

Summary

This chapter discusses SOA as a service model. The chapter then discusses the SOA roles. It provides a brief overview of the technology stack of the SOA. The chapter also explains the primary processes involved in executing the framework and the relationship between the SOA roles. Finally, it discusses the components that make up the value chain of such a Web service.

Part II

Web Services Technology Stack

Chapter 2

XML

IN THIS CHAPTER

- ◆ Introduction to XML
- ◆ XML fundamentals
- ◆ XML namespaces

INTEGRATION SEEMS TO BE THE MOST IMPORTANT TERM in use in the present business industry – and for a good reason. Recently, Tom Berquist, the managing director of research at Goldman Sachs said, "For every dollar spent on an application, corporations spend an additional seven dollars on integration." This statistic is valid as long as a solution for integration problems is found. The present computing generation is close to zeroing in a possible solution for disparate systems that require a long time to make interoperable with each other. That solution? XML.

This chapter provides a substantial overview of e*X*tensible *Markup Language* (XML). It discusses the prerequisites of XML, which helps in you understanding the protocols of the technology stack. The chapter also discusses the fundamentals of XML, including creating the markup document, declarations, and namespaces in the XML fundamentals and XML namespaces sections.

An Introduction to XML

XML, in combination with other essential protocols such as SOAP, provides a comprehensive solution to the problems of data portability and integration standards. XML provides the substantive data-portability standard for application integration, while SOAP provides the channel protocols for sending messages across such ubiquitous technologies as HTTP.

In focusing on Web services, a group of dissimilar systems help you synergize the potential of distributed computing, especially on the Internet. Through the use of Web services, you can enable all clients to access everything from an atomic component that loaded onto a generic-reusable library to a fully blown vertical application that can solve a industry problems, such as problems in banking and supply chain applications. A generic-reusable library is a generic library that can be used by dissimilar systems. A vertical application includes a complete line of activities of an industry. You can commercialize client access to such Web services through use of a subscription channel. The client systems themselves can range from a handheld device running Symbian or Palm to a server running Solaris or Linux.

Enterprises have tried for ages to determine the right balance between homogenous systems built on the same platform and the simulations of homogeneity on different systems. Java is an indispensable platform for maintaining such homogenous simulations on heterogeneous systems. XML is and is sure to become the great leveler in homogenizing data on heterogeneous collaborations.

XML Fundamentals

Although this book does not dig into the intricacies of XML, knowing the fundamentals of XML is important. After gaining a basic knowledge of XML, assimilating other Web-service technologies, such as WSDL and SOAP, becomes quite easy.

XML is an industry standard for creating languages such as HTML or minilanguages such as XPath, and Regular Expressions that represent data. Unlike HTML, which is also a markup language, XML is not limited to just the presentation or display of data. XML is a markup language that you can use as a tool for creating other languages that consist of tags and attributes, which you can then use to represent data in a meaningful way. The advantage of using XML is that you can place such generic data containers into dissimilar applications so that the applications can understand the data format within the containers for easy processing.

As an example, consider representing simple information about stock, such as the stock price for some companies represented by specific ticker symbols. The elements that come into play are listed in Table 2.1.

TABLE 2-1 ELEMENTS REPRESENTING STOCK INFORMATION

Element	Value
Ticker	OPN
Company Name	Open Systems, Inc.
Stock Price	14
Ticker	PROP
Company Name	Proprietary Systems, Inc.
Stock Price	54

You can represent the preceding information in HTML by using the following markup:

```
<HTML>
<BODY>
<H1>
Ticker: OPN<DIV>
Company Name: Open Systems, Inc.<DIV>
Stock Price: 14<DIV>
<HR>
Ticker: PROP<DIV>
Company Name: Proprietary Systems, Inc.<DIV>
Stock Price: 54<DIV>
</BODY>
</HTML>
```

In the preceding code, notice that some tags, such as <H1>, <HR>, and <DIV>, have an opening tag but no closing tag. Even if you write such dirty code, the browsers are tolerant of such markup to display the contents appropriately. Now, suppose that you use this information in your Web site. In addition, assume that your clients depend on such information to build their systems.

I'm going to play the role of a client for a moment. I, as a client, must write an application that actually looks up the site that contains a list of prices for certain stock symbols. More specifically, if I need to find the current closing price of the OPN symbol so that I can use that information in my Web site, I must write a pattern searching code, which looks for a string pattern matching Ticker: OPN on the HTML page. After writing the code to find the matching pattern, I'd write logic that skips the next line (which contains the company name) and gets right to the line displaying the price. That way, I'm writing an algorithm, which searches for a string pattern and eventually skips some lines to find the price. This code (the client code) would work as long as the Web site that contains the stock information does not change its presentation style. That is a tall order. If, for some reason, the stock-price Web site decides to change its presentation from the current one, the client code probably breaks. But that's not the only problem with this approach. Writing code that searches for patterns and then repeatedly skips some lines to find the necessary information is also cumbersome. To understand this concept better, suppose that you change the presentation of the stock information to the following version:

```
<HTML>
  <BODY>
    <H1> Stock Info </H1>
        Symbol: OPN<DIV>
        Price: 14<DIV>
        Name: Open Systems Inc.<DIV>
    <HR>
        Symbol: PROP<DIV>
        Price: 54<DIV>
        Name: Proprietary Systems Inc.<DIV>  </BODY>
</HTML>
```

As you can see, the preceding code includes no string that matches the search pattern `Ticker: OPN`. Therefore, any change in the presentation style of the stock Web site would break the client code on the client's application. If discrepancies can occur with the client code for such a simple application, imagine the chaos that could ensue with a vast, real-time stock tracking system that collates information across many Web sites. Although, you probably wouldn't think of using the preceding logic to track your ticker, you'd be surprised to hear that many actual applications currently run on this strategy. At present, many applications on the Internet search HTML pages for information based on such a predefined pattern. This is a formula for disaster.

If you want an efficient solution for the preceding problem, I advise you to present all your data in an XML application. Following is a sample XML file for the aforementioned scenario:

```
<? xml version="1.0" ?>
<stock>
    <stockinfo ticker="OPN">
        <company>Open Systems Inc.</company>
        <price>14</price>
    </stockinfo>
    <stockinfo ticker="PROP">
        <company>Proprietary Systems Inc.</company>
        <price>54</price>
    </stockinfo>
</stock>
```

Notice that the XML file contains no presentation or display-style information. This file is a pure data container. This file probably cannot be rendered successfully as an HTML page unless you have an exceptional browser. Other technologies in the XML repertoire, however, would handle such information, among them CSS, XSL, XSLT, XSL:FO, and XHTML. (Not that you need a working knowledge of all these technologies, but knowing the acronyms is a good start.)

What purpose, then, would this XML file serve? For one, it is a generic data container in a character format that humans can understand—unlike the RDBMS format. Second and more important, it is very efficient and easy to use to search for appropriate information on a particular ticker. Even if you change the position of company information relative to price, you can be certain that the price tag always calls price, no matter where that information is presented. By using this method, you can write client code that first looks up the `stockinfo` hierarchy to match the appropriate ticker attribute. After the appropriate ticker is found, you can look for a child that states `price` and—voila!—you have the required information.

Creating a parse tree for such an XML file also makes some sense. *Parse trees* are nothing but a hierarchical representation of all elements and their nodes and subnodes as a tree in the memory. Creating a parse tree for XML files is very easy, because they are *well-formed.*

Well-formed XML documents — the rules

A *well-formed XML document* is an XML document that follows the XML syntax and yields a positive test if you parse it. The well-formedness constraints for an XML document are as follows:

- Every opening tag must have an appropriate closing tag.

- All tags and attributes are case-sensitive.

- Empty tags must be closed as standalone tags.

- Tags cannot overlap each other.

- Attribute values must be presented between quotes.

- All tags have only one root. All the tags must either directly or indirectly be the children of the root.

The following sections elaborate these well-formedness constraints.

EVERY OPENING TAG SHOULD HAVE AN APPROPRIATE CLOSING TAG

One of the most important rules determining the well-formedness of an XML document is that an opening tag must always have a closing tag. Following is a valid example:

```
<tag>some info</tag>
<anothertag>some more info</anothertag>
```

In the preceding example, you have an opening tag (`<tag>`), a closing tag (`</tag>`), and some information that is relevant to the tag between the opening and closing tags. All open tags must always be appropriately closed. You cannot leave an open tag unclosed as you can in HTML.

Following is an invalid example:

```
<H1>I am a header
    <H2>A sub header
```

Opening and closing tags are also known as *start* and *end tags*. The use of start and end tags is seemingly more politically correct than that of opening and closing tags.

ALL TAGS AND ATTRIBUTES ARE CASE-SENSITIVE

In a well-formed document, all tags and attributes are case-sensitive. Following is a valid example:

```
<tag>some info</tag>
```

Following is an invalid example:

```
<Tag>some info</tAG>
```

EMPTY TAGS MUST BE CLOSED AS STANDALONE TAGS

An empty tag does not contain any content. In a well-formed XML document, all empty tags must be closed. Following is a valid example of this rule:

```
<H1>Some Info</H1>
<HR/>
```

You can alternatively specify empty tags as follows:

```
<HR></HR>
<H2>Some more info</H2>
```

In the preceding code, <HR> is an empty tag with no content. In such cases, you can create a standalone tag, <HR/>, instead of <HR></HR>, and save yourself some typing.

Following is an invalid example because the <HR> tag lacks the front slash (/):

```
<H1>Some Info</H1>
<HR>
<H2>Some more info</H2>
```

TAGS CANNOT OVERLAP EACH OTHER

Consider the following code:

```
<H1><B>Some Info</B></H1>
```

In the preceding code, notice the layering effect. Some XML authors use the layers of an onion as an example. If you cut a cross-section of an onion, you see that every layer fully contains another. You never see the layers overlapping. The same holds for XML tags. The last tag that you open is the first tag closed and so on, until the first tag becomes the last that you close.

Following is an invalid example:

```
<H1><B>Some Info</H1></B>
```

This well-formedness constraint makes checking the well-formedness of a XML document easier for the parser. Every time that the parser comes across a start tag, it pushes the tag onto a stack. Every time that it comes across a matching end tag, it pops the start tag out of the stack. If no tags are left after the parser pops all start tags, the document is well-formed. If you come across an end tag without a matching start tag at any time during the parsing stage, the document is not well-formed.

ATTRIBUTE VALUES SHOULD BE PRESENTED BETWEEN QUOTES

The values of all attributes must be enclosed in quotes, as shown in the following example:

```
<stockinfo ticker="OPN">...</stockinfo>
```

In the preceding code, the tag – or, more specifically, the element – in consideration is the stockinfo element. As a matter of fact, tags are known as *elements* if you want to be technically precise. The attribute name for the element stockinfo is ticker. The value for the ticker attribute must always appear between quotation marks.

Following is an invalid example:

```
<stockinfo ticker=OPN>...</stockinfo>
```

ALL TAGS HAVE ONLY ONE ROOT

Consider the following example:

```
<HTML>
  <HEAD>
    <TITLE>Welcome page</TITLE>
  </HEAD>
  <BODY>
      Hello World
  </BODY>
</HTML>
```

In the preceding example, notice that the code contains a single root, <HTML>, that encompasses all the other elements in the file.

Following is an invalid example:

```
<HEAD>
  <TITLE>Welcome page</TITLE>
</HEAD>
<BODY>
  Hello World
</BODY>
```

In the preceding code, notice that you have no root element (<HTML>...
</HTML>). Unfortunately, even the current generation of browsers is quite tolerant
in encountering such a piece of code. These browsers would still parse the invalid
code and render the page correctly. But in an XML-ized world, only a single root
element contains all the other elements within its scope. No elements can be presented outside the root element.

Well-formedness constraints ensure that creating parse trees for XML documents
is relatively easy. Parse trees are based on set of rules which are context-free —
or what is known as *context-free grammar (CFG).* You can parse the content of a
context-free grammar language in a single pass without needing to look ahead in
the parsing stack. A language that abides by CFG is a CFG language. The result of
such parsing is always a tree structure. Hence, pinpointing the necessary information down the tree's hierarchy — instead of trying to search a linear list of nodes —
is easy if you create a parse tree. Validating the well-formedness of such parse trees
in a single pass is also easy.

XML documents, therefore, are self-describing data containers that are easy to
parse and assimilate in any application. To make XML even more extensible, you
can create your own context-free grammar (CFG) by creating DTD for your XML
files. (Such CFGs are nothing but Document Type Definitions (DTD) for XML files.)

The advantage of XML is that every document is marked up to present its own
parse tree. It also provides flexibility to either include the DTD in the same XML
document or make it available externally. The DTD is necessary only for validity
constraints. As a matter of fact, you do not need a DTD to check the well-formedness
of an XML document because the document is always correctly marked with the
appropriate elements. As long as you conform to the rules of well-formedness constraints, the parsers churn out a Boolean `true` for the well-formedness of your
documents. The concept behind such constraint checking was elaborated at the time
of explaining the "Tags cannot overlap each other" section.

Consider the following XML document, `stock.xml`:

```
<?xml version="1.0" encoding="UTF-8"?>

<!DOCTYPE stock SYSTEM "stock.dtd">
<stock>
   <stockinfo ticker="OPN">
      <company>Open Systems Inc.</company>
      <price>14</price>
   </stockinfo>
   <stockinfo ticker="PROP">
      <company>Proprietary Systems Inc.</company>
      <price>54</price>
    </stockinfo>
</stock>
```

Context-free grammar, or the DTD `stock.dtd`, for the preceding XML document is as follows:

```
<?xml encoding="UTF-8"?>

<!ELEMENT stock (stockinfo*)>
<!ELEMENT stockinfo (company, price)>
<!ATTLIST stockinfo
    ticker CDATA #REQUIRED>
<!ELEMENT company (#PCDATA)>
<!ELEMENT price (#PCDATA)>
```

In the preceding example, the XML file refers to an external DTD, stock.dtd by using the following code:
```
<!DOCTYPE stock SYSTEM "stock.dtd">
```

Components of an XML document

Before I explain the example in the preceding section, I need to explain some of the formal grammar that you use in creating such XML files and DTDs. First, you need to understand the components of an XML document.

An XML document can contain any of the following components:

- Prolog
  - XML declaration
  - Document-type declaration (DTD)
  - Comments
  - Processing instructions (PI)
- Elements
- CDATA sections
- Attributes
- Entity

The following sections explain these components.

PROLOG

Prolog refers to the first few lines of code that you write in an XML document. It may contain your *XML declaration,* which reads as follows:

```
<?xml version="1.0" encoding="UTF-8"?>
```

The XML declaration is optional. But most of the time, you want to include it. You should specify the version information, the encoding attribute, and a stand-alone attribute that is either yes or no. Version indicates the XML version that you're using, and the encoding attribute indicates the encoding rules for the content. In the preceding code, the value of the encoding attribute is UTF-8. This specifies that the parser should read the document using UTF-8 format. The standalone attribute indicates whether the DTD is included within the XML document or whether the XML document refers to an external DTD. If the standalone attribute is set to yes, it includes the DTD; if you set it to no, the document refers to an external DTD. If you do not provide the attribute, the default is considered as yes.

A *document-type declaration* (DTD) appears as follows:

```
<!DOCTYPE stock SYSTEM "stock.dtd">
```

In the preceding code, the document accesses an external DTD. SYSTEM "stock.dtd" suggests that the document is referring to an external DTD by name "stock.dtd". Notice that your XML declaration does not provide a standalone attribute at all, which normally means that you do not refer to an external document. But the DTD suggests that you *are* referring to an external DTD.

 So the presence of a standalone attribute in the XML declaration functions only as an optimizing feature to tell the parser to optimize the parsing without referring to any external DTD.

In an XML document, you write a *comment* as follows:

```
<!-- This is a comment -->
```

You can also include a comment as a part of the prolog. More specifically, a comment that falls between the XML declaration and the DOCTYPE declaration is considered part of the prolog. Any comment after the DOCTYPE declaration is not considered as part of the prolog. However, you can use a comment throughout an XML document.

Processing instructions (PI) are commands or macros that indicate that an external process or an application such as a graphic rendering engine or a formula transformation engine is to perform computation on behalf of the XML document. The format of a PI is as follows:

```
<?target instruction?>
```

In the preceding code, target is an external application that needs to be called by the application reading the XML (using a parser) to perform some computation on your behalf, and instruction refers to a command that you want to provide to the external application. You use PIs in XML to link the document to a style sheet as shown:

```
<?xml-stylesheet type="text/css"
href="http://www.conceptuniv.com/repository/stock.css" ?>
```

A *style sheet* is any external file that provides the *cascading style sheet* (*CSS*) format to present the XML document in a browser or a WAP device. The `href` attribute indicates the location of the style sheet, and the `type` attribute indicates the format of the resource that the `href` attribute points to.

Following is a simple style-sheet example, `stock.css`, for use with `stock.xml` that you derieved in the preceding section:

```
/* Cascade style sheet based on stock DTD */
stock { display: block }
stockinfo { display: block }
company { display: block }
price { display: block }
```

ELEMENTS

Elements are also known as *tags*. You have *start tags, end tags,* and *empty tags.* Following is a simple example of an element declaration:

```
<!ELEMENT price (#PCDATA)>
```

In the preceding declaration, notice that the element declaration contains the *element name,* which in this case is the `price` element, and a *content specification* for the element, declared here as `PCDATA`..Content specification specifies the data type of content that is used for the element.

You have two different kinds of main data types, *CDATA* and *PCDATA*. PCDATA is parsed character data that contains the markup that needs to be parsed. CDATA is the data that is not parsed. Any data presented within the PCDATA section is subjected to parsing. This situation, however, poses a problem: What if you want to present some markup elements as data in your PCDATA section? In other words, what if you want special characters, such as < or >, in your PCDATA section? If you use them, your parser is likely to confuse them with an end-of-element declaration or the start of a tag. Fortunately, the XML specification provides escape sequences for such special markup elements. If you want to use such special characters, you need to present the predefined names in the &. . . format. This format helps you escape any problems that such special markups may otherwise cause in the PCDATA section. Table 2-2 lists the escape sequences to use in the PCDATA section for these special markup elements.

TABLE 2-2 ESCAPE SEQUENCES FOR SPECIAL MARKUP ELEMENTS

Character	Name	Escape Character
>	Gt	&gt;
<	Lt	&lt;
"	Quot	&quot;
'	Apos	&apos;
&	Amp	&amp;

As I discuss at the beginning of this section, an element declaration consists of an element name and a content specification. The content specification can be any of the following types apart from the main data types, which are CDATA and PCDATA:

◆ EMPTY

◆ Children

◆ Mixed

◆ ANY

The following sections discuss these content-specification types.

EMPTY   EMPTY indicates that you do not have any content that needs presenting. These elements are known as *empty tags*. You can present an empty tag as a stand-alone tag (<hr/>). You can also present it the normal way (<hr></hr>) without any content between the tags.Following is an example :

*.dtd
```
<!ELEMENT hr EMPTY>
```

*.xml
```
<hr></hr>
```

Alternatively, you can present an empty tag as a standalone tag, as shown:

```
<hr/>
```

CHILDREN   *Children content* suggests that you can use other element declarations as *child elements* — for example:

*.dtd

```
<!ELEMENT stock (stockinfo*)>
<!ELEMENT stockinfo (company, price)>
```

In the preceding code, the stock element contains the child element stockinfo. The child element itself contains other children, company and price. One thing to notice is the *, or the *qualifier,* in the section of the stock element declaration. A content particle in general case is a Qname (Qualified Name) used to denote special instructions within an Element declaration. This qualifier indicates that the child element can occur zero or more times in the stock element. Table 2-3 describes qualifiers for the child element:

TABLE 2-3 QUALIFIERS FOR THE CHILD ELEMENT

Qualifier	Meaning
*	Zero or more
+	One or more
?	Zero or one

In the preceding example, the XML file contains a root element, stock, which contains zero or more stockinfo elements as children.

MIXED   *Mixed content* indicates that you can use PCDATA and other possible child elements, such as mixture. You declare PCDATA first, following it with other child elements that you separate with a | symbol, which you follow with a * qualifier on the entire content. Mixed element declaration cannot use other qualifiers except * (as per the W3C document). The pipe, or | symbol, denotes a logical *or* for the content. Consider the following example:

*.dtd

```
<!ELEMENT mixture (#PCDATA | mixture)*>
```

The preceding code is an example of a recursive declaration for the element mixture. A recursive declaration is a declaration where the element uses itself to define its type. In the example, you notice that the element "mixture" is declared with respect to itself in the (#PCDATA | mixture) section. In this scenario, either PCDATA or mixture can occur zero or more times in succession. Notice that the qualifier is tacked to the entire combo — that is, (#PCDATA | mixture), instead of just to mixture.

*.xml

```
<mixture>
   This is a sample
   <mixture> that contains </mixture>
   more than
   <mixture> one child </mixture>
   element in recursion.
   <mixture>
      I can also <mixture> mix </mixture>
      text
   </mixture> more confusingly
</mixture>
```

I advise you to avoid declaring such confusing elements in the mixed-content model. A mixed-content model uses mixed content within the XML. Although mixed-content models are confusing, they serve as a great, flexible model for expressing the complex structures that you need in a business model.

ANY ANY content is a type of mixed-content model that enables you to use PCDATA and other possible elements *in any order*. The order of the child element declaration in the DTD does not matter while creating the respective XML document. You commonly specify the root element as ANY. Consider the following example:

*.dtd

```
<!ELEMENT itemroot ANY>
<!ELEMENT item (subitem*)>
<!ELEMENT subitem (#PCDATA)>
```

The preceding example uses content type ANY, indicating that you can use PCDATA or any possible children in any order of preference. The following example indicates the use of the ANY content type:

*.xml

```
<itemroot>
   I can use text directly here
   <item>
      <subitem>
         some subitem
      </subitem>
   </item>
```

```
and here
<subitem>
    some other subitem directly under the root
</subitem>
and finally here
</itemroot>
```

CDATA SECTIONS

CDATA, as I already discuss in the section "Elements," earlier in this chapter, is the data that the parser doesn't parse. If you use PCDATA extensively in elements, you more likely use CDATA in attributes. If you want to include XML or Java code within an XML document, and you want to display the XML document instead of parsing the content, CDATA also comes in handy. Consider the following code: display_xml.xml

```
<displayxml>
    <![CDATA[
        <stock>
            <stockinfo ticker="OPN">
                <company>Open Systems Inc.</company>
                <price>14</price>
            </stockinfo>
        </stock>
    ]]>
</displayxml>
```

The only thing that you need to make sure of is that your code does not contain the]]> sequence within the CDATA section, because that will end the <![CDATA[section that you opened initially in the code.

Comments, CDATA, and PIs are the different types of data that you actually leave unparsed.

ATTRIBUTES

An *attribute declaration* indicates that a given element has an attribute, which eventually contains some value that is specific to the attribute and relevant to the element. Attributes play a vital role in a validating parser, which checks the structure of an XML document to validate its semantics and determine whether the document is abiding by the context-free grammar (CFG) in the DTD – that is, the validating parser checks to determine whether child elements are created in the order that the DTD declares.

Following is an example of a simple DTD:

```
<?xml encoding="UTF-8"?>

<!ELEMENT stock (stockinfo*)>
<!ELEMENT stockinfo (company, price)>
<!ATTLIST stockinfo
    ticker CDATA #REQUIRED>
<!ELEMENT company (#PCDATA)>
<!ELEMENT price (#PCDATA)>
```

In the case of a validating parser, the parser makes sure that the child elements are in the correct hierarchy as suggested in the DTD. The following example is correctly validated:

```
<?xml version="1.0" encoding="UTF-8"?>

<!DOCTYPE stock SYSTEM "stock.dtd">
<stock>
    <stockinfo ticker="OPN">
        <company>Open Systems Inc.</company>
        <price>14</price>
    </stockinfo>
    <stockinfo ticker="PROP">
        <company>Proprietary Systems Inc.</company>
        <price>54</price>
    </stockinfo>
</stock>
```

The following code, however, returns an invalid status.

```
<?xml version="1.0" encoding="UTF-8"?>

<!DOCTYPE stock SYSTEM "stock.dtd">
<stockinfo>
    <stock ticker="OPN">
        <company>Open Systems Inc.</company>
        <price>14</price>
    </stock>
    <stock ticker="PROP">
        <company>Proprietary Systems Inc.</company>
        <price>54</price>
    </stock>
</stockinfo>
```

The validating parser also checks whether the attribute is providing the suggested values or if it needs to select a default value.

A nonvalidating parser is a parser that checks only the well-formedness constraints of a given XML document. It doesn't check the structural rules of the XML document.

The following example parses without any problems, because the code abides by the well-formedness rule:

```
<?xml version="1.0" encoding="UTF-8"?>

<!DOCTYPE stock SYSTEM "stock.dtd">
<stock>
    <stockinfo ticker="OPN">
        <company>Open Systems Inc.</company>
        <price>14</price>
    </stockinfo>
    <stockinfo ticker="PROP">
        <company>Proprietary Systems Inc.</company>
        <price>54</price>
    </stockinfo>
</stock>
```

Even the following code gets through the nonvalidating parser because the code is well-formed (although it doesn't semantically abide by the CFG in the DTD). Nonvalidating parsers don't need a DTD to parse the document.

A well formed but non-validatable code is as follows:

```
<?xml version="1.0" encoding="UTF-8"?>

<!DOCTYPE stock SYSTEM "stock.dtd">
<stockinfo>
    <stock ticker="OPN">
        <company>Open Systems Inc.</company>
        <price>14</price>
    </stock>
    <stock ticker="PROP">
        <company>Proprietary Systems Inc.</company>
        <price>54</price>
    </stock>
</stockinfo>
```

The following code snippet illustrates how to declare attributes:

```
<!ELEMENT stock (stockinfo*)>
<!ELEMENT stockinfo (company, price)>
```

```
<!ATTLIST stockinfo
    ticker CDATA #REQUIRED>
    . . .
    . . .
```

The declaration in the preceding code begins with ATTLIST and follows it with the name of the element, stockinfo. The element name is followed by the attribute name "ticker". This attribute name is followed by an attribute type CDATA and probably a default declaration #REQUIRED. In the code snippet, the attribute type is CDATA. An attribute can also be a predefined value or values separated by the pipe symbol, including ID, IDREF, ENTITY, ENTITIES, NMTOKEN, or NMTOKENS.

Another example of an attribute declaration is as follows:

```
<!ATTLIST stockinfo ticker (OPN | PROP) #IMPLIED>
```

The preceding example indicates that you can use either OPN or PROP as the value of the attribute.

#REQUIRED and #IMPLIED are attribute-specification parameters that have differing meanings depending on their use. Table 2-4 provides definitions of the attribute specification parameters that you can apply to the end of an attribute declaration.

TABLE 2-4 ATTRIBUTE SPECIFICATION PARAMETERS

Specification	Meaning
#REQUIRED	The attribute value must be specified in the document proper.
#IMPLIED	The attribute value need not be specified. If the attribute value is not specified, "defaultvalue" is used.
"defaultvalue"	The default attribute value is used. For example, "OPN" can be a default value.
#FIXED "fixedvalue"	This attribute value should always use the "fixedvalue" and not any other values in the document proper. For example, "PROP" can be a fixed value.

ENTITY

An *entity* is a distinct individual element that you can include in a XML document. More specifically, entities are *storage units* for data. You can reference entities from the document proper or access them from within the DTDs. The different types of entities that you can refer to are as follows:

- ◆ Character entities
- ◆ General entities
- ◆ Parameter entities

The following sections describe these types of entities.

CHARACTER ENTITIES   You refer to *character entities* by using *Unicode numbers.* To refer to *A,* for example, you use the following character entity:

```
&#65;
```

Similarly, to represent *z,* you use the following character entity:

```
&#122;
```

You can refer to character entities anywhere within an XML document or a DTD without any declarations.

GENERAL ENTITIES   You refer to *general entities,* by their names. For example, instead of a using a &#60, you can use a general entity &lt to denote less than. Also instead of using &#62, you can use a general entity &gt to denote greater than. You refer to general entities only from within an XML document. You can either use the predeclared entities or declare them in your DTD. The following example illustrates the use of general entities:

```
mail.xml

<?xml version="1.0" encoding="UTF-8" standalone="yes"?>

<!DOCTYPE mail [
    <!ELEMENT mail (head, body, ending)?>
    <!ELEMENT head(#PCDATA)>
        <!ELEMENT body(#PCDATA)>
    <!ELEMENT ending(#PCDATA)>
    <!ENTITY from "V V Preetham">
    <!ENTITY mailto "preetham@conceptuniv.com">
]>

<mail>
    <head>
        Some header info...
    </head>
    <body>
        Some mail body goes here...
```

```
          If you would like to get back to me YADA YADA
          Please mail me at &mailto; with a note for &from; and YADA
     YADA...
       </body>
       <ending>
          Regards,
          &from;
          &mailto;
       </ending>
     </mail>
```

In the preceding code, the text that appears in bold is an *entity reference*. The preceding code shows the usage of two general entities by name: &mailto; and &from;. These entities are known as *internal entities*, because you refer to the entity declaration in your DTD. The advantage of such general entities is that you can include multiple references to such general entities in your XML document and, if necessary, you need to change the content of the entity only in one place (the place of declaration), which is then reflected in the XML document. You can also refer to an external entity as shown in the following example:

```
     ...
     <!ENTITY address SYSTEM "address.txt">
     ...
```

In the preceding example, the address.txt file may contain your postal address. The preceding example demonstrates an unparsed reference because the address.txt is a text file. You can also choose to use a parsed external reference such as a *.xml file instead of a *.txt file.

PARAMETER ENTITIES   *Parameter entities* are entities that are similar to general entities but that you declare in a DTD and also refer to from within a DTD. You cannot refer to them from an XML document. Following is an example showing how to declare a parameter entity:

```
     ...
<!ENTITY % someparam "Parameter Value">
     ...
```

In the preceding example, the % symbol in the entity declaration is the only change that you need to make to a general-entity declaration to turn it into a parameter-entity declaration. You should now have the hang of XML, so I move on in the following sections to the concept of *namespaces,* which you use extensively in the SOAP and WSDL specifications.

XML Namespaces

As the preceding sections explain, XML is a tool that you can use for defining your own language to define data. In the defining your own languages, you always face the possibility of defining tags or elements that run into naming conflicts on the Internet. Devising unique names for all your elements, attributes, and entities so that they do not clash or conflict with the languages that other XML authors create is often really hard.

Fortunately, a mechanism exists for preventing such name conflicts for contents in the XML documents and DTDs that you devise: *XML namespaces.*

Before trying to understand the concept of *XML* namespaces, you need to understand the concept of namespaces in general. Namespaces are not a new concept in the industry. Consider, for example, the namespaces that you find in Java. They are technically known as *packages.* What is the purpose of a package? To provide containment for your classes so that you can perform the following tasks:

◆ Create a library for reuse.

◆ Provide a namespace for classes so that you can possibly derive different classes with same class name but that you place in different packages.

If you create a class named `Graph`, for example, that draws some 2D graphs on the monitor and you load it on the Web for reuse by all your clients, your clients can download such a class and use it appropriately. Assume, too, that your clients also have access to some other vendor who also loads a `Graph` class that creates mathematical graphs and lattices for scientific use. If a client happens to use both of these `Graph` classes at the same time, the runtime (JVM) is going to find differentiating one `Graph.class` from another difficult. The Java package specs, therefore, suggest that packaging such classes into unique packages (packages with different name) is a good idea. Unfortunately, coming up with unique package names is also hard. A general notion is to use a reverse URL notion for package names — for example, you can hypothetically think of fully qualified names for the `Graph` classes as follows:

◆ `com.bizgraph.charts.Graph` (for 2D graphs)

◆ `com.mathtools.lattice.Graph` (for graphs and lattices)

The first declaration suggests that com.bizgraph.charts.Graph is a Graph class that belongs to a vendor by name bizgraph (or similar) who happens to have a URL "`www.bizgraph.com`".

The second declaration suggests that com.mathtools.lattice.Graph is a Graph class that belongs to a vendor by name mathtools (or similar) who happens to have a URL "`www.mathtools.com`".

This way, you can carefully avoid name conflicts in Java because the URLs by themselves will always be unique at any point of time. But the problem remains for

XML. The following example poses a general scenario in which you may experience a name conflict in XML. Assume here that I am extending an already existing DTD, as follows:

product.dtd

```
<?xml encoding="UTF-8" ?>

    <!ELEMENT products ANY>
    <!ELEMENT productinfo (name, price)>
        <!ATTLIST productinfo
            partnumber CDATA #REQUIRED>
    <!ELEMENT name (#PCDATA)>
<!ELEMENT price (#PCDATA)>
```

Assume that you need to create a XML document based on this DTD but also want to extend the DTD to add more content. To accomplish this task, you can use the following code:

shipping.xml

```
<?xml version="1.0" encoding="UTF-8"?>

<!-- Look of this document is driven by a CSS referenced by an href
attribute. -->
<?xml-stylesheet type="text/css"
href="http://www.conceptuniv.com/repository/shipping.css" ?>

<!DOCTYPE products SYSTEM "product.dtd" [
    <!ELEMENT shipping(name, address)>
    <!ELEMENT name (firstname, lastname)>
    <!ELEMENT firstname (#PCDATA)>
    <!ELEMENT lastname (#PCDATA)>
    <!ELEMENT address(#PCDATA)>
    ]>

<products>
    <shipping>
        <name xmlns="http://test/">
            <firstname>V V</firstname>
            <lastname>Preetham</lastname>
        </name>
        <address>Some address</address>
    </shipping>
    <productinfo partnumber="004742B">
        <name> productname </name>
```

```
        <price> 500 </price>
    </productinfo>
</products>
```

The problem in the preceding scenario is that the `name` element in the product DTD has a parsed character value. However, you are extending that DTD and trying to redeclare the `name` element in the `shipping.xml` document, which creates trouble when you validate such documents. As a fact, even as the XML author, you may become confused about how to use the `name` element because you will not know whether `name` is now a PCDATA or a element having `firstname` and `lastname` as children.

You can possibly solve this problem by employing a *prefix solution*. In other words, you can assign unique prefixes to elements with common names, as follows:

◆ `prod:name`: The `prod` prefix for the name in `product.dtd`.

◆ `shipto:name`: The `shipto` prefix in the extension.

The updated code, with prefixes, that results is as follows:

product.dtd

```
<?xml encoding="UTF-8" ?>

<!ELEMENT products ANY>
<!ELEMENT productinfo (prod:name, price)>
<!ATTLIST productinfo
    partnumber CDATA #REQUIRED>
<!ELEMENT prod:name (#PCDATA)>
<!ELEMENT price (#PCDATA)>
```

shipping.xml

```
<?xml version="1.0" encoding="UTF-8"?>

<!-- Look of this document is driven by a CSS referenced by an href
attribute. -->
<?xml-stylesheet type="text/css"
href="http://www.conceptuniv.com/repository/shipping.css" ?>
<!DOCTYPE products SYSTEM "product.dtd" [
    <!ELEMENT shipping(shipto:name, address)>
    <!ELEMENT shipto:name (firstname, lastname)>
    <!ELEMENT firstname (#PCDATA)>
    <!ELEMENT lastname (#PCDATA)>
    <!ELEMENT address(#PCDATA)>
```

```
    ]>

<products>
    ...
</products>
```

By using prefixes, you can temporarily solve the problem. The possibility remains, however, that somebody may also come up with exactly the same prefixes for the same elements. That puts you back to ground zero.

To resolve this problem, you can use the namespace mechanism to provide a scope (like the package scope or a local scope of a method) for different elements with the same name. The namespace mechanism is based on a prefix solution but with a twist. In the namespace mechanism, you first assign a prefix to an element. Then you refer the prefix to a unique URI to provide a different scope for the elements. As the URI is always unique (similar to the reverse URL notion in packages), you can be sure that you're successfully providing a different scope for otherwise same-named elements.

Following is the code demonstrating XML namespaces:

product.dtd

```
<?xml encoding="UTF-8" ?>

<!ELEMENT prod:products ANY>
<!ATTLIST prod:products
    xmlns:prod CDATA #FIXED
    "http://www.conceptuniv.com/namespaces/prod/">
<!ELEMENT prod:productinfo (prod:name, prod:price)>
<!ATTLIST prod:productinfo
    partnumber CDATA #REQUIRED>
<!ELEMENT prod:name (#PCDATA)>
<!ELEMENT prod:price (#PCDATA)>
```

shipping.xml

```
<?xml version="1.0" encoding="UTF-8"?>

<!DOCTYPE prod:products SYSTEM "product.dtd" [
    <!ELEMENT shipto:shipping (shipto:name, shipto:address)>
    <!ATTLIST shipto:shipping
        xmlns:shipto CDATA #FIXED
        "http://www.conceptuniv.com/namespaces/shipto/">
    <!ELEMENT shipto:name (shipto:firstname, shipto:lastname)>
    <!ELEMENT shipto:firstname (#PCDATA)>
    <!ELEMENT shipto:lastname (#PCDATA)>
```

```
    <!ELEMENT shipto:address (#PCDATA)>
]>

<prod:products
xmlns:prod="http://www.conceptuniv.com/namespaces/prod/">
    <shipto:shipping
xmlns:shipto="http://www.conceptuniv.com/namespaces/shipto/">
        <shipto:name>
            <shipto:firstname>V V</shipto:firstname>
            <shipto:lastname>Preetham</shipto:lastname>
        </shipto:name>
        <shipto:address>Some address</shipto:address>
    </shipto:shipping>
    <prod:productinfo partnumber="004742B">
        <prod:name> productname </prod:name>
        <prod:price> 500 </prod:price>
    </prod:productinfo>
</prod:products>
```

You may wonder whether this approach isn't overkill. But believe me when I say that you do need to take this level of safety and precaution to avoid name conflicts completely on B2B (Business to Business) solutions.

One thing in particular that you want to notice in the preceding examples is that the xmlns attribute, which derives the prefixes such as prod and shipto, also refers to a URI. This URI must be unique. You don't need to connect to the Internet for your parser to validate this document. It is just a mechanism that you use to make sure that your scope contains unique names without any conflicts. Some people try to type a URI on their browser to check whether any resource is available at that location. They find absolutely nothing, however, because this mechanism is just a logical one (similar to reverse URL notation) that you use to provide unique references.

By using namespaces, you can create extensive mechanisms and template frameworks that are extensible as well as modular. As long as you have a supporting DTD with the predeclared prefixes attached to elements and attributes, your document is likely to go through a validating parser without a hitch.

Summary

In this chapter, you learn about the fundamentals of XML. You discover that XML is easy to read, extensible, and modular. The chapter discusses the various components of XML documents and DTDs and tells you why namespaces are the most crucial concept that you must understand before trying to understand other protocols in the technology stack. Finally, the chapter discusses XML namespaces.

Chapter 3

WSDL

WEB SERVICES DESCRIPTION LANGUAGE (WSDL) provides the capability to define a service-abstraction and also to publish the service to a service broker, such as a UDDI Registry or an ebXML repository. WSDL focuses on defining service abstractions in XML format. The descriptions of such services are within the WSDL document as a set of endpoints that operate on messages. These messages are either document-oriented or procedure-oriented.

 To learn more about ebXML, refer to Chapter 1.

Following is an abstract on WSDL 1.1 from World Wide Web Consortium (W3C):

"WSDL is an XML format for describing network services as a set of endpoints operating on messages containing either document-oriented or procedure-oriented information. The operations and messages are described abstractly and then bound to a concrete network protocol and message format to define an endpoint. Related concrete endpoints are combined into abstract endpoints (services). WSDL is extensible to allow description of endpoints and their messages, regardless of what message formats or network protocols are used to communicate."

WSDL is a proposal that consolidates the efforts of Ariba, IBM, and Microsoft. The current version of this specification (1.1, as of this writing) is available at www.w3.org/TR/wsdl.

WSDL Beginnings

Initially, if people wanted to write network services, they packaged the contents of a message as a POST or a GET request to an HTTP server object. The framework was based on a Request/Response model for carrying messages to and from the clients of such services. This mechanism was considered inefficient for use in integrating large systems, because it lacked standards for modeling the message structure. As the industry matured on the Request/Response model, it wanted a standard protocol for message channels that operate on HTTP. The advent of *SOAP* gave rise to a new industry for network services, where the messages were modeled as XML documents. SOAP was a message-exchange protocol that was envisioned as a wire-neutral protocol. But the early adopters quickly standardized the SOAP bindings to run on HTTP. The advantage of SOAP over HTTP was obvious. HTTP is a ubiquitous standard as a wireprotocol for use on the Internet. Providing message bindings to such ubiquitous standards definitely gained industry acceptance for SOAP. So as time passed, many applications were built using SOAP and XML as their base platforms for system integration.

Soon, the industry noticed that just using SOAP and XML for integrating existing systems was inefficient. The enterprises that were building such network services noticed the lack of a mechanism to publish the interfaces of the server objects. Clients, therefore, had no way to identify the interfaces and tell what operations (or methods) were available on such service-abstractions. SOAP, after all, was just a messaging channel and provided access only to the server objects on the server side. Based on the given case, SOAP can also carry Remote Procedure Call (RPC)-style messages for invocation. This mechanism was not good enough integrating existing systems compared to other distributed computing models such as RMI or CORBA.

In other distributed-computing models, a message channel carries the RPC-style messages and other marshalled parameters to and from the server objects. These distributed-computing models also have certain proxy layers. The advantage of a proxy layer is that it helps clients to programmatically analyze the invocation details, such as methods and arguments of a given service. Programmatic analyzing refers to analyzing dynamic queries at run time. If you consider how such proxy layers work, you notice that a distributed model such as CORBA mandates the use of an *Interface Definition Language (IDL)* to exhibit the operations that the server object provides. Even in the case of RMI, you expose the behavior of server objects by using a remote interface. The reason for such IDLs, or remote interfaces, is to provide a ready reckoner for client-side code. The clients are aware, therefore, of what operations are available at the service end and thus can make the appropriate invocations. IDL also serves the purpose of compile time checks to make sure that the invocation semantics are appropriately bound or matching the semantics of the IDL, or the remote interface.

Early adopters of SOAP noticed that a similar mechanism was necessary to expose the operations of their network service objects for the clients. But no defined standards or proposals were available to address this issue. The only rule of the day was to bundle a set of sample code along with the network services' usage documents for the clients to follow. The enterprises felt, however, that bundling sample codes was not an elegant solution for the problem on hand.

To resolve the issue of exposing a service interface for a given service-abstraction, IBM devised with the following two documents for describing such services:

- Well-Defined Service (WDS)

- Network Accessible Service Specification Language (NASSL)

WDS was a document that described the nonoperational service information, such as the contact information, expiration information, and service category. It also provided the business information for the service provider, such as the name and address of the company providing the service.

NASSL was a document that was considered more crucial in defining the service interface for the service abstraction. NASSL was an IDL-like document that provided operational information about the service, such as its service interface, implementation details, access protocols, and service endpoints. One key initiative of this document was to expose the service interface as an XML description. The service endpoints were also exposed as a set of URIs. This usage inclined toward HTTP as a wire protocol.

NASSL became predominant in the Web Services Toolkit that IBM released. The toolkit was soon accepted by the Java community, as few comprehensive toolkits were available at the time of its release. The early Web-services projects (probably all pilot implementations), therefore, mandated NASSL for use in exposing service-abstractions.

Meanwhile, Microsoft, the first in the industry to embrace XML for Web services, was also working on a mechanism for publishing such services. Microsoft came out with a proposal that it named *Service Contract Language (SCL),* which it soon replaced with *Service Definition Language (SDL).*

Soon IBM and Microsoft realized the necessity for a standard proposal. So eventually, Ariba, IBM, and Microsoft started working together on a standard proposal for service descriptions; the outcome was the Web Services Description Language (WSDL).

Introduction to WSDL

As industry matures in using a technology, it gradually corrects itself by identifying inefficiencies and fixing problems. This maturation process either fixes and standardizes an already existing technology or results in the evolution of an altogether new standard. WSDL is a standard that was consolidated from existing standards such as NASSL, SCL, and SDL. It defines an XML grammar for the description of a service-abstraction as a set of *communication endpoints*. You can consider these communication endpoints as *message ports* on either ends of the messaging channel. You can visualize such messaging channels as eventually connecting to a client and a server, as shown in Figure 3-1.

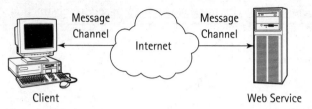

Figure 3-1: The client and the Web service connected through a message channel

As you can see in Figure 3-1, the arrowheads run both ways, indicating that the messages flow to and from the Web service. The message channels can run through the Internet, which is positioned as a cloud service. A cloud service refers to a service that need not be explained or understood by the users.

You probably realize that the service interface is completely different from the implementation of services. WSDL is considered a service interface for a given service-abstraction. The service-interface separates the interface of a given set of operations from its contractual implementation.

For more information on service interface, refer to Chapter 1.

WSDL structure

The following paragraph, extracted from the WSDL 1.1 specification, provides an insight into the structure of a WSDL document:

"A WSDL document defines *services* as collections of network endpoints, or *ports*. In WSDL, the abstract definition of endpoints and messages is separated from their concrete network deployment or data-format bindings. This allows the reuse of abstract definitions: *messages,* which are abstract descriptions of the data being exchanged, and *port types,* which are abstract collections of *operations*. The concrete protocol and data-format specifications for a particular port type constitute a reusable *binding*. A port is defined by associating a network address with a reusable binding, and a collection of ports defines a service."

You always define *services* as a set or a collection of *communication endpoints*. These *endpoints*, in the case of a wire protocol, you can consider as *ports*. *Messages* refer to data that is exchanged on the message channel. *Port types* are a collection of *operations*. *Binding* is a reusable protocol and data-format specification for a given port type.

Based on this definition, the WSDL specification documents the following elements in its definition of Web services:

- ◆ Types

- ◆ Message

- ◆ Operation

- ◆ Port type

- ◆ Binding

- ◆ Port

- ◆ Service

Consider the example in the following section to better understand the preceding elements. (This approach is the same one taken by the WSDL 1.1 specification to deliver the meaning of these stated elements.)

WSDL example

The following example provides a definition of a service that provides details of a book such as title, author, and price information, based on a given ISBN number. The service provides an operation known as GetBookDetails.

Listing 3-1: The GetBookDetails service

```
<?xml version="1.0"?>

<definitions name="BookDetails"

targetNamespace="http://www.conceptuniv.com/bookdetails.wsdl"
xmlns:tns="http://www.conceptuniv.com/bookdetails.wsdl"
xmlns:xsd1="http://www.conceptuniv.com/bookdetails.xsd"
xmlns:soap="http://schemas.xmlsoap.org/wsdl/soap/"
xmlns="http://schemas.xmlsoap.org/wsdl/">

    <types>
        <schema
targetNamespace="http://www.conceptuniv.com/bookdetails.xsd"
            xmlns="http://www.w3.org/2000/10/XMLSchema">
          <element name="BookDetailsRequest">
              <complexType>
                  <all>
                      <element name="ISBN" type="string"/>
                  </all>
              </complexType>
          </element>
```

Continued

Listing 3-1 *(Continued)*

```
            <element name="BookDetails">
                <complexType>
                    <all>
<element name="title" type="string"/>
<element name="author" type="string"/>
<element name="price" type="float"/>
                    </all>
                </complexType>
            </element>
        </schema>
    </types>

    <message name="GetBookDetailsInput">
        <part name="body" element="xsd1:BookDetailsRequest"/>
    </message>

    <message name="GetBookDetailsOutput">
        <part name="body" element="xsd1:BookDetails"/>
    </message>

    <portType name="BookDetailsPortType">
        <operation name="GetBookDetails">
            <input message="tns:GetBookDetailsInput"/>
            <output message="tns:GetBookDetailsOutput"/>
        </operation>
    </portType>

<binding name="BookDetailsSoapBinding"
type="tns:BookDetailsPortType">
        <soap:binding style="document"
transport="http://schemas.xmlsoap.org/soap/http"/>
        <operation name="GetBookDetails">
            <soap:operation
soapAction="http://www.conceptuniv.com/GetBookDetails"/>
            <input>
                <soap:body use="literal"/>
            </input>
            <output>
                <soap:body use="literal"/>
            </output>
        </operation>
    </binding>

    <service name="BookDetailsService">
```

```
        <documentation>My first service</documentation>
        <port name="BookDetailsPort"
binding="tns:BookDetailsSoapBinding">
            <soap:address
location="http://www.conceptuniv.com/bookdetails"/>
        </port>
    </service>

</definitions>
```

The preceding service is deployed using SOAP 1.1 over HTTP, but instead of using SOAP encoding, it sticks to a fixed XML format.

Definitions of the Service-Abstraction

Listing 3-1 gives you a representation of a service definition. The following section explains the elements that make up the service in code Listing 3-1. It also discusses all services that you would define in the future.

The WSDL document in Listing 3-1 is an XML document. The code conforms to the well-formedness constraint of the XML specification. As the XML specification states that you can have one and only one root for an XML document, the WSDL document also has only one root. The name of the root is definitions. This name denotes that the WSDL document is a set of definitions that includes other elements.

WSDL syntax

The following listing provides the grammar for the WSDL document structure (per the WSDL 1.1 specifications document).

Listing 3-2: Grammar for the WSDL document structure

```
<wsdl:definitions name="nmt" targetNamespace="uri">

    <import namespace="uri" location="uri"/>

    <wsdl:documentation .... />

    <wsdl:types>
        <wsdl:documentation .... />
        <xsd:schema .... />
        <-- extensibility element -->
```

Continued

Listing 3-2 *(Continued)*

```
    </wsdl:types>

    <wsdl:message name="nmt">
        <wsdl:documentation .... />
        <part name="nmt" element="mymessage" type="mymessage"?/>
    </wsdl:message>

    <wsdl:portType name="nmt">
        <wsdl:documentation .... />
        <wsdl:operation name="nmt">
            <wsdl:documentation .... />
            <wsdl:input name="nmt" message="mymessage">
                <wsdl:documentation .... />
            </wsdl:input>
            <wsdl:output name="nmt" message="mymessage">
                <wsdl:documentation .... />
            </wsdl:output>
            <wsdl:fault name="nmt" message="mymessage">
                <wsdl:documentation .... />
            </wsdl:fault>
        </wsdl:operation>
    </wsdl:portType>

    <wsdl:binding name="nmt" type="mymessage">
        <wsdl:documentation .... />
        <-- extensibility element -->
        <wsdl:operation name="nmt">
            <wsdl:documentation .... />
            <-- extensibility element -->
            <wsdl:input>
                <wsdl:documentation .... />
                <-- extensibility element -->
            </wsdl:input>
            <wsdl:output>
                <wsdl:documentation .... />
                <-- extensibility element -->
            </wsdl:output>
            <wsdl:fault name="nmt">
                <wsdl:documentation .... />
                <-- extensibility element -->
            </wsdl:fault>
        </wsdl:operation>
    </wsdl:binding>

    <wsdl:service name="nmt">
```

```
        <wsdl:documentation .... />
        <wsdl:port name="nmt" binding="mymessage">
            <wsdl:documentation .... />
            <-- extensibility element -->
        </wsdl:port>
        <-- extensibility element -->
    </wsdl:service>

    <-- extensibility element -->

</wsdl:definitions>
```

As you may notice in Listing 3-2, a WSDL document provides a set of definitions within the definitions root <definitions>...</definitions> defining all the six major elements listed in Table 3-1.

TABLE 3-1 ELEMENTS IN THE WSDL DEFINITION

Elements	Meaning
Types	Provides data-type definitions to make up the message.
Message	Is exchanged on the message channel. Each message consists of logical parts associated with a definition of some type system.
PortType	Represents a set of abstract operation, wherein each operation consists of an input, an output, and a fault message.
Binding	Provides a concrete protocol and data format for a particular PortType.
Port	Provides a communication endpoint for the binding.
Service	Serves as an aggregation of a related set of ports.

 For document naming and linking, and an understanding of the different authoring styles of the WSDL document, please refer to section 2.1.1 and 2.1.2 of the WSDL 1.1 specification, at www.w3.org/TR/wsdl.

WSDL elements

WSDL elements constitute the crucial syntax that constructs the WSDL document. Understanding the meaning of these elements and their grammatical construct helps in comprehending the concept behind the description and usage of such a document. The following sections provide an explanation of all elements of the WSDL document.

TYPES

The `types` element provides the data structure or the data-type definition that makes the messages. The `types` element should follow a schema for describing the data to use to make the data-type structure. The schema for a data-type definition can be any open standard. The WSDL specification uses the W3C *XML Schema Definition (XSD) Language* as its *canonical type system*.

The canonical type system derives from the term *canonical datatype mapping*. Canonical datatype mapping is a specified as datatype mapping that defines a one-to-one correspondence between elements in the syntactical space (also known as lexical space) of XSD and the elements in the value space. Value space refers to the value assigned within the lexical space.

The datatype mapping for the data type `boolean`, for example, is as follows:

```
Value space: {T, F}
Lexical space: {"0", "1", "true", "false"}
Datatype mapping: {<T, "true">, <T, "1">, <F, "0">, <F, "false">}
```

The canonical type mapping for type `boolean` can be represented as follows:

```
Canonical datatype mapping: {<T, "true">, <F, "false">}
```

In Listing 3-1, after the `documentation` element (which provides a human-readable string that explains the service) you can see the `types` elements.

The advantage of such schemas is that you can define wire-protocol-neutral types for message exchange. Because XSD is an abstract data-description schema, the W3C recommends the following guidelines for encoding such abstract data types in using XSD:

♦ Always use elements instead of attributes.

♦ Avoid using wire protocol-specific types such as `soap:root` and `xmi:name`. A wire protocol is a protocol supported by the underlying Transport layer.

♦ Array types should follow the Section 5 encoding schema of the SOAP 1.1 specification. The names of the array should follow the `ArrayOf***` convention, where you replace `***` with the array type.

♦ Use the type `xsd:anyType` to represent a field or parameter whenever you want the type generic or if the type does not matter.

Following the preceding guidelines helps keep you as wire-protocol independent as possible. These guidelines also help you convert any XSD-type format to a given wire format.

The example in Listing 3-2 illustrates how you can derive your `types` elements:

```
<types>
        <schema
targetNamespace="http://www.conceptuniv.com/bookdetails.xsd"
            xmlns="http://www.w3.org/2000/10/XMLSchema">
            <element name="BookDetailsRequest">
                <complexType>
                    <all>
                        <element name="ISBN" type="string"/>
                    </all>
                </complexType>
            </element>
            <element name="BookDetails">
                <complexType>
                    <all>
<element name="title" type="string"/>
<element name="author" type="string"/>
<element name="price" type="float"/>
                    </all>
                </complexType>
            </element>
        </schema>
    </types>
```

In the preceding code, two types, `BookDetailsRequest` and `BookDetails`, are defined. The `BookDetailsRequest` type contains a single child element, `ISBN`, of type `string`. `BookDetails` contains three child elements, `title` and `author`, of the `string` type, and `price`, of the `float` type.

The `types` that you derive in the preceding example follow the XSD-type format. Notice that the description of the `types` conforms to the WSDL specification, Section 2.2, guidelines to make your `types` wire protocol neutral.

MESSAGES

Messages are abstract definitions composed of logical parts, wherein each part associates with the *types* in the type system that you derive (or import). The `message` element constitutes the abstract definition of a given message that you use to exchange information on a message channel.

Every part in the message is associated to a `type` in the type-system by using a message-typing attribute. The syntax for the `message` element is as follows:

```
<definitions>
    ...
    ...
    <message name="nmt">
        <part name="nmt" element="mymessage"? type="mymessage"?/>
```

```
    </message>
</definitions>
```

The following elements are derived as per the WSDL 1.1 specification:

◆ `element`: Refers to an XSD element by using `mymessage`.

◆ `type`: Refers to an XSD `simpleType` or `complexType` by using `mymessage`.

Accordingly, the code Listing 3-1 contains the following `message` element that derives from the WSDL document:

```
<message name="GetBookDetailsInput">
    <part name="body" element="xsd1:BookDetailsRequest"/>
</message>

<message name="GetBookDetailsOutput">
    <part name="body" element="xsd1:BookDetails"/>
</message>
```

The name of the message, or the `name` attribute of the message, signifies that a given message is unique among all other messages in the WSDL document. In the example, two messages, `GetBookDetailsInput` and `GetBookDetailsOutput`, are declared.

The part name provides a unique name among all the parts in a given enclosed message Notice that the part name `body` is reused among different message scopes. You can consider the message scope as a local scope for the parts.

The `GetBookDetailsInput` message has a logical part called `body`, which is associated with `BookDetailsRequest`, wherein `BookDetailsRequest` is an XSD type that derives from the `types` element.

Similarly, the `GetBookDetailsOutput` message has a logical part called `body`, which is associated with `BookDetails`, wherein `BookDetails` is also an XSD type derived from the `types` element.

The `GetBookDetailsInput` message travels from the client to the Web service, as shown in Figure 3-2.

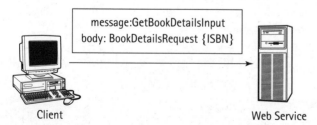

Figure 3-2: The message sent from the client to the Web service

The `GetBookDetailsInput` message contains a logical part by the name of body. The body part is associated with `BookDetailsRequest`, which is an XSD type that derives from the `types` element. The `BookDetailsRequest` type consists of an `ISBN` child element of type `string`.

 The `message` and body prefixes are arbitrary terms in the context of this example. They do not abide to any existing standards. The prefix is used only to enhance the explanation of the text in usage.

The `GetBookDetailsOutput` message travels from the Web service to the client, as shown in Figure 3-3:

message:GetBookDetailsOutput
body: BookDetails {title,author,price}

Client   Web Service

Figure 3-3: The message sent from the Web service to the client

The `GetBookDetailsOutput` message contains a logical part by the name of body. The part body is associated with `BookDetails`, which is an XSD type that derives from the `types` element. The `BookDetails` type consists of `title`, `author`, and `price` as its child elements. They are of type `string`, `string`, and `float`, respectively.

Section 2.3.1 of the WSDL specification provides a detailed list of alternative mechanisms for deriving message parts based on complex type systems.

One thing to notice in Figures 3-2 and 3-3 is that, although the flow of the message from the client to the server and, eventually, from the server to the client is shown, how this flow initiated is not specified. The possible cause of such a message flow could result from the invocation of an operation by the client on the Web service.

PORTTYPES

`PortTypes` is a set of abstract operations with their appropriate messages. You can consider operations as methods. You can consider messages as the arguments and the return values that get marshaled across the Web.

Following is the syntax for defining a `portType` element:

```
<wsdl:portType name="nmt">
<wsdl:operation name="nmt">
```

```
<wsdl:input name="nmt" message="mymessage"/>
<wsdl:output name="nmt" message="mymessage"/>
<wsdl:fault name="nmt" message="mymessage"/>
</wsdl:operation>
</wsdl:portType>
```

The `name` attribute of the `portType` element provides a unique name for a `portType` among all the other `portTypes` in a given WSDL document. An `operation` is a child element of the `portType` element. The `operation` contains a `name` attribute to uniquely identify it among other operations in an enclosing `portType` element.

Operations are also known as *transmission primitives*. The four different kinds of transmission primitives that the WSDL 1.1 specification declares are as follows:

- ◆ One-way

- ◆ Request-response

- ◆ Solicit-response

- ◆ Notification

The following sections describe these transmission primitives.

ONE-WAY   In *one-way operations,* the Web service receives a message but does not respond to such an operation. In these one-way operations, the client sends a message or invokes an operation on a Web service but doesn't expect a response for the invocation. Figure 3-4 illustrates this point much better.

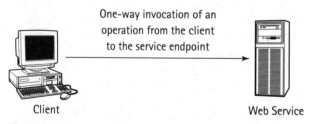

Figure 3-4: One way: Client to service endpoint

The grammar for a one-way transmission primitive is as follows:

```
<wsdl:definitions>
        <wsdl:operation name="nmt">
        <wsdl:input name="nmt" message="mymessage"/>
    </wsdl:operation>
   </wsdl:portType >
</wsdl:definitions>
```

REQUEST-RESPONSE   In a *request-response operation,* the client invokes an operation by sending a message from the client to the service endpoint. The service endpoint or the Web service processes the request and sends a response back to the client. This transmission primitive is similar to the request-response model of the HTTP protocol. This type is the most common transmission primitive that you used in a Web service. Figure 3-5 illustrates the request-response operation.

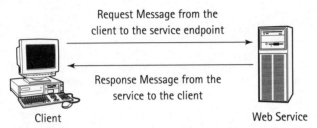

Figure 3-5: Request-response: Client to service endpoint and service endpoint to client

The grammar for a request-response transmission primitive is as follows:

```
<wsdl:definitions .... >
    <wsdl:portType .... >
        <wsdl:operation name="nmt" parameterOrder="nmts">
            <wsdl:input name="nmt" message="mymessage"/>
            <wsdl:output name="nmt" message="mymessage"/>
            <wsdl:fault name="nmt" message="mymessage"/>
        </wsdl:operation>
    </wsdl:portType >
</wsdl:definitions>
```

SOLICIT-RESPONSE   In a *solicit-response operation,* the service endpoint sends a message to a client and expects a response from the client. This type is the inverse of a request-response operation. Figure 3-6 illustrates the solicit-response operation.

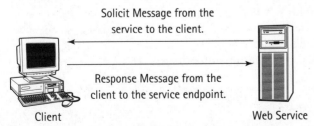

Figure 3-6: Solicit-response: Service to client and client to service endpoint

The grammar for a solicit-response transmission primitive is as follows:

```
<wsdl:definitions .... >
    <wsdl:portType .... >
        <wsdl:operation name="nmt" parameterOrder="nmts">
<wsdl:output name="nmt" message="mymessage"/>
<wsdl:input name="nmt" message="mymessage"/>
<wsdl:fault name="nmt" message="mymessage"/>
        </wsdl:operation>
    </wsdl:portType >
</wsdl:definitions>
```

NOTIFICATION   In a *notification operation,* the service endpoint sends a message to the client and receives no response from the client, as shown in Figure 3-7.

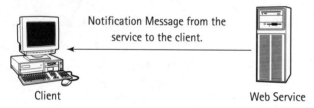

Figure 3-7: Notification: Service to client

The grammar for a notification transmission primitive is as follows:

```
<wsdl:definitions .... >
    <wsdl:portType .... >
        <wsdl:operation name="nmt" parameterOrder="nmts">
<wsdl:output name="nmt" message="mymessage"/>
    </wsdl:operation>
    </wsdl:portType >
</wsdl:definitions>
```

Only one-way and request-response transmission primitives have definitions for their bindings in WSDL, while solicit-response and notification are supported as abstract types in the WSDL base structure. WSDL does not define bindings for these last two operations. Following is the code excerpt from Listing 3-1 that defines a portType with a request-response transmission primitive:

```
<portType name="BookDetailsPortType">
    <operation name="GetBookDetails">
        <input message="tns:GetBookDetailsInput"/>
        <output message="tns: GetBookDetailsOutput"/>
    </operation>
</portType>
```

As you can see, the name of the operation is `GetBookDetails`. The operation is associated with an input message by the name of `GetBookDetailsInput` and an output message by the name of `GetBookDetailsOutput`. The `portType` is also given a unique name, `BookDetailsPortType`.

According to section 2.4.5 of the WSDL 1.1 specification, the `name` attribute of the input and output elements of a `portType` element obtains some defaults based on the operation's name. The document reads that, if "the name attribute is not specified on the input or output messages of a request-response or solicit-response operation, the name defaults to the name of the operation with Request/Solicit or Response appended, respectively." Section 2.4.6 also suggests the parameter-ordering within an operation in an RPC-style binding.

BINDINGS

Given a `portType`, the set of transmission primitives that the `portType` defines and the appropriate messages associated with the transmission primitives make up that `portType`. *Binding* defines the message format and the necessary protocols for these transmission primitives and associated messages in a given `portType`. The grammar of the binding is as follows:

```
<wsdl:definitions .... >
    <wsdl:binding name="nmt" type="mymessage">
        <-- extensibility element (1) -->
        <wsdl:operation name="nmt">
            <-- extensibility element (2) -->
            <wsdl:input name="nmt">
                <-- extensibility element (3) -->
            </wsdl:input>
            <wsdl:output name="nmt">
                <-- extensibility element (4) -->
            </wsdl:output>
            <wsdl:fault name="nmt">
                <-- extensibility element (5) -->
            </wsdl:fault>
        </wsdl:operation>
    </wsdl:binding>
</wsdl:definitions>
```

Notice that the binding has its unique `name` attribute to identify it among all other bindings in an enclosed WSDL document. The `type` attribute of the binding associates the binding to a defined `portType` in the WSDL document. The `extensibility` element indicates the concrete grammar that you use for input, output, and fault messages within a given operation.

An operation name within the `binding` element refers to the transmission primitive that you declare in the `portType`. The operation in the `binding` element and the operation in the `portType` element must be the same. The `name` attribute of the `operation` element within the `binding` element and the `name` attribute of the `operation` element within the `portType` element, therefore, must also match. The `input`, `output`, and `fault` elements must also match with each other. The following code snippet provides a sample declaration of a `binding` element:

```
<binding name="BookDetailsSoapBinding"
type="tns:BookDetailsPortType">
  <soap:binding style="document"
transport="http://schemas.xmlsoap.org/soap/http"/>
    <operation name="GetBookDetails">
      <soap:operation
soapAction="http://www.conceptuniv.com/GetBookDetails"/>
          <input>
            <soap:body use="literal"/>
          </input>
          <output>
            <soap:body use="literal"/>
          </output>
      </operation>
</binding>
```

In the preceding example, the name of the binding element is `BookDetailsSoapBinding`. The `soap` substring within the binding name indicates that the underlying protocol for this binding is of the type SOAP. The three basic protocols for bindings (currently, as of WSDL 1.1) are as follows:

- ◆ SOAP bindings

- ◆ HTTP `GET`/`POST` bindings

- ◆ Multipurpose Internet Mail Extensions (MIME) bindings

The `type` attribute of the `binding` element indicates the `portType` with which the binding is associated. In this case, the `portType` is the already defined `portType` by the name of `BookDetailsPortType`.

The next element, `soap:binding`, is considered an `extensibility` element that indicates the grammar to use for the transmission primitive. The `soap:binding` element suggests that the binding used is of the type SOAP. If you were considering a HTTP request-response-type binding, the `extensibility` element would change to `http:binding`. The `http:binding` can suggest either a `GET` or `POST` request as its verb attribute for the message.

The `soap:binding` element has a `style` attribute that indicates different styles among the SOAP binding. The style can either be of the type `document` or of the type `rpc`. I cover SOAP bindings in the SOAP binding section later in this chapter. For now, consider other elements in the code. Based on the `portType` with which the current binding is associated, you need to refer to the appropriate transmission primitives available through the `portType`. Notice that the `input` and the `output` child elements of the operation conform to the request-response transmission primitive declared in the `portType` element. Furthermore, based on the `style` attribute of the binding, you either have a `soap:body` element within your operation's input and output , which states that the encoding style for the message is `document`. If the `style` attribute changes to `rpc`, you need to conform to a grammar suggesting the rpc-style encoding for the messages.

The `operation` element also has a `style` attribute denoting the encoding style for the messages. Assuming that you did conform to a `document`-style encoding in your `binding` element, the possibility exists that you could override the encoding style with the style that you suggest for the `operation` element.

PORTS

A `port` element is a child element of a `service` element. The `port` element defines a service endpoint for a given binding. It associates the service endpoint to a single address. Following is the grammar for the `port` element:

```
<wsdl:definitions>
    <wsdl:service .... >
        <wsdl:port name="nmt" binding="mymessage">
            <-- extensibility element (1) -->
        </wsdl:port>
    </wsdl:service>
</wsdl:definitions>
```

Notice that you have an `extensibility` element for a given port. The `binding` `extensibility` element is used to provide the address information for the port.

SERVICES

A `service` is an aggregation of related ports. Section 2.7 of the WSDL 1.1 specification provides the following relationships for the ports within a service:

◆ Ports should not interact with each other. You should not pile the output of one port as an input of another port.

♦ A service can provide different bindings to a single `portType`. Such multiple bindings to a single `portType` enable the user of the service to choose the appropriate communication protocol for the interaction.

♦ A client can determine the `portTypes` of a service by examining the ports of the service. This examination enables the client to determine whether to execute the service based on the `portTypes` that it supports.

The grammar for a `service` element is as follows:

```
<wsdl:definitions .... >
    <wsdl:service name="nmt">
        <wsdl:port .... />
    </wsdl:service>
</wsdl:definitions>
```

Putting all preceding explanations together, the following code excerpt provides a sample for defining the BookDetailsService service:

```
<service name="BookDetailsService">
        <documentation>My first service</documentation>
        <port name="BookDetailsPort"
binding="tns:BookDetailsSoapBinding">
            <soap:address
location="http://www.conceptuniv.com/bookdetails"/>
        </port>
</service>
```

In the preceding code, the name of the service is `BookDetailsService`, which needs to be unique among all other services in the WSDL document. It aggregates a single port by the name `BookDetailsPort`, which associates with the SOAP binding `BookDetailsSoapBinding`. The `extensibility` element `soap:address` within the `port` element provides the address for the port.

Binding styles

The WSDL `binding` element provides three different types of protocol bindings as stated earlierfor messages, as follows:

♦ SOAP bindings

♦ HTTP `GET`/`POST` bindings

♦ MIME bindings

The following sections discuss these protocol bindings and provide an explanation for the grammar of usage for the protocols.

SOAP BINDINGS

The SOAP bindings for WSDL provide a SOAP 1.1 protocol binding for the service endpoints. The SOAP binding provides the necessary SOAP 1.1 protocol details, an address for the SOAP service endpoint, an appropriate URI for the `soapAction` header, and necessary definitions for the headers that transmit as part of the `SOAPEnvelope`. One thing to notice is that `soapAction` is an attribute for the `soap:operation` element. `soapAction` suggests the possible combinations for binding SOAP over different wire protocols, such as SOAP/SMTP or SOAP/HTTP.

THE SOAP:BINDING ELEMENT   The `soap:binding` element is a child element of the `binding` element in the WSDL document. The usage of the `soap:binding` element indicates that the messages bind to a SOAP protocol.

Following is the grammar for the ensuring a SOAP protocol for the `binding` element:

```
<definitions .... >
    <binding .... >
        <soap:binding transport="uri" style="rpc|document">
    </binding>
</definitions>
```

The `transport` specifies the wire protocol to use for SOAP. The wire protocol can range from HTTP to SMTP, to FTP, and so on. If the wire is of type `HTTP`, the value of the transport attribute is `http://schemas.xmlsoap.org/soap/http`. You need to specify a different URI if the wire is not of type `HTTP`. The `style` attribute suggests whether an `rpc`-style encoding or a `document`-style encoding is provided for the messages in the operation. The default is `document`.

The following example demonstrates sending SOAP over the SMTP wire protocol:

```
<soap:binding style="document"
transport="http://www.conceptuniv.com/smtp"/>
```

The following example demonstrate sending SOAP over the HTTP wire protocol:

```
<soap:binding style="rpc"
transport="http://schemas.xmlsoap.org/soap/http"/>
```

THE SOAP:OPERATION ELEMENT   The `soap:operation` element provides the necessary details of how the operation binds to the SOAP protocol. The following grammar provides an idea of the attributes involved in encoding this operation:

```
<definitions .... >
    <binding .... >
    <operation .... >
        <soap:operation soapAction="uri" style="rpc|document">
```

```
        </operation>
        </binding>
</definitions>
```

The `soapAction` attribute provides header information for this operation. As a matter of fact, the `soapAction` attribute *must* be used only for the SOAP-over-HTTP protocol bindings. This attribute *must not* be used for SOAP over other wire-protocols. The `soap:operation` element is an optional element for other wire-protocols.

The `style` attribute again suggests the `rpc`- or `document`-style encoding for message formats. The value of the attribute affects the `soap:body` element. In other words, the way that a `soap:body` is constructed is based on the `style` element of `soap:operation`. The value of the `style` attribute of the `soap:operation` element overrides the value of the `style` attribute of the `soap:binding` element.

THE SOAP:BODY ELEMENT   This element provides details on how to assemble the message parts within the SOAP body. You use the `soap:body` element in both `rpc`-and `document`-style messages. The structure of the body differs, based on the encoding style of the message (`rpc | document`). The following list describes the structuring details for the `soap:body` element:

◆ For `rpc`-style operations, the message parts are either an argument or a return value for the operation and should be wrapped within the body with an element name identical to the name of the operation.

◆ For `document`-style operations, you have no requirement for additional wrappers, and the message parts are placed directly under the body.

Following is the grammar for the `soap:body` element:

```
<definitions>
<binding .... >
<operation .... >
        <input>
        <soap:body parts="nmts" use="literal|encoded"
encodingStyle="uri-list" namespace="uri">
        </input>
        <output>
        <soap:body parts="nmts" use="literal|encoded"
encodingStyle="uri-list" namespace="uri">
        </output>
</operation>
</binding>
</definitions>
```

For more information on SOAP, refer to Chapter 4.

THE SOAP:FAULT ELEMENT This element provides the error information of the SOAP `fault` details element. Following is the grammar for the `soap:fault` element:

```
<definitions>
<binding .... >
<operation .... >
      <fault>
      <soap:fault name="nmt" use="literal|encoded"
encodingStyle="uri-list" namespace="uri">
      </fault>
</operation>
</binding>
</definitions>
```

The fault message follows the same convention as a `soap:body` element does, except that the `style` attribute always has a `document` value, and the `soap:fault` has only one part (unlike the multiple parts for `soap:body`).

For more information on SOAP fault, refer to Chapter 4.

THE SOAP:HEADER ELEMENT This element provides the details of the header structure that you include within the SOAP `header` element. I cover SOAP headers in more detail in the following chapter.

Following is the grammar for the `soap:header` element:

```
<definitions>
<binding .... >
<operation .... >
<input>
      <soap:header message="mymessage" part="nmt"
use="literal|encoded" encodingStyle="uri-list" namespace="uri"/>
</input>
<output>
```

```
            <soap:header message="mymessage" part="nmt"
use="literal|encoded" encodingStyle="uri-list" namespace="uri"/>
</output>
</operation>
</binding>
</definitions>
```

The attributes of the `soap:header` element are similar to those of the `soap:body` element.

THE SOAP:HEADERFAULT ELEMENT The `soap:headerfault` element is an optional child element of the `soap:header` element. This element provides the details of the error relating to the `soap:header`. Following is the grammar for the `soap:headerfault` element:

```
<definitions>
<binding .... >
<operation .... >
<input>
        <soap:header .... >
                <soap:headerfault message="mymessage" part="nmt"
use="literal|encoded" encodingStyle="uri-list" namespace="uri"/>
        </soap:header>
</input>
<output>
        <soap:header .... >
                <soap:headerfault message="mymessage" part="nmt"
use="literal|encoded" encodingStyle="uri-list" namespace="uri"/>
        </soap:header>
</output>
</operation>
</binding>
</definitions>
```

THE SOAP:ADDRESS ELEMENT   This element binds the ports that aggregate with a service to a specific URI. The URI scheme should match the `wire-protocol` that the `soap:binding` element specifies. Following is the grammar for the `soap:address` element:

```
<definitions>
<service .... >
        <port .... >
                <soap:address location="uri"/>
        </port>
</service>
</definitions>
```

HTTP GET/POST BINDINGS

The HTTP bindings for WSDL provide HTTP 1.1 protocol binding for the service endpoints. The bindings include a GET and POST verb usage with the WSDL 1.1 document structure to specify the communication method for the service endpoint (the Web server). The client can be any application (and not necessarily a Web browser) that interacts with the Web service. If the client provides the appropriate verb for a HTTP binding within the WSDL document, the Web service doesn't complain.

Per the WSDL 1.1 specification (Section 4), the following protocol specifications apply to the HTTP binding:

◆ An indication that a binding uses HTTP GET or POST.

◆ The address for the port.

◆ The relative address for each operation (relative to the base address defined by the port).

THE HTTP:BINDING ELEMENT This binding, as does soap:binding, indicates that the binding that you use for message transport is of the type HTTP.

Following is the grammar for the http:binding element:

```
<definitions .... >
        <binding .... >
            <http:binding verb="nmt"/>
        </binding>
</definitions>
```

The verb attribute suggests the method of request that is raised. The value can be any of the HTTP methods, such as GET, POST, or PUT. In the preceding example, the value of the verb attribute is nmt, which refers to a name token.

THE HTTP:OPERATION ELEMENT This element is similar to the soap:operation element in that it indicates how a given operation binds to the underlying HTTP protocol.

Following is the grammar for the http:operation element:

```
<definitions .... >
        <binding .... >
            <operation .... >
                <http:operation location="uri"/>
            <operation>
        </binding>
</definitions>
```

The location attribute refers to a relative URI for the operation. This relative URI is intended to combine with the absolute URI that the http:address element provides.

THE HTTP:ADDRESS ELEMENT   The `http:address` element provides the location for the base URI for a specified port.

Following is the grammar for the `http:address` element:

```
<definitions .... >
       <port .... >
              <http:address location="uri"/>
       </port>
</definitions>
```

The `location` attribute of the `http:address` combines with the `location` attribute of the `http:operation` element to provide a full address for a given operation within the `http:operation` element.

THE HTTP:URLENCODED ELEMENT   This element suggests that you encode the message part in the HTTP request by using the standard URI encoding rules. Following is the grammar for the `http:urlEncoded` element:

```
<definitions>
<binding .... >
       <operation .... >
           <http:operation .... />
              <input>
                      <http:urlEncoded/>
              </input>
       </operation>
</binding>
</definitions>
```

MIME bindings

The WSDL specification provides a way to specify the binding of abstract data types to the MIME format. The provided bindings specify different MIME type combinations. Following is a list of the MIME types:

◆ Multipart/related

◆ Text/xml

◆ Application/`x-www-form-urlencoded`

◆ Others

Of the afore mentioned MIME types, Application/`x-www-form-urlencoded` and Others MIME types are still evolving and WSDL 1.1 specification does not provide a XML grammar for them. I discuss the multipart/related and text/xml MIME types in the following sections:

MULTIPART/RELATED

The `mime:multipartRelated` element represents the multipart/related type. This element is used to aggregate different MIME formatted parts as a single message. The concrete format of such a message is described by `mime:multipartRelated` element.

The following is the grammar for `mime:multipartRelated` element

```
<mime:multipartRelated>
    <mime:part>
        <-- mime element -->
    </mime:part>
</mime:multipartRelated>
```

The `mime:part` element represents a single part in a multipart/related message.

TEXT/XML

The `mime:content` element represents the MIME format when no other information is available about the format except for its MIME type string. This element is useful in preventing the creation of additional elements for every MIME format.

The following is the grammar for `mime:content` element

```
<mime:content part="nmtoken"? type="string"?/>
```

The part attribute of the `mime:content` element specifies the name of the message part. As an example, if you are expecting a message as a return value and you are not aware of the schema that would be used to represent the message, then a generic mime element can be used that indicates text/xml as follows:

```
<mime:content type="text/xml"/>
```

Summary

This chapter covers the WSDL 1.1 specification in detail. The chapter provides the XML grammar for the WSDL document. Although many developers would never write such exhaustive XML code for the WSDL document by hand, understanding the intricacies of such documents is good so that, if necessary, you can tweak a tool-generated WSDL document.

Chapter 4

SOAP

IN THIS CHAPTER

- ◆ Introduction to SOAP
- ◆ Message exchange model of SOAP
- ◆ SOAP message
- ◆ SOAP encoding
- ◆ SOAP over HTTP
- ◆ SOAP-RPC

SIMPLE OBJECT ACCESS PROTOCOL (SOAP) is one of the most important standards in building Web services. SOAP forms the backbone of the communication infrastructure of Web services. Using SOAP, disparate components that people build by using different programming languages and component frameworks can talk to each other across HTTP in a distributed, decentralized environment. SOAP defines a framework to initiate request-response-based conversations with UDDI or ebXML repositories. The RPC-style messaging that invokes the methods on the objects residing on the remote server is written using XML as the base data format for e-business frameworks. It mostly uses HTTP to carry the message semantics for its conversations. Although SOAP typically uses HTTP as its wire protocol, you can also use SOAP implementations over SMTP or FTP.

This chapter discusses SOAP concepts that you need to know to build the Web-services infrastructure. It focuses on SOAP version 1.1. The chapter also talks about the design goals, conventions, and semantic structure of SOAP. It demonstrates how to deploy a Web service in a Soap toolkit and discusses how the client SOAP application accesses the deployed service.

The SOAP proposal is a consolidated effort from Develop Mentor, IBM, Lotus Development Corporation, Microsoft, and UserLand Software. You can find the latest version of this proposal at `www.w3.org/TR/SOAP`.

Introduction to SOAP

SOAP is the current industry standard for XML messaging. It is a simple and extensible protocol for exchanging information on the Internet. The information is

83

exchanged in a structured and data-type-specific manner by using XML as its base data format. An advantage of SOAP is that it is wire-protocol neutral. You can implement SOAP over any available wire protocol, ranging from Internet protocols such as HTTP, FTP, or SMTP to GIOP/IIOP or DCE. Because of the ubiquity of HTTP standards on the Internet, the current SOAP specification actually mandates support for HTTP. In addition, most of the industry's XML-based data-interchange models via SOAP are implemented over HTTP.

One of the advantages of SOAP over HTTP is that the XML documents sent by a SOAP client can easily traverse across a firewall on the SOAP server. Most servers block all ports for transport protocols except port 80, which is open to HTTP traffic. The key characteristic of SOAP is that it is operating-system independent. SOAP is not tied to any low-level semantics of any system-level programming model or virtual machine abstractions. In essence, it is a lightweight mechanism for data exchange between heterogeneous component frameworks. SOAP defines only the application semantics necessary for modular packaging and data encoding standards.

You can use SOAP to access legacy systems that can recognize data encoding and structures based on XML formats. You can use SOAP for simple document exchange. You can also use it for remote procedure calls. Because of these advantages, SOAP has gained immense popularity as the standard protocol for Web services. In a typical Web-service scenario, a client application invokes the service method of the server application that provides the Web service. The client request is converted into a SOAP request and is sent across the Web wrapped over HTTP. Similarly, the SOAP server that hosts the Web service sends the service response to the client as a SOAP response wrapped over HTTP.

SOAP mainly consists of the following three functional parts:

- The SOAP envelope
- The SOAP encoding rules
- The SOAP RPC

The *SOAP envelope* is an enclosing construct, which contains zero or more SOAP headers and a mandatory SOAP body. The SOAP envelope is the top element of the XML document. It defines a framework that specifies the details of a message, such as its control information, its address, who should deal with it, and whether it's optional or mandatory. The SOAP headers contain details about the Quality of Service (QoS).

The *SOAP encoding rules* define a way to exchange application-specific data types. This exchange is similar in concept to a distributed programming model such as that of RMI or CORBA. SOAP defines a serialization mechanism for data interchange among disparate systems. It also defines an application-semantic-neutral schema for its data types. This schema is based on the W3C XML schema language.

The *SOAP-RPC* represents a convention for request-response-based model. Using this convention enables you to invoke an RPC-style request, which provides access to a remote procedure exposed by a service interface. SOAP RPC also provides you a convention to obtain responses based on the request that executes. Not using the request-response-based model as a convention gives you document-oriented communication.

The design goals of SOAP

The main focus of SOAP is to act as a simple and lightweight extensible framework. SOAP is also very modular in its design. Because SOAP was designed as a very simple protocol, it omits several features that are relatively supported in other distributed communication models, such as CORBA or DCOM. The following features are *not* supported in SOAP:

◆ **Distributed garbage collection:** Distributed GC is functionality where a remote object is garbage collected when all its local and remote references are lost.

◆ **Batching of messages:** Batching of message is a process where several messages are batched together before they are sent to a message dispatcher. This allows several messages to be put in the same TCP packet. This helps in reducing interrupt and protocol processing overheads.

◆ **Object-by-reference:** Object-by-reference is a feature wherein an object argument is marshaled across as reference instead of a value-object.

◆ **Activation:** Activation is a feature provided by distributed services where a remote server gets lazily activated only when a call to the server is made. This is opposed to a server object always active waiting for a request. The activation feature reduces the unnecessary consumption of memory on the server side.

The concept of object-by-reference is not supported because distributed garbage collection is not supported. The lack of a distributed garbage-collection mechanism creates a lot of confusion at garbage-collection time for local objects because the local garbage-collector algorithm has no way to determine whether a given object is actually being pointed to by a remote reference. This situation causes ambiguity at the time for finalizing such objects. If the garbage collector enforces the finalization on such ambiguous objects, it may leave some remote references in an inconsistent state. To avoid all this mess, SOAP does not implement the object-by-reference mechanism within its framework. Because SOAP does not support object-by-reference, it has no way to support activation mechanisms either. The design goals of SOAP, therefore, consciously eliminated everything that may complicate the SOAP standard, leaving only a simple extensible framework.

Notational conventions

The SOAP notational conventions that I follow throughout this chapter are as described in the following list:

♦ soapenc refers to the encoding namespace as defined by SOAP 1.1. The namespace URI for soapenc is http://schemas.xmlsoap.org/soap/encoding/.

♦ soapenv refers to the envelope namespace as defined by SOAP 1.1. The namespace URI for soapenv is http://schemas.xmlsoap.org/soap/envelope/.*xsi refers to the instance namespace as defined by XSD. The namespace URI for xsi is http://www.w3.org/1999/XMLSchema-instance.

♦ xsd refers to the schema namespace as defined by XSD. The namespace URI for xsd is http://www.w3.org/1999/XMLSchema.

♦ tns refers to this namespace (tns) and is used as a convention to refer to the current document.

♦ URIs starting with www.conceptuniv.com represent some application-dependent or context-dependent URI.

The xsi and xsd prefixes in the WSDL chapter have different namespace URIs. The reason for referring to two separate URIs on the namespaces is to be consistent with the SOAP 1.1 and WSDL 1.1 notational conventions, respectively.

SOAP example

The following example provides a quick preview of a SOAP-enabled service and a SOAP request over HTTP. This example gives you an insight into the anatomy of a SOAP request message.

The following code shows the SOAP message embedded in an HTTP request:

```
POST /bookdetails HTTP/1.1
Host: www.conceptuniv.com
Content-Type: text/xml; charset="utf-8"
Content-Length: n
SOAPAction: "http://www.conceptuniv.com/GetBookDetails"

<?xml version="1.0" encoding="UTF-8"?>
<soapenv:Envelope
xmlns:soapenv="http://schemas.xmlsoap.org/soap/envelope/"
soapenv:encodingStyle="http://schemas.xmlsoap.org/soap/encoding/"
xmlns:xsi="http://www.w3.org/1999/XMLSchema-instance"
xmlns:xsd="http://www.w3.org/1999/XMLSchema">
<soapenv:Body>
<wsns:GetBookDetails xmlns:wsns="http://www.conceptuniv.com/wsns/">
```

```
<ISBN xsi:type="xsd:string">0-7645-8045-8</ISBN>
</wsns:GetBookDetails>
</soapenv:Body>
</soapenv:Envelope>
```

Message Exchange Model of SOAP

The example in the preceding section shows a request for a SOAP message over HTTP. This request seems to be a one-way transmission of a message, but the request eventually evokes a response over HTTP. As a matter of fact, SOAP messages are basically one-way transmissions of messages from a sender to a receiver, but such messages effectively combine to provide more complicated exchange patterns such as request-response.

The SOAP messages always route through a *message path*. A message path consists of one or more intermediary *nodes* for processing the SOAP message. Such SOAP *processing nodes* are also known as *endpoints*. The message path consists of a chain of SOAP processing nodes that provide message-filtering capabilities for the SOAP messages that route through the message path.

According to the SOAP 1.1 specification, an endpoint that receives a SOAP message must process the message by performing the following actions:

◆ The endpoint identifies the message that is addressed to it.

◆ The endpoint verifies the mandatory parts in the message. If the endpoint does not support such messages, it discards them. The endpoint may also ignore the optional parts of the message without affecting the outcome of the processing.

◆ If the endpoint is not the final destination of the message, after processing the message, it removes all the messages addressed to this endpoint before forwarding the messages meant for other endpoints.

The endpoint has the following responsibilities in processing the message:

◆ The endpoint must understand the message exchange pattern that is used in the message path. Some examples of message patterns are *one-way, request-response,* and *multicast.*

◆ The endpoint must understand the role of the recipient in a message pattern.

◆ The endpoint must understand whether the message is engaged in any mechanism, such as RPC-style message exchange.

◆ The endpoint must understand the data-encoding format of the message.

◆ The endpoint must understand any other semantics that are involved in processing the message.

The message-exchange pattern is a message path consisting of intermediaries. The intermediaries have the capability to process the SOAP message in the message path. These intermediaries can act both as receivers and senders of SOAP messages.

Figure 4-1 illustrates different message patterns that are possible in the SOAP message-exchange model.

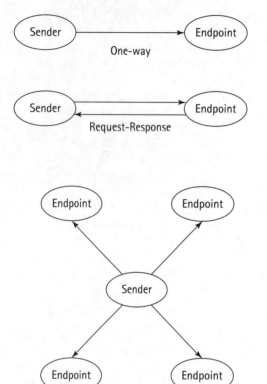

Figure 4-1: Message patterns in the SOAP message–exchange model

According to the SOAP 1.1 specification, certain rules govern the message format for SOAP messages, as follows:

◆ All SOAP messages are encoded by using XML.

◆ SOAP defines two XML namespaces, one for the SOAP envelope and another for SOAP serialization, with the prefixes `soapenv` and `soapenc`, respectively.

◆ A SOAP message must not contain any Document Type Declarations (DTDs).

◆ A SOAP message must not contain any Processing Instructions (PIs).

- SOAP uses the local, unqualified id attribute of type ID to specify the unique identifier of an encoded message.

- SOAP uses the local, unqualified href attribute of type uri-reference to specify a value that conforms to the XML specification, the XML schema specification, and the XML Link Language Specification.

SOAP Message

A SOAP message is an XML document that consists of a SOAP envelope encompassing zero or more headers and a mandatory SOAP body. Figure 4-2 illustrates the main parts of a SOAP message.

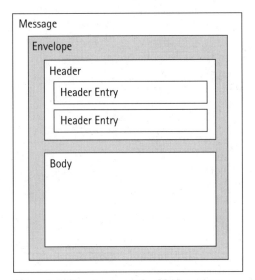

Figure 4-2: The structure of a SOAP message

SOAP envelope

The *SOAP envelope* is the top element in the SOAP XML document that represents the message.

The grammar rules for the envelope are as follows:

- The element name for the SOAP envelope must be Envelope.

- The element must be within a SOAP message.

- The element may contain additional attributes and namespace declarations. The attributes must be namespace qualified. The element may contain subelements and may be namespace qualified.

The SOAP envelope has the following structure:

```
<soapenv:Envelope .... >
      <soapenv:Header name="nmtoken">
            <soapenv:HeaderEntry.... />
      </soapenv:Header>
      <soapenv:Body name="nmtoken">
            [message payload]
      </soapenv:Body>
</soapenv:Envelope>
```

Following is an example highlighting the SOAP Envelope element:

```
<?xml version="1.0" encoding="UTF-8"?>
<soapenv:Envelope
xmlns:soapenv="http://schemas.xmlsoap.org/soap/envelope/"
soapenv:encodingStyle="http://schemas.xmlsoap.org/soap/encoding/"
xmlns:xsi="http://www.w3.org/1999/XMLSchema-instance"
xmlns:xsd="http://www.w3.org/1999/XMLSchema">
      <soapenv:Body>
            <wsns:GetBookDetails
xmlns:wsns="http://www.conceptuniv.com/wsns/">
                  <ISBN xsi:type="xsd:string">0-7645-8045-8</ISBN>
            </wsns:GetBookDetails>
      </soapenv:Body>
</soapenv:Envelope>
```

This example omits the header entry because the header is optional.

SOAP header

The SOAP envelope contains zero or more *headers*. The headers add features to the SOAP messages in an arbitrary fashion without prior agreement between the communicating parties. The features added to the SOAP messages provide a flexible and modular mechanism to make SOAP extensible. The SOAP headers also add details to the message. Such details can specify the address of the endpoint that is to process the message and which parts of the message are optional and mandatory.

Some examples of the extensions that you can add as SOAP header entries are *transaction management, authentication,* and *authorization.*

The grammar rules for the SOAP header are as follows:

◆ The element name for the SOAP header must be Header.

◆ The element must be within a SOAP message. If the element is present, the element must be the first child of a SOAP Envelope element.

◆ The `Header` element can contain child elements indicating the header entries. The header entries must be namespace qualified.

The encoding rules for the SOAP header entries are as follows:

◆ The header entry is identified by its fully qualified element name, qualified by a namespace URI.

◆ The `soapenv:encodingStyle` attribute may be used to specify the serialization rules for the header entries.

◆ The `soapenv:mustUnderstand` and `soapenv:actor` attributes may be used to address who is to process the header entries and how to process them.

The SOAP header has the following structure:

```
<soapenv:Envelope .... >
     <soapenv:Header name="nmtoken">
          <soapenv:HeaderEntry.... />
     </soapenv:Header>
     <soapenv:Body name="nmtoken">
          [message payload]
     </soapenv:Body>
</soapenv:Envelope>
```

The following example illustrates the SOAP `Header` element:

```
<?xml version="1.0" encoding="UTF-8"?>
<soapenv:Envelope
xmlns:soapenv="http://schemas.xmlsoap.org/soap/envelope/"
soapenv:encodingStyle="http://schemas.xmlsoap.org/soap/encoding/"
xmlns:xsi="http://www.w3.org/1999/XMLSchema-instance"
xmlns:xsd="http://www.w3.org/1999/XMLSchema">
     <soapenv:Header>
          <wsns:Transaction
          xmlns:wsns="http://www.conceptuniv.com/wsns/"
soapenv:mustUnderstand="1">
                    5
          </wsns:Transaction>
     </soapenv:Header>
     <soapenv:Body>
          <wsns:GetBookDetails
xmlns:wsns="http://www.conceptuniv.com/wsns/">
                    <ISBN
xsi:type="xsd:string">0-7645-8045-8</ISBN>
```

```
          </wsns:GetBookDetails>
        </soapenv:Body>
</soapenv:Envelope>
```

SOAP body

The SOAP envelope also contains a *body*. The body contains the payload of the
message. It also contains the mandatory information addressed to the recipient of
the message. Some of the uses of the `Body` element include marshalling RPC-style
message calls and error reporting.

The grammar rules for the SOAP body are as follows:

◆ The element name for SOAP body must be `Body`.

◆ The element must be within a SOAP message. If the SOAP `Header` element
  is present, the `Body` element must directly follow the SOAP `Header` element. If the SOAP `Header` element is not present, the `Body` element must
  be an immediate first child of the `Envelope` element.

◆ The element may contain subelements as immediate child elements, indicating a set of body entries for the SOAP message. The child elements of
  the `Body` element may be namespace qualified. The SOAP body also defines
  a SOAP `fault` element that indicates an error in processing the message.
  (See the following section for details on the SOAP `fault` element.)

The encoding rules for SOAP body entries are as follows:

◆ The body entry of the `Body` element is namespace qualified and is identified by its fully qualified name, consisting of the namespace URI and the
  local name.

◆ The `soapenv:encodingStyle` attribute may be used to indicate the serialization rules for encoding the body entries.

The body has the following structure:

```
<soapenv:Envelope .... >
        <soapenv:Header name="nmtoken">
                <soapenv:HeaderEntry.... />
        </soapenv:Header>
        <soapenv:Body name="nmtoken">
                [message payload]
        </soapenv:Body>
</soapenv:Envelope>
```

Following is an example illustrating the SOAP `Body` element:

```
<?xml version="1.0" encoding="UTF-8"?>
<soapenv:Envelope
xmlns:soapenv="http://schemas.xmlsoap.org/soap/envelope/"
soapenv:encodingStyle="http://schemas.xmlsoap.org/soap/encoding/"
xmlns:xsi="http://www.w3.org/1999/XMLSchema-instance"
xmlns:xsd="http://www.w3.org/1999/XMLSchema">
        <soapenv:Header>
                <wsns:Transaction
xmlns:wsns="http://www.conceptuniv.com/wsns/"
soapenv:mustUnderstand="1">
                        5
                </wsns:Transaction>
        </soapenv:Header>
        <soapenv:Body>
                <wsns:GetBookDetails
xmlns:wsns="http://www.conceptuniv.com/wsns/">
                        <ISBN
xsi:type="xsd:string">0-7645-8045-8</ISBN>
                </wsns:GetBookDetails>
        </soapenv:Body>
</soapenv:Envelope>
```

SOAP fault

The SOAP standard provides a SOAP `fault` element to specify the occurrence of error messages at the SOAP processing nodes. During the processing of a message, some of the endpoints may incur some exceptions as they verify header entries. The endpoints may typically incur exceptions while processing the body entry of a SOAP message. The SOAP specification provides a mechanism for the response messages of a request to carry fault codes that specify the error condition. This SOAP `fault` element indicates the error and the status information about the error conditions within a SOAP message. Not only may the response messages carry a `fault` element, but even the request message may carry fault element. Typically, however, a request message may not carry a `fault` element because the request message may not have been processed by the SOAP processing nodes yet.

If the SOAP `fault` element is present, it must appear within the `Body` element as a body entry. The SOAP `fault` element must not, however, appear more than once as a body entry.

The SOAP `fault` element defines the following four subelements within the `soapenv:Fault` element:

◆ The `faultcode` subelement

◆ The `faultstring` subelement

◆ The `faultactor` subelement

◆ The `detail` subelement

The following sections describe each of these subelements.

THE FAULTCODE SUBELEMENT

The `faultcode` subelement indicates a value for the type of error condition that occurs at the time of processing. The values of the fault code are predefined in the SOAP 1.1 specification, Section 4.4.1, and appear in Table 4-1.

TABLE 4-1 SOAP FAULTCODE VALUES

Name	Meaning
VersionMismatch	This faultcode indicates that the namespace of the SOAP envelope is not `http://schemas.xmlsoap.org/soap/envelope`.
MustUnderstand	This faultcode indicates that the endpoint found a mandatory header element that it could not process.
Client	This faultcode indicates that the message received at the endpoint is not well formed or lacks the correct information to succeed.
Server	This faultcode indicates that the message could not be processed at the service endpoint because of reasons that are not directly attributable to the message. A problem may exist at the server end, or a component at the service end may not be working.

You can use these `faultcode` subelements to provide a programmatic control for identifying the errors that may occur at the time of processing the messages. These `faultcode` subelements must be presented within a SOAP `fault` element. The `faultcode` values are flexible and well-defined. Providing an extension for the `faultcode` subelements that existed prior to SOAP 1.1 specification, therefore, is easy.

THE FAULTSTRING SUBELEMENT

The `faultstring` subelement provides a message as string, of the errors that may occur at the time that a message is processed. The `faultcode` subelements are meant for programmatic control of the errors, while the `faultstring` you can use for display purposes. Typically, you use the `faultstring` subelement for displaying and logging errors that may occur at the time a SOAP message is processed.

THE FAULTACTOR SUBELEMENT

Unlike `faultcode` and `faultstring` subelements, the `faultactor` subelement provides information about the SOAP processing node that generates the error status for a given message. The `faultactor` subelement contains a value that specifies the URI of the processing node that raises the error.

This `faultactor` subelement is useful because, in a given message path that consists of multiple endpoints, knowing which of the endpoints issued the error is impossible if an identification mechanism is not available. The Web-services application that uses complex messaging models *must* define the `faultactor` subelement in the SOAP `fault` element. If an error occurs in a complex messaging model and the `faultactor` subelement is not specified in the `fault` element of the resulting error, you can assume that the final-destination endpoint has generated the error.

THE DETAIL SUBELEMENT

The `detail` subelement provides descriptive information about the application-specific error that occurs in the SOAP body. Unlike other subelements, you must not define the `detail` subelement if any processing errors are in the header entries of the message. Instead, the `detail` subelement must be defined only if a processing error occurs in the body entry of the SOAP message. If the `detail` subelement is not present in the `fault` element, you can consider the fault to lie with the header entries of the SOAP message. The presence of the `detail` subelement indicates that the error occurred in the body entry, as opposed to an error occurring in the header entry.

The `detail` subelement has its own subelements. All the immediate child elements of the `detail` subelement are considered as the entries for `detail`. The detail entry has the following encoding rules:

◆ The detail entry consists of the namespace URI and the local URI to form the fully qualified name of the entry. The entry should be namespace qualified.

◆ The use of the `soapenv:encodingStyle` attribute indicates the serialization rule for the detail entry.

SOAP FAULT – AN EXAMPLE

The following example illustrates the use of the `fault` element and its subelements:

```
<soapenv:Envelope
xmlns:SOAP-ENV="http://schemas.xmlsoap.org/soap/envelope/">
    <soapenv:Body>
        <soapenv:Fault>
            <faultcode>soapenv:Client</faultcode>
            <faultstring>Too many parameters</faultstring>
            <detail>
               <wsns:faultdetails
```

```
xmlns:wsns="http://www.conceptuniv.com/wsns/">
                <message>
                        The rpc call that was made on the endpoint
failed due to too many parameters in the Request message
                </message>
                <errorcode>
                        4001
                </errorcode>
            </wsns:faultdetails>
        </detail>
      </soapenv:Fault>
    </soapenv:Body>
</soapenv:Envelope>
```

The preceding example illustrates the faultcode soapenv:Client, with a message stating that too many parameters were sent to execute a SOAP operation.

SOAP Attributes

Clients use SOAP attributes to specify how to process a SOAP message. SOAP attributes indicate who receives the header element of a SOAP message and whether the recipient is to process the header entries. The following sections discuss various SOAP attributes.

The soapenv:encodingStyle attribute

The soapenv:encodingStyle attribute in the Envelope element is a global attribute that indicates the encoding format for the SOAP message. It defines this encoding format for the serialization of the message across the transport protocol. If you do not provide any value for the encodingStyle attribute, no default encoding style is available for the serialization mechanism.

You can provide a list of one or more URIs as the value for the soapenv:encodingStyle attribute. These URIs identify the serialization rules that are necessary for deserializing the SOAP message.

Some examples of values in the order of the most specific to the least specific are http://schemas.xmlsoap.org/soap/encoding/, blank URI(""), and http://some.host/encoding/restricted http://some.host/encoding/.

A blank URI ("") indicates that no claims are made for encoding the message. The SOAP encoding rules are also known as *section-5 encoding* because the serialization rules are provided in the fifth section of the SOAP 1.1 specification.

The soapenv:mustUnderstand attribute

The `soapenv:mustUnderstand` attribute is a global attribute that indicates whether a header entry is mandatory or optional. The recipient of the message should verify the mandatory parts in the message. If the recipient does not support such messages, it discards them. The recipient may also ignore the optional parts of the message without affecting the outcome of the processing. The recipient of the header is defined by the `soapenv:actor` attribute. The value of the `soapenv:mustUnderstand` attribute can be either 0 or 1, with 0 the default value.

If the value of the `soapenv:mustUnderstand` attribute is 1, that indicates that the recipient of the message must obey the semantics of the message and appropriately process the message. Otherwise, the recipient need not process the message.

The soapenv:actor attribute

The `soapenv:actor` attribute indicates the recipient of the header element in the SOAP message. A SOAP message may have a message path consisting of endpoints that form a message chain. These endpoints act as intermediary processing nodes that provide some processing and filtering services for the SOAP message along the message path. The SOAP message can consist of more than one header part specifically addressed to multiple intermediaries along the message path. Such endpoints are both recipients and senders of the SOAP message. The recipient address is provided by the `soapenv:actor` attribute, which indicates the URI of the intermediary processing node. A special case URI, `http://schemas.xmlsoap.org/soap/actor/next`, indicates that the current header element must be processed by the first endpoint that finds the message.

Omitting the `soapenv:actor` attribute suggests that the recipient is the final destination of the SOAP message.

SOAP Encoding

The SOAP 1.1 specification defines a set of serialization rules for marshalling calls on the wire protocol. The encoding style follows a type system that is generally followed by any programming language. You can consider a *type* as either a simple type or a complex type that consists of other entities within the type structure. The following sections provide the encoding rules for serializing data by using the SOAP message format.

Simple types

Based on the encoding rules, *simple types* are always represented as single elements in the SOAP body. Actually, SOAP encoding adopts all the types that you find in the built-in data types of the XML schema specification. The simple type must always derive from an XML schema type.

Following is an example of an XML schema:

```
<element name="name" type="string"/>
<element name="employeeid" type="int"/>
<element name="bankbalance" type="negativeInteger"/>
<element name="eyecolor">
        <simpleType base="xsd:string">
             <enumeration value="Green"/>
             <enumeration value="Black"/>
        </simpleType>
</element>

<name>VVP</name>
<employeeid>1</employeeid>
<bankbalance>-60</bankbalance>
<eyecolor>Black</eyecolor>
```

You can also use the `xsd` prefix to specify the type of a specified value, as follows:

```
<name xsi:type="xsd:string">VVP</name>
```

You can use the `soapenc` prefix, too, as follows:

```
<name xsi:type="soapenc:string">VVP</name>
```

The difference between the first piece of code and the second piece in the preceding example is that the·xsd prefix is associated with the XML schema specification and the `soapenc` prefix is associated with the section-5 encoding of the SOAP specification.

Refer to the SOAP 1.1 specification for an explanation of other simple data types, such as `Strings`, `Enumeration`, and `Byte Arrays`.

Polymorphic accessor

At times, using only simple types may not necessarily provide a sufficient data container for certain arbitrary values with types that are unknown at the time of definition. If you want to define a value for the price of a specified product, for example, and you are aware that such a price instance is defined as an arbitrary type in the service, you must provide an `xsi:type` attribute for the element. Such an element is considered a *polymorphic accessor.* A polymorphic accessor is similar to the `any` type in CORBA. The polymorphic accessor is defined as a placeholder for virtually any type of data.

The following example provides data-type encoding for a polymorphic accessor:

```
<price xsi:type="xsd:float">100.56</price>
```

Alternatively, you can use the following code for a polymorphic accessor:

```
<price xsi:type="xsd:string">100 dollars and 56 cents</price>
```

Compound types

Two compound data types are defined by SOAP encoding: *structs* and *arrays*. A `struct` is a compound type in which every member is uniquely distinguished by its name. An `array` is a compound type in which the members are distinguished by the member's ordinal position. In an array, the members do not have a name.

A compound type is necessary to express complex elements that simple types cannot express. These complex types have child elements. At the time of serialization, a graph of such complex type is marshaled across on the transport.

Following is an example of a struct of type `Author`:

```
<Author>
        <firstname>V V</firstname>
        <lastname>Preetham</lastname>
<Author>
```

The schema fragment describing the preceding structure is as follows:

```
<element name="Author"/>
<complexType>
        <element name="firstname" type="xsd:string"/>
        <element name="lastname" type="xsd:string"/>
</complexType>
```

Following is an example of an array of type `colors`:

```
<colors soapenc:arrayType="xsd:string[4]">
        <color>Black</color>
        <color>Blue</color>
        <color>Green</color>
        <color>Red</color>
</colors>
```

Following is a schema fragment describing the preceding structure:

```
<element name="colors" type="soapenc:Array"/>
```

For a complete explanation of how to define compound types, please refer to section 5.4 of the SOAP 1.1 specification.

SOAP Over HTTP

SOAP over HTTP is almost a default combination that many developers may opt for in choosing a transport protocol for SOAP – mainly because HTTP is a ubiquitous protocol ruling the kingdom of Web transports today. Although you can implement SOAP over other Internet transports, such as FTP or SMTP, HTTP seems to be the choice of the masses. (The fact that SOAP over HTTP is much firewall friendlier than any other transport doesn't hurt either.)

This section explains how to use SOAP over HTTP. SOAP binding to HTTP makes use of the flexibility of SOAP over the HTTP request-response model, which means that the SOAP request parameters are provided in the HTTP request and the SOAP response parameters in the HTTP response. The SOAP intermediaries, however, are not the same as HTTP intermediaries.

If you include the SOAP entity bodies in an HTTP message, the HTTP applications must specify the media type as text/xml.

HTTP request

According to the SOAP specification, section 6.1, the HTTP request for sending the SOAP request parameters is a POST method. The following example binds a SOAP message over the HTTP protocol:

```
POST /bookdetails HTTP/1.1
Host: www.conceptuniv.com
Content-Type: text/xml; charset="utf-8"
Content-Length: n
SOAPAction: "http://www.conceptuniv.com/GetBookDetails"

<?xml version="1.0" encoding="UTF-8"?>
<soapenv:Envelope
xmlns:soapenv="http://schemas.xmlsoap.org/soap/envelope/"
soapenv:encodingStyle="http://schemas.xmlsoap.org/soap/encoding/"
xmlns:xsi="http://www.w3.org/1999/XMLSchema-instance"
xmlns:xsd="http://www.w3.org/1999/XMLSchema">
        <soapenv:Body>
                <wsns:GetBookDetails
xmlns:wsns="http://www.conceptuniv.com/wsns/">
                        <ISBN xsi:type="xsd:string">0-7645-8045-8</ISBN>
```

```
            </wsns:GetBookDetails>
        </soapenv:Body>
</soapenv:Envelope>
```

This example provides the necessary HTTP POST request section that carries the XML document over the HTTP transport. The XML document is a SOAP message that consists of an RPC-style call on a Web service.

SOAPAction

SOAPAction is an HTTP request header field that tells the server that the current HTTP document contains a SOAP message. It also indicates the intent behind such a message. The value of the SOAPAction field is a URI. The presence of the SOAPAction header tells the processing nodes and other firewalls to apply some filtering rules while processing the SOAP message. A zero-length URI ("") means that the intent of the HTTP message can be inferred by the target of the POST. No value indicates *no* intent for the HTTP message.

Following are some valid examples of SOAPAction URIs:

```
SOAPAction: http://www.conceptuniv.com/someservice
```

```
SOAPAction: "urn:Exchange"
```

```
SOAPAction: ""
```

```
SOAPAction:
```

HTTP response

An HTTP request is always followed by an HTTP response. The response contains the *status code* that provides status information about the request made on the server. The status code is an integer that follows the $1xx$, $2xx$, $3xx$, $4xx$ pattern. The $2xx$ status code indicates success, while the $4xx$ status code indicates failure in processing the request. According to the SOAP 1.1 specification, if a SOAP request fails and a SOAP error is generated, the SOAP HTTP server is responsible for generating an HTTP 500 Internal Server Error response. In addition, the HTTP server must also include the SOAP fault message in the response body.

Following is an example of a SOAP response within an HTTP response. The response contains the book's title, its author, and the price of the book as a response. title is of the type string; author is of the type string; and price is of the type float.

```
HTTP/1.1 200 OK
Content-Type: text/xml; charset="utf-8"
Content-Length: n
```

```
<?xml version="1.0" encoding="UTF-8"?>
<soapenv:Envelope
xmlns:soapenv="http://schemas.xmlsoap.org/soap/envelope/"
soapenv:encodingStyle="http://schemas.xmlsoap.org/soap/encoding/"
xmlns:xsi="http://www.w3.org/1999/XMLSchema-instance"
xmlns:xsd="http://www.w3.org/1999/XMLSchema">
<soapenv:Body>
       <wsns:BookDetails
xmlns:wsns="http://www.conceptuniv.com/wsns/">
           <title xsi:type="xsd:string">Book Title</title>
           <author xsi:type="xsd:string">Some Author</author>
           <price xsi:type="xsd:float">45.50</price>
       </wsns:BookDetails>
</soapenv:Body>
</soapenv:Envelope>
```

The following example illustrates an error in processing. This example illustrates a faultcode; soapenv:Client, that has a message stating that too many parameters were sent to execute a SOAP operation.

```
HTTP/1.1 500 Internal Server Error
Content-Type: text/xml; charset="utf-8"
Content-Length: n

<?xml version="1.0" encoding="UTF-8"?>
<soapenv:Envelope
xmlns:soapenv="http://schemas.xmlsoap.org/soap/envelope/"
soapenv:encodingStyle="http://schemas.xmlsoap.org/soap/encoding/"
xmlns:xsi="http://www.w3.org/1999/XMLSchema-instance"
xmlns:xsd="http://www.w3.org/1999/XMLSchema">
<soapenv:Body>
       <soapenv:Fault>
       <faultcode>soapenv:Client</faultcode>
       <faultstring>Too many parameters</faultstring>
       <detail>
       <wsns:faultdetails
xmlns:wsns="http://www.conceptuniv.com/wsns/">
           <message>
                   The rpc call that was made on the endpoint
failed due to too many parameters in the Request message.
           </message>
           <errorcode>
                   4001
```

```
            </errorcode>
         </wsns:faultdetails>
         </detail>
</soapenv:Fault>
</soapenv:Body>
</soapenv:Envelope>
```

SOAP-RPC

RPC over SOAP is the most recent addition to the SOAP standards. This addition is one of the most exciting, however, because it enables developers to make RPC-style calls in the SOAP message over a transport such as HTTP. Simplicity, extensibility, and modularity are the value propositions that SOAP brings to this distributed programming model for remote method calls. SOAP-RPC is simpler to execute over HTTP than RMI or CORBA, which require TCP or GIOP/IIOP transports. Although HTTP is unreliable compared to TCP or IIOP, SOAP-RPC over HTTP is the simplest, yet most extensible framework designed to date. Keep in mind, however, that the purpose of CORBA, RMI, DCOM, or any other distributed programming model is to build complex frameworks that may include features such as Distributed-Garbage Collector (DGC), object-by-reference, or remote-activation mechanisms. SOAP intentionally omits these features from its design. You should acknowledge that, without providing the correct extension mechanisms for SOAP, comparing the SOAP distributed model with CORBA, RMI, and DCOM as is doesn't yield a good argument.

This section explains the use of RPC within SOAP messages over HTTP. The RPC-style calls abide to the section-5 encoding rules of the SOAP 1.1 specification.

In using SOAP-RPC over HTTP, you map an RPC call to an HTTP request and an RPC response is mapped to an HTTP response. The following information is necessary at the time that you place an RPC call over HTTP:

- The URI of the target service

- Name of the operation

- Method signature (optional)

- Parameters list

- Header data (optional)

SOAP actually relies on the underlying wire format for specifying a mechanism to carry the URI. The protocol bindings of SOAP for a specified wire format derive such a mechanism. For SOAP over HTTP, the target URI for the request provides the URI for the resource for which the SOAP request is made.

SOAP Binding Example

Following is an example that relates to different WSDL document structures and
the respective SOAP/HTTP encoding formats. The following WSDL SOAP binding
example uses a document-style binding for the operation, the use attribute being
literal:

bookdetails.wsdl

```xml
<?xml version="1.0"?>

<definitions name="BookDetails"
targetNamespace="http://www.conceptuniv.com/bookdetails.wsdl"
xmlns:tns="http://www.conceptuniv.com/bookdetails.wsdl"
xmlns:xsd1="http://www.conceptuniv.com/bookdetails.xsd"
xmlns:soap="http://schemas.xmlsoap.org/wsdl/soap/"
xmlns="http://schemas.xmlsoap.org/wsdl/">

    <types>
        <schema
targetNamespace="http://www.conceptuniv.com/bookdetails.xsd"
            xmlns="http://www.w3.org/2000/10/XMLSchema">
            <element name="BookDetailsRequest">
                <complexType>
                    <all>
                        <element name="ISBN" type="string"/>
                    </all>
                </complexType>
            </element>
            <element name="BookDetails">
                <complexType>
                    <all>
<element name="title" type="string"/>
<element name="author" type="string"/>
<element name="price" type="float"/>
                    </all>
                </complexType>
            </element>
        </schema>
    </types>

    <message name="GetBookDetailsInput">
        <part name="body" element="xsd1:BookDetailsRequest"/>
    </message>

    <message name="GetBookDetailsOutput">
```

```
            <part name="body" element="xsd1:BookDetails"/>
    </message>

    <portType name="BookDetailsPortType">
        <operation name="GetBookDetails">
            <input message="tns:GetBookDetailsInput"/>
            <output message="tns:GetBookDetailsOutput"/>
        </operation>
    </portType>

<binding name="BookDetailsSoapBinding"
type="tns:BookDetailsPortType">
        <soap:binding style="document"
transport="http://schemas.xmlsoap.org/soap/http"/>
        <operation name="GetBookDetails">
            <soap:operation
soapAction="http://www.conceptuniv.com/GetBookDetails"/>
            <input>
                <soap:body use="literal"/>
            </input>
            <output>
                <soap:body use="literal"/>
            </output>
        </operation>
    </binding>

    <service name="BookDetailsService">
        <documentation>My first service</documentation>
        <port name="BookDetailsPort"
binding="tns:BookDetailsSoapBinding">
            <soap:address
location="http://www.conceptuniv.com/bookdetails"/>
        </port>
    </service>
</definitions>
```

The SOAP request over HTTP for the preceding code is as follows:

```
POST /bookdetails HTTP/1.1
Host: www.conceptuniv.com
Content-Type: text/xml; charset="utf-8"
Content-Length: n
SOAPAction: "http://www.conceptuniv.com/GetBookDetails"

<?xml version="1.0" encoding="UTF-8"?>
```

```
<soapenv:Envelope
xmlns:soapenv="http://schemas.xmlsoap.org/soap/envelope/">
<soapenv:Body>
<ISBN>0-7645-8045-8</ISBN>
</soapenv:Body>
</soapenv:Envelope>
```

Following is an example of a WSDL document that contains an RPC-style oper-ation, with the use attribute having a value of literal:

bookdetails.wsdl

```
<?xml version="1.0"?>
<definitions name="BookDetails" ...
...
...
<soap:binding style="rpc"
transport="http://schemas.xmlsoap.org/soap/http"/>
        <operation name="GetBookDetails">
            <soap:operation
soapAction="http://www.conceptuniv.com/GetBookDetails"/>
            <input>
                <soap:body use="literal"/>
            </input>
            <output>
                <soap:body use="literal"/>
            </output>
        </operation>
    </binding>
...
...
</definitions>
```

The SOAP request over HTTP for the preceding code is as follows:

```
POST /bookdetails HTTP/1.1
Host: www.conceptuniv.com
Content-Type: text/xml; charset="utf-8"
Content-Length: n
SOAPAction: "http://www.conceptuniv.com/GetBookDetails"

<?xml version="1.0" encoding="UTF-8"?>
<soapenv:Envelope
xmlns:soapenv="http://schemas.xmlsoap.org/soap/envelope/">
<soapenv:Body>
<GetBookDetails>
```

```
<ISBN>0-7645-8045-8</ISBN>
            </GetBookDetails>
</soapenv:Body>
</soapenv:Envelope>
```

Following is an example of a WSDL document that contains an RPC-style operation, with the use attribute having a value of encoded:

bookdetails.wsdl

```
<?xml version="1.0"?>
<definitions name="BookDetails" ...
...
...
<soap:binding style="rpc"
transport="http://schemas.xmlsoap.org/soap/http"/>
        <operation name="GetBookDetails">
            <soap:operation
soapAction="http://www.conceptuniv.com/GetBookDetails"/>
            <input>
<soap:body use="encoded"
encodingStyle="http://schemas.xmlsoap.org/soap/http"
namespace="http://www.conceptuniv.com/bookdetails"/>
            </input>
            <output>
<soap:body use="encoded"
encodingStyle="http://schemas.xmlsoap.org/soap/http"
namespace="http://www.conceptuniv.com/wsns"/>
            </output>
        </operation>
    </binding>
...
...
</definitions>
```

The SOAP request over HTTP for the preceding code is as follows:

```
POST /bookdetails HTTP/1.1
Host: www.conceptuniv.com
Content-Type: text/xml; charset="utf-8"
Content-Length: n
SOAPAction: "http://www.conceptuniv.com/GetBookDetails"

<?xml version="1.0" encoding="UTF-8"?>
<soapenv:Envelope
xmlns:soapenv="http://schemas.xmlsoap.org/soap/envelope/"
```

```
soapenv:encodingStyle="http://schemas.xmlsoap.org/soap/encoding/"
xmlns:xsi="http://www.w3.org/1999/XMLSchema-instance"
xmlns:xsd="http://www.w3.org/1999/XMLSchema">
<soapenv:Body>
<wsns:GetBookDetails xmlns:wsns="http://www.conceptuniv.com/wsns/">
<ISBN xsi:type="xsd:string">0-7645-8045-8</ISBN>
</wsns:GetBookDetails>
</soapenv:Body>
</soapenv:Envelope>
```

Now that I've described the structure, the various components, semantics, and uses of a SOAP message, I discuss in the following section how you process SOAP messages in a typical request-response Web-service transaction.

Processing of SOAP Message

You use *SOAP toolkits* to process SOAP messages. A SOAP toolkit enables you to create client-server applications that communicate with each other by using the SOAP protocol. Many vendors provide a wide range of toolkits for processing SOAP requests and responses in compliance with the SOAP specifications. Examples of such toolkits include Apache SOAP toolkit, Microsoft SOAP toolkit, IBM SOAP4J, and Axis. A SOAP toolkit validates the messages necessary for your application. It also checks whether a SOAP message contains the mandatory parts according to the SOAP specification.

To understand what happens in a simple Web-service transaction, consider a client application and a server application. The server application contains service methods that a client application invokes. A client application looks up the discovery document of a server application and invokes its published service method. A SOAP serializer converts this client invocation to a SOAP request. The SOAP request is then wrapped into a HTTP request by a HTTP encoder, and the request is sent to a SOAP server. A servlet in the SOAP server is responsible for decoding the HTTP request. It does so by dispatching the HTTP request to an HTTP/SOAP decoder on the SOAP server. The decoder decodes the request back to the original service call by the client. The service call is then executed. The response that the server application generates is encoded to a HTTP response by a SOAP/HTTP encoder in the SOAP server. This HTTP response passes to the servlet, which in turn dispatches the HTTP response to the client. On the client- side, an HTTP decoder receives the HTTP response and decodes the response to a SOAP message. The SOAP deserializer on the client system decodes the SOAP message and passes the response to the client application.

In this chapter, I use Apache SOAP toolkit to implement a SOAP-based Web service and create a client SOAP application to invoke the Web service.

Implementing SOAP By Using the Apache SOAP Toolkit

In this section, you learn how to create SOAP client and SOAP server applications that use SOAP over HTTP to communicate with each other in a typical Web-service operation. You use the Apache SOAP toolkit to implement the SOAP server application as a Web service. You also create a SOAP client to access deployed Web services. This Web service provides a horoscope based on a client's request.

For this example, you need to download the Tomcat server, the Apache SOAP toolkit, and the Apache Xerces XML parser. You must also install a Java Virtual Machine as part of the Java SDK installation. I use the following version of the Java Standard Development Kit and tools for this example:

- j2sdk-1_3_0_02-win

- Jakarta-tomcat-3.3.1

- soap-bin-2.2

- Xerces-J-bin.2.0.1

You can download the tools from the following links:

- Tomcat server from `http://jakarta.apache.org/builds/`

- Apache Soap toolkit from `http://xml.apache.org/dist/soap/`

- Xerces XML parser from `http://xml.apache.org/dist/xerces-j/`

You also need to download the following JAR files:

- `servlet.jar`

- `mail.jar`

- `activation.jar`

Download `servlet.jar` from `http://java.sun.com/products/jsp/download.html`. For the `mail.jar` file, download the JavaMail package available at `http://java.sun.com/products/javamail/`. Download the JavaBeans Activation Framework 1.0.1 release from `http://java.sun.com/products/javabeans/glasgow/jaf.html` for the `activation.jar` file.

After you download the necessary tools and files, the next step is to set the environment variables. Set the environment variable `TOMCAT_HOME` to the home directory of the installed Tomcat server. Similarly, set `JAVA_HOME` to the home directory of your Java Standard Edition installation. If you install the Java SDK and the

Tomcat server in your C: drive in a Windows system, for example, set the environment variable as follows:

```
JAVA_HOME=C:\jdk1.3.0_02TOMCAT_HOME=C:\Jakarta-tomcat-3.3.1
```

Set the path variable pointing to the bin folder of your Java installation and the bin folder of your Tomcat installation. Set the `CLASSPATH` to include `xercesImpl.jar`, `xercesSamples.jar`, `xmlParserAPIs.jar`, `soap.jar`, `servlet.jar`, `mail.jar`, and `activation.jar`.

The `xercesImpl.jar`, `xercesSamples.jar`, and `xmlParserAPIs.jar` files are in Xerces installation directory. You find `soap.jar` in the `lib` folder of the Apache SOAP toolkit installation.

 You must set `xercesImpl.jar` prior to any JAR file in the `CLASSPATH`.

After setting the environmental variables, execute the following command:

```
echo %CLASSPATH%
```

On executing the command, the `CLASSPATH` appears, as shown:

```
C:\xerces-2_0_1\xercesImpl.jar;C:\xerces-2_0_1\xercesSamples.jar;C:\xerces-
2_0_1\xmlParserAPIs.jar;
C:\soap-2_2\lib\soap.jar;C:\javamail-1_2\javamail-1.2\mail.jar;
C:\servlet\servlet.jar;C:\jaf-1.0.1\activation.jar;C:\example\
```

 The `C:\example` that appears in the `CLASSPATH` is the directory where you keep the server-application CLASS file.

Now edit the `tomcat.bat` file to include your `CLASSPATH` prior to its classes. To do so, open `tomcat.bat`, which is in the `bin` directory of your Tomcat installation and edit the `set CLASSPATH=%TOMCAT_INSTALL%\lib\tomcat.jar` statement as follows:

```
set CLASSPATH=%CLASSPATH%;%TOMCAT_INSTALL%\lib\tomcat.jar
```

Save the changes.

Now edit `server.xml` in the `conf` folder of your Tomcat installation to include the following code:

```
<Context
path="/soap"
docBase="C:/soap-2_0/webapps/soap"
reloadable="true">
</Context>
```

Save the `server.xml` file.

Create the service application to deploy in the Apache SOAP toolkit. This application is a simple Java class that takes a `String` parameter representing the zodiac sign of a client. By using this `string` parameter, the application generates a horoscope message based on the appropriate zodiac sign by using if ... else statements. The code of the server class is as follows:

```
public class HoroscopeService
  {
  public String getHoroscope( String zodiac)
    {

    if (zodiac.equalsIgnoreCase("Aries"))

    return "You may be sensitive to comments made by family or
friends today. Opportunities for investment should be considered.
Keep on the move.";


    else if (zodiac.equalsIgnoreCase("Taurus"))

    return "Your mind will be on old memories. Some of the memories
that surface will prompt you to readdress what you have done with
your life. A good day for travelling.";


    else if (zodiac.equalsIgnoreCase("Gemini"))

    return "You will feel the need to guard and protect all
possessions and people you love. Today you will fight for what you
believe is right. You are courageous, caring and certainly
charismatic.";


    else if (zodiac.equalsIgnoreCase("Cancer"))

    return "Today you will want to get up and speak on behalf of
those who can't. The more you do to help a worthy cause the more
```

likely you will be to get ahead. Go out for a party with your
friends.";

    else if (zodiac.equalsIgnoreCase("Leo"))

    return "Today you will want to surge ahead. You can do that if
you are true to yourself and honest about what your intentions are.
The more you push yourself, the farther you will go.";

    else if (zodiac.equalsIgnoreCase("Virgo"))

    return "Give a bit of discipline to your creative side today.
You will get a chance to start a new project.";

    else if (zodiac.equalsIgnoreCase("Libra"))

    return "You have the power to work extremely efficiently and
effectively today. Make a plan and get it done.";

    else if (zodiac.equalsIgnoreCase("Scorpio"))

    return "Charge ahead with a romantic pursuit today. But do not
let things discourage you.";

    else if (zodiac.equalsIgnoreCase("Sagittarius"))

    return "Your private life may be feeling very much 'not your
own' today. Do not let this discourage you. Instead free your mind
and go for a stroll.";

    else if (zodiac.equalsIgnoreCase("Capricorn"))

    return "You will be bubbling with energy today. Romance has its
rewarding and promising sides today.";

    else if (zodiac.equalsIgnoreCase("Aquarius"))

    return "Misunderstanding may creep up between your friends
today. But you will eventually move out of it with your brilliant
diplomacy and tact.";

```
    else if (zodiac.equalsIgnoreCase("Pisces"))
```

```
    return "You may want to keep a close eye on your investments
today. Today the more you work, the better you will feel about
yourself";
```

```
else
```

```
return "Please enter a valid zodiac sign.";
```

```
}
  }
```

Create a folder that you name `example` and compile the `HoroscopeService.java` file in it. You are now ready to deploy your Web service in the Apache SOAP toolkit. To deploy the Web service, start the Tomcat server by executing the following command at the command line:

```
tomcat run
```

 You can stop the Tomcat server by executing the following command:

```
shutdown.
```

Now open the browser and type the following address in the address bar:

```
http://localhost:8080/soap
```

The Apache-Soap welcome page appears. Click the `Run the admin client` hyperlink to open the Apache Soap Admin page. Click the `Deploy` link. In the table Service Deployment Descriptor Template that appears, add the following entries:

```
ID: urn:example:horoscopeService
Scope: Request
Methods: getHoroscope
Provider Type: Java
Provider Class: HoroscopeService
Static? No
```

After you add the preceding data, click the Deploy button. If your service deploys, the following message appears:

```
Service urn:example:horoscopeService deployed
```

After you successfully deploy the horoscope service, you need to create a SOAP client to access the deployed service.

To do so, create a Java application that you name `HoroscopeClient.java` and import the following classes and packages in your application:

```
import java.io.*;
import java.net.*;
import java.util.*;
import org.apache.soap.util.xml.*;
import org.apache.soap.*;
import org.apache.soap.rpc.*;
```

Add the static method `callHoroscopeService (URL url, String zodiac, String urn)` to the `HoroscopeClient` class. This method takes the URL of the `RPCrouter` endpoint, the parameter that you provide for the `service` method, and the `String` representation of the `ID` attribute value of your deployed service. As you deploy your service on the local machine, the URL is `http://localhost:8080/soap/servlet/rpcrouter/`. In the `callHoroscopeService (URL url, String zodiac, String urn)` method, create a `Call` object. Using the `Call` instance, set the URI of the target object with the `string` parameter `urn` of the method. Set the encoding style to `Constants.NS_URI_SOAP_ENC`, as shown in the following code snippet:

```
Call call = new Call();
call.setTargetObjectURI(urn);
call.setMethodName( "getHoroscope" );
call.setEncodingStyleURI( Constants.NS_URI_SOAP_ENC );
```

Set the parameter of the `Call` object by using the `Parameter` object with the argument name `zodiac`, the argument type `String.class`, the value of the argument `zodiac`, and the encoding style set to `null`. The following code shows how to set the parameter of the `Call` object:

```
Vector params = new Vector();
    params.addElement( new
Parameter("zodiac",String.class,zodiac,null));
    call.setParams(params);
```

To send your SOAP request for the service, call the `invoke()` method as follows:

```
Response response = call.invoke( url, "");
```

If no fault is generated, store the `response` value in a `String`, as follows:

```
Response response = call.invoke( url, "");
        if(!response.generatedFault())
```

```
            {
            Parameter param = response.getReturnValue();
            horoscope=(String) param.getValue();
            }
```

If a fault is generated, print the fault code along with the fault message, as follows:

```
else
            {
             System.out.println("Result= Fault");
            Fault f = response.getFault();
            System.err.println("Fault= " + f.getFaultCode() + ", " +
            f.getFaultString());
            }
```

Catch any exception that may arise and return the String that contains the response value, as follows:

```
catch( SOAPException e )
            {
            System.out.println("Exception");
            System.err.println("Exception="+ e.getFaultCode() +
            e.getMessage() );
            }
return horoscope;
```

Inside the main method, create the URL that you provide as parameter to the callHoroscopeService (URL url, String zodiac, String urn) method. Call the callHoroscopeService (URL url, String zodiac, String urn) method, passing the URL that you created, the string representation of the zodiac sign that a client provides at the command prompt, and the string representation of the Web-service identifier. (The Web service identifier is the ID of your Web service that you specify on deploying the Web service.) The following code shows the main() method of the HoroscopeClient class:

```
public static void main( String[] args )
{
if (args.length == 0) {
                        System.out.println("Provide your zodiac
sign");
                        return;
                        }
try
        {
            URL url=new
```

```
URL("http://localhost:8080/soap/servlet/rpcrouter");
        String zodiac= args[0];
         String urn = "urn:example:horoscopeService";
        String check = callHoroscopeService(url,zodiac,urn);
        System.out.println(check);
    }
  catch (Exception e)
     {
       e.printStackTrace();
     }
 }
```

The complete source code of the client SOAP application is as follows:

```
import java.io.*;
import java.net.*;
import java.util.*;
import org.apache.soap.util.xml.*;
import org.apache.soap.*;
import org.apache.soap.rpc.*;

public class HoroscopeClient
   {
static String horoscope;
   public static String callHoroscopeService (URL url, String
zodiac, String urn) throws Exception
     {

    Call call = new Call();
    call.setTargetObjectURI(urn);
    call.setMethodName( "getHoroscope" );
    call.setEncodingStyleURI( Constants.NS_URI_SOAP_ENC );
    Vector params = new Vector();
    params.addElement( new
Parameter("zodiac",String.class,zodiac,null));
    call.setParams(params);

    try
      {

      Response response = call.invoke( url, "");
      if(!response.generatedFault())
        {
       Parameter param = response.getReturnValue();
       horoscope=(String) param.getValue();
```

```
            }
        else
          {
           System.out.println("Result= Fault");
           Fault f = response.getFault();
           System.err.println("Fault= " + f.getFaultCode() + ", " +
           f.getFaultString());
           }
         }
      catch( SOAPException e )
         {
         System.out.println("Exception");
         System.err.println("Exception="+ e.getFaultCode() +
         e.getMessage() );
         }
return horoscope;
       }
public static void main( String[] args )
       {
if (args.length == 0) {
                   System.out.println("Enter your zodiac sign");
                   return;
                   }
try
           {
            URL url=new
URL("http://localhost:8080/soap/servlet/rpcrouter");
           String zodiac= args[0];
                   String urn = "urn:example:horoscopeService";
           String check = callHoroscopeService(url,zodiac,urn);
           System.out.println(check);
        }
    catch (Exception e)
       {
         e.printStackTrace();
       }
 }
 }
```

Compile the client SOAP application. Run the application by using the following command:

```
java HoroscopeClient aries
```

You see the output of the horoscope corresponding to the zodiac sign that you specify.

Summary

This chapter provides the complete syntax for and an explanation of the SOAP 1.1 standards. The chapter explains the design goals of SOAP and provides an explanation of what makes SOAP modular and extensible. In addition, the chapter provides explanations of different message-exchange models and patterns of message flow. The chapter also details how to define a SOAP message based on its envelope, header, and body elements. The chapter provides a detailed list of SOAP faults and their appropriate subelements. It also explains the encoding rules of a SOAP message. The chapter describes how to process SOAP requests and responses. It also provides descriptions of the SOAP bindings over HTTP along with a set of examples explaining how to carry SOAP messages over HTTP for a WSDL document. Finally, the chapter shows how to deploy server applications in the Apache SOAP toolkit and how a client SOAP application invokes the service method of the server application.

Chapter 5

UDDI

IN THIS CHAPTER

- ◆ What is UDDI?

- ◆ Why is UDDI important?

- ◆ UDDI technical framework

- ◆ UDDI data structures

- ◆ UDDI programmer's API

- ◆ UDDI best practices

- ◆ UDDI workarounds

- ◆ WSDL with UDDI – an example

UNIVERSAL DESCRIPTION, DISCOVERY, AND INTEGRATION, OR UDDI, is the core of the Web-services integration stack. UDDI is a registry specification for Web services. UDDI provides a distributed information store that you can access across the Internet by using a standard protocol such as SOAP. The information repository of UDDI holds the references to the programmable elements of the Web-services architecture.

UDDI specification in general describes a method in which enterprises can publish and discover the Web-services interface that provides the invocation details of a service-abstraction. UDDI acts as a distributed centralized repository, which UDDI operators manage. A UDDI operator act as caretakers of huge data stores.

The very presence of a standardized data repository gives rise to a global electronic marketplace that almost all the businesses that provide and utilize Web services can use. Enterprises can dynamically discover each other's services and invoke those services at runtime. The businesses that like to contribute to such a dynamic market place may lie in any sector or may serve any segment of the market in the economy.

UDDI started as an initiative from three companies: Ariba, IBM, and Microsoft. Currently, hundreds of companies are joining the initiative to specify the UDDI standards. The current version of the UDDI specification is 2.0. You can find the UDDI specification at `www.uddi.org`. This chapter provides details of the technical architecture of UDDI, the data structures, and the APIs that you use in implementing the specification.

What Is UDDI?

Until recently, the number of enterprises sharing services with one another in the electronics data integration frameworks was limited. Eventually, the industry realized that such marketplaces, built on proprietary integration standards, were limiting opportunities for businesses to interact with other businesses outside the scope of the marketplace. The cost of interoperability with other businesses, along with the cost of implementing a framework that invoked the services of other business entities, outweighed the benefits of this invocation of services.

The evolution of Web services has given rise to a global electronic market that provides interoperability among differing services and reduces the relative cost of business interactions. The prime motivation that is driving enterprises toward this service-oriented framework is the Return On Investment (ROI) that this framework brings to them. A significant amount of cost reduction is sure to be realized in making such services interoperate with the disparate service frameworks that exist on the Internet today. The advantages of this framework in maintaining a dynamic relationship with such distributed, disparate services is a major reason for the success of today's business-to-business (B2B) marketplace.

Web Services are now used as one of the most potential B2B integration tools. If, for example, a company participating in a B2B exchange wants to make the details of its procurement needs available through a Web service, other companies involved in the exchange can electronically query the Web service to identify potential opportunities for supplying materials to that company. Consider a scenario in which a material-processing company, Materials, Inc., is interested in seeking out opportunities on the Internet. If Materials, Inc., wants to find all the companies that provide their procurement details as Web services where should it look for this information? This question is exactly what UDDI answers.

UDDI is a *directory,* much like a typical yellow-pages directory, for all the businesses involved in these exchanges. It publicizes some of or all its services as a Web service. UDDI is an industry standard to publish or register such businesses in a central database. UDDI manages all such registered businesses in the form of business taxonomy, such as the Thomas Register, which is explained in the section "UDDI Programmer's API."

UDDI sits in the center of the Web services stack. Compared to other distributed service models such as Remote Method Invocation (RMI) or Common Object Request Broker Architecture (CORBA), UDDI plays the same part as the RMI registry-server in the RMI framework or plays a part like the interface repository in the CORBA framework. UDDI acts as a central repository for the service interfaces that the service providers publish.

For more information on architectural processes of the Web services stack, refer to Chapter 1. Refer to Chapter 3 to know more about WSDL.

The architectural processes of the Web-services stack explain the primary processes that you invoke as you execute the service.. The primary steps in the architectural process are *description, discovery,* and *invocation.* You define a service interface in WSDL.

After you are through defining a service interface, you may eventually publish the service interface to a central registry. This central registry is also known as a *service broker.* The service broker is a place where you can find a list of references to businesses interested in providing services. The service broker enables users of the service to look up and identify an appropriate service so that the users can invoke that service. Within the sequence of steps necessary to execute a service implementation, you must go through many different processes, as shown in Figure 5-1.

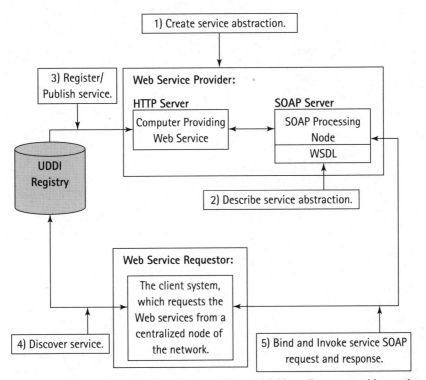

Figure 5-1: Process flow showing the description, publishing, discovery, and invocation of a service abstraction

The process flow shown in Figure 5-1 summarizes the high-level sequence of steps that you use in invoking a service on the provider nodes. The description of the service within a WSDL file exists in a standard XML format. SOAP acts as a message channel and connects the service provider, the service broker, and the service requestor. You can also overlay SOAP on a transport protocol such as HTTP. Figure 5-2 gives you a high-level view of the relationship between the standards that different service roles use.

For information on service roles, refer to Chapter 1.

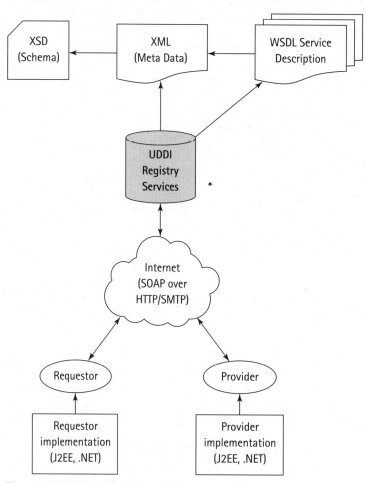

Figure 5-2: Relationship between different service roles

UDDI is not a fully-blown directory service, like DNS, or a search engine, like one that you use on the Internet for searching content. UDDI is a specification for a "technical-discovery" layer that defines the following:

◆ Structure for business registries

◆ Application Programming Interfaces (APIs) for the programmers

The business registry forms the backbone of the UDDI specification that describes the service-abstraction in a data-neutral XML format. The programmer APIs provide a way to publish or inquire about services in the UDDI framework. UDDI is like an industry initiative to create a standard specification to perform the following tasks:

♦ Describe and publish services

♦ Look up and discover services

♦ Bind and integrate your services with other business services

Why Is UDDI Important?

Until a couple of years ago, businesses used different mechanisms to locate service partners to perform business exchanges on the Web.

Now, appropriate vendors can provide the exact service that an enterprise is looking for at an economical cost and at the speed of the Internet. This description seemed way too ideal in an era where there no real interoperability standards were defined for integrating services. Until recently, the digital marketplace consisted of custom-defined standards proprietary to a given marketplace. Only those businesses enlisted into such marketplaces could use that custom standard in the marketplace. Later, as Electronic Data Interchange (EDI X12), United Nations Rules For Electronic Data Interchange for Administration, Commerce, and Transport (UN/EDI-FACT), and other data-interchange formats became established as standards, the industry started to work together in its efforts to implement its service frameworks by using standards, such as EDI-X12. Yet, the industry noticed that integrating services based on such standards was too costly, time-consuming, and complex.

Over time, the XML formats started to mature and evolved within the industry as a standard data-neutral and platform-neutral data format. Eventually, the development of XML-RPC provided organizations with a way to implement pilot projects for testing XML message formats that carried invocation semantics to a service-abstraction. This situation gave rise to messaging formats such as SOAP. As SOAP matured, the industry wanted to use the tried-and-tested model of dynamic-service discovery over SOAP. Dynamic discover is the ability to query a central repository to expose all the necessary interface details of a service at run time. SOAP is, of course, a simple framework that deliberately omits many complex issues in its design. The decision to so limit SOAP also limited its dynamic-discovery capabilities, which led to the need for a protocol that could provide the same features (such as dynamic discovery feature) as an interface repository in the CORBA architecture. Dynamically querying a centralized repository that could provide the details of a service abstraction poses certain requirements. Based on the need for the dynamic discovery of Web services, the industry started investigating newer approaches to aid in building a repository to expose the metadata necessary for service discovery. One of these initiatives was UDDI.

UDDI is a platform-neutral, distributed, global specification built on top of SOAP. UDDI uses XML schemas as its format for describing these Web services. UDDI provides a way for organizations across the globe to quickly look up and discover the right businesses with which to integrate their own services. The look-up process can be directly based on some of the following criteria:

◆ The name of the organization

◆ The geographic taxonomy or some industry-specific code of an organization

◆ The service that a business is declaring that it can provide

The UDDI framework consists of business registries that hold the preceding information in different structures. These business registries are as follows:

◆ **White Pages:** This registry provides a directory mechanism for registering Web services specific to the name of the business entity, contact information, IDs, or any other human-readable description of such services. So, if the requestors have any of the preceding information, they can inspect the white pages of the UDDI to look up an appropriate service based on the same information.

◆ **Yellow Pages:** This registry provides a directory mechanism for registering Web services specific to the services and product index of the service. The provider can categorize the service provision under geographic location or under a specific industry code for the business entity.

◆ **Green Pages:** This registry provides a directory mechanism for registering Web services specific to the functionality of the service provision. The service provider must publish such service-abstractions based on e-business rules, operational descriptions, invocation descriptions, and data-binding aspects of the service-abstraction. This registry enables the service requestor to look up a service based on the required functionality.

After the organization that's searching a central repository such as UDDI finds a business that suits the current needs of the organization, it needs a standard way to bind to such a service provider. UDDI provides a programmatic interface that enables a company to dynamically discover and bind to the business process of the service provider. In this way, the organization that wants to conduct business with the service provider can smoothly integrate its processes with the services of the service provider. Some of the benefits of using a centralized repository such as UDDI are as follows:

◆ Global visibility of your business

◆ New partnerships on a global scale, where trading of goods and commerce can occur automatically by finding these processes on the Internet

◆ Ad-hoc service integration

◆ Data and platform independence

◆ Economic scalability for future expansion of services

The UDDI Technical Framework

The UDDI framework is based on business registries; the registration, look-up, and discovery of services; and the process of binding to services. *Business registration* is a process in which a service provider publishes an XML document containing descriptions of its services. The *registration* occurs in any of the directories referred by the *business registry,* such as White Pages, Yellow Pages, or Green Pages. Publishing a service interface occurs through a Web portal or through any of the vendor-defined tools that enable you to programmatically hook up to the service broker to publish the service. The vendor tools use the UDDI's programmer APIs to register provider services to the centralized nodes of the registry.

UDDI is a distributed datastore that maintains many such nodes across the Internet. The concept is the same as that of Light Weight Directory Access Protocol (LDAP). Many players in the industry take care of such distributed nodes of the UDDI framework. The nodes are all distributed in the Internet space and share data and context with one another. The businesses that maintain and administer such nodes are known as *node operators*. The node operators are responsible for maintaining the distributed context within the UDDI business registries. Node operators are also responsibility for replicating data among some nodes. Several node operators are taking care of various UDDI root nodes across the Internet. Among the players are IBM, Microsoft, and Hewlett Packard (HP). After a service provider chooses a particular node to register, the provider gets free registration to publish the service interface to the nodes that any of these node operators maintain. The provider does not need to reregister to other nodes that different operators maintain. The operator who maintains the node automatically takes care of data replication. In this way, the service interface that you register is freely available to all requestors across the globe who want to integrate their processes with your services.

UDDI semantics derive from the UDDI specification, available at `www.uddi.org/specification.html`. The UDDI version 2.0 specification is classified in the following documents:

◆ UDDI Version 2.0 Data Structure Specification

◆ UDDI Version 2.0 XML Schema

◆ UDDI Version 2.0 Programmer's API Specification

◆ UDDI Version 2.0 Replication Specification

◆ UDDI Version 2.0 XML Replication Schema

- ◆ UDDI Version 2.0 XML Custody Schema
- ◆ UDDI Version 2.0 Operator's Specification

UDDI Data Structures

The business registries of the UDDI technical layer use a schema format based on XML. The XML schema provides much flexibility and extensibility for defining the services contained in these business registries. The four information types that these business registries hold are as follows:

- ◆ Information about the business
- ◆ Information about the service
- ◆ Information about the binding
- ◆ Information about the specification for services

The following sections describe these types of information in detail.

Information about business

A business' registration is defined in an XML format. Information about the business becomes an element within the XML file, which provides the registration information to the business registry. The *businessEntity* element represents the information about the business. The information about your business can be the name of your business, the name of the person to contact, business identifiers, or categories to which your business belongs. (The *business identifiers* can be further classified into Dun & Bradstreet (D&B) numbers and tax numbers.) The businessEntity element serves as the topmost structure to provide this related information about the business. Information about the business identifiers or the categorization of the business is used in a Yellow Pages registry to provide taxonomies so that requestors can search the registry. The information about the business name, the name of the person to contact, and the address can be used in a White Pages registry.

The following code provides the schema for a businessEntity element:

```
<element name="businessEntity" type="uddi:businessEntity" />
<complexType name="businessEntity">
<sequence>
        <element ref="uddi:discoveryURLs" minOccurs="0" />
        <element ref="uddi:name" maxOccurs="unbounded" />
        <element ref="uddi:description" minOccurs="0"
maxOccurs="unbounded" />
        <element ref="uddi:contacts" minOccurs="0" />
```

```
        <element ref="uddi:businessServices" minOccurs="0" />
        <element ref="uddi:identifierBag" minOccurs="0" />
        <element ref="uddi:categoryBag" minOccurs="0" />
</sequence>
<attribute name="businessKey" use="required" type="uddi:businessKey"
/>
<attribute name="operator" use="optional" type="string" />
<attribute name="authorizedName" use="optional" type="string" />
</complexType>
```

The following code example illustrates the use of the businessEntity element:

```
<?xml version="1.0" encoding="utf-8" ?>
<businessDetail generic="2.0" xmlns="urn:uddi-org:api_v2"
operator="www.ibm.com/services/uddi" truncated="false">
        <businessEntity businessKey="929F5AB0-3150-11D6-9E2B-
000629DC0A2B" operator="www.ibm.com/services/uddi"
authorizedName="1000004DBR">
        <discoveryURLs>
            <discoveryURL useType="businessEntity">

https://www.ibm.com/services/uddi/v2beta/uddiget?businessKey=929F5AB
0-3150-11D6-9E2B-000629DC0A2B
            </discoveryURL>
        </discoveryURLs>
        <name xml:lang="en">ConceptUniv, LLC</name>
        <description xml:lang="en">
                Default description
        </description>
        <contacts>
                <contact useType="Software Architect">
                <description xml:lang="en">Default contact
description</description>
                <personName>V V Preetham</personName>
                <phone useType="Dummy phone">123 456 7989</phone>
                <email useType="">preetham@conceptuniv.com</email>
                </contact>
        </contacts>
        <businessServices>
                <!-- businessServices skipped -->
        </businessServices>
        <categoryBag>
                <keyedReference tModelKey="UUID:C1ACF26D-
9672-4404-9D70-39B756E62AB4" keyName="Categorization (taxonomy)"
keyValue="categorization" />
```

```
    </categoryBag>
  </businessEntity>
</businessDetail>
```

Information about the service

You use the *businessService* element to depict the service information that a business publicizes. These descriptions provide the technical definitions of the service. The businessService element is actually a subelement of the businessEntity element. This businessService subelement provides a description of services relating to the high-level business processes of the business, such as procurement services and inventory services. The businessEntity element can contain one or more businessService subelements that describe more than one service available to a business.

You can further classify businessService based on the business category or the geographic category of the business. You can also classify the business services into industry-based taxonomies, such as SIC, UN/SPSC (ECMA), and NAICS, or geographic taxonomies based on ISO 3166 standards. The businessService element contains descriptions such as the address of the Web service to communicate with, optional information about a specific marketplace hosting such services, the quality of services such as load balancing, and other such service specifications that the Web services applications can use.

The following code provides the schema for a businessService element:

```
<element name="businessService" type="uddi:businessService" />
<complexType name="businessService">
      <sequence>
            <element ref="uddi:name" maxOccurs="unbounded" />
            <element ref="uddi:description" minOccurs="0"
maxOccurs="unbounded" />
            <element ref="uddi:bindingTemplates" />
            <element ref="uddi:categoryBag" minOccurs="0" />
      </sequence>
<attribute name="serviceKey" use="required" type="uddi:serviceKey"
/>
<attribute name="businessKey" use="optional" type="uddi:businessKey"
/>
</complexType>
```

The following code example illustrates the use of the businessService element:

```
<businessService serviceKey="896FF100-876E-22E7-670A-0041DC679C1E"
businessKey="929F5AB0-3150-11D6-9E2B-000629DC0A2B">
      <name>SomeService</name>
      <description xml:lang="en">
          Default service description
```

```
        </description>
        <bindingTemplates>
                <bindingTemplate bindingKey="xxxxxxxx-xxxx-xxxx-xxxx-
xxxxxxxxxxxx" serviceKey="xxxxxxxx-xxxx-xxxx-xxxx-xxxxxxxxxxxx">
                <description xml:lang="en" />
                <accessPointURLType="http">
                http://www.conceptuniv.com/somerouter
                </accessPoint>
                <!-- tModelInstance reference skipped -->
                </bindingTemplate>
        </bindingTemplates>
        <categoryBag>
                <keyedReference
tModelKey="UUID:28B85030-3154-11D6-9E2B-000629DC0A2B"
keyName="TestModel"/>
        </categoryBag>
</businessService>
```

Information about the binding

You use the *bindingTemplate* element to provide the semantic-level definitions for how to invoke the service. The information available in the bindingTemplate element helps the requestors discover the binding and invocation semantics of the service-abstraction. (The bindingTemplate element is actually a subelement within the businessEntity element.) If the businessService element provides the address details of a particular service, the bindingTemplate element provides the details of how to bind to the provided address and, eventually, the service that is offered. If businessService provides an address for an inventory service, for example, the binding template provides the necessary information about how to obtain a bill of material for a particular product from such an inventory service. The information may include the protocol of access, security considerations, and message patterns.

The following code provides the schema for a bindingTemplate element:

```
<element name="bindingTemplate" type="uddi:bindingTemplate" />
<complexType name="bindingTemplate">
        <sequence>
                <element ref="uddi:description" minOccurs="0"
maxOccurs="unbounded" />
                <choice>
                        <element ref="uddi:accessPoint" minOccurs="0"
/>
                        <element ref="uddi:hostingRedirector"
minOccurs="0" />
                </choice>
                <element ref="uddi:tModelInstanceDetails" />
```

```
        </sequence>
<attribute name="serviceKey" use="optional" type="uddi:serviceKey"
/>
<attribute name="bindingKey" use="required" type="uddi:bindingKey"
/>
</complexType>
```

The following code example illustrates the use of bindingTemplate:

```
<bindingTemplate bindingKey="xxxxxxxx-xxxx-xxxx-xxxx-xxxxxxxxxxxx"
serviceKey="xxxxxxxx-xxxx-xxxx-xxxx-xxxxxxxxxxxx">
        <description xml:lang="en" />
        <accessPoint URLType="http">
                http://www.conceptuniv.com/somerouter
    </accessPoint>
<tModelInstanceDetails>
                <tModelInstanceInfo
                tModelKey="UUID:28B85030-3154-11D6-9E2B-
000629DC0A2B">
                    <instanceDetails>
                        <overviewDoc>
                        <overviewURL>

http://www.conceptuniv.com/wsdl/dummy.wsdl
                        </overviewURL>
                        </overviewDoc>
                        <instanceParms>
                                <port name="SomePort"
binding="SomeBinding"/>
                        </instanceParms>
                    </instanceDetails>
                </tModelInstanceInfo>
        </tModelInstanceDetails>
</bindingTemplate>
```

Information about the specification for services

The bindingTemplate element in the preceding section provides information about how to access the Web service. You, as a programmer, probably want to know more about the service invocation, such as the methods involved in the invocation and the structures that you use in information exchange. To make these specifications available, the bindingTemplate element contains the tModelInstanceDetails element that references information about the behavior and the programming interface of the service. The tModelInstanceDetails element refers to a tModel element. You can consider the tModel element as the metadata for a specification.

The tModel element contains URL pointers to the centralized specification that the provider nodes maintain.

The following code provides the schema for a tModel element:

```
<element name="tModel" type="uddi:tModel" />
<complexType name="tModel">
        <sequence>
                <element ref="uddi:name" />
                <element ref="uddi:description" minOccurs="0" maxOc
                curs="unbounded" />
                <element ref="uddi:overviewDoc" minOccurs="0" />
                <element ref="uddi:identifierBag" minOccurs="0" />
                <element ref="uddi:categoryBag" minOccurs="0" />
        </sequence>
<attribute name="tModelKey" use="required" type="uddi:tModelKey" />
<attribute name="operator" use="optional" type="string" />
<attribute name="authorizedName" use="optional" type="string" />
</complexType>
```

The following code example illustrates the use of tModel:

```
<tModel authorizedName="..." operator="..." tModelKey="...">
        <name>GetBookDetails</name>
        <description xml:lang="en">
                WSDL description of a book details service interface
        </description>
        <overviewDoc>
                <description xml:lang="en">
                        WSDL source document.
                </description>
                <overviewURL>
                        http://www.conceptuniv.com/bookdetails.wsdl
                </overviewURL>
        </overviewDoc>
        <categoryBag>
                <keyedReference tModelKey="UUID:C1ACF26D-
9672-4404-9D70-39B756E62AB4"
                keyName="TestModel"
                keyValue="wsdlSpec"/>
        </categoryBag>
</tModel>
```

Publisher assertion

The publisherAssertion element is a new data structure that the UDDI version 2.0 adds to the specification. The publisherAssertion data structure provides a way in which you can depict relationships between businesses. If an enterprise consists of more than one *businessEntity,* the publisher assertion comes in handy in providing a relationship model for such entities. According to the specification, two business entities can represent their relationship by using the ***_publisherAssertion messages. Both businessEntities should publish the exact publisher assertion so that no confusion exists over resolving the relationship.

The following code provides the schema for a publisherAssertion element:

```
<element name="publisherAssertion" type="uddi:publisherAssertion" />
<complexType name="publisherAssertion">
        <sequence>
                <element ref="uddi:fromKey" />
                <element ref="uddi:toKey" />
                <element ref="uddi:keyedReference" />
        </sequence>
</complexType>
```

 Please refer to the UDDI Version 2.0 Data Structure Specification for a detailed explanation of all the keywords that I use in the current section.

Figure 5-3 gives you an overall idea of the relationships between the different data structures that I explain in the preceding sections.

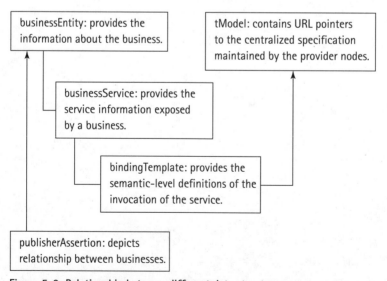

Figure 5-3: Relationship between different data structures

UDDI Programmer's API

The *UDDI API* provides access for enterprises so that they can publish any number of classifications to their business registrations. This access helps the requestors to discover services based on business name, product code, or service type. The UDDI 2.0 specification adds the capability to manage validated taxonomies. Following are the two types of taxonomies that the UDDI 2.0 specification supports:

- **Unchecked taxonomies:** Unchecked taxonomies provide unrestricted references to themselves. You use these taxonomies without an associated validator. Publishers can register such taxonomies by classifying a newly registered tModel as a categorization taxonomy.

- **Checked taxonomies:** Checked taxonomies restrict the references to themselves. You use these taxonomies with an associated validator that validates the value of the saved data, which contains references to such taxonomies.

 The taxonomy-provider specification available on www.uddi.org provides a detailed approach to understanding the six steps for a checked taxonomy.

Through taxonomies, the requestors discover the relevant businesses and services with which to integrate. So taxonomies and business identifiers play a very crucial role within the UDDI framework.

Following are some of the taxonomies that you can use in the UDDI framework:

- **Standard Industrial Classification (SIC):** Classifies the industry based on the type of activity in which the industry is engaged.

- **North American Industry Classification System (NAICS):** Replaces SIC. This mechanism specifies the classification code for industries.

- **United Nations/Standards Products and Services Classification (UN/SPSC (ECMA)):** A global categorization for products and services used in electronic-service documents.

- **Location:** A geographical taxonomy based on ISO 3166 or any other taxonomy similar to GeoWeb from Microsoft.

Architecture and design

The UDDI programmer API specification is actually based on a request-response message pattern for the discovery and binding of services. The messaging format for such a request and response is XML-based SOAP messages that can transmit across HTTP or any other available transport protocol. The design goal of the UDDI framework is to concentrate on simplicity. Security aspects were taken care of at the time the publishing API was designed. Although UDDI does not mandate any particular type of authentication protocols at the operator's end, it states that authenticating access is required at the time the user uses the publishing APIs. The operator needs to validate the user credentials of the programmer before permitting the programmer to publish any interface to the registry. The operator can assign credentials to the users by permitting them to sign up to the registry before publishing any context. Inquiry APIs (see the following section) do not require any authentication to use the registry. The UDDI specification also taken care of versioning and whitespace issues. Messaging and error handling are based on SOAP. SOAP's `fault` elements report any errors that occur at the registry's end.

API reference

The following two different types of APIs are available for the programmer through the UDDI specification:

◆ The *inquiry API,* which you can use to look up the registry and perform an inquiry on it.

◆ The *publishing API,* which you can use to publish business interfaces and services to the business registry.

Before exploring the API section within the UDDI framework, you need to understand the meaning of some values that the API syntax of UDDI uses. Table 5-1 presents the meaning of the values that the API syntax uses.

TABLE 5-1 MEANING OF SPECIAL VALUES IN THE API SYNTAX

Representation	Meaning
uuid_key	This key represents a globally unique identifier (GUID). A special algorithm, as agreed on by the operator council, generates the key. The tModelKey values are the exception in which an urn prefix is used with the uuid.
Generic	This attribute represents the version of a given API. The valid values for this attribute are 1.0 and 2.0. Any other value now raises an error, because the attribute presently supports version 1.0 and 2.0 only and also because no versions higher than 2.0 are available.
Xmlns	This attribute is a namespace qualifier.

Representation	Meaning
FindQualifiers	You use this qualifier to represent special meaning during a search. You use this qualifier in the inquiry APIs.
MaxRows	You use this qualifier to limit the number of rows that return for a particular request. You also use this qualifier in the inquiry APIs.
Truncated	This attribute indicates that the result returned does not contain the complete rowset. It indicates that the results were truncated.
CategoryBag	You use this element to represent a list of category references.
IdentifierBag	You use this element to represent a list of business-identifier references.
TmodelBag	You use this element to search for businesses with bindings that expose a specific fingerprint within the tModelInstanceDetails collection.

The inquiry API

The *inquiry API* provides the following three forms of query patterns:

◆ **The browse pattern:** Exploration of data requires the capability to browse through data from a broader range of information in an informal way until you pinpoint the results you are looking for. The browse pattern enables you to start from a large base of information to search. After you obtain results, you can eventually drill down to any specific information you are looking for. The UDDI specification provides the browse pattern through `find_***` API calls, where *** represents a wildcard pattern.

◆ **The drill-down pattern:** Four major data structures are specifically declared in the UDDI specification: `businessEntity`, `businessService`, `bindingTemplate`, and `tModel`. If you search the registry by using the browse pattern, you obtain a list of business structures. You can obtain a `businessKey` for any of the four data structures from the business list, and you can pass the key to any of the `get_***` API calls to obtain specific information on a given data instance.

◆ **The invocation pattern:** The `bindingTemplate` value of a business provides details of the address for the instance of an interface, as well as other such technical details. After you obtain the `bindingTemplate` from the business registry, you can use the information in the `bindingTemplate` to invoke a method on the remote Web service. The invocation patterns deal with such invocation of methods on the Web-services processing node.

The following sections list the publicly accessible queries that can be used for querying. These messages are used as an HTTP POST method, which is usually a synchronous call.

THE FIND_BINDING CALL

You use the find_binding call to obtain specific bindings within a registry. The API call returns the bindingDetail message that contains zero or more instances of bindingTemplate.

Following is the syntax for the find_binding call:

```
<find_binding serviceKey="uuid_key" [maxRows="nn"] generic="2.0"
xmlns="urn:uddi-org:api_v2" >
[<findQualifiers/>]
<tModelBag/>
</find_binding>
```

THE FIND_BUSINESS CALL

You use the find_business call to obtain a list of business structures. The API call returns a businessList message that matches the conditions in the argument.

Following is the syntax for the find_business call:

```
<find_business [maxRows="nn"] generic="2.0" xmlns="urn:uddi-
org:api_v2" >
[<findQualifiers/>]
[<name/> [<name/>]...11]
[<discoveryURLs/>]
[<identifierBag/>]
[<categoryBag/>]
[<tModelBag/>]
</find_business>
```

THE FIND_RELATEDBUSINESSES CALL

You use the find_relatedBusinesses call to obtain a list of business structures that are related to the businessEntity. The API call returns a relatedBusinessList message.

Following is the syntax for the find_relatedBusinesses call:

```
<find_relatedBusinesses generic="2.0" xmlns="urn:uddi-org:api_v2" >
[<findQualifiers/>]
<businessKey/>
[<keyedReference/>]
</find_relatedBusinesses>
```

THE FIND_SERVICE CALL

The find_service call you use to obtain a list of business services. The API call returns a serviceList message.

Following is the syntax for the `find_service` call:

```
<find_service businessKey="uuid_key" " [maxRows="nn"] generic="2.0
xmlns="urn:uddi-org:api_v2" >
[<findQualifiers/>]
[<name/> [<name/>]...13]
[<categoryBag/>]
[<tModelBag/>]
</find_service>
```

THE FIND_TMODEL CALL

The `find_tModel` call you use to obtain a list of `tModels`. The API call returns a list of abbreviated information about the `tModel` that is referenced as a `tModelList` message.

Following is the syntax for the `find_tModel` call:

```
<find_tModel [maxRows="nn"] generic="2.0" xmlns="urn:uddi-
org:api_v2" >
[<findQualifiers/>]
[<name/>]
[<identifierBag/>]
[<categoryBag/>]
</find_tModel>
```

THE GET_BINDINGDETAIL CALL

The `get_bindingDetail` call you use to obtain the `bindingTemplate` of `businessEntity` to invoke a service. The API call returns a `bindingDetail` message.

Following is the syntax for the `get_bindingDetail` call:

```
<get_bindingDetail generic="2.0" xmlns="urn:uddi-org:api_v2" >
<bindingKey/> [<bindingKey/> ...]
</get_bindingDetail>
```

THE GET_BUSINESSDETAIL CALL

The `get_businessDetail` call you use to obtain the information about the business. The API call returns a `businessDetail` message.

Following is the syntax for the `get_businessDetail` call:

```
<get_businessDetail generic="2.0" xmlns="urn:uddi-org:api_v2" >
<businessKey/> [<businessKey/> ...]
</get_businessDetail>
```

THE GET_BUSINESSDETAILEXT CALL

The `get_businessDetailExt` call you use to obtain the extended business information for more than one `businessEntity` registrations. The API call returns the `businessDetailExt` message.

Following is the syntax for the `get_businessDetailExt` call:

```
<get_businessDetailExt generic="2.0" xmlns="urn:uddi-org:api_v2" >
<businessKey/> [<businessKey/> ...]
</get_businessDetailExt>
```

THE GET_SERVICEDETAIL CALL

The `get_serviceDetail` call you use to obtain the business-structure information. The API call returns the `serviceDetail` message.

Following is the syntax for the `get_serviceDetail` call:

```
<get_serviceDetail generic="2.0" xmlns="urn:uddi-org:api_v2" >
<serviceKey/> [<serviceKey/> ...]
</get_serviceDetail>
```

THE GET_TMODELDETAIL CALL

The `get_tModelDetail` call you use to obtain the complete information about a `tModel`. The API call returns a `tModelDetail` message.

Following is the syntax for the `get_tModelDetail` call:

```
<get_tModelDetail generic="2.0" xmlns="urn:uddi-org:api_v2" >
<tModelKey/>
[<tModelKey/> ...]
</get_tModelDetail>
```

The publishing API

The `publishing APIs` are the calls that you make on the business registry to access and change the information about a business. You use these calls to register an interface to a business registry or to make necessary changes to the name, service, or any such technical specification of the business entity. As discussed in the section "Architecture and design," the UDDI security specification states that the node operator must authenticate the API calls. The node operator is responsible for authenticating the correct user credentials before permitting changes to the business registry.

The publishing APIs that the UDDI specification supports are as I describe in the following sections.

THE ADD_PUBLISHERASSERTIONS CALL

The `add_publisherAssertions` call is used in adding one or more `publisherAssertions` data structures into the publisher's assertion collections. The API call, if successful, returns a `dispositionReport` message.

Following is the syntax for the `add_publisherAssertions` call:

```
<add_publisherAssertions generic="2.0" xmlns="urn:uddi-org:api_v2" >
<authInfo/>
<publisherAssertion>
<fromKey/>
<toKey/>
<keyedReference/>
</publisherAssertion>
[<publisherAssertion/> ...]
</add_publisherAssertions>
```

THE DELETE_BINDING CALL

The `delete_binding` call is used in deleting one or more `bindingTemplate` from the business registry. The API call, if successful, returns a `dispositionReport` message.

Following is the syntax for the `delete_binding` call:

```
<delete_binding generic="2.0" xmlns="urn:uddi-org:api_v2" >
<authInfo/>
<bindingKey/> [<bindingKey/> ...]
</delete_binding>
```

THE DELETE_BUSINESS CALL

The `delete_business` call is used in deleting one or more `businessEntity` data from the business registry. A successful API call returns a `dispositionReport` message.

Following is the syntax for the `delete_business` call:

```
<delete_business generic="2.0" xmlns="urn:uddi-org:api_v2" >
<authInfo/>
<businessKey/>
[<businessKey/> ...]
</delete_business>
```

THE DELETE_PUBLISHERASSERTIONS CALL

The `delete_publisherAssertions` call you use to delete one or more `publisherAssertion` elements from the publisher's assertion collection. The API call, on success, returns a `dispositionReport` message.

Following is the syntax for the `delete_publisherAssertions` call:

```
<delete_publisherAssertions generic="2.0" xmlns="urn:uddi-
org:api_v2" >
<authInfo/>
<publisherAssertion>
```

```
<fromKey/>
<toKey/>
<keyedReference/>
</publisherAssertion>
[<publisherAssertion/> ...]
</delete_publisherAssertions>
```

THE DELETE_SERVICE CALL

The delete_service call you use to delete one or more businessService from the business registry. The API call, on success, returns a dispositionReport message.

Following is the syntax for the delete_service call:

```
<delete_service generic="2.0" xmlns="urn:uddi-org:api_v2" >
<authInfo/>
<serviceKey/>
[<serviceKey/> ...]
</delete_service>
```

THE DELETE_TMODEL CALL

The delete_tModel call you use to logically delete one or more tModel from the registry. Such logical deletions actually only hide the tModel structures from discovery. They aren't physically removed from the registry. The API call, on success, returns a dispositionReport message.

Following is the syntax for the delete_tModel call:

```
<delete_tModel generic="2.0" xmlns="urn:uddi-org:api_v2" >
<authInfo/>
<tModelKey/> [<tModelKey/> ...]
</delete_tModel>
```

THE DISCARD_AUTHTOKEN CALL

The discard_authToken call you use to tell the site operator to end the active session. The API call informs the operator to discard the authentication token. For sites that do not manage session state, the API call is rejected by the operator. The API call, on success, returns a dispositionReport message.

Following is the syntax for the discard_authToken call:

```
<discard_authToken generic="2.0" xmlns="urn:uddi-org:api_v2" >
<authInfo/>
</discard_authToken>
```

THE GET_ASSERTIONSTATUSREPORT CALL

The get_assertionStatusReport call you use to obtain an assertionStatusReport that determines the status of the current, outstanding publisher assertions involving any of the business registrations that the individual publisher account manages. The API call returns an assertionStatusReport message.

Following is the syntax for the `get_assertionStatusReport` call:

```
<get_assertionStatusReport generic="2.0" xmlns="urn:uddi-org:api_v2"
>
<authInfo/>
[<completionStatus/>]
</get_assertionStatusReport>
```

THE GET_AUTHTOKEN CALL

The `get_authToken` call you use to obtain an authentication token. The API call returns an `authToken` message.

Following is the syntax for the `get_authToken` call:

```
<get_authToken generic="2.0" xmlns="urn:uddi-org:api_v2"
userID="someLoginName"
cred="someCredential" />
```

THE GET_PUBLIHERASSERTIONS CALL

The `get_publisherAssertion` call you use to obtain a list of publisher assertions associated with an individual publisher account. The API call returns the `publisherAssertions` message.

Following is the syntax for the `get_publisherAssertions` call:

```
<get_publisherAssertions generic="2.0" xmlns="urn:uddi-org:api_v2" >
<authInfo/>
</get_publisherAssertions>
```

THE GET_REGISTEREDINFO CALL

The `get_registeredInfo` call you use to obtain information about the business and the service specification. The API call returns a `registeredInfo` message. The returned message contains the list of `businessInfo` elements and `tModelInfo` elements.

Following is the syntax for the `get_registeredInfo` call:

```
<get_registeredInfo generic="2.0" xmlns="urn:uddi-org:api_v2" >
<authInfo/>
</get_registeredInfo>
```

THE SAVE_BINDING CALL

The `save_binding` call you use to update a `bindingTemplate` data structure. The API call returns a `bindingDetail` message.

Following is the syntax for the `save_binding` call:

```
<save_binding generic="2.0" xmlns="urn:uddi-org:api_v2" >
<authInfo/>
```

```
<bindingTemplate/> [<bindingTemplate/>...]
</save_binding>
```

THE SAVE_BUSINESS CALL

The save_business call you use to update the business information in the businessEntity. The API call returns a businessDetail message.

Following is the syntax for the save_business call:

```
<save_business generic="2.0" xmlns="urn:uddi-org:api_v2" >
<authInfo/>
<businessEntity/> [<businessEntity/>...]
</save_business>
```

THE SAVE_SERVICE CALL

The save_service call you use to update the service provided by the business. The API call returns the serviceDetail message.

Following is the syntax for the save_service call:

```
<save_service generic="2.0" xmlns="urn:uddi-org:api_v2" >
<authInfo/>
<businessService/> [<businessService/>...]
<F/save_service>
```

THE SAVE_TMODEL CALL

The save_tModel call you use to update one or more tModel structures. The API call returns the tModelDetail message.

Following is the syntax for the save_tModel call:

```
<save_tModel generic="2.0" xmlns="urn:uddi-org:api_v2" >
<authInfo/>
<tModel/> [<tModel/>...]
</save_tModel>
```

THE SET_PUBLISHERASSERTIONS CALL

The set_publisherAssertions call you use to save the complete set of publisher assertions. The API call returns the publisherAssertions message.

Following is the syntax for the save_tModel call:

```
<set_publisherAssertions generic="2.0" xmlns="urn:uddi-org:api_v2" >
<authInfo/>
<publisherAssertion>
<fromKey/>
<toKey/>
<keyedReference/>
</publisherAssertion> [<publisherAssertion>...]
</set_publisherAssertions>
```

Refer to the UDDI version 2.0 programmer's API appendix A for a set of error codes for the programmer APIs.

UDDI Best Practices

UDDI is a data-neutral, platform-neutral specification used across the globe to publish, discover, and invoke service interfaces that you implement at the provider nodes. The description of a business and its relevant services are depicted using different data structures in UDDI. As I describe earlier in this chapter, WSDL is an XML-based service-interface description specification. The WSDL file describes the service type, ports, binding, and other details of service-abstraction. The WSDL is an abstract definition of the protocol bindings of the services that you implement on top of a network transport. This technology complements the UDDI specification. Using WSDL with UDDI to register a service interface is a best practice in the industry. This section provides an understanding of the relationship between WSDL and UDDI.

Of the different types of UDDI data structures that I explain in the preceding sections, the businessService and the tModel data structures are important in explaining the relationship between UDDI and WSDL.

The businessService element within the business registry represents the service related to a business, while the bindingTemplate element represents the technical entry point and construction specifications of the service. The following syntax gives an idea of a businessService:

```
<businessService>
(...)
    <bindingTemplates>          <bindingTemplate>
                    (...)
                    <accessPoint urlType="http">
                            http://www.etc.com/
                    </accessPoint>
                    <tModelnstanceDetails>
                        <tModelnstanceInfo tModelKey="...">
                        </tModelnstanceInfo>
                    (...)
                    </tModelnstanceDetails>
        </bindingTemplate>
        (...)
    </bindingTemplates>
</businessService>
```

The WSDL XML structure provides an extensible mechanism in which you can import the definitions of types from a secondary file. This structure provides a modular mechanism for WSDL definitions to separate the concerns between the service-interface definition and the service-implementation definition. You can consider the service-interface definition as the reusable portion of the WSDL definition that contains the details of message-formats, portTypes, and protocol bindings. The service-implementation portion can contain details of the port and the service-binding information.

After you gain knowledge about the separation of concerns in the WSDL definitions, you can understand how to use WSDL and UDDI together.

Initially, you create the WSDL service-interface definition. You then register the service-interface definition as a tModel in the UDDI business registry. The overviewDoc element of tModel should point to the WSDL service-interface definition file. Next, you can build the service-abstractions that implement the service interface. In the end, you must deploy and register the new service into the UDDI business registry.

UDDI Workarounds

WSDL is the best option to use to work with UDDI. Instead of needing to look up WSDL service-definitions through some other techniques (such as publishing them in a proprietary B2B portal), you have a workaround for accessing a WSDL file by using tModel.

The following procedure provides a step-by-step approach for creating, registering, and accessing a WSDL file from the UDDI directory:

1. Create the WSDL service-interface definition. The service interface defines a set of service types and describes them with one or more service-interface definition WSDL documents. The WSDL service's interface definitions you then register as UDDI tModels.

2. Use some UDDI-aware tool to retrieve the tModel information. The tool helps in parsing the overviewDoc link within the tModel. By using the link, you obtain the WSDL service-definition document. After you obtain the WSDL definition document, the you can generate a WSDL-to-language binding (where the language is Java, C++, or Visual Basic). By using the standard interfaces and binding that you generate, you can provide standard implementations that use your favorite programming language.

3. Use WSDL and a UDDI-aware tool to create a UDDI businessService data structure and then register it in the UDDI repository.

Using WSDL with UDDI — An Example

In this section, I provide an example that illustrates how to use WSDL with UDDI. The following example illustrates a WSDL service interface:

Bookdetails.wsdl

```xml
<?xml version="1.0"?>

<definitions name="BookDetails"

targetNamespace="http://www.conceptuniv.com/bookdetails.wsdl"
xmlns:tns="http://www.conceptuniv.com/bookdetails.wsdl"
xmlns:xsd1="http://www.conceptuniv.com/bookdetails.xsd"
xmlns:soap="http://schemas.xmlsoap.org/wsdl/soap/"
xmlns="http://schemas.xmlsoap.org/wsdl/">

    <types>
        <schema
targetNamespace="http://www.conceptuniv.com/bookdetails.xsd"
                xmlns="http://www.w3.org/2000/10/XMLSchema">
            <element name="BookDetailsRequest">
                <complexType>
                    <all>
                        <element name="ISBN" type="string"/>
                    </all>
                </complexType>
            </element>
            <element name="BookDetails">
                <complexType>
                    <all>
<element name="title" type="string"/>
<element name="author" type="string"/>
<element name="price" type="float"/>
                    </all>
                </complexType>
            </element>
        </schema>
    </types>

    <message name="GetBookDetailsInput">
        <part name="body" element="xsd1:BookDetailsRequest"/>
    </message>
```

```
    <message name="GetBookDetailsOutput">
        <part name="body" element="xsd1:BookDetails"/>
    </message>

    <portType name="BookDetailsPortType">
        <operation name="GetBookDetails">
            <input message="tns:GetBookDetailsInput"/>
            <output message="tns:GetBookDetailsOutput"/>
        </operation>
    </portType>

<binding name="BookDetailsSoapBinding"
type="tns:BookDetailsPortType">
        <soap:binding style="document"
transport="http://schemas.xmlsoap.org/soap/http"/>
        <operation name="GetBookDetails">
            <soap:operation
soapAction="http://www.conceptuniv.com/GetBookDetails"/>
            <input>
                <soap:body use="literal"/>
            </input>
            <output>
                <soap:body use="literal"/>
            </output>
        </operation>
    </binding>
</definitions>
```

If you place the preceding WSDL file under www.conceptuniv.com/
bookdetails.wsdl, the corresponding tModel for the WSDL service interface is
as follows:

```
<tModel authorizedName="..." operator="..." tModelKey="...">
    <name>GetBookDetails</name>
    <description xml:lang="en">
        WSDL description of a book details service interface
    </description>
    <overviewDoc>
        <description xml:lang="en">
            WSDL source document.
        </description>
        <overviewURL>
            http://www.conceptuniv.com/bookdetails.wsdl
        </overviewURL>
    </overviewDoc>
    <categoryBag>
```

```
            <keyedReference tModelKey="UUID:C1ACF26D-
9672-4404-9D70-39B756E62AB4"
            keyName="TestModel"
            keyValue="wsdlSpec"/>
    </categoryBag>
</tModel>
```

The corresponding business-service structure is as follows:

```
<businessService businessKey="..." serviceKey="...">
    <name>BookDetailsService</name>
    <description> (...) </description>
    <bindingTemplates>
        <bindingTemplate>
            (...)
            <accessPoint urlType="http">
            http://www.conceptuniv.com/bookdetails
            </accessPoint>
            <tModelnstanceDetails>
            <tModelnstanceInfo tModelKey="...">
            </tModelnstanceInfo>
            </tModelnstanceDetails>
        </bindingTemplate>
    </bindingTemplates>
</businessService>
```

After you create the `tModel` and the `businessService` structures, you can register the structures to a UDDI repository, such as an IBM UDDI business registry. The IBM Test Registry is available at the following URL:

`https://www-3.ibm.com/services/uddi/testregistry/`

Following are the steps that the test registry site lists to help you register the services:

1. Obtain an IBM username and password for the registry.

2. Log on by using the username and the password.

3. Register the businesses and services by using the Add New Business and Add New Service Type wizards.

4. After you finish, log off and disconnect.

This last step concludes your registration and publishing process.

Summary

This chapter explains UDDI Version 2.0 in detail. It explains the UDDI discovery process, the description process, and the invocation process for a business registry. In addition, the chapter provides a detailed explanation of the UDDI data structures. The chapter also explains the UDDI architecture and the design specification of its framework. It explains, too, the UDDI Version 2.0 programmer API. In addition, the chapter lists all the inquiry APIs and the publishing APIs available in the programmer-API specification. The chapter also provides an explanation of the different query patterns that you use in the inquiry API. Finally, the chapter provides information about the relationship between WSDL and UDDI and explains how to use WSDL within the UDDI business registry.

Part III

The Java Web Services Architecture

Chapter 6

Introduction to JavaServer Pages and Java Servlets

IN THIS CHAPTER

- ◆ An overview of system architecture
- ◆ What are servlets?
- ◆ Session Tracking
- ◆ Overview of Java Server Pages

SERVICE-ORIENTED ARCHITECTURE (SOA) is the buzzword in the industry. E-business solutions require dynamic interoperability and integration services to solve the needs of today's industry. To achieve such a level of service polymorphism the technology leaders of the current industry need to work together to achieve the requirement of the current market.

Java seems an obvious choice for a platform and XML as an interoperability standard for building Web services. Java provides code portability, and XML provides data portability. A combination of these technologies is the preferred choice of developers to build Web-services.

An Overview of System Architecture

Java Platform 2 Enterprise Edition (J2EE) is an architectural specification that details the application programming interfaces and component frameworks of the J2EE platform, which developers use for developing an enterprise system. J2EE is not itself a single product or a tool but is a collation of APIs, guidelines and blueprints, design patterns, and best practices that combine to provide an effective architecture to develop enterprise applications. Before understanding the J2EE architecture, however, you need to understand different system architectures.

Different types of system architectures provide a distributed service framework to satisfy certain types of business needs. System architectures can be based on two-tier, three-tier, or n-tier models. The following sections describe these models in detail.

The two-tier model

The *two-tier model* employs a simple client and a server in an enterprise system, as shown in Figure 6-1.

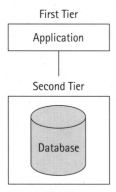

First Tier

Application

Second Tier

Database

Figure 6-1: The two-tier model

The client side of a two-tier model consists of the *user interface, client-side validations, business logic,* and *network interfaces* that enable the client to interface with the server-side application. The server side of the two-tier model is typically a relational database that provides *data storage, data retrieval, indexing, querying,* and *stored procedure logic* for the client-side code.

Two-tier models were typically the most preferred models at the beginning of the client-server era. Later, the limitations of two-tier models became obvious. In a distributed environment that uses communication protocols to network hundreds of clients, maintaining client-side logic on every client is very difficult. To begin with, the installation of a client-side application on hundreds of clients is a difficult task. Even if an automated tool assists the administrator in such deployments, tracking failures and recovering from failed events is not an easy task. After installation, maintaining the latest versions on every client is again a laborious task.

Above all, an inherent problem in the two-tier model is the architecture of the model. The client-side application of the model is a static bundle of presentation logic and business logic. Every client implementation, therefore, has the same set of UI and business logic copied across all the clients. In addition, tight coupling of business logic with presentation logic makes the client-side code very brittle. Changing the user interface of such client-side applications is really hard without breaking business logic or vice versa. Such brittleness in any architecture is uncalled for. Moreover, the implementation of the two-tier model in a dynamic enterprise environment calls for changing business logic very frequently, because in a dynamic business environment, business rules change too often. Because of these limitations, the two-tier model was considered unfit for a dynamic Web-services environment.

The three-tier model

The *three-tier model* employs a client-side user interface, a middle tier that consists of business logic, and the back-end data tier. The three-tier model is as shown in Figure 6-2.

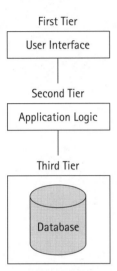

Figure 6-2: The three-tier client-server model

The industry overcame some of the limitations of the two-tier model by separating business logic from the user interface. The two-tier model redundantly copied the same business logic to call clients. In the three-tier model, you separate business logic from the user interface and implement the business logic in a middle tier. This separation of concerns provides flexible and scalable architecture compared to that provided by the two-tier model. The separation of business logic ensures that all clients share a single implementation of business logic on the middle tier. In a dynamic business environment, if business rules change frequently, changing the current implementation of business logic to a new version that portrays the current set of rules is relatively easy. An administrator needs to worry about updating only the middle tier. His has no need to update the client-side code because the client-side implementation does not carry any business logic. The administrative overhead on the three-tier model is relatively low compared to that of the two-tier model. The segregation of the logics into different tiers comes at the cost of increased complexity in the code. Such a tradeoff between complexity and flexibility, however, is a worthwhile investment.

The n-tier model

The *n-tier model* is a multitiered model that consists of more than three tiers of system layers. Figure 6-3 shows a representation of the n-tier model.

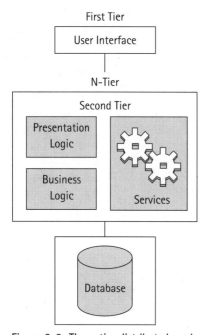

Figure 6-3: The n-tier distributed services model

In the three-tier model, business logic is separate from the user interface. This separation provides a flexible framework for distributed services. The three-tier model does, however, have some limitations. The three-tier model bundles the client-side user interface (UI) with the client-side presentation logic and validation logic. This approach is again redundant. If the validation logic on the three-tier model needs updating, the system administrator faces a nightmare in rolling out a new version of the client-side code on all clients.

An n-tier model overcomes this limitation. In an n-tier model, presentation logic is separate from the UI of the client. The abstracted presentation logic moves to a separate logical layer. The presentation layer eventually interfaces with the business logic layer to map the workflow of the system to the client UI. This separation of concerns from the client-side UI makes the maintenance of client-side validation easy. The n-tier model is the most preferred model today. The side effect of the model is increased complexity. As the number of logical layers increases in the system architecture, the need to effectively integrate these layers becomes increasingly complex. Some of the criteria to keep in mind before deploying n-tier models are as follows:

◆ System integration and responsiveness of multinodal systems

◆ Scalability of the complete framework

◆ Robustness or the capability to rely on multitiered systems

◆ Overall complexity of the architecture

◆ Security and access control among different layers

Now that you know the basics of system architecture, you can take a look at how to implement it in the current business scenario. Consider a situation where you want to register yourself with a Web site to get a free subscription to newsletters. To register with the Web site, you need to provide such information as your first name, last name, and the name of your organization. In addition, you can also choose an ID for yourself to use in logging on to the Web site. After you enter the details and click the Submit button, the data is forwarded to the Web server for processing. This processing can involve checking whether the ID is already in use or checking for invalid values. If the ID is already in use, the user is asked to choose a different ID. To reduce the overhead on the server and the network, such validations as checking for blank fields and negative values can occur on the client-side itself. Small programs that you write for such purposes are known as *client-side scripts*. VBScript and JavaScript are two languages that you can use for client-side scripting. The programs that process data on the Web server are known as *server-side scripts*. Web applications also demand more functionality from the Web server. This demand has triggered the development of tools that enable efficient server-side programming – tools such as servlets, Java Server Pages (JSP), Active Server Pages (ASP), and Hypertext Preprocessor (PHP).

What Are Servlets?

Servlets are Java programs that you can deploy on a Java-enabled Web server to enhance and extend the functionality of the Web server. For example, you can write a servlet to add a messenger service to a Web site. You can also use servlets to add dynamic content to Web pages. You can, for example, use a servlet to retrieve from an information database the latest gift offers that a Web site provides and display the information on the home page of another Web site.

You can use servlets to develop a variety of Web-based applications. Because you write servlets by using Java, they can use the extensive power of the Java API, including networking and URL access, multithreading, database connectivity, internationalization, remote method invocation (RMI), and object serialization. The characteristics of servlets that have gained them widespread acceptance are as follows:

◆ **Servlets are efficient:** The initialization code for a servlet executes only as the servlet executes for the first time. Subsequently, the requests that the servlet receives are processed by its `service()` method. This process helps to increase the efficiency of the server by avoiding creation of unnecessary processes.

◆ **Servlets are robust:** As servlets are based on Java, they provide all the powerful features of Java, such as exception handling and garbage collection, which make them robust.

◆ **Servlets are portable:** Servlets are also portable because you develop in Java them. This development enables easy portability across Web servers.

◆ **Servlets are persistent:** Servlets help to increase the performance of the system by preventing frequent disk access. If a customer logs on to a bank's Web site, for example, the customer can perform many activities, such as checking for a balance and applying for a loan. At every stage, the site needs to authenticate the customer by checking the account number against the database. Instead of checking for the account number against the database every time, servlets retain the account number in memory till the user logs out of the Web site.

◆ **Servlets can be implemented to maintain state:** One of the disadvantages of using HTTP as the transport protocol of the Web is its incapability to maintain its state. You can use servlets, however, to overcome the problem of statelessness. Servlets can maintain state and track sessions over the Web by using certain techniques that I discuss in the section "Session Tracking," later in the chapter.

Applets are Java programs that you embed in Web pages. If someone opens a Web page containing an applet, the byte code of the applet downloads to the client computer. This process is time-consuming if the size of the applet is large. As servlets execute on the Web server, they help overcome problems that users face with download time while using applets. Unlike applets, servlets do not require a browser to be Java-enabled, because they execute on the Web server and send the results back to the client or the browser. Having learned the basics of servlets, you can now take a look at some alternative technologies.

Servlets and other alternative technologies

Common Gateway Interface (CGI) scripts, PHP, ColdFusion, and Active Server Pages (ASP) are alternatives to servlets and have their own advantages and disadvantages. The following sections briefly discuss these alternative technologies.

CGI SCRIPTS

A *CGI script* is a program written in C, C++, or Perl. A CGI script executes at the server side. After a server receives a request from the client for processing data, the server passes the request to the CGI script. The CGI script processes the request and sends the output to the server in the form of HTML. The server, in turn, passes the request to the client.

The disadvantages of using a CGI script are as follows:

- ◆ Whenever a CGI script is invoked, the server creates a separate process for it. The server is limited in the number of processes that it can create simultaneously. If the number of requests is too high, the server can't accept the requests. In addition, creating too many processes also reduces the efficiency of the server.

- ◆ The most popular platform for writing a CGI script is Perl. Although Perl is a very powerful language for writing CGI applications, the server needs to load the Perl interpreter for each request that it receives. Thus, for an incoming request, the executable file of the CGI script and the Perl interpreter both load, which reduces the efficiency of the server.

Unlike CGI scripts, the servlet initialization code executes only once. In the case of servlets, a separate thread in the Web server handles each request. This setup helps make the Web server more efficient by preventing the creation of unnecessary processes.

ACTIVE SERVER PAGES (ASP)

ASP is a server-side scripting language developed by Microsoft. ASP enables a developer to combine both HTML and a scripting language in the same Web page. JavaScript and VBScript are two scripting languages that ASP supports. You can also use VBScript and JavaScript for server-side scripting by using the runat tag in the ASP page.

The limitation of ASP is that it is not compatible with all the Web servers. Most Web servers need certain plug-ins installed to support ASP. Adding plug-ins, however, can decrease the performance of the system.

HYPERTEXT PREPROCESSOR (PHP)

PHP is a server-side scripting language that combines script commands and HTML to provide, dynamic Web pages that can be displayed across any platform. PHP was originally developed by Rasmus Lerdorf and gradually matured with the help of many developers into a prominent scripting language on the Internet.

The popularity of PHP lies in the fact that its syntax is easy to learn, and being open source, it can be freely downloaded. A PHP script file is a text file consisting of script commands and HTML codes. After a Web server receives a request for a PHP file, it processes the PHP scripts and then sends the response to the client.

COLDFUSION

ColdFusion is an application server of Allaire that processes .cfm pages. A .cfm page uses CFML (Cold Fusion Markup Language) along with HTML codes. CFML is a server-side markup language consisting of tags, expressions, and functions. In addition to its supported tags, you can also create your own custom tags in CFML. After the ColdFusion application server receives a request for a .cfm file, it processes the page, executes the ColdFusion code, and then sends the response to the client.

Having discussed the alternative technologies to servlets, I now look at the working of a servlet.

Working of a servlet

Having discussed the alternative technologies to servlets in the preceding sections, I now look at the working of a servlet in this section.

The client or the browser passes requests to the server by using the GET or the POST methods. For example, a servlet can be invoked as the result of clicking a user-interface component, such as button on a form, or by following a hyperlink in a Web page. After the servlet processes the request, the output returns to the client as an HTML page.

The client request consists of the following components:

♦ *The protocol* that you use for communication between the server and the client, such as HTTP.

♦ *The request type*, which is GET or POST.

♦ *The URL* of the document you're retrieving.

♦ *A query string* that contains additional information, such as login name, password, and registration details.

Consider the following example:

```
GET http://www.EarnestBank.com/login.html?username="Carol"&passwd= ↵
"3445H"
```

The preceding URL you can use to display the mailbox of the user "Carol". The different components of the URL are as follows:

♦ http: The protocol for communication between the server and the client.

♦ www.EarnestBank.com: The name of the Web site.

♦ login.html: The name of the form that appears to the user.

♦ username="Carol"&passwd="3445H": The values that pass to the server-side program.

THE GET AND POST METHODS

As a client sends a request to the server, the client can also use the GET method to pass additional information along with the URL to describe what exactly is necessary as output from the server. The additional sequence of characters that you append to the URL is known as a *query string*. The length of the query string, however, is limited to 240 characters. Moreover, the query string is visible on the browser and can, therefore, become a security risk. To overcome these disadvantages, you can use the POST method. The POST method sends the data as packets through a separate socket connection. The complete transaction is invisible to the client. The disadvantage of this method is that it is slower than the GET method, because it sends data to the server as separate packets.

The javax.servlet package

Java supports the implementation of servlets through the `javax.servlet` and `javax.servlet.http` packages. The `javax.servlet.Servlet` interface provides the general framework for a creating a servlet. A servlet can directly implement this interface or indirectly implement the same by extending the `javax.servlet.GenericServlet` or the `javax.servlet.http.HTTPServlet` classes.

You use the `GenericServlet` class of the `javax.servlet` package to create servlets that can work with any protocol. The `javax.servlet.http` package you use to create HTTP servlets that provide the output in the form of HTML pages. The class that you use to create HTTP servlets is `HTTPServlet` and derives from the `GenericServlet` class. *Serialization* is also possible in servlets because `GenericServlet` implements the `java.io.Serializable` interface.

 Serialization is the process of writing an object into a persistent storage medium, such as a hard disk.

Some of the classes and interfaces that you use for the creation of servlets are as follows:

- `HttpServlet` **class:** Provides an HTTP-specific implementation of the servlet interface. This class extends the `GenericServlet` class that provides a framework for handling other types of network and Web services.

- `HttpServletRequest` **interface:** Provides methods to process the requests from the clients. Assume, for example, that the client browser consists of a form with two fields. After you submit the values to the server for processing, they are extracted by using methods in the `HttpServletRequest` interface.

- `HttpServletResponse` **interface:** Response to the client is sent in the form of an HTML page through an object of the `HttpServletResponse` interface.

- `ServletConfig` **class:** Used to store the servlet's startup configuration values and the initialization parameters. You use the `getServletConfig()` method of the servlet interface to obtain information about the configuration values of a servlet.

The following code sample creates a servlet by the name `MyFirstServlet`. I discuss the elements of this code in detail in the section Life cycle of a servlet later in this chapter.

```
import java.io.*;
import javax.servlet.*;
```

```
import javax.servlet.http.*;
public class MyFirstServlet extends HttpServlet
 {
 public void doGet(HttpServletRequest req, HttpServletResponse res)
               throws ServletException, IOException
          {
                    String name=req.getParameter("username");
                    String pswd=req.getParameter("passwd");
                    res.setContentType("text/html");
                    PrintWriter out = res.getWriter();
 out.println("<HEAD><TITLE> My First Servlet</TITLE></HEAD><BODY
bgcolor=pink>");
                    out.println(" Hello "+name +"! Your Password
is "+ pswd+".");
                    out.println("</BODY>");
                    out.close();
          }
 }
```

Life cycle of a servlet

A servlet loads into the memory only once and is initialized in the init() method. After the servlet is initialized, it starts accepting requests from the client and processes them through the service() method until is the destroy() method shuts it down. The service() method executes for every incoming request. The life cycle of a servlet is as shown in Figure 6-4.

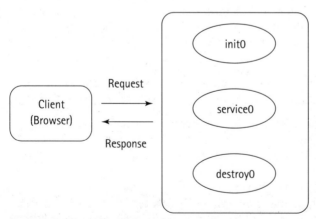

Figure 6-4: Life cycle of a servlet

Table 6-1 describes a few methods that you use in creating a servlet.

TABLE 6-1 METHODS TO USE IN CREATING A SERVLET

Method Name	Description
Servlet.init(ServletConfig config) throws ServletException	Contains the initialization code for the servlet and is invoked as the servlet first loads.
Servlet.service()	Receives all requests from clients, identifies the type of the request, and dispatches them to the `doGet()` or `doPost()` methods for processing.
Servlet.destroy()	Executes only once as the servlet is removed from server. The cleanup code for the servlet must be provided in this method.
HttpServletResponse.getWriter()	Returns a reference to a `PrintWriter` object. The `PrintWriter` class is used to write formatted objects as a text-output stream onto the client.
HttpServletResponse.setContentType (String type)	Sets the type of content that is to go out as response to the client browser. For example, `setContentType ("text/html")` is used to set the response type as text.

Deploying a servlet

For a servlet or an HTML page (that may contain a link to a servlet) to be accessible from the client, first you must deploy it on the Web server.

You can deploy a servlet on any of the following:

◆ Java Web Server (JWS)

◆ Tomcat

◆ Apache

◆ Java 2 Enterprise Edition (J2EE) server

JWS is a Web server from Sun Microsystems that is based on the servlet technology and that you can use to deploy servlets.

You can also use *Tomcat* and *Apache* to deploy and run servlets. Tomcat, which is a servlet /JSP container, is a product of Jakarta. It provides the implementation of the servlets and JSP specifications along with other functionality for deploying Web applications. Apache is a Web server, from an organization also known as Apache, that you can use to deploy servlets. A few features of Apache that have made it popular are its freely distributed code, robustness, and the security that it offers.

Java 2 Enterprise Edition (J2EE) is a set of specifications that defines the standards for creating distributed objects. J2EE also specifies how you can integrate these technologies to provide a complete solution. It is also a standard architecture that defines a multitier programming model. The multitier programming model is discussed in the section, The n-tier model. The J2EE server is a product from Sun Microsystems that is based on the Java 2 Enterprise Edition (J2EE). You use the J2EE server to deploy servlets and JSP files. It enables users to access the deployed servlets and JSP files by implementing appropriate security.

Creating, deploying, and testing a servlet

Consider a scenario where an online music company, SanguineTunes, has a Web site providing information about music. A user must register at its Web site to access the information. A registration form should appear to the user so that the user can enter the necessary details to register. The user details should be recorded in the database, and the user should be informed that he is registered.

The application must be created by using a servlet. You can access the servlet by using an HTML page. The HTML page can accept the user's details, and the servlet records them in the database. This servlet also informs the user that the user is registered.

Following is the code for the HTML page that calls the servlet:

```
<HTML>
    <HEAD>
        <TITLE>SanguineTunes </TITLE>
    </HEAD>
    <BODY bgcolor=blue>
        <CENTER><H1>Registration Form</H1></CENTER>
        <HR>
        <BR><BR>
        <FORM    method=post
action="http://localhost:8000/registercontext/RegisterAlias">
            <CENTER>
                <TABLE>
                    <TR><TD>First Name:</TD>
                    <TD><INPUT type=text name="firstname"></TD>
                    </TR>
                    <TR><TD>Last Name:</TD>
                    <TD><INPUT type=text name="lastname"></TD>
                    </TR>
                    <TR><TD>PassWord:</TD>
                    <TD><INPUT type=password
name="password"></TD>
                    </TR>
                    <TR><TD>Address:</TD>
```

```
                        <TD><INPUT type=text name="address"></TD>
                        <TR><TD>Phone Number:</TD>
                        <TD><INPUT type=text
name="phonenumber"></TD>
                        </TR></TR>
                        <TR><TD>Email ID:</TD>
                        <TD><INPUT type=text name="emailid"></TD>
                </TABLE>
                <BR><BR>
                <CENTER><INPUT type=SUBMIT value=SUBMIT></CENTER>
            </CENTER>
        </FORM>
    </BODY>
</HTML>
```

After a user enters the details and clicks the Submit button, the RegisterServlet servlet with the alias name MyRegisterAlias receives the details. The request method type is POST as specified in the following code snippet of the HTML page:

```
<FORM
method="post"action=http://localhost:8000/registercontext/RegisterAl
ias>
```

The code for the servlet, RegisterServlet, is as follows.

```
import java.io.*;

import javax.servlet.*;
import javax.servlet.http.*;
import javax.sql.*;
import java.sql.*;

    public class RegisterServlet extends HttpServlet
    {
        Connection  con;
        PreparedStatement stat;
        public void doPost(HttpServletRequest req,
HttpServletResponse res) throws ServletException, IOException
    {
            try
                {

Class.forName("sun.jdbc.odbc.JdbcOdbcDriver");
con=DriverManager.getConnection("jdbc:odbc:MyDataSource","sa","");
```

```
System.out.println("Connection established");

            }
             catch(ClassNotFoundException e)
                {
                          System.out.println("Database driver    not
found"+e);

            }
      catch (Exception e)
          {
              System.out.println(e.toString());
          }

            res.setContentType("text/html");
            PrintWriter out=res.getWriter();
             String firstname=req.getParameter("firstname");
             String lastname=req.getParameter("lastname");
             String password=req.getParameter("password");
             String address=req.getParameter("address");
             String phonenumber=req.getParameter("phonenumber");
             String emailid=req.getParameter("emailid");
        int upd=0;
         try
         {
             stat=con.prepareStatement("insert into registration
values(?,?,?,?,?,?)");
      stat.setString(1,firstname);
      stat.setString(2,lastname);
             stat.setString(3,password);
             stat.setString(4,address);
      stat.setString(5,phonenumber);
             stat.setString(6,emailid);
             upd=stat.executeUpdate();
         }
         catch (Exception e)
         {
             System.out.println(e.toString());
         }
         if (upd==0)
         {
            System.out.println("Error inserting data in the
registration table");
         }
```

```
        else
        {
                System.out.println("The values have been inserted in
the table successfully");
                out.println("<html>");
          out.println("<head><title>SanguineTunes</title></head>");
                out.println("<body bgcolor=pink>");
                out.println( "Welcome! "+firstname +", you have been
successfully registered.   " );
        out.println("<BR>");
                out.println("<BR>");
                out.println("</body></html>");
          try
          {
          con.close();
          }
          catch(Exception e)
          {
                System.out.println(e.toString());
          }
      }
   }
}
```

COMPILING THE SERVLET

To compile the servlet, the `path` and the `CLASSPATH` variables must be set by invoking the following commands at the command prompt. The `path` variable must be set to the folder where the Java compiler is present. The `CLASSPATH` variable must be set to the folder where all the system class files are present. If you change the name of the JDK folder, you must ensure that the same name is specified in the `path` and `CLASSPATH` variables, as follows:

```
set path=.;<System Drive>:<root directory>\<JDK Folder>\bin;<System ↵
Drive>:<root directory>\<Java Enterprise Edition Folder>\bin
set classpath=.;<system Drive>:<root directory>\<JDK Folder> ↵
\lib;<System Drive>:<root directory>\<Java 2 Enterprise Edition ↵
Folder>\lib\j2ee.jar
```

If you can't compile the program, check whether the `path` and the `CLASSPATH` variables are set appropriately. Ensure, too, that the current working directory in the command prompt is correct before you compile the program.

DEPLOYING THE SERVLET

The application file that you create in J2EE is known as the *Enterprise Archive File (EAR)*. The servlets and the JSP components that you need to add in an application are known as the *Web components*. The Web components combine with the HTML files to create a *Web Archive File (WAR)* file. The WAR file is then added to the EAR file.

This application is deployed and tested by using the Java 2 SDK Enterprise Edition (J2EE) application server. Before starting the application server, you need to set the environment variable JAVA_HOME to the folder where JSDK is installed and J2EE_HOME to the folder where J2EE server is installed.

Assuming that JSDK and the J2EE application server are installed in the C: drive, in the folders JDK1.3 and J2SDKEE1.2.1, respectively, you set the environment variables as follows:

```
Set JAVA_HOME=C:\JDK1.3
Set J2EE_HOME=C:\J2SDKEE1.2.1
```

The following steps illustrate how you can deploy your HTML file and servlet class file as an application in the J2EE server:

1. Start the J2EE server by typing **J2EE –verbose.**

    The -verbose option starts the J2EE application server in the verbose mode.

2. Type **deploytool** at the command prompt. The Application Deployment Tool window appears, as shown in the Figure 6-5.

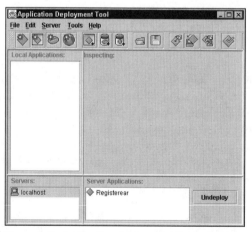

Figure 6-5: Application Deployment Tool window

3. Choose File → New → Application in this window to open the New Application dialog box. Click the Browse button. The New Application dialog box appears.

4. From the Look in drop-down list, select the working directory and edit the File Name text box to **Registerear,** as shown in the Figure 6-6. Click the New Application button.

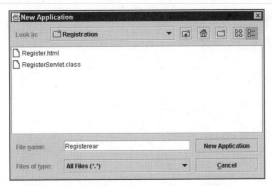

Figure 6-6: The New Application dialog box

 The working directory is the folder where you store the files that you want to deploy.

5. Click OK to close the New Application dialog box.

6. From the Application Deployment Tool window, choose File → New Web Component to open the New Web Component Wizard – Introduction dialog box and click Next to open the New Web Component Wizard – WAR File General Properties dialog box.

7. Click the Add button in this dialog box to open the Add Files to .WAR – Add Content Files dialog box.

 You use this dialog box to add the HTML, JSP, and GIF files into a WAR file that you want to deploy on the Web server.

8. In the Add Files to .WAR – Add Content Files dialog box, click the Browse button. The Choose Root Directory dialog box appears as shown in Figure 6-7. From the Look in drop-down list, select the root directory. The root directory specifies the location of the servlet and other files deployed on the Web server. After you select the root directory, click the Choose Root Directory button. The Choose Root Directory dialog box closes and the Add Files to .WAR – Add Content Files dialog box reappears.

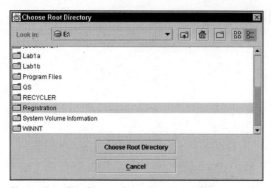

Figure 6-7: The Choose Root Directory dialog box

9. In the Add Files to .WAR – Add Content Files dialog box select the appropriate HTML file – in this case, `Register.html` – and click Add. Observe that the file is added to the list of files.

10. In the Add Files to .WAR – Add Content Files dialog box, click Next to open the Add Files to .WAR – Add Class Files dialog box. In the Add Files to .WAR – Add Class Files dialog box, click the Browse button. The Choose Root Directory dialog box appears. In this dialog box select the root directory and click the Choose Root Directory button. The Choose Root Directory dialog box closes.

11. In the Add Files to .WAR – Add Class Files dialog box, select the servlet class file – in this case, `RegisterServlet` class. Click Add and then click Finish. The Add Files to .WAR – Add Class Files dialog box closes.

12. In the New Web Component Wizard – WAR File General Properties dialog box that appears, type **Registerwar** in the WAR Display Name text box and click Next.

13. The New Web Component Wizard – Choose Component Type dialog box appears. Click Next to open the New Web Component Wizard – Component General Properties dialog box.

14. In the New Web Component Wizard – Component General Properties dialog box, select `RegisterServlet` from the Servlet Class list. In the Web Component Display Name text box, type **Register.** Click Next. The New Web Component Wizard – Component Initialization Parameters dialog box appears. In this dialog box click Next.

15. In the New Web Component Wizard – Component Aliases dialog box that appears, click Add. The focus moves to the Aliases text box. Type **RegisterAlias** in the Aliases text box.

You use the alias name to access Web components. Type a meaningful name, therefore, that is easy to remember.

16. Click Finish. The Application Deployment Tool window appears.

Sometimes, you may need to click Next and then in the next dialog box that appears click Finish. Otherwise, the `deploytool` may not accept the alias name.

17. In the Application Deployment Tool window, click the Web Context tab and type **registercontext** in the Context Root text box.

The Web context specifies the name of a directory structure, created by the server, inside which all the Web components are deployed. You use the Web context name while calling the Web component.

The preceding steps package the Web files into a .WAR file, which is ready for deployment. Perform the following steps to complete the deployment process:

1. In the Application Deployment Tool window choose Tools → Deploy Application to open the Deploy Registerear – Introduction dialog box and then click Next. The Deploy Register - .WAR Context Root dialog box appears.

2. Observe that the context root that you specified in the Context Root text box under the Web Context tab of the Application Deployment Tool window appears. Click Next. The Deploy Register – Review dialog box appears.

3. Click Finish to open the Deployment Progress dialog box, which displays the deployment progress, as shown in Figure 6-8.

4. Click OK. The application is deployed.

If the deployment process fails, review all the information that you entered. In some cases, you may need to restart the J2EE server.

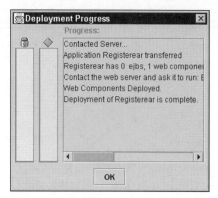

Figure 6-8: The Deployment Progress dialog box

 To add a J2EE server to the deployment tool, choose Add and then specify the server name. If you change the servlet or HTML files after deploying, you need not go through the entire deployment process. You can choose Tools ' Update and Redeploy from the menu bar in the Application Deployment Tool window.

TESTING THE SERVLET

Open a browser and type `http://localhost:8000/registercontext/ Registration.html` in the address bar. Figure 6-9 shows the Registration form that opens.

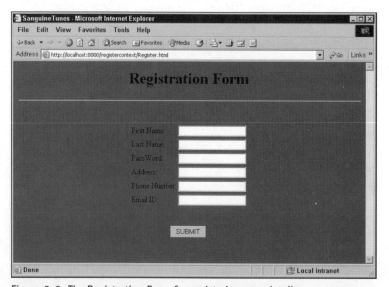

Figure 6-9: The Registration Form for registering user details

After you fill out the form and click the Submit button, you see a page similar to that shown in Figure 6-10.

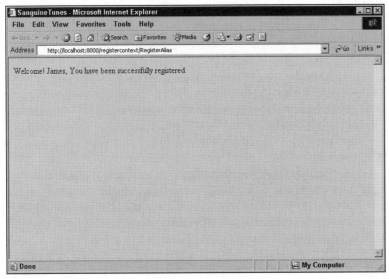

Figure 6-10: The successful registration notification page

Session Tracking

A *session* is a group of activities that a user performs while accessing a particular Web site. The process of keeping track of settings across sessions is known as *sessions tracking.* Consider the example of an online shopping mall: The user can choose a product and add it to the shopping cart. If the user moves to a different page, the details in the shopping cart are retained so that the user can still check the items in the shopping cart and then place the order.

You can also use sessions tracking to keep track of the user's preferences. If the user selects more novels than anything else, for example, more novels then appear to the user as recommendations.

Techniques to keep track of sessions in servlets

By default, you cannot store data across sessions by using HTTP, because HTTP is a stateless protocol. Certain techniques, however, help store session data by using HTTP. They are *URL rewriting, hidden form fields, cookies,* and *the HTTPSession interface,* as the following sections describe.

URL REWRITING

This technique is one by which you modify the URL to include the session ID of a particular user and send it back to the client. In any subsequent transactions, the client must use the session ID whenever it sends a request to the server. If the session ID does not exist, one is created and used in subsequent communication between the client and the server.

Consider the following example:

Original URL:

```
http://<host address>:<port number>/servletcontext/sampleservlet
```

Rewritten URL:

```
http://<host address>:<port
number>/servletcontext/sampleservlet/1000
http://<host address>:<port number> /servletcontext
/sampleservlet?sessionid=1000
```

HIDDEN FORM FIELDS

This technique is one that you can use to keep track of users by placing hidden fields in a form. The values that you entered in these fields remain hidden from the user. The values of the hidden fields are sent to the server after the user submits the form. As far as the server is concerned, no difference exists between hidden form fields and the other fields in the form.

Consider the example of a shopping mall: The items that the user selects can be tracked by the values of the hidden form fields and submitted to the server to process the details.

Consider the following example:

```
< -- Hello.html -- >
<HTML>
       <TITLE> A Form with Hidden Fields> </TITLE>
       <BODY>
          <FORM>
              <INPUT TYPE="HIDDEN" NAME="text1">
          </FORM>
       </BODY>
</HTML>
```

USING THE HTTPSESSION INTERFACE

The Servlet API consists of few classes and interfaces that help to implement sessions tracking in servlets. The Java Servlet API provides an interface called HTTPSession that you can use to keep track of sessions in the current servlet context.

Every user who logs on to a Web site automatically associates with an HttpSession object. The servlet can use this object to store information about the user's session. The HttpSession object enables the user to maintain two types of data: *state* and *application*. You use the state data in a servlet to maintain and retrieve details about the user's connection. A user's connection details could consist of the time at which the session was created or last accessed. You use application data in a servlet to store details, such as the items that the user added to the shopping basket. You can manipulate the application data by using the getValue() and the putValue() methods of the HttpSession interface. Table 6-2 lists the functions that you can use to manipulate application data.

TABLE 6-2 FUNCTIONS TO MANIPULATE APPLICATION DATA

Method name	Functionality
getSession()	HttpSession HttpServletRequest.getSession (boolean)
	You use this method to retrieve the current HttpSession that is associated with the user. If a session does not exist, you can create a session by using getSession(true).
getValue()	Object getValue(String name)
	You use this function to retrieve the value in a session object. For example, if you have a session object named itemselected, you can retrieve the value in the session object by using getValue(itemselected).
putValue()	void putValue(String name, Object value)
	This function you use to add an item to the session.
getCreationTime()	long getCreationTime()
	This function returns the time, in milliseconds, when the session was created.
getLastAccessedTime()	long getLastAccessedTime()
	This function returns the previous time a request was made with the same session ID. The session manager uses the return value of this function to optimize the activity of the server.
getID()	String getID()
	Returns the session ID. If you use URL rewriting, the session can be retrieved by using this function and passed onto the client.
isNew()	boolean isNew()
	Returns a true value if a new session ID was created recently and not sent to the client.

COOKIES

Cookies are pieces of state information that a Web server sends to clients to keep track of client information. The server creates them and sends them to the client with the HTTP response headers as text strings. The cookie is stored in the client's browser's memory. On subsequent requests to the server, the cookie is sent along with the HTTP request headers. If a user exits the site before the cookie expires, the cookie is stored in the user's machine for any further reference. If a cookie with the same name already exists, the key is overwritten with the new value. A server can send one or more cookies to the client. A Web browser, which is the client software, is expected to support 20 cookies per host, and the size of each cookie can be a maximum of four bytes.

Following are some characteristics of cookies:

◆ Cookies only go back to the server that created them and not to any other server. If a cookie is created by the Web server at www.macromedia.com, for example, and sent to the client or a browser, the cookie can be sent back only to that same server.

◆ The server can use cookies to determine the name, IP address, or other details of the client computer.

The javax.servlet.http.Cookie class

The Servlet API provides a class known as Cookie, which it uses to represent a cookie. You use the Cookie class for implementing session tracking in servlets. The values of the cookies are stored in the client computers. A cookie has a name, which you refer to as *key*, and the data stored in the cookie you refer to as *value*.

A cookie is sent by the client through an HTTPServletRequest object. The servlet sends the cookie to the client through an HTTPServletResponse object.

Table 6-3 lists some of the methods of the Cookie, HTTPServletRequest, and HTTPServletResponse classes that you use to implement the concept of session tracking by using cookies:

TABLE 6-3 METHODS OF THE COOKIE, HTTPSERVLETREQUEST, AND
            HTTPSERVLETRESPONSE CLASSES

Method name	Functionality
Cookie.Cookie(String, String)	You use the constructor of the Cookie class to create a cookie and assign a value to it.
Cookie.getValue(String name)	Each cookie that you create has a name and a value. This function returns the value stored in the given cookie.

Method name	Functionality
Cookie.setValue(String)	You use this function to assign a value of type `String` to the given cookie.
Cookie.getName()	You use this method to retrieve the name of a cookie.
Cookie.setMaxAge(int)	You use this method to specify the maximum amount of time for which the client browser retains the cookie value.
HttpServletResponse. addCookie()	The servlet passes cookies on to the client through an `HTTPServletResponse` object. You use the `addCookie()` method to add a cookie to the response. This method can be called more than once to add different cookies to the response that is sent to the client.
HTTPServletRequest. getCookie()	The client sends data to the server in the form of a request, which is received by the server in the form of a `HTTPServletRequest` object. You use this method to retrieve the cookie values from the request.

Overview of Java Server Pages

With the gradual shift of modern enterprise application toward *n-tier architecture*, Web-based clients gradually began playing a major role in enterprise application. Sun Microsystems' *JavaServerPages (JSP)* API provides the mechanism for creating such application.

In n-tier architecture, the components that make up the enterprise application are separated into different layers. This partitioning of layers across different processes and on different machines across the network enables people working on different layers to enhance and change a particular layer without disturbing the other layers. In typical n-tier architecture, the presentation layer, the business layer, and the data access layer are separate from one another. Refer to the section, "The n-tier model," of this chapter, for more details on n-tier architecture.

The JSP technology enables Web developers to generate dynamic content for the Web by using server-side scripting. As JSP uses Java as its scripting language, it enjoys the benefits of the Java language.

The JSP technology separates the presentation part (HTML) from the actual business logic (Java code) of a Web page. This separation helps in differentiating between the role of a Web designer and a Web developer. A Web designer can change the look and feel of the JSP page without needing to understand the coding part of it.

JSP files are basically a combination of HTML (or XML) and JSP tags. Java Server Pages are built on servlet technology. After a JSP page is first requested, it is translated and compiled into a servlet by the JSP engine. The servlet engine then loads the servlet, and the servlet then handles any subsequent requests. A JSP source file is processed after the JSP gets translated and compiled into a servlet for the first time. After a user sends requests to the JSP, the server executes the compiled servlet by using the request values provided by the user.

A JSP page uses the `javax.servlet.jsp` package, which has the following two classes.

- `JspPage`

- `HttpJspPage`

These classes specify that the compiled JSP page must have the following three methods.

- `jspInit()`

- `jspDestroy()`

- `_jspService(HttpServletRequest request, HttpServletResponse response)`

The following example is a simple JSP code, which displays a simple welcome greeting:

```
<%@ page import="java.util.*" %>
<HTML>
<HEAD>
<TITLE>
SanguineTunes
</TITLE>
</HEAD>
<BODY bgcolor=pink>
Today is :
<% =new Date();%>
</BODY>
</HTML>
```

After the preceding JSP code is called, it displays the page shown in Figure 6-11.

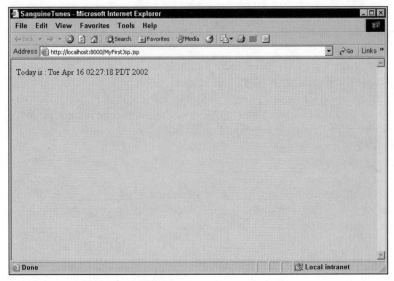

Figure 6-11: Output of the JSP page

JSP components

JSP technology provides various components, such as scripting element (scriptlet), JSP actions, and JSP implicit objects that you use to script and design a JSP page. The following is a list of various JSP components:

- JSP directives
- JSP declarations
- JSP scriplets
- JSP expressions
- JSP implicit objects
- JSP actions

The following sections describe these components.

JSP DIRECTIVES

You use *JSP directive* elements to provide information about a JSP page. In the directive elements, you can perform operations such as importing packages that the JSP files need or specifying error-handling pages.

The syntax of JSP directives is as follows:

```
< %@directive attribute="value"%>
```

The following sections describe the three types of JSP directives.

JSP PAGE DIRECTIVES   You use this directive to provide information to the server about the JSP page. The attributes may be as follows:

- language= "java": You use this attribute to define the language the page is written in. Following is an example showing the use of the language attribute:

  ```
  <:%@page language="java">
  ```

- extends= "packagename.classname": You use this attribute to import classes and packages for use in the JSP page. The following example shows the use of the extends attribute:

  ```
  < %@page  language="java" extends="java.util.Date">
  ```

- session="true|false": This attribute specifies whether session data is available for the particular JSP page. The following example shows the use of the session attribute:

  ```
  < %@page language="java" extends="java.util.Date"
  session="true">
  ```

- errorpage="url": You use this attribute to specify the URL of a file, which is used to handle exceptions. The following example shows the use of the errorpage attribute:

  ```
  < %@page language="java" errorpage="ErrorPage.jsp">
  ```

- isErrorPage="true|false": You use this attribute to specify whether you're using that particular JSP page as an error page. Its default value is false.

JSP INCLUDE DIRECTIVE   You use this directive to include the content of a file in a JSP page whenever the JSP file is translated into a servlet. The following example shows the use of the include directive:

```
< %@include file="/banner.jsp">
```

JSP TAGLIB DIRECTIVE   You use this directive if you are using custom tags in the JSP page. The following example shows the use of the taglib directive:

```
<%@ taglib uri="Tld.tld" prefix="MyTag">
```

JSP DECLARATIONS

You use *JSP declarations* to define page-level variables and methods that the rest of a JSP page can use. Declarations are processed during request-processing time.

The syntax of JSP declaratives is as follows:

```
<%! declaration%>
```

The following example shows the use of JSP declaratives:

<%! INT I=0>JSP SCRIPLETS

Scriplets are Java code fragments embedded within the `<% %>` JSP tag. This code gets inserted in the service method of the generated servlet during the request-processing time. Following is an example of a JSP scriplet:

```
<%
for (int i=0; i<=5; i++)
out.println("Hello");
%>
```

JSP EXPRESSIONS

You use a *JSP expression* to directly insert Java values into the output page. A JSP expression is evaluated, the result is cast as a string, and then it is displayed.

JSP expressions start with `<%=` and ends with `%>`. Following is an example of a JSP expression:

```
<%="Welcome"%>
```

JSP IMPLICIT OBJECTS

To simplify codes in JSP, the JSP container provides some implicit objects that you can use in expressions and scriplets. Following is a list of some of the JSP implicit objects that you can readily use:

- ◆ `request`: This implicit object represents a `HttpServletRequest` object and encapsulates the client request. You use it to retrieve request data of the client. You can use it, for example, to retrieve the request parameters in a scriplet, as follows:
  ```
  <%
  String str="";
   str= request.getParameter("name");
  %>
  ```
- ◆ `response`: This implicit object represents a `HttpServletResponse` object. You use this object to provide responses to the client.
- ◆ `session`: This implicit object represents the `HTTPSession` object associated with the request.

- **out:** This implicit object represents a `JspWriter` object that you use to write an output to the output stream.

- **config:** This implicit object represents the `ServletConfigObject` for the page.

JSP ACTIONS

You use *JSP actions* to perform tasks such as dynamically inserting a file, reusing a JavaBean component, and forwarding requests without using Java code. Some of JSP actions are as follows:

- `jsp:include`: You use this action to insert a file at the time the page is requested. The syntax of the `jsp:include` action is `<jsp:include page="banner.jsp" flush="true" />`.

- `jsp:useBean`: You use this action to load and use a bean. The syntax of the `jsp:useBean` object is `<jsp:useBean id="name" class="package.class" scope="session" />`. You can use this action to create a reference of an existing instance of the bean class, specified by the `class` attribute. The reference is specified by the `id` attribute. You can set the scope of the associated bean with the `scope` attribute with one of the following values: `page`, `request`, `session`, and `application`. These values determine the scope from where the bean object is accessible.

- `jsp:setProperty`: You use the `jsp:setProperty` action to set the property of a JavaBean that was referenced. The syntax of this action is `<jsp:setProperty name="name" property="property" value="value"/>`.

- `jsp:getProperty`: You use this action to retrieve the property of a specified bean. The syntax of this action is `<jsp:getProperty name="name" property="propertyname" value="value"/>`.

Implementing JSP by using a JavaBean component

In server-side application development, a JSP page can use a JavaBean component, which embeds the business logic of the application. As a JavaBean is a reusable component, any other JSP can use it.

 A JavaBean is a Java class that follows certain conventions. All JavaBean classes are public, for example, with a public constructor, and the JavaBean class has private members known as *properties*. To change and read these properties, you must define methods known as the *mutator* and *accessor* methods.

Going back to the SanguineTunes example from earlier sections in this chapter, consider a scenario in which a registered user forgets the password necessary to access the company's Web site. A form should appear to the user where the user fills in his unique e-mail ID. On submitting the form, the user should receive an e-mail containing his name and his password. For this application, you use a HTML form, where the user enters the e-mail ID; a JSP page, which uses a bean; and a JavaBean class to retrieve the user's name and password from the database. The JSP page displays the name and the password to the user.

The following code is for the HTML page that calls the JSP page:

```
<HTML>
     <HEAD>
          <TITLE>SanguineTunes</TITLE>
     </HEAD>
     <BODY bgcolor=blue>
          <BR><BR>
          <CENTER>
               <H4>Please enter your emailID to retrieve your
username
               and password.</H4>
          </CENTER>
          <BR><BR><BR>
          <FORM  method=post
action="http://localhost:8000/CallBean.jsp">
          <CENTER>
          <TABLE>
               <TR><TD>Email ID:</TD>
               <TD> <INPUT type=text name="emailid"></TD>
               </TR>
               <TR></TR>
               <TR><TD></TD>
               <TD><INPUT type=SUBMIT value="SUBMIT"></TD>
               </TR>
          </CENTER>
          </TABLE>
          </FORM>
     </BODY>
</HTML>
```

The following code is for the JSP page CallBean.jsp, which uses a bean component to perform the password retrieval operation and then display it to the user:

```
<%@ page language = "java" %>
 <jsp:useBean id="RB" scope="application" class="RetrievalBean" />
 <jsp:setProperty name="RB" property="*"/>
```

```
<HTML>
    <HEAD>
        <TITLE>SanguineTunes</TITLE>
    </HEAD>
    <BODY>
        <% String s=RB.getInfo();%>
        <%=s %>
    </BODY>
</HTML>
```

The JavaBean class `RetrievalBean` sets the e-mail ID of the user and uses it to retrieve the user's name and password from the database. It then returns a string to the JSP page. This string contains the username and the password that appears to the user. The JavaBean code is as follows:

```
import java.io.*;
import java.sql.*;
public class RetrievalBean
 {
     private String emailid=" ";
    Connection con = null;
    PreparedStatement stat = null;
    ResultSet result = null;

    public RetrievalBean()
     {}

    public void setEmailid(String emailid)
    {
        this.emailid=emailid;
    }

    public String getInfo()
    {
        String str="Reenter Your email ID";
        String str2=" ";
        try
          {

            Class.forName("sun.jdbc.odbc.JdbcOdbcDriver");

con=DriverManager.getConnection("jdbc:odbc:MyDataSource","sa","");
            System.out.println("Value of emailid : "+emailid);
        }
```

```
                catch(ClassNotFoundException e)
                {

                        System.out.println("Database driver    not
found"+e);
                }
                catch (Exception e)
                {
                        System.out.println(e.toString());
                }

        try
        {
            stat=con.prepareStatement("Select * from registration
where EMAILID=?");
                stat.setString(1,emailid);
                result=stat.executeQuery();

                while(result.next())
                {
                    String name=result.getString(1);
                    String pswd=result.getString(3);
                    str2+="Your User Name is "+name +"and your password
is "+pswd+"\n";
                }
            return str2;
        }
        catch(Exception e)
                {
                    System.out.println("Exception in database value
retrieval");
                    return "Record does not exist: Please check your
email id";
                }


        }
}
```

To test this application, follow these steps:

1. Compile the bean class by typing **javac RetrievalBean.java.** Place the
   class file in the `classes` folder of the J2EE servers `lib` folder. If your
   J2EE server is installed in the C drive, place the `RetrievalBean.class` in
   `C:\j2sdkee1.2.1\lib\classes`. Put your HTML file and your JSP file in
   the `public_html` folder inside the `j2sdkee1.2.1` folder.

2. Start the J2EE server by typing **J2EE –verbose** in the command line.

3. Open your browser and type **http://localhost:8000/PasswordInfo.html** in the browser's address bar.

Type your email ID in the text box and click the submit button. The JSP page displays your user name and password that is retrieved by the bean.

JSP custom tags

You use the JSP tags to perform various tasks on a JSP page. Sometimes you may need to perform a task repeatedly across various JSP page. JSP technology enables you to define your own tags to describe such repeated tasks. Tags that you define yourself are known as *custom tags*. You may, for example, display a particular output many times across pages; then you can define a custom tag to represent such output. By using the custom tags, you can separate the presentation logic from the business logic to a greater extent.

You define all the custom tags in a file known as the *tag library descriptor,* or *TLD*. The TLD is an XML file that defines the various characteristics of custom tags, such as the name of the tag, the attributes of the tag, the class file, and the body content.

You also need to define a Java class file to handle the tag. This class file is known as the *tag handler*. The tag handler is usually a JavaBean class. The following section describes the TLD file and tag handlers.

THE TLD FILE

This section provides an example of a TLD file that defines the tag `Welcome`.

You always write the first few lines in the TLD file as shown in the following code:

```
<?xml version ="1.0" encoding="ISO-8859-1" ?>
<!DOCTYPE taglib PUBLIC "-//Sun Microsystems, Inc.//DTD JSP Tag
Library 1.1//EN"
"http://java.sun.com/j2ee/dtds/web-jsptaglibrary_1_1.dtd">
```

In the TLD file, you specify the `tlibversion`, `uri` (or uniform resource information), `info` tags, and other information tags. The following code snippet shows how you specify the `<tlibversion>`, `<info>` and other information tags, such as `<jspversion>` and `<shortname>`:

```
<taglib>
    <tlibversion>1.0</tlibversion>
    <jspversion>1.1</jspversion>
    <shortname>WelcomeTags</shortname>
    <info>A tag library for demonstration</info>
```

You then define the custom tags. Most of the tags that you use are obvious – for example, the `name` tag defines the name of the custom tag and the `tagclass` tag specifies the name of the tag handler class. The `bodycontent` tag specifies whether the custom tag has a body. Some custom tags may also have attributes. You can also use the `attributes` tag to define the attributes that you need to specify for a particular tag. The following code snippet shows the custom tag for this example:

```
<tag>
    <name>Welcome</name>
    <tagclass>WelcomeTag</tagclass>
    <info>Will display a Welcome page</info>
    <bodycontent>JSP</bodycontent>
</tag>

</taglib>
```

TAG HANDLER CLASS

You define the activities of the custom tag in the tag handler class. If you examine an HTML tag, such as the `BODY` tag, you observe that it has a defined structure, as in the following example:

```
<BODY  bgcolor=pink>
    This is the body of the BODY tag.
</BODY>
```

In the preceding example, the `BODY` tag has a start tag, `<BODY>`; an attribute, `bgcolor`; the body content `This is the body of the BODY tag.`; and the end tag, `</BODY>`. To interpret this tag, the browser must perform the following activities:

1. Carry out initializations.

2. Start processing at the start of the tag.

3. Process the body content.

4. Perform certain processes at the end of the tag.

5. Release any resources currently in use.

As you write a tag handler for a custom tag, therefore, you must perform the preceding activities on the custom tag in the class file. The tag handler that you write implements either the `Tag` interface or extends the `TagSupport` or `BodyTagSupport` class of the `javax.servlet.tagext` package. These classes implement the `Tag` interface, which has methods that you can map to the activities that I mention in the preceding steps. These methods are as follows:

◆ The doStartTag() method is called when a JSP engine encounters a tag. You use this method to initialize the tag handler class. This method returns one of the following integer values: SKIP_BODY, EVAL_BODY_INCLUDE, or EVAL_BODY_TAG. If the return is SKIP_BODY, the JSP engine directly calls the doEndTag() method. The EVAL_BODY_INCLUDE value specifies that the body content must be processed. The EVAL_BODY_TAG value specifies that the tag body must be processed.

◆ The doBeforeBody() method is called before evaluating the body.

◆ The doAfterBody() method is called on completing the evaluation of the body.

◆ The doEndTag() method is called on encountering the end tag.

◆ The release() method removes the instance of the tag handler and is called after the doEndTag() method.

The TagSupport class is extended to define a bodyless tag, while the BodyTagSupport class is extended to define a tag with a body.

 A *bodyless tag* has a starting tag but does not have a matching end tag. A *tag with a body* has a start tag and a matching end tag.

The following code shows the implementation of the custom tag:

```
import javax.servlet.jsp.*;
import javax.servlet.jsp.tagext.*;
import java.io.*;
public class WelcomeTag extends TagSupport{
     public WelcomeTag()
      {}
     public int doStartTag() throws JspTagException
     {
        try{
                JspWriter out =pageContext.getOut();
                out.println("Welcome to the world of tunes that
make you happy : SanguineTune ");
             }
```

```
        catch(Exception e){}
     return SKIP_BODY;
  }
  public int doEndTag(){
     try{}
        catch(Exception e){}
     return 1;
  }
}
```

In the JSP page, you use the `taglib` directive to specify the `uri` and the `prefix` attributes. The `uri` attribute defines the TLD file, and the `prefix` attribute specifies the name of the TLD file that you use in the JSP page. You can then use the custom tag as you use any other tags.

The following code illustrates the JSP page CustomTagDisplay.jsp that uses your custom tag to display a message:

```
<%@ taglib uri="WelcomeTLD.tld" prefix="MyTag">
<!DOCTYPE HTML Public "-//W3C//DTD HTML 4.0 Translational//EN ">
<HTML>
<HEAD>
<TITLE>
SanguineTune
</TITLE>
</HEAD>
<BODY bgcolor=pink>
Here goes my tag!<BR>
<MyTag:Welcome/><BR>
I have used  my tag.<BR>
</BODY>
</HTML>
```

To test this example, copy the JSP file and the TLD file in the `public_html` folder inside `j2sdkee1.2.1`. Now put the class file of the tag handler class file in the `classes` folder of the J2EE servers `lib` folder. Start the J2EE server by typing **J2EE –verbose**. In the address bar of your browser type the following address:

```
http://localhost:8000/ CustomTagDisplay.jsp
```

The JSP page displays the welcome message.

Summary

In this chapter, you learn the different kinds of system architectures that you can use to build distributed application frameworks. This chapter explained what servlets are, servlets alternate technologies, and how a servlet works. This chapter also discussed the life cycles of a servlet and explained how to create, deploy, and test a servlet. In this chapter, you learned various ways to track session. This chapter also provided an overview of JSP. You also learned about various JSP components, and custom tags.

Chapter 7

J2EE and Web Services

IN THIS CHAPTER

- ◆ Introduction to J2EE architecture
- ◆ Web components
- ◆ J2EE and Web services

YOU CAN EASILY BUILD THE WEB SERVICES MODEL by using J2EE specifications. A large number of B2B collaboration models are already using J2EE architecture. Developers can now model XML-based Web services by using J2EE initiatives, because the current version of the J2EE API includes the XML pack for XML-centric collaboration frameworks. J2EE provides the capability to quickly build a framework without re-engineering the existing Java-based implementation.

The J2EE specification is available at `http://java.sun.com/j2ee/download.html`.

Introduction to J2EE Architecture

The J2EE specification details different technologies and component frameworks that enable a developer to implement the n-tier system model in an enterprise. As the name suggests, J2EE is a Java technology that uses the Java platform to solve all enterprise needs. The J2EE specification consists of numerous specifications, as shown in Figure 7-1.

Refer to Chapter 6 for more information on the n-tier system model.

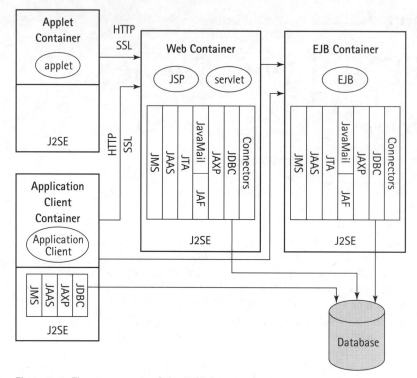

Figure 7-1: The components of the J2EE framework

According to the J2EE specification, on a higher level, J2EE has the following elements:

- ◆ **J2EE platform:** This element is the standard Java platform where n-tier application models are implemented.

- ◆ **J2EE compatibility test suite:** This suite provides the test tools that verify an implemented application to determine whether the application adheres to J2EE guidelines.

- ◆ **J2EE reference implementation:** This reference implementation provides an operational prototype of the J2EE specification.

- ◆ **J2EE BluePrints:** These blueprints are a set of design patterns and best practices for implementing a distributed n-tier model.

The J2EE Platform

The J2EE platform logically consists of the following services:

- ◆ Runtime component services
- ◆ Runtime infrastructure services

COMPONENT SERVICES

J2EE supports four runtime application-component specifications, as shown in Figure 7-1. These runtime application-component specifications are as follows:

- **Application client:** Application clients are the Java applications that you implement to execute as a standalone context. The application client can directly integrate with the business-logic layer for invoking the workflow. The UIs on such applications are usually very complex and rich, and you can probably bundle them with presentation logic (similar to three-tier clients).

- **Applets:** Applets are Java programs that execute within a browser's context. Applets are downloadable from the Internet, unlike application clients that you must preinstall on every client node. Applets serve the purpose of dynamic client downloads. Applets are, again, client-side applications that can also directly invoke the workflow on the business-logic layer.

- **JSP and servlets:** Java Server Pages (JSP) and servlets are server-side programs that execute on the application server. JSPs serve the purpose of representing a dynamic client-side UI that is served to the client at run-time. Servlets provide presentation logic and event-management and filtering capabilities for the JSP layer. If you consider the MVC architecture as an analogy, the servlet component acts as a controller between the JSP and the business-logic layer.

- **Enterprise Java Beans (EJBs):** Enterprise Java Beans are the server-side components that execute within an application server. EJBs are implemented on the business-logic tier of the n-tiered system architecture. EJBs model the workflow logic of the business layer. The three kinds of EJBs are known as *session beans, entity beans,* and *message-driven beans.* The session bean manages the workflow logic of the business tier. The entity bean manages entity relationships with the datastore and exposes an interface for data manipulation. The message-driven bean provides an interface for session beans to communicate with any asynchronous messaging model.

THE INFRASTRUCTURAL SERVICES

J2EE supports the following infrastructural services:

- **J2EE container:** A J2EE container is a runtime context for the application components of the J2EE platform. Figure 7-1 provides an overview of the different containers that are available in the J2EE platform. A container is a runtime context that injects primary services such as transaction, concurrency, persistence, distributedness, naming, and security into the components that execute within the container context. The container is responsible for maintaining the life cycle of the components that execute within the container context. Four container specifications are presently available, as shown in Figure 7-1. The *applet container* provides a runtime context for the applet components to execute. The *application-client container* provides the necessary infrastructural and runtime support for Java application clients to execute. The *Web container* provides the runtime context for JSP and servlets to execute. The *EJB container* provides the runtime context for EJBs to execute.

◆ **J2EE server:** A J2EE server is a server that has the capability to host JSPs, servlets, and EJB components within the server framework. To accommodate the hosting of these different server-side application components, the server must support the Web container as well as the EJB container. The J2EE specification provides a container-component contract for the containers to adhere to. It also provides a server-container contract for the servers to adhere to. The server-container contract suggests the demarcation between a server and a container. For example, a J2EE server takes care of system-level initiatives, such as providing a interface for underlying communication protocols, supporting adapters for messaging, and providing system-level APIs for security, transactions, and threads. The J2EE server is a combination of a Web server, a message server, a transaction monitor, and a request broker. As of today, a J2EE server is known as an *application server*. The application servers in the present market should also support XML-based frameworks so that the servers are Web services–enabled.

The J2EE platform provides a distinct set of APIs that enables the developer to make use of the J2EE server implementation. Figure 7-1 provides an overview of how the technologies fit into the overall picture of the J2EE architecture. The following list presents the different APIs available in J2EE:

◆ Java Servlet

◆ Java Server Pages (JSP)

◆ Enterprise JavaBean Architecture

◆ JDBC

◆ Java Naming and Directory Interface (JNDI)

◆ Java Transaction API (JTA)

◆ Java Transaction Service (JTS)

◆ Java Messaging Service (JMS)

◆ Java Interface Definition Language (Java IDL)

- ◆ Remote Method Invocation-Internet Inter ORB Protocol (RMI-IIOP)

- ◆ JavaMail

The J2EE architecture is based on J2SE APIs. *J2SE* stands for *Java Platform 2 Standard Edition*. The Standard Edition provides the base set of APIs that is always present in any Java-enabled environment. Additional sets of APIs provide core extensions of the base J2SE set. These additional sets of APIs provide support for authentication, authorization, cryptography, and management extensions. The most important addition to the J2SE API set is the various Java APIs for accessing Web services. Following is a list of the Java APIs that you can use for accessing Web services:

- ◆ Java API for XML Processing (JAXP)

- ◆ Java API for XML Binding (JAXB)

- ◆ Java API for XML Messaging (JAXM)

- ◆ Java API for XML-based RPC (JAX-RPC)

- ◆ Java API for XML Registries (JAXR)

The APIs in the preceding list are based on XML technology. These APIs are also known as the *JAX-Pack*. The JAX-Pack is a new addition to the J2EE family. JAX-Pack also comes bundled with the *Java Web Services Developer Pack,* or *JWSDP*. The JWSDP is a bundling of the JAX-Pack, JSP Standard Tag Library (JSTL), a Tomcat Web container, a registry server, and a build tool known as Ant, from Apache. Before you begin understanding JWSD-Pack, you need to understand other technologies in the J2EE repertoire.

Web Components

The most important technologies of the J2EE architecture are the Web-container and Web-component technologies of J2EE. The Web-oriented technologies available in J2EE are Java Server Pages (JSP) and servlets. These technologies are important, because in the Web-services architecture, the service that the provider presents to the external world is facing outside, toward the Internet. The capability to expose the service to the Internet becomes possible through the J2EE Web-oriented technologies. Figure 7-2 provides a perspective of the Web container's role in J2EE Web services.

As Figure 7-2 shows, the Web container plays an important role in the Web-services provider architecture. It is essential that you understand the roles of Web containers and components before I discuss J2EE Web services.

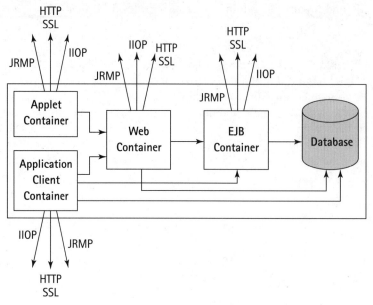

Figure 7-2: Web container's role in the J2EE Web-services architecture

Servlets

Servlets are the Java Web components that execute within a Web container. They are Java programs that execute on the server side of system architecture. Servlets execute in the presentation layer of the system architecture.

 The servlet specification details the entire API of the servlet 2.3 architecture. The specification is available at `http://java.sun.com/products/servlet`.

 To know more about servlets, refer to Chapter 8.

You mainly use servlets as a replacement for technologies similar to CGI. CGI programs are those programs that generate dynamic Web content, which you need to present to a Web client. Servlet technology has overcome various limitations of CGI programming. Table 7-1 compares the features of CGI and servlets.

TABLE 7-1 CGI VS. SERVLETS

CGI	Servlets
CGI programs are typically written in Perl but can also be written in C and Python.	Servlets are always written in Java.
Every client invocation starts a new process for the CGI program.	Every client invocation starts only a separate thread on a single servlet object.
Programs run as a separate process and, therefore, they consume a lot of memory.	Because the clients are served by using separate threads, memory consumption is much less.
Separate processes for every client slow the service substantially.	Threads are lightweight and significantly faster than processes.
Uses HTTP as the base for communication	Uses HTTP as the base for communication. Can also communicate literally across any other communication channel with ease.
Mostly procedural logic	Because servlets are Java programs, they are 100-percent object-oriented.

Although you can use both technologies appropriately in a given context, you can apply servlets, in general, to almost every conceivable context in Web services.

Servlets are Web components managed by Web containers that also are known as *servlet engines*. A Web container is a runtime context for the servlet that manages the life cycle of the servlet. The Web container also injects necessary services, such as concurrency, persistence, and resource pooling. Because servlets are Java programs, they are platform-neutral, as is Java itself. Similar to any other Java program, you always compile servlet codes to a system-neutral intermediary, known as *byte code*. Servlet technology also employs a standard programming model based on the servlet API from the J2EE architecture. The J2EE specification dictates that all J2EE-compliant Web servers must expose the same programming model for Web components. This exposure mandates a level of comfort for the servlets to feel at home within any Web server. Because Web-container vendors expose the servlet programming model within their products, servlets can safely execute within any Web server without needing to be rewritten or recompiled. In other words, the majority of the servlet codes not only are cross-platform, but are also cross-vendor. Servlet technology is generally Web-oriented. Because the Internet uses HTTP as its ubiquitous protocol, you also generally implement servlets on HTTP for communication, which means that servlets employ HTTP request and response methods for communication between a Web client and a servlet.

Servlets are based on a request-response programming model. The request-response model dictates that the servlet-programming model has synchronous messaging architecture. This requirement is key for most of the service-abstractions that you implement within the Web-services model. A service requestor communicates with a service provider by using SOAP. SOAP messages eventually execute over the HTTP communication layer. SOAP messages also carry XML-RPC-style message-invocation mechanisms that are synchronous. Because both SOAP message invocation and the servlet-programming model employ the request-response messaging model, servlet technology maps as a natural fit to the Web-services model. Servlets are the most preferred option for providing Web services across HTTP. You can also use other (nonservlet) Java programs to expose a service to the Internet. Servlets are regularly used as an RPC-Router in the service architecture. You also use servlets in requestor architecture to look up a service description in the registry. I limit the discussions on these mechanisms for now. I explain the role of the servlet in the service-provision architecture and service-requestor architecture after covering the servlet-programming model and the JAX-Pack in detail.

SERVLET-PROGRAMMING MODEL

J2EE accommodates the servlet API in its architecture. The servlet API contains the necessary interfaces and classes that are easy to conceive, as they are designed to work on any kind of underlying communication model. The Servlet interface is the main interface and is implemented by two servlet classes, GenericServlet and HttpServlet. Usually, if a developer wants to create a servlet, the developer should use either the GenericServlet class or the HttpServlet class without worrying about implementing the Servlet interface. You extend the GenericServlet class while creating a generic servlet that is applicable to any protocol providing a request-response model. You use the HttpServlet class only if you're sure of using the servlet only on the HTTP communication layer. The following code gives you an idea how to use the GenericServlet class:

```
import javax.servlet.*;

public class SimpleServlet extends GenericServlet {
    public void service(ServletRequest request, ServletResponse
response) throws ServletException, java.io.IOException {
        response.setContentType("text/html");
        java.io.PrintWriter out = response.getWriter();
        out.println("<html>");
        out.println("<head>");
        out.println("<title>Hello World Servlet</title>");
        out.println("</head>");
        out.println("<body>");
        out.println("<h1>Hello World</h1>");
        out.println("</body>");
        out.println("</html>");
```

```
        out.close();
    }
    public String getServletInfo() {
        return "The servlet generates a HTML that displays a Hello
World message on the client browser";
    }
}
```

In the preceding example, the code extends the `GenericServlet` class. The `javax.servlet.*` package contains all the interfaces and classes that help you create a generic servlet class, which you can program for any communication protocol. The preceding code overrides only a `service` method in which you embed application logic. The service method manually outputs an HTML page by statically hard-coding the HTML page within the embedded logic. The `ServletRequest` and `ServletResponse` parameters that you declare in the `service` method represent the request message and the response message, respectively. Notice that, by using the `ServletResponse`, you can obtain the output stream of the servlet. This output stream, `PrintWriter`, provides the outlet to stream the contents of the HTML page that you intend to display. The `getServletInfo` method returns a short description of the servlet to a tool, such as an IDE, which wants to host the servlet. The method does not come in handy for any other documentation purposes except for providing a short description at runtime.

After you write the source code, you normally use the standard Java compiler to compile the servlet. Take care in setting up the environment before compiling the servlet. After you compile the servlet, deploy the servlet into a servlet container. The process of deploying the servlet into the servlet container depends on which servlet container you are using. In Chapter 4, I showed you how to deploy the servlet into a Tomcat servlet container. Assuming that you take the necessary steps for deploying the servlet within a servlet container, you are ready to execute the servlet from a client browser. Assuming that the Web server is running on a local host on the port 8080, invoke the servlet from within your Web browser by typing the following URL:

`http://localhost:8080/servlet/SimpleServlet`

This URL breaks down into the elements shown in Table 7-2.

TABLE 7-2 ELEMENTS OF THE SERVLET INVOCATION URL

Element	Value	Purpose
Protocol	http	The primary protocol used for transport, such as HTTP, FTP, and RMI.

Continued

TABLE 7-2 ELEMENTS OF THE SERVLET INVOCATION URL *(Continued)*

Element	Value	Purpose
Server	Localhost	The name of the host on which the Web container is executing.
Port	8080	The service port on which the Web container is listening.
Loader	Servlet	The default servlet loader that bootstraps your servlet object.
Name	SimpleServlet	Usually the name of your servlet.

The following code illustrates how to use a `HttpServlet` class:

```
import javax.servlet.*;
import javax.servlet.http.*;

public class MyHttpServlet extends HttpServlet {
    public void init(ServletConfig config) throws ServletException {
        super.init(config);
    }

    protected void processRequest(HttpServletRequest request,
HttpServletResponse response)
        throws ServletException, java.io.IOException {
        response.setContentType("text/html");
        java.io.PrintWriter out = response.getWriter();
        String greeting = request.getParameter("greeting");
        String user = request.getParameter("user");
        out.println("<html>");
        out.println("<head>");
        out.println("<title>Http Servlet</title>");
        out.println("</head>");
        out.println("<body>");
        out.println("<h1>" + greeting + " " + user + "</h1>");
        out.println("</body>");
        out.println("</html>");
        out.close();
    }

    protected void doGet(HttpServletRequest request,
HttpServletResponse response)
        throws ServletException, java.io.IOException {
```

```
        processRequest(request, response);
    }

    protected void doPost(HttpServletRequest request,
HttpServletResponse response)
    throws ServletException, java.io.IOException {
        processRequest(request, response);
    }

    public String getServletInfo() {
        return "This servlet displays a user greeting message on ↵
the client browser";
    }
}
```

The preceding example shows you how to extend the HttpServlet class. You use the HttpServlet class specifically on the HTTP protocol. You start by importing the javax.servlet.* and javax.servlet.http.* packages. These packages contain the necessary interfaces and classes to create an HTTP-specific servlet code. This code overrides two special methods, doGet() and doPost(). These two methods participate in the life cycle of the servlet. You provide application logic in a developer-defined method, processRequest(). The doPost() and the doGet() methods invoke the processRequest() method. The processRequest() method manually outputs an HTML page by dynamically coding the HTML page within the embedded logic. The output of the preceding servlet changes depending on the value of the parameters that pass to the servlet. The init() method is another overridden method that accepts the ServletConfig object from the container for use within the servlet. The ServletConfig object provides the configuration details that are necessary for the correct initialization of the servlet.

After compiling the servlet, you need to deploy the servlet into a servlet container. This process is similar to that of deploying the GenericServlet class. Then you need to invoke the servlet from within your Web browser by typing the following URL:

`http://localhost:8080/servlet/MyHttpServlet?greeting=Hello&user=preetham`

This URL breaks down into the elements shown in Table 7-3.

TABLE 7-3 ELEMENTS OF THE SERVLET INVOCATION URL

Element	Value	Purpose
Protocol	http	The primary protocol used for transport, such as HTTP, FTP, and RMI.

Continued

TABLE 7-3 ELEMENTS OF THE SERVLET INVOCATION URL *(Continued)*

Element	Value	Purpose
Server	Localhost	The name of the host on which the Web container is executing.
Port	8080	The service port on which the Web container is listening.
Loader	Servlet	The default servlet loader that bootstraps your servlet object.
Name	MyHttpServlet	Usually the name of your servlet.
Query string initiator	?	This signifies the beginning of the query string.
Parameter1 name-value pair	Greeting=Hello	*Greeting* specifies the first parameter name, and *Hello* specifies its value.
Parameter separator (appendage)	&	The ampersand signifies the addition of more parameters.
Parameter2 name-value pair	User=preetham	*User* specifies the second parameter name, and `preetham` specifies its value.

SERVLET CONCURRENCY

A servlet, as opposed to a CGI program, provides multithreaded access to a single servlet object to handle the requests that multiple service clients raise. The Web container manages the concurrency issues of sending the request messages to the service method of the servlet. It becomes the responsibility of the developer to make sure that the state of the servlet does not conflict with such multithreaded access. The servlet specification cautions developers not to flag the service method as synchronized. Doing so slows the servlet drastically, and the container does not pool the servlets that are using synchronized methods.

If any probable cause appears for an inadequate state-management mechanism within the servlet, the developer can implement the `SingleThreadModel` interface. The implementation of this interface signals to the Web container to disallow concurrent access to the servlets. Instead, the Web container can choose to create number of objects of the same servlet and can resource-pool these instances among different clients. Choosing whatever logic is appropriate for their products is entirely at the discretion of the Web-container vendors.

SESSION MANAGEMENT

Servlets are Java programs that use HTTP as the transport layer. HTTP is a *stateless protocol*. What is statelessness? Given the communication between a Web client and a Web server, the incapability to manage an active conversational state of the session is known as *statelessness*. Servlets have been discussed in Chapter 6.

The advantage of having a stateless protocol working for you is that such a protocol is definitely simpler and lighter than any other transport protocol. The disadvantage of statelessness is that no inherent mechanism is available to maintain the conversational state between two endpoints. So every time that the client invokes a service on the Web server, the client needs to declare its identity to the server. Why? Because the stateless protocol does not inherently maintain the state of a session. If the server also does not provide any mechanism to maintain a session state, you can call the server a stateless server. A stateless server never remembers the identity of the client it is conversing with. A constant reminder about the client's identity assists every client invocation.

You can introduce *statefulness* into the architecture by manually designing the application to manage a state. In object-oriented design, you probably use state fields to maintain a conversational state with an object. In other words, to maintain a conversational state with an object across multiple method invocation, you declare attributes that hold the state of the conversation. By the same principle, you may presume that a servlet can also have state fields that can eventually maintain the conversational state of a session. This philosophy works as long as you have a one-to-one relationship between a servlet and a client. To begin, HTTP not only is a stateless protocol, but it is also a *connectionless protocol*. No active connection is maintained between one request and another. Such connectionless access to the servlet raises the possibility of timing out the servlet. Even if you had a mechanism to disallow the expiry of a servlet, you still face a bigger problem – state maintenance. This problem involves the design of the servlet architecture. The servlet architecture or the Servlet specification dictates that a single servlet object is used by the servlet container in serving multiple clients. These clients are served by the servlet container using separate threads. As soon as you consider concurrent access to a shared resource such as a servlet, you confront the problem of sharing the state of the resource with multiple threads. You may think that this issue is not a big one and that accessing this shared state in a "synchronized" way can solve it. Before you jump to that conclusion, notice that the servlet specification prevents you from using the synchronized keyword for the service. You may think that flagging the servlet as `SingleThreadModel` solves the problem. By making the servlet a `SingleThreadModel`, you achieve one-to-one access to a servlet object from the resource pool. The problem is really not solved, however, because HTTP is a connectionless protocol. How can you identify a client request from another so that you can always map the consequent requests from a given client to the same servlet in the resource pool? This question is hard to answer on a connectionless protocol. Following, however, are the probable ways out of this problem:

♦ Flag the HTTP protocol between the client and the server to `KEEP_ALIVE`. Setting the `KEEP_ALIVE` attribute of the HTTP protocol to true never drops a session. In this way, you can possibly achieve a connection-oriented approach to the problem.

♦ Use some other state management mechanisms such as hidden form fields, cookies, URL-rewriting, or `HttpSession` objects.

In the preceding list, the first option seems appropriate only if you directly manage the client boxes that you network to the Internet. This option is literally impossible to employ on an ad-hoc service-request architecture such as that of Web services, because you are really not aware of the client that may make such requests. If you are not aware of the clients who can connect to your server, you cannot manage a client session as a connection-oriented session.

The second option seems more appropriate, as that option provides freedom of expression. You are not limited to implementing a `SingleThreadModel` to maintain the state. You do not need to worry about connectionless access to your servlets. All you need to concern yourself with is a tiny piece of metadata that is served to you every time a request is made. This metadata can be in the form of a cookie, a hidden field, or a query string from your rewritten URL. Whatever the case, you can still use the metadata that may possibly carry a unique session ID for a given client. This unique session ID helps you to discern between client requests. You are also free to implement `HashMap`, which holds session IDs as a key and the appropriate-state object as the value. The consequence is a flexible, extensible implementation of session management architecture within your application.

The best mechanism to maintain the conversational state of a session is to use an `HttpSession` object to maintain the state. The following code provides an overview of state management within a servlet:

```java
import javax.servlet.*;
import javax.servlet.http.*;
import java.util.*;

public class ShoppingCartServlet extends HttpServlet {
    public void init(ServletConfig config) throws ServletException {
        super.init(config);
    }

    protected void processRequest(HttpServletRequest request,
HttpServletResponse response) throws ServletException,
java.io.IOException {
        response.setContentType("text/html");
        java.io.PrintWriter out = response.getWriter();
        out.println("<html>");
        out.println("<head><title>Shopping Cart
Servlet</title></head>");
        out.println("<body>");
        out.println("<form action=
'http://localhost:8080/servlet/ShoppingCartServlet' method=
'post'>");
        out.println("<h1>Shopping Cart Example</h1><hr/><br/>");
        out.println("Enter an item into the cart:<br/><input
type=text name=item><br/><br/>");
        out.println("<input type=submit value='Add to
cart'></form><hr/>");
```

```
        HttpSession session=request.getSession(true);
        if(session.isNew())
            session.setAttribute("CART", new Vector());
        Vector cart = (Vector) session.getAttribute("CART");
        String item=request.getParameter("item");
        if(item!=null)
            cart.addElement(item);
        if(!cart.isEmpty()) {
            out.println("<h2>The current items in cart
are:</h2><hr/><ul>");
            for(Iterator
iterator=cart.iterator();iterator.hasNext();out.println("<li>" +
iterator.next() + "</li>"));
        } else
            out.println("<h2>There are currently no items in the
cart<h2>");
        out.println("</ul><hr/>");
        out.println("</body>");
        out.println("</html>");
        out.close();
    }

    protected void doGet(HttpServletRequest request,
HttpServletResponse response)
        throws ServletException, java.io.IOException {
        processRequest(request, response);
    }

    protected void doPost(HttpServletRequest request,
HttpServletResponse response)
        throws ServletException, java.io.IOException {
        processRequest(request, response);
    }
}
```

The preceding code uses the HttpSession object to maintain the state of the session. You obtain the HttpSession object by enquiring the HttpServletRequest object. The HttpServletRequest object is obtained as an argument for service methods such as doGet() and doPost(). The request.getSession(true) call results in HttpSession.

The request.getSession(true) call works on the following principles if you pass true as a Boolean argument:

◆ If no active session is assigned to the client thread, create a new session and return a new HttpSession object that contains the new session ID.

◆ If a session ID is already assigned to the requesting client thread, simply return the HttpSession object that is already assigned to the thread.

The `request.getSession(false)` call works on the following principles if you pass `false` as a Boolean argument:

♦ If no active session is assigned to the client thread, return `null`.

♦ If a session ID is already assigned to the requesting client thread, simply return the `HttpSession` object that is already assigned to the thread.

As you go along the servlet path, you come across a lot of other concepts that were recently added to the Servlet 2.3 specification. These new concepts, such as filters and application events, help you write complex programming logic for Web services. For now, understanding the JSP technology helps you to write the client-side presentation logic.

Java Server Pages

JSP, a mixture of the HTML programming script and the Java programming language, gives you the capability to embed Java code within an HTML script. You mainly use JSPs for writing presentation logic for a client. JSP code still resides on the presentation layer on the server side. JSP code provides an expressive combination of syntax and semantics to mix and match both HTML and Java code within a single presentation code. As you may notice in the preceding section, the code for the servlet aimed at displaying or generating HTML content from within the servlet logic. This approach looked a little weird. Writing display logic, which is eventually HTML code, from within your servlet is almost obscure. Writing presentation code as HTML in an HTML file rather than in a servlet is much better. Writing Java code within an HTML file would also prove interesting, if you could do so. That way, you can introduce dynamism into your code at the place where you require it. Writing Java code within an HTML script is also advantageous in that HTML authoring tools can still work on the HTML file for the purposes of content management and presentation.

The bottom line is that a JSP is just an inside-out logic of a servlet code. In a servlet, you write HTML within Java code. In JSP, you write Java code within HTML. At the end of the day, a JSP code is eventually converted by the Web container to a servlet for you. The Web container makes sure that it converts the JSP file that you are trying to deploy into the Web container to a servlet code. The reason behind this conversion is that the container can then compile the servlet code and launch the servlet as an object within the runtime environment. This way, the container can remain object-oriented in its management style. This approach seems simple, yet effective for tool vendors, because all the code that you write, whether JSP or servlet, is eventually converted into a servlet object at runtime. Web containers thus need only to concentrate on managing a dynamic servlet object at runtime.

The following code gives an overview of a simple JSP code:

HelloUser.jsp

```
<%@page contentType="text/html"%>
<html>
```

```
<head><title>JSP Page</title></head>
<body>
<form action='http://localhost:8080/HelloUser.jsp' method='POST'>
    <%
        String user = request.getParameter("user");
        if(user==null) {
    %>
            <h2>Hello user, please enter your name :</h2>
            <input type=text name='user'>
    <%
        } else {
    %>
            <h2>Hello <%= user %> </h2>
    <%
        }
    %>
</form>
</body>
</html>
```

After you finish writing the source code, save the source as a `*.jsp` file. The preceding code you save as `HelloUser.jsp`. You usually save the code under the Web-server `root`. Just saving the code to an appropriate place, depending on the Web container that you are using, deploys the JSP file into the Web container.

After you finish deploying the JSP file, you can usually execute it from within your Web browser by typing the following address in the address bar:

```
http://localhost:8080/HelloUser.jsp
```

The JSP programming model is the same as the servlet programming model because JSP is a servlet at the time of execution. The Web container is responsible for converting a JSP file into a servlet. The Web container converts the JSP file to a servlet only once. The conversion happens only on the first call to the JSP file. Every other subsequent call to the same JSP file is routed to the servlet that the container created from the JSP file. The Web container also converts the JSP to a servlet if the JSP code changes. The Web container maintains a timestamp of the JSP and the servlet code. If a mismatch occurs in the timestamp, the Web container goes through the conversion process again.

For more information on JSPs, refer to Chapter 7.

Various `taglib` directives are used in JSP. Table 7-4 provides a list of the `taglib` directives available in JSP:

TABLE 7-4 JSP TAGLIB SYNTAX

Syntax	Term	Meaning
`<jsp:include>`	Include taglib	This taglib provides a way to include the output of another JSP, text, or HTML page within the current JSP. The execution context is within the current JSP.
`<jsp:forward>`	Forward taglib	Provides capability to forward the request and response objects of the current JSP to another JSP. The execution context jumps from the current JSP to the other JSP.
`<jsp:usebean>`	UseBean taglib	You use this taglib if you want to include a JavaBean instance with the current JSP context.
`<jsp:setProperty>`	SetProperty taglib	This taglib sets the property of the JavaBean that the setProperty tag is referring to.
`<jsp:getProperty>`	GetProperty taglib	You use this taglib to include the obtained property value of a JavaBean into the current JSP context.
`<jsp:plugin>`	Plugin taglib	You use this taglib to execute an applet in the specified plug-in.

You use the action tags in Table 7-4 within the JSP context to easily manage the creation of beans, forward the execution context to another JSP, including the output of another file, or start an applet within a plug-in.

J2EE and Web Services

After you understand the fundamentals of J2EE and the Web components of J2EE architecture, you can understand the role that J2EE plays in the Web services architecture.

Usually, on the server side, servlets play the part of an RPC-Router while you can use JSP in the presentation logic. Most Web-services architectures use a servlet as a front controller. The following steps provide a high-level overview of a servlet acting as a router for an RPC-style XML document accessing a service that the J2EE architecture makes available:

1. The service requestor queries a UDDI registry and obtains the reference of a WSDL file from within the business registry of UDDI.

2. The WSDL file provides the location to which the service is bound.

3. The requestor sends a SOAP request over HTTP to the provider location.

4. The provider receives the SOAP message (an XML file) through the servlet, which listens on the bound address.

5. The servlet routes the RPC call to the appropriate EJB components within the J2EE architecture.

6. The EJB components then process the call and send a response to the servlet.

7. The servlet may need to use some filters to convert the response that it obtains into an appropriate XML message.

8. The servlet returns the XML file to the requestor as a SOAP message over HTTP.

The preceding steps are the high-level steps that a developer must design at the time of architecting a Web-services framework. Further chapters delve into the details involved in creating such a framework by using the JAX-Pack.

SunONE – an overview

SunONE stands for *Sun Open Net Environment*. It is Sun Microsystems' strategy for providing a framework for the Web-services architecture. The framework includes Sun's own products and the protocols in the Web-services stack. Sun recommends a delivering strategy that it calls *Service on Demand* to take its Web-services offerings to the industry. Service on Demand is a strategy, while SunONE is a platform offering a number of Sun products. Sun claims to possess the products and expertise to deliver its Web services vision to the industry based on its successful J2EE platform. Sun professional services provide architectural solutions for most of the top business players in the industry. SunONE actually provides a framework for independent ISVs to build industrial-strength Web services platform either from scratch or from the existing systems they already possess.

The Service on Demand strategy that Sun is marketing is based on an open standard, which, if implemented, promises vendor-neutral capabilities as offered by the J2EE platform. Because SunONE is based on Java, most of its interoperability, vendor neutrality, and integration inherently mature with the language.

The product offerings in the SunONE strategy range from the Solaris Operating Environment to the publicly (read freely) available Forte tools that Sun is having in its repertoire. The focal point of the strategy is the SunONE range of products like such as SunONE Application Server, SunONE Directory Server, SunONE Integration Server, SunONE Portal Server, and SunONE commerce applications. SunONE also has a range of service offerings such as iForce and SunTone.

DART

Sun uses the *DART* diagram that explains the positioning of the SunONE offerings in the industry. DART stands for *D*ata, *A*pplications, *R*eports, and *T*ransactions, which I discuss as follows:

- **Data:** Sun uses the concept of directories to represent data. The Service on Demand framework considers that aggregated data from all the players in the industry, such as partners, suppliers, vendors, and customers, is vital for the Web-services architecture. Controlling data within a directory seems to be the strategy that Service on Demand is using. Sun uses the iPlanet Directory Server to control, aggregate, and manage data within the Web-services model.

- **Applications:** Sun uses the iPlanet Application Server to deliver application service on the Web. The iPlanet Application Server is going to provide a stable, scalable, and dynamic delivery environment for all the service provisions that a service provider needs to expose on the Internet.

- **Reports:** The capability to track and report organizational services is considered another important component within your Web-services stack. Such tracking and reporting service should remain available 24 hours a day and seven days a week on the Internet. Sun uses the iPlanet Web Server to constantly provide such reporting services on the Internet.

- **Transactions:** Transactions, or trading, is considered the primary and most crucial requirement for commerce on the Internet. The capability to conduct business on the Internet is accommodated through a range of services such as iPlanet Communication Services, iPlanet Commerce Services, and the SunONE Webtop.

To conclude, DART is a strategy for effectively utilizing the information assets that already exist within an organization. The DART strategy composes everything about an organization starting from focusing on the business relations with partners, trade merchants, and ending with focusing on interactions with customers, community, vendors, and employees.

Summary

In this chapter, you learn about the J2EE architecture and the services that are available within the J2EE platform. The chapter provides an overview of the different J2EE Web components that play an important role within the Web-services framework. Finally, the chapter discusses the Service on Demand strategy that Sun is providing on its SunONE platform.

Chapter 8

JAXP

IN THIS CHAPTER

- ◆ Introduction to JAXP
- ◆ The SAX API
- ◆ The DOM API

WEB SERVICES ON THE Java platform use XML as their data format. XML is the preferred data format because it is platform independent, portable, and extensible. Moreover, XML encodes data in such a manner that you can easily create and process XML documents. Java Web services use the Standard Object Access Protocol (SOAP) to exchange information on the Web. Because SOAP is XML-based, it provides the information exchange by transporting XML documents across the Web. SOAP also uses the XML-RPC-style messaging framework for invoking remote methods. In addition, WSDL and UDDI, both of which are important components in the Java Web-services model, are based on XML.

As discussed in the preceding paragraph, all these protocols and standards of the Java Web-services framework are heavily based on XML and XML-related technologies. Whenever you implement a Java-based Web-services framework, you need to process all these XML-related technologies from within the implemented code. This capability to access, convert, and process XML documents from within a Java-based system is provided by the JAXP specification.

Java API for XML Processing (JAXP) is among the specifications available in the JAX-Pack. JAXP provides you with an easy way to process XML documents. With the introduction of JAXP, you can now easily create Java applications that use the JAXP API to parse and transform XML documents.

The current JAXP specification is at version 1.1, final specification. At the time of this writing, the 1.2 specification with 1.2.0 EA1 for the reference implementation was out. JAXP is an effort by JavaSoft and the Java Community Process (JCP) to provide a standard API for processing and transforming XML documents. The JCP initiative is constantly working to improve on JAXP and related specifications in the JAX-Pack. The current JAXP specification is available at the JCP.org site as a JSR-63 document. You can find JSR-63 at `http://java.sun.com/aboutJava/communityprocess/jsr/jsr_063_jaxp.html`.

Introduction to JAXP

JAXP is an API that you use to generate, transform, and process XML documents from Java applications. Although JAXP is an API standard, it is more like an abstraction layer that provides access to different XML parsers in a vendor-neutral fashion. Actually, JAXP itself does not process XML documents. Instead, JAXP makes use of the Simple API for XML parsing (SAX) and Document Object Model (DOM) specifications. Without a parsing API, you cannot parse XML documents. JAXP simplifies the tasks of using the SAX and DOM APIs to parse XML documents.

The SAX parser enables you to access the XML-related documents serially, using a data stream. The DOM-related parsers enable you to access the XML documents by building an object tree. In short, SAX provides serial access while DOM provides a tree-based hierarchical access to the data in XML documents. According to your need, you can use the JAXP API from your Java application and use a particular parser — say, a SAX parser or a DOM parser — to parse an XML document.

The JAXP specification also provides support for XML Stylesheet Language Transformations (XSLT). XSLT is an XML standard that enables the developer to transform XML data into other formats. As a matter of fact, the SAX, DOM, and XSLT specifications were maturing in the industry before JAXP was introduced. These existing specifications are considered very raw or primitive for use within a J2EE implementation. The SAX parser specs or the DOM parsers enable a programmer to access XML-based documents from their applications. Because of the primitive API structure of these parsers, however, using these specifications as is within Web-services architecture is a little inconvenient. To counter this inconvenience, the JAXP APIs provide an easy-to-manage, flexible API structure that provides a native Java interface to easily process and transform XML documents. JAXP is considered flexible because it provides a pluggability layer to plug in either the SAX or the DOM parsers within the Web-services infrastructure. The pluggability layer can also accommodate an XSL processor to transform XML data to a presentation style by using the XSLT framework. Therefore, you always use the JAXP as the base API on which you actually build the Web-service interfaces.

JAXP endorses the following set of standards:

- W3C XML 1.0 Recommendation (Second edition)
- W3C XML Namespaces 1.0 Recommendation
- Simple API for XML Parsing (SAX) 2.0
- Document Object Model (DOM) Level 2
- XSLT 1.0

Now that you know about the XML specifications and namespaces, I can discuss the SAX and DOM API specifications and also the XSLT specification for presentation control. After you get a clear understanding of the preceding specifications, understanding the JAXP API is very simple and easy.

The SAX API

As I discuss in the introduction of this chapter, Java Web services rely on XML to exchange information on the Web. You provide information and create tags to structure your information in an XML document. To consume information, you create an application and use the SAX or DOM API, implemented by an XML parser, to access the information encoded in an XML document.

SAX stands for *Simple API for XML*. Some people also call it as *Serial Access for XML*. SAX is an API and a parser standard for accessing XML documents in a serial mode. The SAX programming model is an event-driven model, which relies heavily on the runtime events that occur during the parsing of the XML documents. These runtime events are very important, because they provide callback mechanisms for the application-specific code. If an event occurs at the time of parsing the XML documents, the parsers use the call-back mechanism to invoke the application-specific code.

As a SAX parser reads an XML document, for example, it generates an event whenever the parser encounters an open element tag. This event invokes a call-back function, `startElement()`. Similarly if the parser encounters other things in the XML document, such as close element tags, a #PCDATA section, and comments, it invokes their corresponding callback functions. You basically implement these callback methods in your application according to the required logic.

To accomplish all these tasks, you first create a `SAXParser` instance in your application. Then you provide the required logic for each of the callback functions and finally start parsing the XML document.

Suppose that you want to change your parser to another vendor specific parser. For that, you must again instantiate the specific vendor class to get a parser instance. You can also use the SAX helper class `ParserFactory` and provide the name of the parser class to it. But in both the cases, you must change and recompile your application. With the introduction of JAXP, these complications are removed. By using JAXP, you can provide a parser as a Java system property. On doing so, you do not need to recompile your code each time that you swap between different vendor-specific parsers.

The SAX APIs are bundled with the JWSDP (Java Web Services Developer Pack) kit. The current version of the SAX APIs bundled with JWSDP Early Access 1 is version 2.0 r2 prerelease. Before discussing the SAX programming model, I need to discuss the different Java packages that you use in your application. Table 8-1 provides all the SAX packages that you use in your Web-services framework.

TABLE 8-1 THE JAVA SAX PACKAGES

Package	Description
org.xml.sax	Bundles all the base interfaces of SAX 2.0 r2 prerelease and the `HandlerBase` and `InputSource` classes.
org.xml.sax.helpers	Bundles all the helper classes such as `ParserAdapter`, `NamespaceSupport`, and `XMLFilterImpl`, which make the SAX programming easier.
javax.xml.parsers	Bundles the `SAXParser` and `SAXParserFactory` classes that you use in obtaining a parser and parsing XML documents.
org.xml.sax.ext	Defines the SAX extension APIs that you use in advanced SAX processing. It currently bundles two interfaces, `LexicalHandler` and `DeclHandler`.

The current version of the JAXP is at version 1.2 and Reference Implementation (RI) 1.2.0 EA1. You need to understand the difference between a specification version and the RI version. The specification version always has an $x.x$ format in the version number, while the RI always has an $x.x.x$ format for its versioning. The specification is a blueprint of what the API framework eventually contains. It theoretically provides the API guidelines, endorsements, and details of a given standard. The RI attempts to implement the given specification. The RI contains both the specification version number (the first two x's in the $x.x.x$ format) and an implementation version number (the last x in the $x.x.x$ format). The implementation version can change for the same specification. These changes occur because of bug fixes in the RI for a given specification.

You can categorized the JAXP specification into the following two main standards:

♦ **The parsing API:** Contains the parser specifications and how-tos for accessing different parsers available in the industry.

♦ **The transformation API (TrAX):** Contains the transformation specifications to transform an XML document.

JAXP 1.1.1 RI uses the *Crimson parser,* which was created in joint collaboration between Apache and JavaSoft. JAXP 1.1.1 RI also uses the Xalan XSL Transformer for XML transformations. JAXP 1.2.0 RI EA1 uses the latest Xerces 2 version 2.0.0 beta3 as its default XML parser, while it uses Xalan classic version 2.2.D14 as its default XSLT engine.

You may wonder about all these different specifications, RIs, and version numbers. You may also get confused about all these different parsers from the same organization, Apache. To understand things better, you need to go back to history.

To begin, Apache accepted a specification donated by IBM (XML4J) and named it *Xerces*. Apache also accepted the Project X from the Sun's JCP community and named the specification Crimson. Therefore, Apache needed to support two parser specs, Xerces and Crimson. Later, Apache came out with a rewrite of its Xerces parser and named it Xerces2. Xerces2 claims to have advanced capabilities compared to Xerces (or Xerces1, to be politically correct) and Crimson. According to Apache, Xerces2 is a next-generation parser that is compliant with Xerces1 and Crimson. Xerces2 actually includes a Xerces Native Interface (XNI), which is a framework to build parser components and configurations. It provides maintainability and very high modularity. XNI is actually a standard from Apache, which provides the framework for serially communicating a document over a stream and constructing generic parser configurations.

Setting up JWSDP

The first step to set up JWSDP is to download the JWSDP EA1 from the following location:

`http://java.sun.com/Webservices/downloads/Webservicespack.html`.

If you are running Windows on your computer, you can install the kit directly in your `root` directory. The C: drive is a good location for installation. After you install the kit under the `root`, you can normally locate a folder on your computer as follows:

`c:\jwsdp-1_0-ea1`

As you install JWSDP EA1 on your computer, JAXP 1.2.0 EA1 RI is automatically installed as well. As I state in the preceding section, the JAXP 1.2.0 EA1 comes with Xerces2 as its default parser and Xalan as the default XSLT engine. Before you can begin coding, you need to make sure that you do an appropriate setup on your computer. You need to set the following environment variable (referring to the appropriate documentation of your operating system to learn exactly how to set up the variable):

`set JWSDP_HOME=c:\jwsdp-1_0-ea1`

For all future references, I use `%JWSDP_HOME%` as the home directory for all JWSDP-related examples. You can normally identify the following JAR files in the `%JWSDP_HOME%\common\lib` directory:

- ◆ `xerces.jar`: Contains all the packages relating to the Xerces2 parser from Apache.
- ◆ `xalan.jar`: Contains all the necessary packages relating to the Xalan XSLT engine from Apache.

You need to set your CLASSPATH to refer to the preceding two JAR files. To set the CLASSPATH environment variable, type the following code:

```
set CLASSPATH=%CLASSPATH%;%JWSDP_HOME%\common\lib\xerces.jar;
%JWSDP_HOME%\common\lib\xalan.jar;
```

If you are using Java platform version 1.4, the SDK comes prebundled with the Crimson API. To override the preexisting API, ignore the preceding instruction and copy the JAR files into the following directory:

```
%JAVA_HOME%/jre/lib/endorsed
```

The preceding code snippets set up the environment for the execution of JAXP RI 1.2.0 EA1 on your computer.

The XML document

To begin using a SAX API, you need to make sure that you have an XML document. The XML document can be sent across a SOAP message channel, or for the sake of learning SAX, you can also create an XML file on your computer. I take the latter approach in this chapter. Consider, then, a simple example involving reading a stock quote from an XML file and displaying a formatted result of the readings on the console. To read an XML file that contains some stock quotes and display the listings of the XML file on your console, you begin by creating the necessary XML file. You first need to create the DTD for the XML file so that the XML file can rely on the grammatical structure of the DTD.

On your computer, create an XML file, stock.xml, by using the following code:

```
<?xml version="1.0" encoding="UTF-8"?>

<!DOCTYPE stock SYSTEM "stock.dtd">
<stock>
        <stockinfo ticker="OPN">
                <company>Open Systems Inc</company>
                <price>14</price>
        </stockinfo>
        <stockinfo ticker="PROP">
                <company>Proprietary Systems Inc</company>
                <price>54</price>
        </stockinfo>
        <stockinfo ticker="CPT">
                <company>Concept Solutions</company>
                <price>73</price>
        </stockinfo>
```

```
<stockinfo ticker="ABC">
        <company>ABC Systems Inc</company>
        <price>67</price>
</stockinfo>
<stockinfo ticker="XYZ">
        <company>XYZ MicroSystems</company>
        <price>81</price>
</stockinfo>
</stock>
```

The DTD for the preceding code must also be present in the same folder as the XML file. The DTD, stock.dtd, is as follows:

```
<?xml encoding="UTF-8"?>

<!ELEMENT stock (stockinfo*)>
<!ELEMENT stockinfo (company, price)>
<!ATTLIST stockinfo
     ticker CDATA #REQUIRED>
<!ELEMENT company (#PCDATA)>
<!ELEMENT price (#PCDATA)>
```

After you save the XML file and the DTD, you can write the code to parse the XML file by using SAX parsers.

Parse and display

To parse the XML document that you create in the preceding section, you must create a Java application that uses the Xerces2 parser available within the JWSD pack. The following example shows you how to parse the stock.xml file. The code that follows is hardcoded to work with the stock.xml file:

```java
import java.io.*;
import org.xml.sax.*;
import org.xml.sax.helpers.*;
import javax.xml.parsers.*;

public class DisplayStockDetails {
  public static void main(String[] args) {
    try {
      DefaultHandler docHandler = new StockContentHandler();
      SAXParserFactory factory = SAXParserFactory.newInstance();
      SAXParser saxParser = factory.newSAXParser();
      saxParser.parse(new File("stock.xml"), docHandler);
```

```
      } catch (Exception e) {
        e.printStackTrace();
      }
  }
}


class StockContentHandler extends DefaultHandler {

 public void startDocument() throws SAXException {
    System.out.println("\nDisplaying Stock details");
    System.out.println("------------------------\n");
  }

  public void endDocument() throws SAXException {
    System.out.println("\nEnd of details");
    System.out.println("-----------------------\n");
  }

  public void startElement(String uri, String lName, String qName,
Attributes attrs) throws SAXException {
    if(!lName.equals("stock")) {
      if (attrs != null) {
      for (int i = 0; i < attrs.getLength(); i++) {
System.out.println("[Ticker : " + attrs.getValue(i) + "]");
        }
       }
    }
  }

  public void endElement(String uri, String lName, String qName)
throws SAXException {
    System.out.println();
  }

  public void characters(char[] ch, int start, int length) throws
SAXException {
    System.out.println(new String(ch, start, length));
  }
}
```

After you compile and execute the preceding code, it should generate the output shown in Figure 8-1.

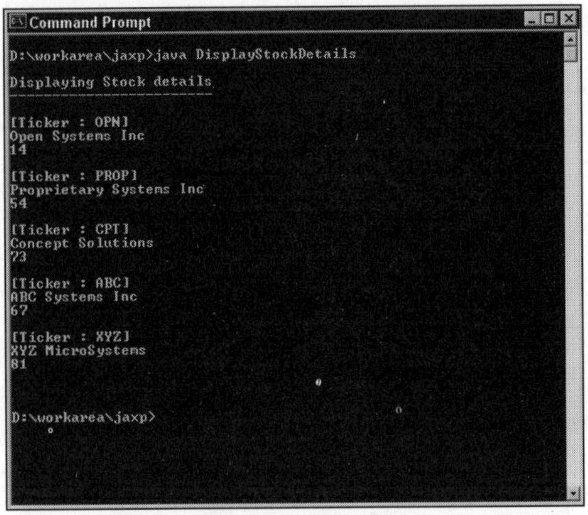

```
Command Prompt                                            _ □ X

D:\workarea\jaxp>java DisplayStockDetails

Displaying Stock details
_____

[Ticker : OPN]
Open Systems Inc
14

[Ticker : PROP]
Proprietary Systems Inc
54

[Ticker : CPT]
Concept Solutions
73

[Ticker : ABC]
ABC Systems Inc
67

[Ticker : XYZ]
XYZ MicroSystems
81


D:\workarea\jaxp>
```

Figure 8-1: Output of the stock.xml file

In the preceding code, you create two classes, DisplayStockDetails and StockContentHandler. The DisplayStockDetails class creates the appropriate parser object and also creates the content-handler object to parse the stock.xml file.

To create a parser, you first need to obtain a SAXParserFactory instance. The SAXParserFactory class enables you to change different parser implementations. The SAXParserFactory class also enables you to set various configuration properties of your SAX parsers. The following code provides the SAXParserFactory object:

SAXParserFactory factory = SAXParserFactory.newInstance();

Create the SAXParser object by using the SAXParserFactory object as follows:

SAXParser saxParser = factory.newSAXParser();

The SAXParser object refers to a default parser, which in your case is a Xerces2 parser. After creating the parser object, call its parse() method to parse your XML document. You provide the stock.xml XML document to parse and the content handler that you create as arguments to the parse() method. After you invoke the parse() method, the parser parses the stock.xml document and invokes the various callback functions that you implemented in the StockContenthandler class. The following code creates the content handler, provides the XML document to the parser, and also registers the content handler to the parser:

```
DefaultHandler docHandler = new StockContentHandler();
saxParser.parse(new File("stock.xml"), docHandler);
```

StockContentHandler is the default handler, which listens to the events generated from the parser. The StockContentHandler handler provides the callback mechanism, which contains the application logic that you need to execute. The following section explains the ContentHandler interface.

Content Handlers

In the preceding section, you wrote a code that enables you to parse and display an XML file on the console. A StockContentHandler class occupies the major chunk of the code. You can also implement the ContentHandler interface to provide logic for the callback functions.

If your Java application needs to handle any of the parsing events that generate at the time of parsing, your class needs to implement the ContentHandler interface. You then need to provide in your application an implementation for the callback methods that are available within this interface. After you write the code for the class, you register an instance of ContentHandler with a SAX parser that you create within your application. By registering the content handler to the parser, you are using the handler to receive events that the specific parser generates at parse time.

Following is the code for the ContentHandler interface:

```
package org.xml.sax;

public interface ContentHandler {
 public void characters(char[] ch, int start, int length) throws
SAXException;
 // Receive notification of character data.

 public void endDocument() throws SAXException;
 // Receive notification of the end of a document.

 public void endElement(java.lang.String namespaceURI,
java.lang.String localName, java.lang.String qName) throws
SAXException;
 // Receive notification of the end of an element.

 public void endPrefixMapping(java.lang.String prefix) throws
SAXException;
 // End the scope of a prefix-URI mapping.

 public void ignorableWhitespace(char[] ch, int start, int length)
throws SAXException;
 // Receive notification of ignorable whitespace in element content.

 public void processingInstruction(java.lang.String target,
java.lang.String data) throws SAXException;
```

```
//Receive notification of a processing instruction.

public void setDocumentLocator(Locator locator) ;
//Receive an object for locating the origin of SAX document events.

public void skippedEntity(java.lang.String name) throws
SAXException;
// Receive notification of a skipped entity.

public void startDocument() throws SAXException;
// Receive notification of the beginning of a document.

public void startElement(java.lang.String namespaceURI,
java.lang.String localName, java.lang.String qName, Attributes atts)
throws SAXException;
// Receive notification of the beginning of an element.

public void startPrefixMapping(java.lang.String prefix,
java.lang.String uri) throws SAXException;
// Begin the scope of a prefix-URI Namespace mapping.


}
```

Different types of content handlers are available in the SAX specification. `ContentHandler` is just one of the interfaces. Figure 8-2 illustrates different handler interfaces.

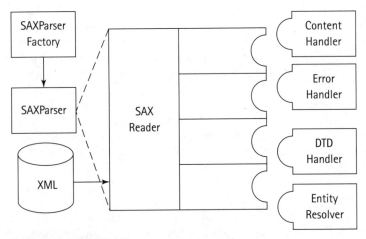

Figure 8–2: The SAX APIs

THE STARTDOCUMENT AND ENDDOCUMENT CALL

The ContentHandler interface provides a callback mechanism to indicate the beginning and end of an XML document while parsing the XML document. Logically, any given document should always have only one beginning and one end.

You use the startDocument() call-back function to implement any startup logic as parsing begins on the document. The startDocument()function is the first that is called as soon as the parser begins parsing the XML file. The endDocument() function is a callback that is called after the parser parses the entire XML file. The endDocument() function is an ideal place to provide clean-up code for your SAX-based application. The endDocument() function is also called if any unrecoverable error occurs at the time the XML file is parsed.

The following code uses the startDocument() and endDocument() call mechanisms:

```
public void startDocument() throws SAXException {
   System.out.println("\nDisplaying Stock details");
   System.out.println("-----------------------\n");
}

public void endDocument() throws SAXException {
   System.out.println("\nEnd of details");
   System.out.println("-----------------------\n");
}
```

Notice that both the functions throw a SAXException exception.

THE STARTELEMENT AND ENDELEMENT CALL

The ContentHandler interface also provides callback functions to indicate the start and end of XML elements. Logically, more than one element can exist within your XML file. The root element is always the first element that the parser encounters.

startElement() is a call-back function that is called whenever the parser comes across the beginning of an element. The complete method signature of the startElement() function is as follows:

```
public void startElement(java.lang.String namespaceURI,
java.lang.String localName, java.lang.String qName, Attributes
attrs) throws SAXException;
```

As you see, the startElement() function accepts a namespaceURI as a string argument. The namespaceURI is a URI that is provided at the time that you declare an xmlns attribute for a given element. The xmlns attribute is an XML namespace prefix that indicates that a given element belongs to a namespace, as the URI suggests.

The `localName` argument is the name of the element without the namespace prefix. This name is the true element name that you intend to use.

The `qName` argument is the fully qualified name of your element. The `qName` element consists of the URI prefix and the local name of your element.

Finally, the `Attributes` argument provides you with a list of attributes of the element. The element may or may not have any attributes declared. If an element contains any attributes, you can use the `Attributes` argument to access the attributes by an index or by the name of the attribute. The following code shows the structure of the `Attribute` interface:

```
public interface Attributes {
        int getIndex(java.lang.String qName) ;
        int getIndex(java.lang.String uri, java.lang.String
localName) ;
        int getLength() ;
        java.lang.String getLocalName(int index) ;
        java.lang.String getQName(int index) ;
        java.lang.String getType(int index) ;
        java.lang.String getType(java.lang.String qName) ;
        java.lang.String getType(java.lang.String uri,
java.lang.String localName) ;
        java.lang.String getURI(int index) ;
        java.lang.String getValue(int index) ;
        java.lang.String getValue(java.lang.String qName) ;
        java.lang.String getValue(java.lang.String uri,
        java.lang.String localName) ;
}
```

As you can see, the interface contains the various methods that help you in querying the attribute of an element. `endElement()` is a call-back function that gets invoked whenever the parser encounters the end of an element while parsing the XML document. The complete signature of `endElement()` function is as follows:

```
public void endElement(java.lang.String namespaceURI,
java.lang.String localName, java.lang.String qName) throws
SAXException;
```

Notice that the `endElement()` function also provides different parameters to identify the namespace prefix, the local name and the `qName` of an element. Obviously, you don't need the attribute list while closing the element, as XML documents do not include attributes for the ending tags of an element.

In the following code, you implement the `startElement()` and `endElement()` functions:

```
public void startElement(String uri, String lName, String qName,
Attributes attrs) throws SAXException {
    if(!lName.equals("stock")) {
      if (attrs != null) {
         for (int i = 0; i < attrs.getLength(); i++) {
                System.out.println("[Ticker : " + attrs.getValue(i)
+ "]");
           }
          }
      }
  }

  public void endElement(String uri, String lName, String qName)
throws SAXException {
    System.out.println();
  }
```

The startElement() function checks whether lName is stock. The reason to do so is because you want to avoid displaying any details for the root element in the stock.xml document. If the element parsed is not a stock element, the startElement() function displays the value of the attribute of a stockinfo element. The endElement() function is just adding a new line statement at the end of an element.

DATA OF THE ELEMENT

Generally, an element in an XML document contains data that needs to be parsed. The data contained in the element can consist of some other elements or textual data such as PCDATA. Whenever the parser encounters an element as the data for another element, it calls the startElement() callback function for the beginning of the new element. If an element contains textual data, the data needs to be parsed and should become available to the parsing application. To accommodate the parsing of the textual data, the SAX API provides the characters() callback function. Following is a complete signature for the characters() function:

```
public void characters(char[] ch, int start, int length) throws
SAXException;
```

The characters() callback function declares three parameters. The first parameter is the character buffer that contains the textual data as a stream of characters. The second argument provides the offset within the character buffer where the text begins. The third parameter provides the length of the textual information within the character buffer. You can use these parameters to constructively create a String structure for use in your Web-services application. The following code shows how to use the characters() callback to display the PCDATA within the elements:

```
public void characters(char[] ch, int start, int length) throws
SAXException {
  System.out.println(new String(ch, start, length));
}
```

Notice that the StockContenthandler class of your application does not directly implement the ContentHandler interface. Instead, you extend a helper class available from the org.xml.sax.helpers package. The name of the class is DefaultHandler. The DefaultHandler class implements the ContentHandler interface and provides blank implementation for the event-handler methods of the interface.

The SAX APIs provides multitude of interfaces and classes that help you write complex Web-services architecture. The SAX 2.0 core specification plays a major role within the JAXP specification. SAX parsers are less memory intensive than their DOM counterparts. In addition, SAX parser serially parses the XML document and generates the events during the parsing stage. It does not parse the entire document and then generate the events. SAX parsers, therefore, are favored in most Web-services implementations where speed, flexibility, and memory consumption are the primary issues.

The DOM API

The *Document Object Model (DOM)* API is a product of the World Wide Web Consortium (W3C). DOM API is a parser specification that you can use in the Web-services framework to read and work with the content and structure of an XML document. Although the DOM API is also a parser specification like the SAX API, DOM parsers that implement the DOM API work in a completely different manner than do the SAX parsers. As discussed in the "Introduction to JAXP" section, the JAXP specification provides a pluggability layer to accommodate both SAX and DOM parsers within the Web-services framework. You choose DOM over SAX for several reasons that I make clear in this section. Both the parser specifications have their own advantages and disadvantages. You, as a programmer, can usually trade off the advantages over the disadvantages.

DOM parsers, after parsing the XML documents, present a data object tree in the memory so that an application can work with the hierarchical data in a random mode. Unlike SAX, which actually provides a serial access to the XML document, the DOM parser provides a somewhat random access for the XML content. The DOM tree structure contains nodes that represent the elements and texts of the XML document. The DOM API provides different functionality to remove or change the content of the nodes. The DOM API also provides functionality to traverse the node up and down in memory.

Because DOM is a specification from the W3C, unlike SAX, DOM is a better-matured standard that provides platform-neutral and language-neutral features.

The advantage to SAX is that it is less memory intensive and you can serially access the XML structure at runtime. Also, its events are based on the runtime parsing of the XML document. The advantage to DOM is that you can write simple code for XML processing, although it is very memory intensive. DOM parsers provide you with a document tree, which you can traverse at your convenience. In addition, you can serialize such documents to a file and retrieve the document model later for further query.

DOM specifications are available as different levels of recommendations, such as level 1 and level 2. The current level of the DOM specification is level 2. Level 1 actually provides details of navigability through a document structure. Level 2 adds more functionality for level-1 APIs to provide better content handling and specific parsing functionalities for different content formats such as XML, HTML, and CSS. DOM level 3 is currently in the development phase, and it aims to extend level 2 by enhancing various types of functionality such as namespace support, DTD, and XML schema loading. The DOM Level 2 Core API, which is a component API of the JAXP API, is provided in the `org.w3c.dom` package.

The DOM structure is a tree model of the XML document within memory. Unlike SAX, DOM first parses the entire XML document and then provides a hierarchical representation of the document in memory. Figure 8-3 provides an overview of the DOM structure.

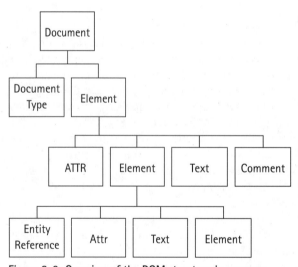

Figure 8-3: Overview of the DOM structure in memory

This section discusses how you can work with the DOM APIs for the same example that you use in "The XML Document" section, earlier in this chapter. The stock-quote data is available as a XML file, and the relevant DTD for the file is also present, as follows:

```
<?xml version="1.0" encoding="UTF-8"?>

<!DOCTYPE stock SYSTEM "stock.dtd">
<stock>
        <stockinfo ticker="OPN">
                <company>Open Systems Inc</company>
                <price>14</price>
        </stockinfo>
        <stockinfo ticker="PROP">
                <company>Proprietary Systems Inc</company>
                <price>54</price>
        </stockinfo>
        <stockinfo ticker="CPT">
                <company>Concept Solutions</company>
                <price>73</price>
        </stockinfo>
        <stockinfo ticker="ABC">
                <company>ABC Systems Inc</company>
                <price>67</price>
        </stockinfo>
        <stockinfo ticker="XYZ">
                <company>XYZ MicroSystems</company>
                <price>81</price>
        </stockinfo>
</stock>
```

The DTD for preceding code should also be present in the same folder as the XML file. The DTD, stock.dtd, is as follows:

```
<?xml encoding="UTF-8"?>

<!ELEMENT stock (stockinfo*)>
<!ELEMENT stockinfo (company, price)>
<!ATTLIST stockinfo
     ticker CDATA #REQUIRED>
<!ELEMENT company (#PCDATA)>
<!ELEMENT price (#PCDATA)>
```

Using the same stock-quote data, I can show you how to parse the XML file by using the DOM API so that the same output format for the display is generated on the console.

You don't need to set up the JWSDP package again, as you already did so once in the section, "Setting up JWSDP," earlier in this chapter. You use the Xerces2 parser spec that is compatible with the DOM level-2 specification. The following code parsers the XML document and creates a Document object in memory:

```java
import java.io.*;
import org.w3c.dom.*;
import javax.xml.parsers.*;

public class DOMDemo {
    public static void main(String[] args) {
      try {
            DocumentBuilderFactory factory =
DocumentBuilderFactory.newInstance();
            DocumentBuilder builder = factory.newDocumentBuilder();
        Document doc = builder.parse("stock.xml");
        DisplayDOM displayDOM= new DisplayDOM();
        displayDOM.displayNode(doc, System.out);
        } catch (Exception e) {
          e.printStackTrace();
        }
    }
}
class DisplayDOM {
    public void displayNode(Node node, PrintStream out) throws
IOException {
        switch (node.getNodeType()) {
            case Node.DOCUMENT_NODE:
                out.println("\nDisplaying Stock details");
                out.println("-----------------------");
                NodeList nodes = node.getChildNodes();
                if (nodes != null) {
                    for (int i=0; i<nodes.getLength(); i++) {
                        displayNode(nodes.item(i), out);
                    }
                }
                break;

            case Node.ELEMENT_NODE:
                String name = node.getNodeName();
                NamedNodeMap attributes = node.getAttributes();
                for (int i=0; i<attributes.getLength(); i++) {
                    Node current = attributes.item(i);
                    out.print("[Ticker : " + current.getNodeValue() +
"]");
                }

                NodeList children = node.getChildNodes();
                if (children != null) {
                    for (int i=0; i<children.getLength(); i++) {
```

```
                    displayNode(children.item(i), out);
                }
            }
            break;

        case Node.TEXT_NODE:
            out.print(node.getNodeValue());
            break;
        }
    }
}
```

In the preceding code, you use the DisplayDOM file to parse the tree in memory and display the structure on the console, as shown in Figure 8-4.

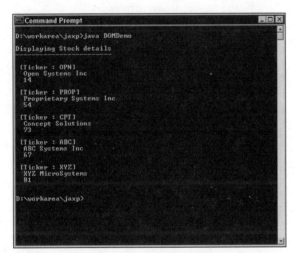

Figure 8-4: The output of the DisplayDOM code

Notice that the output of the DisplayDOM application is almost the same as the output of the SAX example. The aim of this example is to provide a comparison between the SAX and the DOM code examples.

The preceding code is using two classes, DOMDemo and DisplayDOM. The DOMDemo class is the main class that uses the DisplayDOM object to parse the DOM tree. The first thing that you do in the DOMDemo class is to create a DOM parser. To create a DOM parser, you need to obtain a factory object. The JAXP API provides a DocumentBuilderFactory class to construct the DOM-parser factory object. You create the DocumentBuilderFactory instance in your application as follows:

```
DocumentBuilderFactory factory =
DocumentBuilderFactory.newInstance();
```

The preceding code assists you in creating a factory for the default DOM parser, which in this case is Xerces2. After you obtain a factory object, you are free to build the parser by itself. You use the `DocumentBuilderFactory` instance to create a `DocumentBuilder` object. The `DocumentBuilder` object parses the XML document to create a document that represents the parsed XML document. For the sake of simplicity, I hardcoded the parsing of the `stock.xml` document by the `DocumentBuilder` object. The following code shows how to create the `DocumentBuilder` object to parse the `stock.xml` document:

```
DocumentBuilder builder = factory.newDocumentBuilder();
Document doc = builder.parse("stock.xml");
```

Figure 8-5 gives you an overview of the DOM APIs.

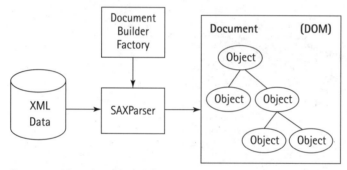

Figure 8-5: Overview of the DOM APIs

The parse method of the `builder` object is overloaded to accept multiple arguments. Following are the different overloaded versions of the `parse()` method in the `builder` object:

```
public Document parse(java.io.File f) throws SAXException,
java.io.IOException ;

public abstract Document parse(InputSource is) throws SAXException,
java.io.IOException ;

public Document parse(java.io.InputStream is) throws SAXException,
java.io.IOException ;

public Document parse(java.io.InputStream is, java.lang.String
systemId) throws SAXException, java.io.IOException ;

public Document parse(java.lang.String uri) throws SAXException,
java.io.IOException;
```

Notice that the `parse()` method takes differing arguments and always returns a Document object. The `parse()` method also throws SAXException and IOException exceptions. You may wonder about the SAXException. Why not DOMException? Actually, the DOM API is built on top of the SAX API specification. The DOM API provides you an easy way to handle XML documents by presenting a tree model of the XML document, but the DOM internally uses SAX to create the tree in the first place. Because of this nature of DOM parsers, the exception that the SAX parsers propagate eventually surfaces at the DOM API level.

The Document object that you obtain from the `parse()` method is the most important object in the DOM API. Document is an interface that actually represents the parsed XML file. The specification states that Document is the root of the document tree that gives you access to the data within the document.

Following is the code for the Document interface:

```
package org.w3c.dom;

public interface Document extends Node {
 public Attr createAttribute(java.lang.String name) throws
DOMException;

 public Attr createAttributeNS(java.lang.String namespaceURI,
java.lang.String qualifiedName) throws DOMException;

 public CDATASection createCDATASection(java.lang.String data)
throws DOMException;

 public Comment createComment(java.lang.String data) ;

 public DocumentFragment createDocumentFragment() ;

 public Element createElement(java.lang.String tagName) throws
DOMException;

 public Element createElementNS(java.lang.String namespaceURI,
java.lang.String qualifiedName) throws DOMException;

 public EntityReference createEntityReference(java.lang.String name)
throws DOMException;

 public ProcessingInstruction
createProcessingInstruction(java.lang.String target,
java.lang.String data) throws DOMException;

 public Text createTextNode(java.lang.String data) ;
```

```
    public DocumentType getDoctype() ;

    public Element getDocumentElement() ;

    public Element getElementById(java.lang.String elementId) ;

    public NodeList getElementsByTagName(java.lang.String tagname) ;

    public NodeList getElementsByTagNameNS(java.lang.String
namespaceURI, java.lang.String localName) ;

    public DOMImplementation getImplementation() ;

    public Node importNode(Node importedNode, boolean deep) throws
DOMException;

}
```

Notice that Document is actually extending the Node interface. The code for the Node interface is as follows:

```
package org.w3c.dom;

public interface Node {
 public final static short ATTRIBUTE_NODE ;
 // The node is an Attr.

 public final static short CDATA_SECTION_NODE ;
 // The node is a CDATASection.

 public final static short COMMENT_NODE ;
 // The node is a Comment.

 public final static short DOCUMENT_FRAGMENT_NODE ;
 // The node is a DocumentFragment.

 public final static short DOCUMENT_NODE ;
 // The node is a Document.

 public final static short DOCUMENT_TYPE_NODE ;
 // The node is a DocumentType.

 public final static short ELEMENT_NODE ;
 // The node is an Element.

 public final static short ENTITY_NODE ;
```

```
// The node is an Entity.

public final static short ENTITY_REFERENCE_NODE ;
// The node is an EntityReference.

public final static short NOTATION_NODE ;
// The node is a Notation.

public final static short PROCESSING_INSTRUCTION_NODE ;
// The node is a ProcessingInstruction.

public final static short TEXT_NODE ;
// The node is a Text node.

public Node appendChild(Node newChild) throws DOMException ;
// Adds the node newChild to the end of the list of children of
this node.

public Node cloneNode(boolean deep) ;
// Returns a duplicate of this node, i.e., serves as a generic copy
constructor for nodes.

public NamedNodeMap getAttributes() ;
// A NamedNodeMap containing the attributes of this node (if it is
an Element) or null otherwise.

public NodeList getChildNodes() ;
// A NodeList that contains all children of this node.

public Node getFirstChild() ;
// The first child of this node.

public Node getLastChild() ;
// The last child of this node.

public java.lang.String getLocalName() ;
// Returns the local part of the qualified name of this node.

public java.lang.String getNamespaceURI() ;
// The namespace URI of this node, or null if it is unspecified.

public Node getNextSibling() ;
// The node immediately following this node.

public java.lang.String getNodeName() ;
```

```
// The name of this node, depending on its type; see the table
above.

public short getNodeType() ;
// A code representing the type of the underlying object, as
defined above.

public java.lang.String getNodeValue() throws DOMException;
// The value of this node, depending on its type; see the table
above.

public Document getOwnerDocument() ;
// The Document object associated with this node.

public Node getParentNode() ;
// The parent of this node.

public java.lang.String getPrefix() throws DOMException;
// The namespace prefix of this node, or null if it is unspecified.

public Node getPreviousSibling() ;
// The node immediately preceding this node.

public boolean hasAttributes() ;
// Returns whether this node (if it is an element) has any
attributes.

public boolean hasChildNodes() ;
// Returns whether this node has any children.

public Node insertBefore(Node newChild, Node refChild) throws
DOMException;
// Inserts the node newChild before the existing child node
refChild.

public boolean isSupported(java.lang.String feature,
java.lang.String version) ;
/* Tests whether the DOM implementation implements a specific
feature and that feature is supported by this node. */

public void normalize() ;
/* Puts all Text nodes in the full depth of the sub-tree underneath
this Node, including attribute nodes, into a "normal" form where
only structure (e.g., elements, comments,     processing
instructions, CDATA sections, and entity references) separates Text
```

nodes,   i.e., there are neither adjacent Text nodes nor empty
Text nodes. */

```
 public Node removeChild(Node oldChild) throws DOMException;
 // Removes the child node indicated by oldChild from the list of
 children, and returns it.

 public Node replaceChild(Node newChild, Node oldChild) throws
 DOMException;
 // Replaces the child node oldChild with newChild in the list of
 children, and returns the oldChild node.

 public void setNodeValue(java.lang.String nodeValue) throws
 DOMException ;
 // The value of this node, depending on its type; see the table
 above.

 public void setPrefix(java.lang.String prefix) throws DOMException;
 // The namespace prefix of this node, or null if it is unspecified.


}
```

The Node interface is the most primitive of the structures in the whole of the DOM model. The Document interface extends the Node interface and also adds more functionality to the Node interface. This way, Node represents a single node in the document tree, while conceptually Document can represent a tree model. Relatively speaking, you can use a Document object interchangeably with Node. Nodes may or may not have children in the Document tree. Some of the methods in the Node interface, such as nodeValue() or nodeName(), you use to query for more information about the Node object.

Table 8-2 provides a list of attributes and nodeValue and nodeName values based on the type of the node.

**TABLE 8-2 VALUES OF NODENAME, NODEVALUE, AND ATTRIBUTES
BASED ON THE NODE TYPE**

Interface	nodeName	nodeValue	Attributes
Attr	name of attribute	value of attribute	Null
CDATASection	"#cdata-section"	content of the CDATA Section	Null

Continued

**TABLE 8-2 VALUES OF NODENAME, NODEVALUE, AND ATTRIBUTES
BASED ON THE NODE TYPE** *(Continued)*

Interface	nodeName	nodeValue	Attributes
Comment	"#comment"	content of the comment	Null
Document	"#document"	Null	Null
DocumentFragment	"#document-fragment"	Null	Null
DocumentType	document type name	Null	Null
Element	tag name	Null	NamedNodeMap
Entity	entity name	Null	Null
EntityReference	name of entity referenced	Null	Null
Notation	notation name	Null	Null
ProcessingInstruction	target	entire content excluding the target	Null
Text	"#text"	content of the text node	Null

The `DisplayDOM` class in the code example uses the `Node` and the `Document` objects to parse through the document tree model that you obtain by requesting the `builder` object.

The `DisplayDOM` class works with different node types and appropriately displays the content on the console. To begin, build the generic method `displayNode()`, that accepts two arguments, as shown in the following code:

```
public void displayNode(Node node, PrintStream out) throws
IOException
```

The `displayNode()` method uses a `Node` object as the first argument and a `PrintStream` object, which represents an output stream, as the second argument. Within the `displayNode()` method, you need to first determine the type of node that is sent across as an argument. The following types of nodes are available:

```
public final static short ATTRIBUTE_NODE ;
 // The node is an Attr.

 public final static short CDATA_SECTION_NODE ;
```

```
// The node is a CDATASection.

public final static short COMMENT_NODE ;
// The node is a Comment.

public final static short DOCUMENT_FRAGMENT_NODE ;
// The node is a DocumentFragment.

public final static short DOCUMENT_NODE ;
// The node is a Document.

public final static short DOCUMENT_TYPE_NODE ;
// The node is a DocumentType.

public final static short ELEMENT_NODE ;
// The node is an Element.

public final static short ENTITY_NODE ;
// The node is an Entity.

public final static short ENTITY_REFERENCE_NODE ;
// The node is an EntityReference.

public final static short NOTATION_NODE ;
// The node is a Notation.

public final static short PROCESSING_INSTRUCTION_NODE ;
// The node is a ProcessingInstruction.

public final static short TEXT_NODE ;
// The node is a Text node.
```

These node types are declared as fields in the Node interface. Within the displayNode() method, you write a switch case, which uses the node type as an integral selector and different Node fields as integral values to choose from. In the following code, only few of the node types are used. This approach is just a simple one to help you understand the DOM API without getting entangled too much in the complexity of DOM specifications:

```
switch (node.getNodeType()) {
        case Node.DOCUMENT_NODE:
                out.println("\nDisplaying Stock details");
                out.println("------------------------");
            NodeList nodes = node.getChildNodes();
            if (nodes != null) {
                for (int i=0; i<nodes.getLength(); i++) {
```

```
                    displayNode(nodes.item(i), out);
                }
            }
            break;

        case Node.ELEMENT_NODE:
            String name = node.getNodeName();
            NamedNodeMap attributes = node.getAttributes();
            for (int i=0; i<attributes.getLength(); i++) {
                Node current = attributes.item(i);
                    out.print("[Ticker : " +
current.getNodeValue() + "]");
            }

            NodeList children = node.getChildNodes();
            if (children != null) {
                for (int i=0; i<children.getLength(); i++) {
                    displayNode(children.item(i), out);
                }
            }
            break;

        case Node.TEXT_NODE:
            out.print(node.getNodeValue());
            break;
        }
    }
```

Notice that, to obtain the node type, the node.getNodeType() method call on the Document object passes as a argument. You can use the Document object interchangeably with Node, as Document extends the Node interface. The getNodeType() method actually returns an integer value, which the code is comparing against a set of predefined constants.

Now to explain the logic in the switch construct. In the first case, the code uses the node type Node.DOCUMENT_NODE, as follows:

```
case Node.DOCUMENT_NODE:
    out.println("\nDisplaying Stock details");
    out.println("------------------------");
    NodeList nodes = node.getChildNodes();
    if (nodes != null) {
      for (int i=0; i<nodes.getLength(); i++) {
    displayNode(nodes.item(i), out);
      }
    }
    break;
```

This section of the code checks whether the node type is a `Document` node. The `Document` node type indicates that the node is a `Document` object and is the root for all other nodes. In the code, you first provide the appropriate startup logic. Then you check for the children of the nodes. To obtain a list of child nodes, you invoke the `node.getChildNodes()` method. This invocation returns a `NodeList` object that contains an `Enumeration` of the child nodes. After you obtain the `NodeList` object, you iterate through the `NodeList` object. You use the `nodes.getLength()` method to obtain the number of child nodes of the `NodeList` object so that you can iterate through the list without causing `OutOfBound` scenarios.

In the iteration code, you recursively call the `displayNode()` method by passing the current node item in the list and the `PrintStream` object. This recursive call has the power to build the DOM tree by using recurred stacks of the call.

The `Node.ELEMENT_NODE` case you use to identify the elements in the XML document. While you are recurring through the DOM tree, you eventually hit on an element node. The following code parses such elements.

```
case Node.ELEMENT_NODE:
    String name = node.getNodeName();
    NamedNodeMap attributes = node.getAttributes();
    for (int i=0; i<attributes.getLength(); i++) {
        Node current = attributes.item(i);
        out.print("[Ticker : " + current.getNodeValue() + "]");
    }

    NodeList children = node.getChildNodes();
    if (children != null) {
      for (int i=0; i<children.getLength(); i++) {
        displayNode(children.item(i), out);
      }
    }
    break;
```

In the preceding code, you use the `Node.ELEMENT_NODE` field to identify an element. After you obtain an element, you may want to obtain the name of the element and the name of the attributes, if any. To obtain the name of the element, you use the `node.getNodeName()` method. The `node.getAttributes()` method provides you with a list of attributes. You can store the attributes in a `NodeMap` structure. `NodeMap` provides you an interface to iterate through the attributes just as `NodeList` does. You can iterate through `NodeMap` and obtain the value of the attributes by calling the `getNodeValue()` method for the current node (attribute) in the `NodeMap`.

After you display all the attributes, you query the element node to determine whether any more child nodes are within the given element node. If any child nodes of the element node are there, you need to recursively parse through the subtree of the element node until you display all the nodes in the subtree. The code achieves the recursive call by again invoking the `displayNode(children.item(i), out)` call.

The `TEXT_NODE` node represents the textual information. The textual information carries data, which is helpful for the user of the system. To display the textual information, the following code uses `Node.TEXT_NODE` as follows:

```
case Node.TEXT_NODE:
  out.print(node.getNodeValue());
  break;
```

The preceding code displays the textual information of the node on your console by using the `getNodeValue()` method.

In this way, you can successfully parse through all the nodes within the `Document` object and display the content of the nodes appropriately on the console.

A key point to notice here is that, although the preceding SAX and DOM examples provide a very simple code structure, that structure is very effective if you apply it within the Web services implementation. It provides your Web services' SOAP-message-router-servlets to correctly decipher the XML message, understand the message based on a prebuilt template, and appropriately route the messages to different components in the workflow.

Notice that using the DOM parser specifications is much easier than using the SAX counterpart. The advantage of using SAX is that it is less memory intensive, and you can serially access the XML structure at runtime. Its events are also based on the runtime parsing of the XML document. The advantage of using DOM is that you can write simple code for XML processing, but it is very memory intensive. DOM parsers provide you with a document tree, which you can traverse at your convenience. You can also serialize such documents to a file and retrieve the document model later for further query.

Summary

This chapter gives you an overview of the JAXP architecture. The chapter focuses on the SAX API and the SAX programming model. It explains the `ContentHandler` specification of the SAX API. The chapter also focuses on the DOM level-2 API. The chapter explains different node types in the DOM API and how to work with those node types. The chapter also highlights the differences between the SAX and the DOM parsers.

Chapter 9

JAXB

IN THIS CHAPTER

- ◆ Introduction to JAXB
- ◆ Unmarshalling, validation, and marshalling
- ◆ Working with JAXB

IN THE CURRENT WEB-SERVICES framework, XML is considered the standard for developing robust and interoperable Web services. With Sun Microsystems embracing XML standards as its data format, you can now build powerful Web service applications enjoying the benefits of both Java and XML platforms. Sun Microsystems has released several APIs for developing Java Web services with XML. Sun Microsystems has also released the Java Web Services Developer Pack to simplify the development of XML-based Web services using the J2EE platform.

The complete suite of Java APIs for XML includes the following:

- ◆ Java API for XML Messaging (JAXM)
- ◆ Java API for XML Processing (JAXP)
- ◆ Java API for XML Registries (JAXR)
- ◆ Java API for XML-based RPC (JAX-RPC)
- ◆ Java API for Web Service Description Language (JWSDL)
- ◆ Java API for XML Binding (JAXB)

 The Java Community Process (JCP) is currently working on the Java API for Web Service Description Language (JWSDL). It is yet to be released.

This chapter discusses the Java Architecture for XML Binding (JAXB).

Introduction to JAXB

JAXB is an architecture that enables mapping between Java objects and XML documents. It enables applications to build Java objects to represent XML documents. These Java objects can then be modified to regenerate XML documents. JAXB does so by taking a DTD and an XML schema, known as the *binding schema*, as input. By using this DTD and binding schema, the schema compiler generates Java source files. You then compile the source files by using a Java compiler to create Java classes. These classes hide the complexities of XML parsing and processing codes from the developer. By using these classes, you can develop applications to convert a XML document into an *object tree*. This process is known as *unmarshalling*. You can then work with the objects and persist them back to a XML document. This process is known as *marshalling*. A developer can thus easily work with the generated classes to format and create XML documents based on the schema by using the Java Architecture for XML Binding (JAXB), Early Access Implementation version 1.0. It is being developed through the Java Community Process program under JSR-31 (where *JSR* stands for *Java Specification Request*). The Early Access Implementation version 1.0 (EAI v1.0) contains the necessary tools and API for supporting the mapping mechanism.

Before I discuss the working of JAXB, I need to discuss the concept of *data binding*. The industry has recognized XML as a primary data format for Web applications. For an object-oriented language such as Java to seamlessly work and process XML, a need arises for data binding. Data binding basically means mapping objects by using XML. Data binding enables the creation of a class hierarchy corresponding to an XML document. This class hierarchy represents the structure of the XML document. Data binding enables you to use object-oriented programming (OOP) to work with the XML data without needing to worry about the underlying XML structure. You can modify the data and create new objects. You can then persist them as XML documents. JAXB provides the capability to map XML elements to Java classes in a binding schema. Simple DTD elements, which do not have subelements, map to *values*. Elements in a DTD that contain subelements map to *classes*.

Document Type Definition (DTD)

The *Document Type Definition* (DTD) defines how to use an element in an XML document. A DTD, which is a text file, defines the tags in an XML document. A valid XML document must conform to its DTD. An XML document must always contain a `root` element, and other elements should lie between the starting and the ending tags of the root element. The syntax for declaring elements in a DTD is as follows:

```
<!ELEMENT elementName (element contents)>
```

Following is an example of an XML document:

```
<Validation>
            <Name>Robert</Name>
            <Password>password</Password>
</Validation>
```

Following is the code for the *Validation DTD,* the DTD file for the preceding XML document:

```
<! Element Validation(Name, Password) >
<! Element Name (#PCDATA)>
<! Element Password (#PCDATA)>
```

 The notation #PCDATA(Parseable Character DATA) represents characters. An element with content that defines PCDATA can contain only text.

Table 9-1 describes the symbols that DTDs commonly use.

TABLE 9-1 SYMBOLS USED IN DTD

Symbol	Examples	Description
,	Name, Password	Signifies *and.* Both Name and Password elements should be present in the XML document in the specified order.
|	Name | Password	Signifies *or.* Either the Name or Password element must be present in the XML document.
?	Address?	Signifies that the Address element may not be present but that, if it is present, only a single element is permitted.
*	Address*	Implies that any number of Address elements may be present. However, it is not necessary that the Address element be present in the XML document.
+	Address+	Implies that at least one Address element must be present in the XML document.

The binding schema

As I discuss in the section "Introduction to JAXB," earlier in this chapter, JAXB requires an *XML-Java binding schema (XJS)* called the binding schema. This schema defines how you want to translate your XML document into Java classes and vice versa. The binding schema maps elements of an XML document to the Java class.

JAXB provides a schema compiler, known as `xjc`. The schema compiler interprets the binding schema and the DTD to generate the Java source files. You provide information (in the form of declarations) in the binding schema. The schema compiler uses this information to decide how to bind a source schema that is a DTD to a set of derived classes. The schema compiler interprets the declarations and creates the derived classes accordingly.

You can create a binding schema by providing minimum binding declarations. Such a schema is known as a *minimal binding schema.* If the schema compiler encounters such a schema, it creates the derived classes based on certain assumptions. In such a case, all simple elements in a DTD map to *strings,* and all complex elements that have subelements map to *classes.* The names of the derived classes correspond to their element names.

Following is the code for `Validation.xjs`, a minimal binding schema for the Validation DTD file that I show you in the preceding section:

```
<xml-java-binding-schema version="1.0ea">
<element name="Validation" type="class" root="true" />
</xml-java-binding-schema>
```

If you run the schema compiler, providing the Validation DTD and the binding schema, the schema compiler creates a Java source file, `Validation.java`, the code of which is similar to the following example:

```
import java.io.IOException;
import java.io.InputStream;
import javax.xml.bind.ConversionException;
import javax.xml.bind.Dispatcher;
import javax.xml.bind.InvalidAttributeException;
import javax.xml.bind.LocalValidationException;
import javax.xml.bind.MarshallableRootElement;
import javax.xml.bind.Marshaller;
import javax.xml.bind.MissingContentException;
import javax.xml.bind.RootElement;
import javax.xml.bind.StructureValidationException;
import javax.xml.bind.UnmarshalException;
import javax.xml.bind.Unmarshaller;
import javax.xml.bind.Validator;
import javax.xml.marshal.XMLScanner;
```

```
import javax.xml.marshal.XMLWriter;


public class Validation
    extends MarshallableRootElement
    implements RootElement
{

    private String _Name;
    private String _Password;

    public String getName() {
        return _Name;
    }

    public void setName(String _Name) {
        this._Name = _Name;
        if (_Name == null) {
            invalidate();
        }
    }

    public String getPassword() {
        return _Password;
    }

    public void setPassword(String _Password) {
        this._Password = _Password;
        if (_Password == null) {
            invalidate();
        }
    }

    public void validateThis()
        throws LocalValidationException
    {
        if (_Name == null) {
            throw new MissingContentException("Name");
        }
        if (_Password == null) {
            throw new MissingContentException("Password");
        }
    }

    public void validate(Validator v)
```

```
            throws StructureValidationException
    {
    }

    public void marshal(Marshaller m)
        throws IOException
    {
        XMLWriter w = m.writer();
        w.start("Validation");
        w.leaf("Name", _Name.toString());
        w.leaf("Password", _Password.toString());
        w.end("Validation");
    }

    public void unmarshal(Unmarshaller u)
        throws UnmarshalException
    {
        XMLScanner xs = u.scanner();
        Validator v = u.validator();
        xs.takeStart("Validation");
        while (xs.atAttribute()) {
            String an = xs.takeAttributeName();
            throw new InvalidAttributeException(an);
        }
        if (xs.atStart("Name")) {
            xs.takeStart("Name");
            String s;
            if (xs.atChars(XMLScanner.WS_COLLAPSE)) {
                s = xs.takeChars(XMLScanner.WS_COLLAPSE);
            } else {
                s = "";
            }
            try {
                _Name = String.valueOf(s);
            } catch (Exception x) {
                throw new ConversionException("Name", x);
            }
            xs.takeEnd("Name");
        }
        if (xs.atStart("Password")) {
            xs.takeStart("Password");
            String s;
            if (xs.atChars(XMLScanner.WS_COLLAPSE)) {
                s = xs.takeChars(XMLScanner.WS_COLLAPSE);
            } else {
```

```
                s = "";
            }
            try {
                _Password = String.valueOf(s);
            } catch (Exception x) {
                throw new ConversionException("Password", x);
            }
            xs.takeEnd("Password");
        }
    xs.takeEnd("Validation");
}

public static Validation unmarshal(InputStream in)
    throws UnmarshalException
{

    return unmarshal(XMLScanner.open(in));
}

public static Validation unmarshal(XMLScanner xs)
    throws UnmarshalException
{

    return unmarshal(xs, newDispatcher());
}

public static Validation unmarshal(XMLScanner xs, Dispatcher d)
    throws UnmarshalException
{

    return ((Validation) d.unmarshal(xs, (Validation.class)));
}

public boolean equals(Object ob) {
    if (this == ob) {
        return true;
    }
    if (!(ob instanceof Validation)) {
        return false;
    }
    Validation tob = ((Validation) ob);
    if (_Name!= null) {
        if (tob._Name == null) {
            return false;
        }
        if (!_Name.equals(tob._Name)) {
            return false;
        }
    }
```

```
        } else {
            if (tob._Name!= null) {
                return false;
            }
        }
        if (_Password!= null) {
            if (tob._Password == null) {
                return false;
            }
            if (!_Password.equals(tob._Password)) {
                return false;
            }
        } else {
            if (tob._Password!= null) {
                return false;
            }
        }
        return true;
    }

    public int hashCode() {
        int h = 0;
        h = ((127 *h)+((_Name!= null)?_Name.hashCode(): 0));
        h = ((127 *h)+((_Password!= null)?_Password.hashCode(): 0));
        return h;
    }

    public String toString() {
        StringBuffer sb = new StringBuffer("<<Validation");
        if (_Name!= null) {
            sb.append(" Name=");
            sb.append(_Name.toString());
        }
        if (_Password!= null) {
            sb.append(" Password=");
            sb.append(_Password.toString());
        }
        sb.append(">>");
        return sb.toString();
    }

    public static Dispatcher newDispatcher() {
        Dispatcher d = new Dispatcher();
        d.register("Validation", (Validation.class));
        d.freezeElementNameMap();
```

```
        return d;
    }

}
```

Notice that the name of the derived class is the same as the name specified in the binding schema. As the class derives from the root element, `Validation`, it extends the `MarshallableRootElement` class. The XML elements `<Name>` and `<Password>`, which were declared in the DTD, appear as private String variables `_Name` and `_Password`, respectively. Corresponding to the variables, you also see the accessor methods, *getxxx()* and *setxxx()*.

The binding schema can have the following declarations:

- Element declaration
- Content-property declaration
- Model-based content-property declaration
- Conversion declaration
- Attribute-property declaration
- Enumeration declaration
- Constructor declaration
- Interface declaration
- Options declaration

The following sections describe each of these declarations.

ELEMENT DECLARATION

An *element declaration* can be either an *element-class* declaration or an *element-value* declaration. An element-class declaration has the following syntax:

```
<element name="Validate" type="class"
            [class="MyValidate"]  [root="{true|false}"]>
```

For the preceding declaration, you must have a `Validate` element in the DTD. You can specify the class name of the generated Java source file by using the `class` attribute. If you do not specify the attribute, the compiler creates a class with the name specified in the `name` attribute. The `root` attribute determines whether the generated class is a `root` element class.

CONTENT-PROPERTY DECLARATION

You must declare the *content-property* inside the *element-name* declaration. The content-property declaration has the following syntax:

```
< content property="prop"
                [collection="{array|list}"]
                [supertype=""type"] />
```

On interpreting the preceding declaration, the compiler creates a *property* in the generated class with the name as specified in the `property` attribute. This property represents contents of all elements. You can declare a class or interface in the `supertype` attribute that acts as the base type for the property. Consider the following code of the element type `album`:

```
<! Element album (Name, Singer, Songs+, Code?, Date?)>
```

You can use a content-property declaration in its element-class declaration, as shown in the following binding schema:

```
<element name="album" type="class" root="true">
<content property="prop"/>
```

The generated class `Album` now contains three methods, `getProp()`, `deleteProp()`, and `emptyProp()`, as shown in the following code:

```
public class Album{
                    public List getProp();
                    public void deleteProp();
                    public void emptyProp();
                                        }
```

MODEL-BASED CONTENT-PROPERTY DECLARATION

The *model-based content-property declaration* appears within the element-class declaration. Whenever the schema compiler interprets this expression, it defines the properties of the generated element class, according to the properties set in the declaration. A model-based content-property declaration has the following syntax:

```
<element name="elt" type="class">
<content>
<element-ref name="ref-elt" [property="prop"] [collection="coll"]/>
<choice property="prop" [collection="coll"] [supertype="type"]/>
<sequence property="prop" [collection="coll"] [supertype="type"]/>
<rest property="prop" [collection="coll"] [supertype="type"]/>
```

CONVERSION DECLARATION

In the conversion declaration, you specify a valid Java type to which the conversion takes place. A conversion declaration has the following syntax:

```
< conversion name="conversionName"
[type="conversionType"] [parse="conversionParse"]
```

```
[print="conversionPrint"]
[whitespace="{preserve|normalize|collapse}"] />
```

In the preceding code, you use the `parse` attribute to declare how the conversion of a string type takes place to the specified Java type. You can specify how to convert a Java type back to a string type by using the `print` attribute.

After the compiler interprets the conversion declaration, it defines a binding conversion with the specified name in the `name` attribute. This binding conversion contains the target type of the conversion, a `parse` method, and a `print` method.

Before calling the `parse` method, the `whitespace` in the input strings is processed. You specify it by using the `whitespace` attribute.

ATTRIBUTE-PROPERTY DECLARATION

Whenever the schema compiler generates the derived class, it creates a property. This property represents the value of the attribute. The *attribute-property* declaration should appear within the element-class declaration. An attribute-property declaration has the following syntax:

```
<attribute name="attr" [convert="cnv"]
[property="prop"] [collection="array"]/>
```

ENUMERATION DECLARATION

The schema compiler, on interpreting the *enumeration* declaration, creates an `Enumeration` class of the specified name. The *enumeration declaration* has the following syntax:

```
<enumeration name="Name" members="member1, member2....membern"/>
```

CONSTRUCTOR DECLARATION

You use the *constructor declaration* within an element-class declaration. The compiler creates a constructor in the generated class with parameters specified in the `properties` attribute. A constructor declaration has the following syntax:

```
<constructor properties="p1,p2....pn" />
```

 The *constructor* declaration is not yet supported by JAXB.

INTERFACE DECLARATION

Whenever the schema compiler interprets the *interface declaration,* it creates an interface specified by the `name` attribute. The interface specifies the methods according to the properties specified in the `properties` attribute. It then declares

Java classes that implement the interface as specified in the `members` attribute. An *interface declaration* has the following syntax:

```
<interface name="name"
       members="m1,m2...mn"
    [properties="p1,p2....pn"] />
```

OPTIONS DECLARATION

You can use the *options declaration* only once. In this declaration, you specify the `package` attribute with a package name that contains the compiler-generated classes and interfaces. The options declaration has the following syntax:

```
< options [package="package"]
  [default-reference-collection-type="{array|list}"]
  [property-get-set-prefixes="{true|false}"]
 [marshallable="{true|false}"] [unmarshallable="{true|false}"] />
```

The `property-get-set-prefixes` attribute specifies whether the accessor methods of the properties are declared in the Java bean or in C++ style.

You can specify whether the generated class should support marshalling by using the `marshallable` attribute. Marshalling is the generation of a XML document from a Java object tree. Marshalling is discussed in details in the "Unmarshalling, validation, and marshalling" section of this chapter. If you specify the value of the `marshalling` attribute as `false` and try calling the `marshal` method of the derived class, an `UnsupportedOperationException` is thrown.

You can specify whether the `derived` class supports unmarshalling by using the `unmarshallable` attribute. Unmarshalling is the generation of a Java object tree from a XML document. Unmarshalling is discussed in details in the "Unmarshalling, Validation, and Marshalling" section of this chapter. If you specify the value of the `unmarshallable` attribute as `false` and try to invoke the `unmarshal` methods of the `derived` class, an `UnsupportedOperationException` is thrown.

Advantages of JAXB

The advantages of the Java API for XML Binding *JAXB* are as follows:

◆ JAXB uses Java and XML technologies and, therefore, enjoys the benefits of both platforms. Because Java and XML complement each other very well, mapping Java objects and XML data with each other becomes easy. The JAXB schema compiler achieves this task by compiling a XML schema to corresponding sets of Java source files. Moreover, Java, being a platform-independent language, merges well with XML, which is also a platform-independent data format.

- **JAXB is faster and easier than other XML parsers.** *Simple API for XML (SAX)* and *Document Object Model (DOM)* are two APIs that are used for parsing XML documents. But using these APIs has certain disadvantages over using the JAXB architecture. JAXB performs faster parsing than does the SAX parser, because it works with compiled Java classes that already contain the schema logic. Moreover, as the generated classes contain all the necessary codes necessary for processing a XML document, a developer using JAXB is freed from working with complex conversion codes.

- **JAXB ensures valid data.** To create Java objects, you require a binding schema. By using the information of this binding schema, JAXB binds the components of the source schema to a set of Java classes. If an XML document does not correspond to the defined schema, JAXB does not enable you to generate the corresponding Java objects.

- **JAXB performs type conversions.** JAXB converts data in XML documents to Java data types. If necessary, you can specify the data-type conversion in the binding schema. In the schema, you can also specify the class names, interface names, and package names that appear in the generated class. In addition, you can assign the method types of the generated class. You can also create customized constructor and interfaces in the Java classes by using the schema.

Limitations of JAXB

JAXB, being a new architecture, has certain limitations, as follows:

- JAXB supports only the DTD sublanguage of the XML 1.0 recommendation as the schema language.

- The schema compiler does not support all the defined JAXB specifications.

- Certain declarations in the binding schema are not enforced.

- The code generated by the schema compiler for the derived classes is not very efficient.

Components of JAXB

The primary components of JAXB are as follows:

- **Schema compiler:** A binding schema and a DTD represent the structure of your XML document. A schema compiler generates a set of Java source files based on the DTD and the binding schema. The schema compiler also assumes certain mappings if you do not specify any. The JAXB distribution provides the `jxc` schema compiler. The working of a schema compiler is as shown in Figure 9-1.

- ♦ **Binding language:** The *binding language* defines the binding of the schema to the generated classes. It is an XML-based language. You use the binding language to define the binding schema.

- ♦ **Binding framework:** The *binding framework* is a set of Java interfaces and classes. The derived Java classes extend them to provide three primary functionalities: *unmarshalling, marshalling,* and *validation.* The JAXB runtime library provides the classes and the interfaces that the binding framework uses.

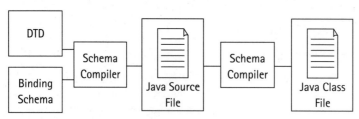

Figure 9-1: The working of a schema compiler

The JAXB Runtime Library

The *JAXB runtime library* consists of two packages, the `javax.xml.bind` and the `javax.xml.marshal`. The following sections discuss the interfaces and classes in these packages.

THE JAVAX.XML.BIND PACKAGE

The `javax.xml.bind` package comprises a set of Java interfaces and classes. The derived classes implement these interfaces and classes and, therefore, exhibit the unmarshalling, validation, and marshalling functionalities.

THE ELEMENT INTERFACE   All the classes that derive from the element-class declaration in the binding schema implement the `Element` interface. You use the `validateThis()` method of an object to ensure that the object abides by the local structural constraints. Following is the structure of the `Element` interface:

```
interface Element {
void validateThis() throws LocalValidationException;
}
```

THE IDENTIFIABLEELEMENT INTERFACE   If your element has an ID attribute, then its derived class implements the `IdentifiableElement` interface. The `id()` method returns a string that represents the identifier value of the element. The structure of the `IdentifiableElement` interface is as follows:

```
interface IdentifiableElement
extends Element
{
String id();
}
```

THE ROOTELEMENT INTERFACE All the root-element classes implement the `RootElement` interface. You use the `validate()` method of this interface to validate the `root` object's content tree. The structure of the `RootElement` interface is as follows:

```
interface RootElement extends Element
{
void validate() throws StructureValidationException;
}
```

 Root-element classes are classes generated by the schema compiler that correspond to the `root` element of the XML document.

THE JAVAX.XML.BIND.DISPATCHER CLASS The `javax.xml.bind.Dispatcher` *class* maps the element names that you provide to the derived class names. The Dispatcher class does so by using an element-name map and a class map. This class also initiates the unmarshalling process. The structure of the `javax.xml.bind.Dispatcher` class is as follows:

```
final class Dispatcher {
Dispatcher();
void freezeClassMap();
void freezeElementNameMap();
Class lookup(Class mobClass);
Class lookup(String elementName)
throws UnrecognizedElementNameException;
void register(Class mobClass, Class userClass);
void register(String elementName, Class elementClass);
RootElement unmarshal(java.io.InputStream in) throws
UnmarshalException;
RootElement unmarshal(javax.xml.marshal.XMLScanner xs)
throws UnmarshalException;
RootElement unmarshal(javax.xml.marshal.XMLScanner xs, Class
```

```
rootClass)
throws UnmarshalException;
}
```

THE JAVAX.XML.BIND.MARSHALLABLEOBJECT CLASS   All classes with objects that you can marshal and unmarshal extend the `javax.xml.bind. MarshallableObject` class either directly or indirectly. The `marshal(Marshaller m)` method uses `Marshaller` to marshal the object against which it is invoked. This method is invoked by the marshalling process. The `unmarshal(Unmarshaller u)` method uses the `Unmarshaller` to convert an element into the object against which it is invoked. The structure of the `javax.xml.bind.MarshallableObject` class is as follows:

```
abstract class MarshallableObject
extends ValidatableObject
{
protected MarshallableObject();
void marshal(Marshaller m) throws java.io.IOException;
abstract void unmarshal(Unmarshaller u) throws UnmarshalException;
}
```

THE JAVAX.XML.BIND.MARSHALLABLEROOTELEMENT CLASS   All root-element classes with objects that you can only marshal and unmarshal extend the `javax. xml.bind.MarshallableRootElement` class. This class defines two methods to perform marshalling. As the root-element class extends this class, the unmarshalling methods must be static. However, the `MarshallableRootElement` class, being abstract, cannot contain static methods. Therefore, the schema compiler generates four static methods to perform unmarshalling in the derived classes. The structure of the `javax.xml.bind.MarshallableRootElement` class is follows:

```
abstract class MarshallableRootElement
extends MarshallableObject // ValidatableObject
implements RootElement
{
protected MarshallableRootElement();
final void marshal(java.io.OutputStream out) throws
java.io.IOException;
final void marshal(javax.xml.marshal.XMLWriter xw)
throws java.io.IOException;
}
```

THE JAVAX.XML.BIND.MARSHALLER CLASS   The `javax.xml.bind.Marshaller` class is primarily responsible for the process of converting a content tree into an XML document. The `marshal(MarshallableObject mob)` method marshals the `MarshallableObject` passed to it. For this process, it uses the writer provided by the `writer()` method. The structure of the `javax.xml.bind.Marshaller` class is follows:

```
final class Marshaller {
void marshal(MarshallableObject mob) throws java.io.IOException;
javax.xml.marshal.XMLWriter
writer();
}
```

THE JAVAX.XML.BIND.PCDATA CLASS If an element contains simple character contents or mixed contents, the object of the `PCData` class is used to represent the character data. The structure of the `javax.xml.bind.PCData` class is as follows:

```
final class PCData
extends MarshallableObject // ValidatableObject
implements Comparable
{
PCData();
PCData(String chars);
String chars();
void chars(String chars);
int compareTo(Object ob);
boolean equals(Object ob);
String getChars();
int hashCode();
void marshal(Marshaller m) throws java.io.IOException;
void setChars(String chars);
void unmarshal(Unmarshaller um) throws UnmarshalException;
void validateThis() throws MissingContentException;
}
```

THE JAVAX.XML.BIND.UNMARSHALLER CLASS The `javax.xml.bind.Unmarshaller` class is primarily responsible for converting an XML document into a content tree. It validates the tree while constructing it. This class defines methods for unmarshalling a content tree. The structure of the `javax.xml.bind.Unmarshaller` class is as follows:

```
final class Unmarshaller {
javax.xml.marshal.XMLScanner
scanner();
MarshallableObject unmarshal() throws UnmarshalException;
MarshallableObject unmarshal(Class mobClass) throws
UnmarshalException;
Validator validator();
}
```

THE JAVAX.XML.BIND.VALIDATABLEOBJECT CLASS   The methods of `javax.xml.bind.ValidatableObject`, along with the methods of the `Validator` class, define how a content tree is validated. The structure of the `javax.xml.bind.ValidatableObject` class is as follows:

```
abstract class ValidatableObject {
final void invalidate();
final void validate() throws StructureValidationException;
void validateThis() throws LocalValidationException;
void validate(Validator vd) throws StructureValidationException;
}
```

The method `invalidate()` marks the object, against which it is invoked, as invalid. If this method is invoked, you cannot marshal the content tree to a XML document. The method `validate()` validates the content tree of an object. The object against which this method is invoked should be an object of a root class. The method actually creates a `Validator` instance.

THE JAVAX.XML.BIND.VALIDATOR CLASS   The `javax.xml.bind.Validator` class validates a content tree. The `validate(ValidatableObject)` method of this class is primarily responsible for the validation process. Following is the structure of the `javax.xml.bind.Validator` class:

```
final class Validator {
void reference(IdentifiableElement elt) throws
MissingIdentifierException;
void reference(String id, Validator.Patcher p);
void validate(ValidatableObject vob) throws
StructureValidationException;
}
```

THE JAVAX.XML.BIND.VALIDATOR.PATCHER CLASS   The `javax.xml.bind.ValidatorPatcher` class is used to provide reference to an unmarshalled element object during the process of unmarshalling. The `patch(IdentifiableElement target)` method is called after the reference is provided during the unmarshalling process. The structure of the `javax.xml.bind.Validator.Patcher` class is as follows:

```
static abstract class Validator.Patcher {
Validator.Patcher();
abstract void patch(IdentifiableElement target);
}
```

THE JAVAX.XML.MARSHAL PACKAGE

The `javax.xml.marshal` package contains classes that are used for scanning and writing XML documents. Some of the important classes of this package I discuss in the following sections.

THE JAVAX.XML.MARSHAL.DOCUMENTSCANPOSITION CLASS The `javax.xml.marshal.DocumentScanPosition` class describes the position of a scanner in a DOM tree. The `node()` method returns the scan position of the DOM node in a DOM tree. The structure of the `javax.xml.marshal.DocumentScanPosition` class is as follows:

```
final class DocumentScanPosition
extends ScanPosition
{
DocumentScanPosition(org.w3c.dom.Node node);
org.w3c.dom.Node node();
}
```

THE JAVAX.XML.MARSHAL.STREAMSCANPOSITION CLASS The class `javax.xml.marshal.StreamScanPosition` represents the scanner's position in an input stream. The scan position in an input stream consists of a line number, a column number, and a source URI. The column number and source URI are optional. The structure of the `javax.xml.marshal.StreamScanPosition` class is as follows:

```
final class StreamScanPosition
extends ScanPosition
{
StreamScanPosition(int line);
StreamScanPosition(int line, int col);
StreamScanPosition(int line, int col, String uri);
int column();
int line();
String toString();
String uriString();
}
```

The following method signatures can be used to create a new scan position:

◆ `StreamScanPosition(int line)`

◆ `StreamScanPosition(int line, int col)`

◆ `StreamScanPosition(int line, int col, String uri)`

If the source URI and the column number are not known, the method takes 0 or null against it. The `column()` and `line()` methods return the column number and line number, respectively. The `toString()` method returns the scan position as a string, and the `uriString()` method returns the source URI of the position as a string.

THE JAVAX.XML.MARSHAL.XMLSCANNER CLASS   During the process of unmarshalling an XML document to a content tree, the XML document must be a well-formed XML document. The schema-derived class enforces all validity constraints. The derived classes also enforces the Element type Match and the Unique Att Spec well-formedness constraints of the XML 1.0 specification. The XML scanner enforces the remaining well-formedness constraints of the XML 1.0 specification.

The `XMLscanner` object can be in one of the following states:

- `Start`

- `AttributeName`

- `AttributeValue`

- `AttributeValueToken`

- `Chars`

- `End`

- `EndOfDocument`

The scanner position can be checked by using methods that return a Boolean value declared in the `javax.xml.marshal.XMLScanner` class. The `atStart()` method checks whether the scanner is at the position of the `start` tag. If it is in that state, the method returns `true`. The `position()` method returns a `scan-position` object that provides information on the scanner's current position. The structure of the `javax.xml.marshal.XMLScanner` class is follows:

```
abstract class XMLScanner {
static final int WS_COLLAPSE;
static final int WS_NORMALIZE;
static final int WS_PRESERVE;
XMLScanner();
abstract boolean atAttribute();
abstract boolean atAttributeValue();
abstract boolean atAttributeValueToken();
abstract boolean atChars(int whitespace) throws ScanException;
abstract boolean atEnd() throws ScanException;
abstract boolean atEndOfDocument()
throws javax.xml.bind.InvalidContentException,
ScanException;
```

```
abstract boolean atEnd(String name) throws ScanException;
abstract boolean atStart() throws ScanException;
abstract boolean atStart(String name) throws ScanException;
abstract void close() throws ScanIOException;
static XMLScanner open(java.io.InputStream in) throws ScanException;
static XMLScanner open(org.w3c.dom.Document doc) throws
ScanException;
abstract String peekStart()
throws javax.xml.bind.InvalidContentException,
ScanException;
abstract ScanPosition position();
abstract String takeAttributeName()
throws javax.xml.bind.InvalidContentException,
ScanException;
final String takeAttributeValue()
throws javax.xml.bind.InvalidContentException,
ScanException;
abstract String takeAttributeValue(int whitespace)
throws javax.xml.bind.InvalidContentException,
ScanException;
abstract String takeAttributeValueToken()
throws javax.xml.bind.InvalidContentException,
ScanException;
abstract String takeChars(int whitespace)
throws javax.xml.bind.InvalidContentException,
ScanException;
final void takeEmpty(String name)
throws javax.xml.bind.InvalidContentException,
ScanException;
abstract String takeEnd()
throws javax.xml.bind.InvalidContentException,
ScanException;
abstract void takeEndOfDocument()
throws javax.xml.bind.InvalidContentException,
ScanException;
abstract void takeEnd(String name)
throws javax.xml.bind.InvalidContentException,
ScanException;
final String takeLeaf(String name, int whitespace)
throws javax.xml.bind.InvalidContentException,
ScanException;
abstract String takeStart()
throws javax.xml.bind.InvalidContentException,
ScanException;
abstract void takeStart(String name)
```

```
throws javax.xml.bind.InvalidContentException,
ScanException;
abstract void tokenizeAttributeValue()
throws javax.xml.bind.InvalidContentException,
ScanException;
}
```

THE JAVAX.XML.XMLWRITER CLASS   The `javax.xml.XMLWriter` class is used to write XML output streams. The structure of the `javax.xml.XMLWriter` class is as follows:

```
class XMLWriter {
XMLWriter(java.io.OutputStream out) throws java.io.IOException;
XMLWriter(java.io.OutputStream out, String enc)
throws java.io.UnsupportedEncodingException, java.io.IOException;
XMLWriter(java.io.OutputStream out, String enc, boolean declare)
throws java.io.UnsupportedEncodingException, java.io.IOException;
void attributeName(String name) throws java.io.IOException;
void attribute(String name, String value) throws
java.io.IOException;
void attributeValue(String value) throws java.io.IOException;
void attributeValueToken(String token) throws java.io.IOException;
void chars(String chars) throws java.io.IOException;
void close() throws java.io.IOException;
void doctype(String root, String dtd) throws java.io.IOException;
void end(String name) throws java.io.IOException;
void flush() throws java.io.IOException;
void inlineLeaf(String name) throws java.io.IOException;
void inlineLeaf(String name, String chars) throws
java.io.IOException;
void leaf(String name) throws java.io.IOException;
void leaf(String name, String chars) throws java.io.IOException;
void setQuote(char quote);
void start(String name) throws java.io.IOException;
}
```

Unmarshalling, Validation, and Marshalling

As I discuss in the section "The binding schema" earlier in this chapter, the schema compiler generates the Java source files by using the DTD and the binding schema. These source files are then compiled by using the Java compiler to create Java class files. The generated Java classes extend the classes and interfaces of the binding framework to provide the following functionalities:

◆ Unmarshalling

◆ Validation

◆ Marshalling

The following sections describe these three functionalities.

Unmarshalling

Unmarshalling is the process of generating a tree of Java objects from a corresponding XML document. This object tree is also known as a *content tree*. You can unmarshal a XML document into a content tree by using the unmarshal() method that is present in the JAXB-generated root class. The root class is the class that corresponds to the root element of the XML document. The typical signature of the unmarshal methods of a root class, Test, is as follows:

```
public static Test unmarshal(XMLScanner xs, Dispatcher d) throws
UnmarshalException;

public static Test unmarshal(XMLScanner xs) throws
UnmarshalException;
public static Test unmarshal(InputStream is) throws
UnmarshalException;
```

The first method takes an XMLScanner object for scanning the document. It also takes a Dispatcher object for mapping the elements name to the element classes. The other two methods use a default Dispatcher.

If you invoke any of the preceding methods, the Unmarshal class gets instantiated and its instance is responsible for creating the content tree.

For unmarshalling elements, Dispatcher first maps the element's name to the corresponding class of the element. It then instantiates that particular class and invokes its unmarshal(Unmarshaller) method. This method is responsible for unmarshalling the subelements that the element possesses.

Validation

Validation is the process of ensuring that the content tree corresponds with the constraints of the schema. All the derived classes extend either directly or indirectly from the abstract class ValidatableObject. The ValidatableObject class shown in the following code provides the necessary methods for validating content trees:

```
public abstract class ValidatableObject
{
    public void validatethis()
        throws LocalValidationException;
  public void validate(Validator v)
        throws StructurevalidationException;
  public final void validate()
            throws StructurevalidationException;
public final void invalidate();
}
```

You can validate a content tree by using the `validate()` method of the derived root class. If you call the `validate()` method, the `Validator` class gets instantiated. This instance is responsible for validation of the content tree. It does so by invoking each object's `validateThis()` method and the `validate(Validator)` method, where it passes itself.

Marshalling

Marshalling is the process of creating a new XML document from a Java object tree. You may use the `marshal` method present in the JAXB-generated class to perform marshalling. A derived content class directly or indirectly extends the `MarshallableObject` abstract class. This class defines methods for marshalling and unmarshalling, as shown in the following code:

```
public abstract class MarshallableObject
        extends  ValidatableObject
    {
        protected MarshallableObject();
        public void marshal(Marshaller m)
          throws IOException;
         public void unmarshal (Unmarshaller u)
           throws UnmarshalException;
    }
```

The root class extends the `MarshallableRootElement` abstract class. The `MarshallableRootElement` class receives the functionality of the `MarshallableObject` class by extending it.

The typical signature of the `marshal` methods of the `MarshallableRootElement` class is as follows:

```
public final void marshal(XMLWriter xw)
  throws IOException;
```

```
public final void marshal(OutputStream out)
  throws IOException;
```

If you invoke one of these methods of the `root` class, the `Marshaller` class gets instantiated. The instance then invokes the `marshal` methods of each object of the content tree. Figure 9-2 shows the process of marshalling and unmarshalling.

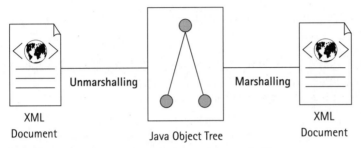

Figure 9-2: The process of marshalling and unmarshalling

Working with JAXB

In this section, you work with an XML document containing information about books. You use data binding to see how the data in the XML document can be mapped to Java objects. To do so, you create a DTD and a binding schema. You use the schema compiler to generate the derived classes that you use to process the XML document. You then create a JAXB application to unmarshal an XML document to the Java object tree. You also create a JAXB application to validate the object tree and to marshal the object tree back to an XML document.

For this section, you need to download the Java Architecture for XML Binding (JAXB) Implementation 1.0 Early Access from `http://java.sun.com/xml/downloads/jaxb.html`. You need an implementation of the Java 2 platform, Standard Edition, version 1.3 or later. After you download the release, copy the jar files `jaxb-rt-1.0-ea.jar` and `jaxb-xjc-1.0-ea.jar` into the `jre/lib/ext` directory of your J2SE distribution. Now copy the `xjc` script from the `bin` folder of the JAXB release download into the `~/bin` directory of your J2SE distribution. Open the `xjc` script file and uncomment the line beginning with `#JAVA` and change it to point to the location of your Java virtual machine.

You also create a JAXB application for processing the XML document. Create the XML file as follows:

```
<?xml version="1.0" ?>
<book code="1369">
<name>Learning XML</name>
<author>Jack walsh</author>
<authoraddress>
<addressline>14,Park Street,NY.</addressline>
<state>NY.</state>
```

```
<zipcode>35724</zipcode>
</authoraddress>
<price>45</price>
</book>
```

Create a `Books` folder and save the XML file as `Book.xml`. Now perform the following steps:

1. Create a DTD that describes the structure of the XML document. For the `BookList` example, create a DTD to describe the components of a book. Save the file as `BookDTD.dtd`. Following is the code for the BookDTD file:

```
<? xml version="1.0" encoding="UTF-8">
<!ELEMENT book (name, author, authoraddress+, price)+ >
<!ATTLIST book
          code CDATA #REQUIRED >
<!ELEMENT name (#PCDATA) >
<!ELEMENT author (#PCDATA) >
<!ELEMENT authoraddress (addressline, state, zipcode) >
<!ELEMENT addressline (#PCDATA) >
<!ELEMENT state (#PCDATA) >
<!ELEMENT zipcode (#PCDATA) >
<!ELEMENT price (#PCDATA) >
```

The DTD `BookDTD.dtd` has the `root` element `book`. The `book` element has an attribute code and subelements `name`, `author`, `authoraddress`, and `price`. The `authoraddress` element has the subelements `addressline`, `state`, and `zipcode`.

2. Define a binding schema that the schema compiler needs to generate the derived classes. Save the binding schema as `BookBS.xjs`. Following is the structure of BookBS.xjs:

```
<? xml version="1.0" encoding="UTF-8" ?>
<xml-java-binding-schema version="1.0ea">
<options package="examples.books" />
<element name="book" type="class" root="true">
<attribute name="code" convert="long" />
</element>
</xml-java-binding-schema>
```

In the binding schema, the element declaration declares the `book` element as the `root` element and specifies that the `root` element should be mapped to a class. The attribute tag in the binding schema declares that the `code` attribute should be mapped to a `long` value.

3. After you create the DTD and the binding schema, you generate the `derive` classes that contain the processing codes. To generate processing codes, run the following command at the command prompt:

```
xjc  BookDTD.dtd  BookBS.xjs
```

The schema compiler generates the derived classes for you. The derive class `Book.java` generated by the compiler will look similar to the following class:

 There is no xjc launcher for Windows. To work around this problem, create a batch file xjc.bat in your folder that contains the DTD and the binding schema. The xjc.bat file has the following code:

```
rem set JAXB=C:\jaxb-1.0-ea
rem Add to your PATH C:\jaxb-1.0-ea\BIN;
rem set JAVA_HOME C:\jdk1.3.0_02
set JAVACMD=%JAVA_HOME%\bin\java
%JAVA_HOME%\bin\java com.sun.tools.xjc.Main %1 %2 %3 %4
```

```java
import java.io.IOException;
import java.io.InputStream;
import java.util.ArrayList;
import java.util.Iterator;
import java.util.List;
import javax.xml.bind.Dispatcher;
import javax.xml.bind.DuplicateAttributeException;
import javax.xml.bind.InvalidAttributeException;
import javax.xml.bind.InvalidContentObjectException;
import javax.xml.bind.LocalValidationException;
import javax.xml.bind.MarshallableObject;
import javax.xml.bind.MarshallableRootElement;
import javax.xml.bind.Marshaller;
import javax.xml.bind.MissingAttributeException;
import javax.xml.bind.MissingContentException;
import javax.xml.bind.PredicatedLists;
import javax.xml.bind.PredicatedLists.Predicate;
import javax.xml.bind.RootElement;
import javax.xml.bind.StructureValidationException;
import javax.xml.bind.UnmarshalException;
import javax.xml.bind.Unmarshaller;
import javax.xml.bind.ValidatableObject;
import javax.xml.bind.Validator;
import javax.xml.marshal.XMLScanner;
```

```
import javax.xml.marshal.XMLWriter;


public class Book
    extends MarshallableRootElement
    implements RootElement
{

    private String _Code;
    private List _Content =
PredicatedLists.createInvalidating(this, new
ContentPredicate(), new ArrayList());
    private PredicatedLists.Predicate pred_Content = new
ContentPredicate();

    public String getCode() {
        return _Code;
    }

    public void setCode(String _Code) {
        this._Code = _Code;
        if (_Code == null) {
            invalidate();
        }
    }

    public List getContent() {
        return _Content;
    }

    public void deleteContent() {
        _Content = null;
        invalidate();
    }

    public void emptyContent() {
        _Content = PredicatedLists.createInvalidating(this,
pred_Content,
 new ArrayList());
    }

    public void validateThis()
        throws LocalValidationException
    {
        if (_Code == null) {
```

```
            throw new MissingAttributeException("code");
        }
        if (_Content == null) {
            throw new MissingContentException("content");
        }
    }


    public void validate(Validator v)
        throws StructureValidationException
    {
        for (Iterator i = _Content.iterator(); i.hasNext(); )
{
            v.validate(((ValidatableObject) i.next()));
        }
    }


    public void marshal(Marshaller m)
        throws IOException
    {
        XMLWriter w = m.writer();
        w.start("book");
        w.attribute("code", _Code.toString());
        for (Iterator i = _Content.iterator(); i.hasNext(); )
{
            m.marshal(((MarshallableObject) i.next()));
        }
        w.end("book");
    }


    public void unmarshal(Unmarshaller u)
        throws UnmarshalException
    {
        XMLScanner xs = u.scanner();
        Validator v = u.validator();
        xs.takeStart("book");
        while (xs.atAttribute()) {
            String an = xs.takeAttributeName();
            if (an.equals("code")) {
                if (_Code!= null) {
                    throw new
DuplicateAttributeException(an);
                }
                _Code = xs.takeAttributeValue();
                continue;
            }
```

```
                         throw new InvalidAttributeException(an);
               }
               {
                       List l = PredicatedLists.create(this,
           pred_Content, new ArrayList());
                       while
           (((xs.atStart("authoraddress")||xs.atStart("name"))||xs.atSta
           rt("author"))||xs.atStart("price")) {
                              l.add(((MarshallableObject) u.unmarshal()));
                       }
                       _Content =
           PredicatedLists.createInvalidating(this, pred_Content,
            l);
               }
               xs.takeEnd("book");
           }

       public static Book unmarshal(InputStream in)
           throws UnmarshalException
       {
           return unmarshal(XMLScanner.open(in));
       }

       public static Book unmarshal(XMLScanner xs)
           throws UnmarshalException
       {
           return unmarshal(xs, newDispatcher());
       }

       public static Book unmarshal(XMLScanner xs, Dispatcher d)
           throws UnmarshalException
       {
           return ((Book) d.unmarshal(xs, (Book.class)));
       }

       public boolean equals(Object ob) {
           if (this == ob) {
               return true;
           }
           if (!(ob instanceof Book)) {
               return false;
           }
           Book tob = ((Book) ob);
           if (_Code!= null) {
               if (tob._Code == null) {
```

```
                return false;
            }
            if (!_Code.equals(tob._Code)) {
                return false;
            }
        } else {
            if (tob._Code!= null) {
                return false;
            }
        }
        if (_Content!= null) {
            if (tob._Content == null) {
                return false;
            }
            if (!_Content.equals(tob._Content)) {
                return false;
            }
        } else {
            if (tob._Content!= null) {
                return false;
            }
        }
        return true;
    }

    public int hashCode() {
        int h = 0;
        h = ((127 *h)+((_Code!= null)?_Code.hashCode(): 0));
        h = ((127 *h)+((_Content!= null)?_Content.hashCode():
0));
        return h;
    }

    public String toString() {
        StringBuffer sb = new StringBuffer("<<book");
        if (_Code!= null) {
            sb.append(" code=");
            sb.append(_Code.toString());
        }
        if (_Content!= null) {
            sb.append(" content=");
            sb.append(_Content.toString());
        }
        sb.append(">>");
        return sb.toString();
```

```
        }

        public static Dispatcher newDispatcher() {
            return Author.newDispatcher();
        }


        private static class ContentPredicate
            implements PredicatedLists.Predicate
        {


            public void check(Object ob) {
                if (!(ob instanceof MarshallableObject)) {
                    throw new InvalidContentObjectException(ob,
        (MarshallableObject.class));
                }
            }
        }
    }
```

Notice that, according to the element declaration in the binding schema, the class is named Book. As the class derives from the root element of the DTD, book, it is the root element class and extends the MarshallableRootElement class. As I discuss in the section "The javax.xml.bind.MarshallableRootElement" class earlier in this chapter, the class MarshallableRootElement is abstract and cannot contain static methods. Therefore, the four static unmarshalling methods that you notice in the class are generated by the schema compiler. The derived class is a root element class and also implements the RootElement interface. In addition, notice that various methods that I discussed in the JAXB runtime library section, such as methods for unmarshalling, validating, and marshalling, are present in the compiler-generated class. You call some of these methods from your JAXB application to perform the required operations. Notice that, in the class Book, the private class variable _Code corresponds to the attribute declaration that you made in the DTD. Also notice the two corresponding accessor and mutator methods, getCode() and setCode(String _code), in the class. The remaining methods of the generated classes are used to encapsulate the complexities of processing an XML document.

The derived class Author.java that the compiler generates looks similar to the following class:

```
import java.io.IOException;
import java.io.InputStream;
import javax.xml.bind.ConversionException;
import javax.xml.bind.Dispatcher;
import javax.xml.bind.Element;
```

```
import javax.xml.bind.InvalidAttributeException;
import javax.xml.bind.LocalValidationException;
import javax.xml.bind.MarshallableObject;
import javax.xml.bind.Marshaller;
import javax.xml.bind.StructureValidationException;
import javax.xml.bind.UnmarshalException;
import javax.xml.bind.Unmarshaller;
import javax.xml.bind.Validator;
import javax.xml.marshal.XMLScanner;
import javax.xml.marshal.XMLWriter;


public class Author
    extends MarshallableObject
    implements Element
{

    private String _Content;

    public String getContent() {
        return _Content;
    }

    public void setContent(String _Content) {
        this._Content = _Content;
        if (_Content == null) {
            invalidate();
        }
    }

    public void validateThis()
        throws LocalValidationException
    {
    }

    public void validate(Validator v)
        throws StructureValidationException
    {
    }

    public void marshal(Marshaller m)
        throws IOException
    {
        XMLWriter w = m.writer();
        w.start("author");
```

```
            if (_Content!= null) {
                w.chars(_Content.toString());
            }
            w.end("author");
        }

        public void unmarshal(Unmarshaller u)
            throws UnmarshalException
        {
            XMLScanner xs = u.scanner();
            Validator v = u.validator();
            xs.takeStart("author");
            while (xs.atAttribute()) {
                String an = xs.takeAttributeName();
                throw new InvalidAttributeException(an);
            }
            {
                String s;
                if (xs.atChars(XMLScanner.WS_COLLAPSE)) {
                    s = xs.takeChars(XMLScanner.WS_COLLAPSE);
                } else {
                    s = "";
                }
                try {
                    _Content = String.valueOf(s);
                } catch (Exception x) {
                    throw new ConversionException("content", x);
                }
            }
            xs.takeEnd("author");
        }

        public static Author unmarshal(InputStream in)
            throws UnmarshalException
        {
            return unmarshal(XMLScanner.open(in));
        }

        public static Author unmarshal(XMLScanner xs)
            throws UnmarshalException
        {
            return unmarshal(xs, newDispatcher());
        }

        public static Author unmarshal(XMLScanner xs, Dispatcher d)
```

```
        throws UnmarshalException
{
        return ((Author) d.unmarshal(xs, (Author.class)));
}

public boolean equals(Object ob) {
    if (this == ob) {
        return true;
    }
    if (!(ob instanceof Author)) {
        return false;
    }
    Author tob = ((Author) ob);
    if (_Content!= null) {
        if (tob._Content == null) {
            return false;
        }
        if (!_Content.equals(tob._Content)) {
            return false;
        }
    } else {
        if (tob._Content!= null) {
            return false;
        }
    }
    return true;
}

public int hashCode() {
    int h = 0;
    h = ((127 *h)+((_Content!= null)?_Content.hashCode(): 0));
    return h;
}

public String toString() {
    StringBuffer sb = new StringBuffer("<<author");
    if (_Content!= null) {
        sb.append(" content=");
        sb.append(_Content.toString());
    }
    sb.append(">>");
    return sb.toString();
}

public static Dispatcher newDispatcher() {
```

```
        Dispatcher d = new Dispatcher();
        d.register("author", (Author.class));
        d.register("authoraddress", (Authoraddress.class));
        d.register("book", (Book.class));
        d.register("name", (Name.class));
        d.register("price", (Price.class));
        d.freezeElementNameMap();
        return d;
    }


}
```

Notice that the class corresponds to the subelement author as declared in the DTD. The Author class extends the MarshallableObject class. This enables the object of the Author class to be marshaled and unmarshalled. The Author class is an element class and implements the Element interface, unlike the root element class Book, which implements the RootElement interface. Notice the various methods that are required for unmarshalling, validation, and marshalling its object. The other derived classes that are generated by the compiler (corresponding to the name and price elements declared in the DTD) are Name.java and Price.java.

The derived class Authoraddress.java generated by the compiler looks similar to the following class:

```
import java.io.IOException;
import java.io.InputStream;
import javax.xml.bind.ConversionException;
import javax.xml.bind.Dispatcher;
import javax.xml.bind.Element;
import javax.xml.bind.InvalidAttributeException;
import javax.xml.bind.LocalValidationException;
import javax.xml.bind.MarshallableObject;
import javax.xml.bind.Marshaller;
import javax.xml.bind.MissingContentException;
import javax.xml.bind.StructureValidationException;
import javax.xml.bind.UnmarshalException;
import javax.xml.bind.Unmarshaller;
import javax.xml.bind.Validator;
import javax.xml.marshal.XMLScanner;
import javax.xml.marshal.XMLWriter;
public class Authoraddress
    extends MarshallableObject
    implements Element
{

    private String _Addressline;
```

```java
private String _State;
private String _Zipcode;

public String getAddressline() {
    return _Addressline;
}

public void setAddressline(String _Addressline) {
    this._Addressline = _Addressline;
    if (_Addressline == null) {
        invalidate();
    }
}

public String getState() {
    return _State;
}

public void setState(String _State) {
    this._State = _State;
    if (_State == null) {
        invalidate();
    }
}

public String getZipcode() {
    return _Zipcode;
}

public void setZipcode(String _Zipcode) {
    this._Zipcode = _Zipcode;
    if (_Zipcode == null) {
        invalidate();
    }
}

public void validateThis()
    throws LocalValidationException
{

    if (_Addressline == null) {
        throw new MissingContentException("addressline");
    }
    if (_State == null) {
        throw new MissingContentException("state");
    }
```

```
            if (_Zipcode == null) {
                throw new MissingContentException("zipcode");
            }
        }


    public void validate(Validator v)
            throws StructureValidationException
        {
        }

    public void marshal(Marshaller m)
            throws IOException
        {

            XMLWriter w = m.writer();
            w.start("authoraddress");
            w.leaf("addressline", _Addressline.toString());
            w.leaf("state", _State.toString());
            w.leaf("zipcode", _Zipcode.toString());
            w.end("authoraddress");
        }


    public void unmarshal(Unmarshaller u)
            throws UnmarshalException
        {

            XMLScanner xs = u.scanner();
            Validator v = u.validator();
            xs.takeStart("authoraddress");
            while (xs.atAttribute()) {
                String an = xs.takeAttributeName();
                throw new InvalidAttributeException(an);
            }
            if (xs.atStart("addressline")) {
                xs.takeStart("addressline");
                String s;
                if (xs.atChars(XMLScanner.WS_COLLAPSE)) {
                    s = xs.takeChars(XMLScanner.WS_COLLAPSE);
                } else {
                    s = "";
                }
                try {
                    _Addressline = String.valueOf(s);
                } catch (Exception x) {
                    throw new ConversionException("addressline", x);
                }
                xs.takeEnd("addressline");
```

```
        }
    if (xs.atStart("state")) {
        xs.takeStart("state");
        String s;
        if (xs.atChars(XMLScanner.WS_COLLAPSE)) {
            s = xs.takeChars(XMLScanner.WS_COLLAPSE);
        } else {
            s = "";
        }
        try {
            _State = String.valueOf(s);
        } catch (Exception x) {
            throw new ConversionException("state", x);
        }
        xs.takeEnd("state");
    }
    if (xs.atStart("zipcode")) {
        xs.takeStart("zipcode");
        String s;
        if (xs.atChars(XMLScanner.WS_COLLAPSE)) {
            s = xs.takeChars(XMLScanner.WS_COLLAPSE);
        } else {
            s = "";
        }
        try {
            _Zipcode = String.valueOf(s);
        } catch (Exception x) {
            throw new ConversionException("zipcode", x);
        }
        xs.takeEnd("zipcode");
    }
    xs.takeEnd("authoraddress");
}

public static Authoraddress unmarshal(InputStream in)
    throws UnmarshalException
{
    return unmarshal(XMLScanner.open(in));
}

public static Authoraddress unmarshal(XMLScanner xs)
    throws UnmarshalException
{
    return unmarshal(xs, newDispatcher());
}
```

```
    public static Authoraddress unmarshal(XMLScanner xs, Dispatcher
d)
        throws UnmarshalException
    {
        return ((Authoraddress) d.unmarshal(xs,
(Authoraddress.class)));
    }

    public boolean equals(Object ob) {
        if (this == ob) {
            return true;
        }
        if (!(ob instanceof Authoraddress)) {
            return false;
        }
        Authoraddress tob = ((Authoraddress) ob);
        if (_Addressline!= null) {
            if (tob._Addressline == null) {
                return false;
            }
            if (!_Addressline.equals(tob._Addressline)) {
                return false;
            }
        } else {
            if (tob._Addressline!= null) {
                return false;
            }
        }
        if (_State!= null) {
            if (tob._State == null) {
                return false;
            }
            if (!_State.equals(tob._State)) {
                return false;
            }
        } else {
            if (tob._State!= null) {
                return false;
            }
        }
        if (_Zipcode!= null) {
            if (tob._Zipcode == null) {
                return false;
            }
            if (!_Zipcode.equals(tob._Zipcode)) {
```

```
                         return false;
                 }
         } else {
             if (tob._Zipcode!= null) {
                 return false;
             }
         }
         return true;
    }

    public int hashCode() {
         int h = 0;
         h = ((127 *h)+((_Addressline!=
null)?_Addressline.hashCode(): 0));
         h = ((127 *h)+((_State!= null)?_State.hashCode(): 0));
         h = ((127 *h)+((_Zipcode!= null)?_Zipcode.hashCode(): 0));
         return h;
    }

    public String toString() {
         StringBuffer sb = new StringBuffer("<<authoraddress");
         if (_Addressline!= null) {
             sb.append(" addressline=");
             sb.append(_Addressline.toString());
         }
         if (_State!= null) {
             sb.append(" state=");
             sb.append(_State.toString());
         }
         if (_Zipcode!= null) {
             sb.append(" zipcode=");
             sb.append(_Zipcode.toString());
         }
         sb.append(">>");
         return sb.toString();
    }

    public static Dispatcher newDispatcher() {
         return Author.newDispatcher();
    }
}
```

The AuthorAddress class is an element class, as is the Author class, and it therefore extends the MarshallableObject class and implements the Element interface.

However, notice that three private class variables _AddressLine, _State, and _ZipCode appear in the class. These variables correspond to the sub elements addressline, state, and zipcode of the author element that you declared in the DTD. The class also contains the methods required for unmarshalling, validation, and marshalling operations. You now unmarshal the XML file Book.xml. To do so, create an application, BookApp.java. In the BookApp class, create the instance myBook, of the class that the schema compiler generated. Create the File object bookFile, of the XML document that you're to unmarshal. Open FileInputStream. Call the unmarshal method, passing FileInputString. Now print the output, calling myBook's toString() method. Your BookApp.java file should look similar to the following code:

```
import java.io.File;
import java.io.FileInputStream;
public class BookApp{
public static Book myBook=new Book();
static FileInputStream fileInStream;
public static void main(String args[])throws Exception{
try{

    File bookFile=new File("Book.xml");
fileInStream=new FileInputStream(bookFile);
    myBook=myBook.unmarshal (fileInStream);
    fileInStream.close();
    }
catch(Exception ex)
    {
    fileInStream.close();
    ex.printStackTrace();
    }
    System.out.println(myBook.toString());
}
}
```

Compile the application and run it. You see the following output:

```
<<book code=1369 content=[<<name content=Learning XML>>, <<author content=Jack
walsh>>, <<authoraddress addressline=14,Park Street,NY. state=NY. zipcode=35724>>
, <<price content=45>>]>>
```

After you unmarshal your XML document, you validate the object tree that is created corresponding to your XML document. To validate the object tree, add a validateBook method in BookApp.java. Following is the code for the method:

```
public String validateBook(){
try{
        myBook.validate();
        System.out.println("myBook Validated");
    }
catch(Exception e){
 e.printStackTrace();
}
}
```

Call the `validateBook()` method from the `main()` method of your `BookApp`.
`java` application. Run the application. Notice the output `myBook Validated`.

You now marshal the content tree back to a XML document. To do so, create the
method `marshalBook()` in your `BookApp.java`. In this method, create the new
`File` object `bookFile`, of the XML document that you intend to marshal to. Open
`FileOutputStream`, passing the `File` object. Now call the `marshal()` method that
takes the `FileOutputStream` object. Your code should look similar to the following
example:

```
public void marshalBook() throws Exception{
try{
File bookFile=new File("MarshalBook.xml");
FileOutputStream fileOS=new FileOutputStream(bookFile);
myBook.marshal(fileOS);
System.out.println("Marshalling Complete");
}
catch(Exception e){
e.printStackTrace();
}
```

Call the `marshalBook()` from the `main()` method of BookApp.java. Compile and
run the Application. You see the following output:

```
Marshal<<book code=1369 content=[<<name content=Learning XML>>,
<<author
 content=Jack walsh>>, <<authoraddress addressline=14,Park
Street,NY. state=NY.
 zipcode=35724>>, <<price content=45>>]>>


MyBook Validated
Marshalling Complete
```

Notice the new MarshalBook.xml document that gets automatically generated in
your folder. The BookApp application first unmarshals the Book.xml document that

you created. The application then validates the generated object tree and finally the object tree is marshaled to a new XML document MarshalBook.xml.

Summary

This chapter introduces you to Java Architecture for XML Binding (JAXB). In this chapter, you learn the need for Java-XML binding. The chapter discusses DTDs and binding schemas in detail. It then discusses the advantages, disadvantages and components of JAXB. The chapter also discusses unmarshalling, validation, and marshalling in detail. Finally, the chapter illustrates how to use JAXB.

Chapter 10

JAXM

IN THIS CHAPTER

♦ Overview of JAXM

♦ J2EE Messaging

♦ JAXM Architecture

♦ JAXM Programming Model

WITH THE ADVENT OF Web services, businesses can now exchange their documents across the Web for business interaction. Java Web services enable business message transactions through the Java API for XML Messaging (JAXM). JAXM is a standard for exchanging XML messages on the Java platform. By using the JAXM API, you can develop a Java application to create, send, and receive XML messages. JAXM is based on the SOAP 1.1 and SOAP with attachment specifications. You typically use it within the Web-services architecture for exchanging XML-based documents as SOAP messages. JAXM also enables the use of standard implementations, such as ebXML Transport, Routing, and Packaging V1.0 Message Service Specification, on SOAP.

 You can download the JAXM specification from `http://java.sun.com/Download5`.

Overview of JAXM

Messaging is a primitive component within the Web-services architecture. Business-to-business (B2B) exchange generally involves a heavy flow of message traffic between interacting businesses. The B2B messaging facility needs to function in a smooth and seamless manner so that the parties involved in the exchange do not need to wait for long periods of time for the messages to reach the other endpoint. JAXM supports some typical messaging scenarios to meet this requirement, as follows:

♦ **Scenario 1:** A sender sends an update message to the receiver. The receiver receives the update and sends an acknowledgement to the sender. The sender receives the acknowledgement.

♦ **Scenario 2:** A sender sends a request message to the receiver. The receiver receives the message and sends a corresponding response to the sender. The sender receives the response.

♦ **Scenario 3:** A sender sends a message to the receiver and does not expect a response.

In Scenario 1 and Scenario 2, the exchange of messages is either a *synchronous* exchange or an *asynchronous* exchange. In a synchronous exchange, the sender of an update or message waits until it receives an acknowledgement or a response from the receiver. In an asynchronous exchange, no time is bound for the receiver to send the acknowledgement or the response. The receiver sends the response or acknowledgment as a separate operation. In such asynchronous exchange, the client does not wait for the response.Both synchronous and asynchronous messaging styles are common scenarios in the Web-services architecture. All the preceding messaging scenarios use a messaging provider to manage messages that route through the messaging channel. The messaging provider takes care of the routing and traversal of the messages to the appropriate recipients on behalf of the JAXM client. The messaging provider ensures that message sent is handed over to the appropriate recipient whenever the recipient is available. In this way, a sender can hand over the message to the messaging provider, and the sender can concentrate on other activities on hand without waiting for a reply from the receiver. However, you use a messaging provider only if the JAXM client supports it. A standalone JAXM client can also send synchronous messages to a specified URL without using a messaging provider. In most of these cases, an application server vendor (such as WebLogic or WebSphere) incorporates the messaging provider.

JAXM is a standard that provides a definition for the communication of messages between two endpoints. The endpoints are either a JAXM client communicating with a servlet running within a Web container or a JAXM client interacting with a messaging provider. The provider is an implementation of the JAXM protocol, which exposes a standard JAXM API for the sender. Either way, you can use JAXM to specify the interactions between these endpoints. Using a messaging provider within the architecture, however, is not always necessary. You can use a standalone client based on the J2SE platform to communicate with a servlet or other components within a J2EE container. Using J2SE, however, is not an absolute must. You can use any architecture that supports request-response-based messaging. You can use JAXM APIs to provide a standard interface to use any kind of implementation of message routing and traversal architecture in a transparent fashion.

You can use JAXM in almost all the industry scenarios where you need to send a document from one component to another across the Internet. As an analogy, you can use JAXM to send invoices, purchase orders, mail, memos, and engineering documents or inventory requirements across from one business component to another via the Web.

According to the JAXM specification, all implementations that are JAXM-compatible must support SOAP 1.1 specifications and the SOAP message with attachment specifications. In addition, the JAXM specification states that the JAXM 1.0 does not mandate any use of a specific XML messaging standard. Instead, the JAXM specification uses an abstract term, *Profile,* to refer to the protocols based on the SOAP 1.1 standards. JAXM, therefore, provides a set of APIs for the Web-services client such that the client can send a message payload on any underlying protocol in a transparent mode. The client is not bound to use SOAP, ebXML, or any other standard for messaging.

As discussed in Chapter 8 and Chapter 9, JAXP and JAXB provide you with enough details to access and process an XML message. JAXM provides the details for sending and carrying this message across from one endpoint to the other regardless of the underlying message channels. Figure 10-1 shows a conceptual model of the JAXM messaging components and their relationship with each other.

 Please refer to Chapter 8 for JAXP and Chapter 9 for JAXB.

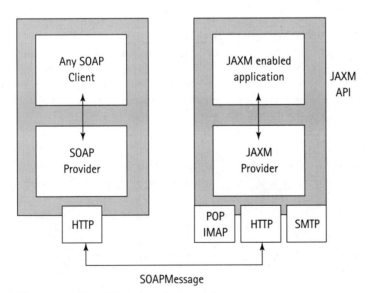

Figure 10-1: The JAXM conceptual model

In the conceptual model, notice a SOAP client interacting with a SOAP provider to send an XML document by using SOAP over HTTP. The SOAP message is sent to an endpoint that implements the JAXM provider architecture. You may wonder about the differences between SOAP-enabled service and a JAXM-enabled service. Practically, the difference lies in the way that you program for each of the provider architectures. In SOAP-based provider architecture, you need to specifically implement the service over SOAP as a message channel. In JAXM-based provider architecture, which implementation is available for, messaging does not matter. JAXM can work with SOAP or any other underlying messaging protocols. In addition, the JAXM API makes sticking to a standard interface for accessing XML-based documents from the Web much easier for the developer. JAXM is a lightweight protocol for business interaction. The messaging provider takes care of managing the routing and transmission control primitives of the payload over a particular messaging protocol.

Types of messaging

The messaging between the Web-services endpoints is of the following five types:

- Asynchronous request-response
- Asynchronous request-acknowledgement
- Synchronous request-response
- Synchronous request-acknowledgement
- One way with no reply (fire-and-forget)

ASYNCHRONOUS REQUEST-RESPONSE

In asynchronous messages, the client does not wait for an immediate reply after sending a request. The reply to such requests may even take days. Asynchronous messages, therefore, are considered one-way operations. The JAXM implementation should, therefore, withstand such inordinately prolonged transactions in the model. Figure 10-2 illustrates the asynchronous request-response model.

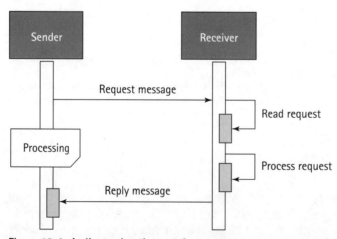

Figure 10-2: A client using the asynchronous request-response model

ASYNCHRONOUS REQUEST-ACKNOWLEDGEMENT

This model is the same as asynchronous except that the client waits for an acknowledgement from the messaging provider instead of a reply message.

Figure 10-3 illustrates the asynchronous request-acknowledgement model.

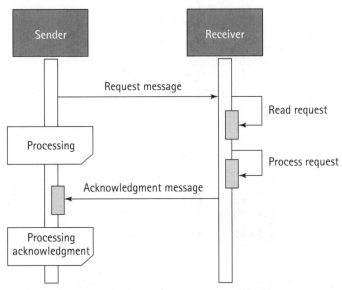

Figure 10-3: A client using the asynchronous request-acknowledgement model

SYNCHRONOUS REQUEST-RESPONSE

In this model, the client actually waits until it receives a response from the recipient of the message. The client is considered in a blocked state while waiting for the response. In this model, you have no absolute necessity for a messaging provider. Figure 10-4 illustrates the synchronous request-response model.

SYNCHRONOUS REQUEST-ACKNOWLEDGEMENT

This model is similar to the synchronous request-response model. In this model, the client sends the message payload and expects an immediate acknowledgement from the recipient. The client does not, however, wait for an appropriate response for the request that is sent.

Figure 10-5 illustrates the synchronous request-acknowledgement model.

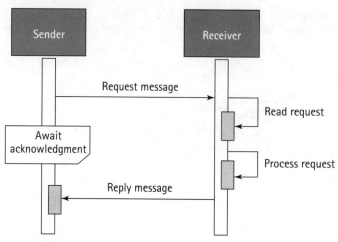

Figure 10-4: A client using the synchronous request–response model

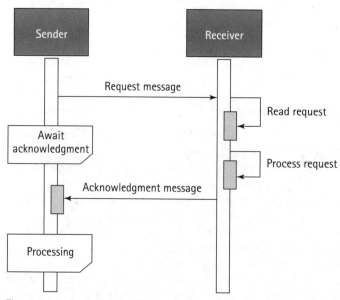

Figure 10-5: A client using the synchronous request–acknowledgement model

ONE-WAY WITH NO REPLY

In the one-way with no reply model, the client sends a message and does not expect a reply or an acknowledgement from the recipient. Figure 10-6 illustrates the one-way with no reply model.

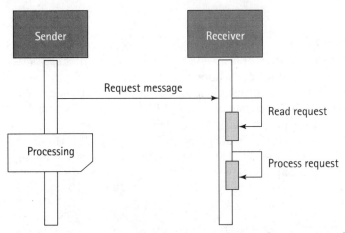

Figure 10-6: A client using the one way with no reply (fire-and-forget) model

Whenever the sender uses a messaging provider, all the messages sent go through the provider. In other words, the client needs to open a `Connection` object to the messaging provider to send the message across to the recipient. The messaging provider, at runtime, sends and receives the messages on the sender's behalf.

In fact, all the JAXM implementations should support all the five types of messaging models. A client can use different types of messaging implementations at any given point of time. Figure 10-7 gives an overview of a client architecture that uses both a synchronous and an asynchronous messaging protocol to send a message.

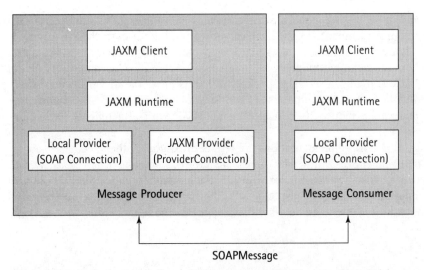

Figure 10-7: A client using both synchronous and asynchronous provider models

Interoperability

The prime motto of a Web-services model is to provide integration between disparate systems. For such integration of disparate business systems, *interoperability* is the key issue. The capability of the applications to interoperate with each other in a way that the applications can exchange payload, invoke operations, and process each other's request is the main advantage in the Web-services architecture. To provide such a level of interoperability, the JAXM-enabled service should be capable of interacting with other services, which may or may not be JAXM-enabled. According to the JAXM specification, JAXM accommodates such levels of interoperability because of the following principles:

◆ A transport-neutral packaging model

◆ Agreements on message-header structures and manifests

The JAXM specification mandates the use of SOAP 1.1 and SOAP with attachment specifications to be implemented by JAXM providers. JAXM providers can also incorporate support for other message protocols within the implementation. JAXM providers are also free to implement transport protocols such as HTTP, FTP, SMTP, POP, or IMAP for the traversal of messages. JAXM makes the default assumption that SOAP-based messages traverse through the transport endpoints. The specification states: "In order for a JAXM client (or service) to interoperate with a JAXM or non-JAXM service (or client), the parties must first agree on SOAP transport bindings and messaging profiles."

SOAP packaging

SOAP has two packaging models: SOAP messages with attachment and SOAP messages without attachment. JAXM enables you to work with both these packaging models. Figure 10-8 illustrates a standard SOAP packaging model, the SOAP messages without attachment model.

SOAP also provides a different packaging for its envelope in which more than one MIME attachment is within the package. Such packaging is known as *multipart/related messaging*. Figure 10-9 illustrates the SOAP with attachments packaging model.

Ideally, all JAXM implementations are required to support the packaging shown in Figure 10-9. The JAXM sender is responsible for choosing whether to send a SOAP message with attachments or without attachments. In either case, the JAXM implementation should be ready to handle the package and route it accordingly. The multipart attachments in SOAP with attachments model are either XML-related or non-XML-related.

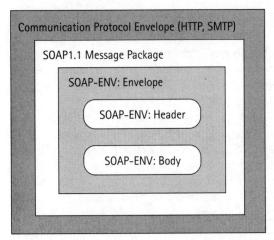

Figure 10-8: SOAP package without attachments model

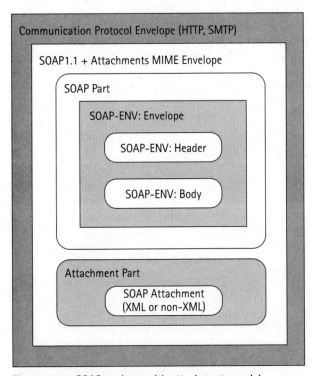

Figure 10-9: SOAP package with attachments model

J2EE Messaging

Java 2 Platform Enterprise Edition (J2EE) has Java Messaging Services (JMS) and JavaMail API messaging models available within its architecture. So how different is JAXM from these models? To answer this question, you need to look under the hood of these three different specifications.

Basically, all these technologies provide messaging functionality to the Java platform by projecting the messaging model from different perspectives. The JMS APIs provide a standard set of interfaces to access any given *Message Oriented Middleware (MOM)* without worrying about the specifics of their implementation. In a sense, JMS is a vendor-neutral standard that provides a common set of APIs for enterprise messaging. The JMS architecture provides two messaging models: *publish-and-subscribe messaging (pub/sub)* and *point-to-point messaging (P2P)*. The pub/sub messaging model is based on the broadcast messaging architecture, while the P2P messaging is based on a one-to-one messaging architecture. Although you can use JMS for sending XML-based messages, it is not the best fit for Web services because the API semantics of JMS does not expose any interfaces that support SOAP-based messaging. As JMS does not provide support to work with SOAP messages, Web services programming is a bit harder. Using JMS Writing applications by using only JMS, which can programmatically manipulate SOAP messages, is difficult.

The JavaMail API provides a standard set of APIs to access e-mail-based protocols such as POP3 or IMAP. You use The JavaMail API for corporate mailing solutions. Although you can send XML messages via e-mail by using JavaMail, it still is not a best fit for Web-services messaging architecture for the same reasons that I give for JMS. The API semantics of JavaMail do not expose any interfaces that support SOAP-based messaging.

The JAXM technology is a technology that befits the Web-services scenario. Within the Web-services model, SOAP is the most definitive protocol that you use to communicate across the Web. If SOAP is a major benefactor for the Web services framework, however, you should have an easier way to incorporate SOAP access within the Java framework. You should be able to easily use the SOAP-based APIs to send and receive messages on a SOAP-provider architecture. To accommodate this level of ease and service within the Java platform, JAXM exposes a set of Java interfaces to the Java-based Web-services application so that the application can make use of the SOAP message protocols.

In essence, although all three APIs share a single theme conceptually, they all satisfy different criteria of messaging. Each protocol is optimized to take care of one and only one perspective of the Web-services messaging framework. In fact, you quite possibly can have mixed-mode systems that support all these flavors of messaging within a single application. One of the advantages of choosing JAXM is that it provides a standard message access protocol such as SOAP, which can bind to any kind of transport protocol, such as HTTP, FTP, or SMTP. Just one protocol, however, may not satisfy all the criteria on hand. The three protocols should coexist with each other within a Web-services framework. And a mixed-mode hybrid implementation of these protocols is actually becoming the order of the day. You can find e-mail systems based on MOMs, for example, or you can find SOAP messages transported across a MOM infrastructure. They are all valid hybrid implementations of the JAXM, JMS, and JavaMail specifications.

JAXM Architecture

A messaging provider is a component that implements the JAXM specification and exposes the standard JAXM API to the users of the system. Currently different vendors are providing messaging providers by implementing the JAXM API. The application that uses JAXM-based messaging component you can term a *JAXM client.*

   A JAXM client can either act as a provider of the messages (sender) or consumer of the messages (receiver). Don't confuse the term JAXM client, therefore, with anything except a conceptual indication to refer to a JAXM application.

JAXM clients

As I discuss in the Overview of JAXM section, a JAXM client mayor may not use a messaging provider. The following two scenarios can classify the two different types of JAXM clients:

- ◆ A JAXM client using the JAXM provider

- ◆ A standalone JAXM client

JAXM CLIENT USING THE JAXM PROVIDER

A JAXM client generally uses a JAXM provider that acts as a messaging provider to send and receive messages either synchronously or asynchronously. If the client needs to access the JAXM provider, the client opens a `Connection` object with the JAXM provider. An easy way to implement this scenario is to execute a JAXM client within a J2EE Web container or a J2EE Enterprise JavaBean (EJB) container that exposes the JAXM API to the client components, which are running within the container framework. In this way, you have a crisply defined contract that can distinguish the relationship between the client and the container and also between the container and the JAXM provider. The client talks to the container only about operations such as receiving or sending messages and obtaining connections. The container is responsible for handling these complex issues. In addition, the container can manage the life-cycle events of such clients at runtime. You can use deployment tools available from different vendor frameworks to deploy such JAXM clients into a Web-services container. During the deployment of the JAXM client, you specify the name of the provider so that the JAXM client can obtain and maintain a connection with the JAXM provider. You do so by registering the provider in a Java Naming and Directory Interface (JNDI) naming service.

As I discussed in the Overview of JAXM section earlier in this chapter, the implementation of the JAXM provider that acts as a messaging provider is vendor-specific. Given a certain vendor, that vendor may choose to provide some specific message-routing algorithms that may or may not be available within other vendor products. The only thing that is vendor-neutral in the framework is the JAXM APIs that the client accesses. For the JAXM client, the messaging traversal and routing is completely transparent. All that the client needs to do is to send and receive messages from a JAXM provider by using the standard JAXM APIs. The client can query further vendor-specific information about the provider by utilizing some metadata interfaces available within the JAXM API specifications.

STANDALONE JAXM CLIENTS
In the case of a point-to-point, synchronous Web-services messaging model, you do not need a JAXM provider handling the messages for you. Such a messaging provider is unlikely to add any value to the messaging architecture. Instead, using such providers may increase the complexity of the code for simple synchronous message semantics.

A messaging client that does not use the JAXM provider component is a *standalone JAXM client.* You can implement a standalone JAXM client as a Java application by using the J2SE platform. The standalone client just needs to connect to the service URL directly. The message semantics on such a model are those of the synchronous request-response model.

JAXM Message Profiles

The JAXM specification is based on the SOAP 1.1 and SOAP with attachments specifications but is not strictly bound to any specific message structure or semantics for the routing or traversal of messages between endpoints. The JAXM implementation provides the addressing scheme for message-routing semantics by using the concepts of *Profiles.*

Profiles operate on the SOAP message protocol. JAXM does not mandate any specific content structure (such as XML) for use in any of the SOAP message semantics. JAXM does not, for example, specify what kind of XML content to place within a SOAP header, SOAP body, or SOAP attachments. Instead, a Profile can specify an appropriate usage of a SOAP header. As an example, a Profile can specify that the SOAP header can carry a sender ID and a date stamp telling when the message was sent. Typically, the developers specify the critical information about a message, such as sender ID, receiver ID, message ID, and the correlation information of a message.

Following is a brief outline of a SOAP message structure without any attachments:

```
SOAP message
    SOAP part
        SOAP envelope
            SOAP header (optional)
            SOAP body
```

Typically, you use such a structure if you need to send messages that specify a content structure similar to that of XML. In other words, if you can format and unformat the content that you need to send by using XML-like syntax, you can use the preceding outline.

If the content that you send contains a format that is not similar to that of XML or that you cannot represent as an XML-like syntax, you use a SOAP attachment. A message that you need to send may, for example, include some images (gifs, jpegs). Such a message consists of a SOAP part that contains the XML-like content and a SOAP attachment, which contains the images. A brief outline for this scenario is as follows:

```
SOAP message
    SOAP part
        SOAP envelope
            SOAP header (optional)
            SOAP body
    Attachment part (image file)
```

The manner in which this information maps to the message structure is based on the Profile that the developer may be using to send the message. JAXM does not provide any mechanism for mapping. The JAXM client should establish a connection with a message provider by providing the Profile string indicating the Profile to use at runtime. You can set up such strings within a deployment descriptor at deployment time or can also obtain them from other datastores at runtime. In fact, if you don't specify an application Profile, the JAXM provider suggests a default Profile to use for mapping the contents within the message structure. You, as a developer, need to decide on the messaging provider component (or product) and the default Profile that the vendor chooses to use within the product.

JAXM is free to choose any standard industry Profile that may exist at the time of usage. Whenever the JAXM client uses an appropriate Profile, the client's becomes responsible for suggesting the URI of the schema associated with the industry Profile that the client is using. For two applications to understand the message, the endpoints must first confirm to use the same Profile; only then can the endpoints make sense of the information encoded within the structure of the message.

Finally, the JAXM clients don't handle the security considerations of the message routing and traversal information and the authentication of such a messaging framework. According to the specification, the JAXM provider is solely responsible for taking care of the security considerations of the messaging framework.

JAXM Programming Model

The JAXM programming model is based on two Java packages, `javax.xml.messaging` and `java.sml.soap`. These Java-based APIs enable the JAXM client to interact with XML-related documents.

The javax.xml.messaging package

The `javax.xml.messaging` package is a high-level abstraction of the messaging model. The `javax.xml.messaging` package consists of the following interfaces:

- `OnewayListener`
- `ProviderConnection`
- `ProviderMetaData`
- `ReqRespListener`

The `javax.xml.messaging` package consists of the following classes:

- `Endpoint`
- `JAXMServlet`
- `ProviderConnectionFactory`
- `URLEndpoint`

The `javax.xml.messaging` package also consists of the `JAXMException` exception.

As I discuss in the section Types of Messaging, JAXM has different styles of messaging. The JAXM message model uses the Profiles concept to manage the mapping of the message content for a specified structure of a message. The usage of similar Profiles on two endpoints provides you with a notion of an interoperable Web-services messaging framework.

THE ENDPOINT AND URLENDPOINT CLASSES

The `Endpoint` class represents an application endpoint of a Web-services framework. The `URLEndpoint` is a direct subclass of the `Endpoint` class. The `URLEndpoint` is considered a special case of the `Endpoint` class, which wants to interact with another SOAP-based application directly instead of going through a JAXM provider. The messaging semantics used in this case is a direct request-response-based messaging. The calling client is considered in a blocked state whenever such messaging semantics occur. These messaging semantics are also known as *synchronous messaging models.*

THE PROVIDERCONNECTIONFACTORY AND PROVIDERCONNECTION OBJECTS

Within the JAXM messaging models are asynchronous messaging model types that free the JAXM client from waiting for a reply from the recipient of a request. To accommodate such a style of messaging, you use a messaging provider that manages the message flow for you. In addition, such messaging providers are vendor-specific implementations that expose a standard JAXM API for the JAXM clients.

The clients communicate with the provider object by using the JAXM APIs. In this section, you discover how to communicate with the JAXM provider component that is available to you.

The easiest way to implement a JAXM client by using an asynchronous messaging model is to deploy client components within a Web-services container (such as J2EE). The container is responsible for providing access to the JAXM provider for all the clients deployed within the container. The container exposes the JAXM API to the clients. The `ProviderConnection` object is an object that clients need to create to communicate with the JAXM provider.

To create the `ProviderConnection` object, you first need to obtain access to a `ProviderConnectionFactory` object. The `ProviderConnectionFactory` object helps you to create a `ProviderConnection` with the JAXM provider. The Web-services container manages the `ProviderConnectionFactory` object. Because you deploy JAXM clients within the container, the clients need to query the container to obtain the `ProviderConnectionFactory` object. The `ProviderConnectionFactory` object is actually set up in the container at the time you install the container (the default provider and Profiles), or you can specify the `ProviderConnectionFactory` object at the time of deployment. At runtime, you can obtain the `ProviderConnectionFactory` object either through a vendor-specific datastore or a standard JNDI-based object tree. Typically, most containers always provide a JNDI-based interface for obtaining a `ProviderConnectionFactory` object by looking up a unique name for the object.

After you obtain a factory object and create the appropriate `ProviderConnection` object, you are free to communicate with the JAXM provider. Typically, you use the `MessageFactory` object based on a given Profile to create `SOAPMessage` objects.

Whenever you have a message to send, you can call the `ProviderConnection.send()` method to send a `SOAPMessage` from one endpoint to another.

THE ONEWAYLISTENER AND REQRESPLISTENER INTERFACES

Whenever a JAXM client is planning to implement a specific messaging style, it has two broad options from which to choose: *synchronous* or *asynchronous* style of messaging.

If a JAXM client chooses to implement a synchronous messaging style, the application client must implement a marker interface known as the `ReqRespListener` interface. The implementation of the `ReqRespListener` interface indicates that the client intends to participate in a request-response-based point-to-point synchronous message call.

If a JAXM client wants to implement an asynchronous messaging style, the application client must implement the `OnewayListener` marker interface.

The `OnewayListener` interface and the `ReqRespListener` interface contain an `onMessage()` method signature that the JAXM clients need to implement. The `onMessage()` method is a callback mechanism that contains the application logic to handle the messages that it receives. The container actually invokes the callback mechanism based on a message-received event.

THE JAXMSERVLET CLASS

JAXMServlet is a class that extends the `javax.servlet.http.HTTPServlet` class. The JAXMServlet class is a utility class that embeds a `MessageFactory` field, which you can use within the service logic of the method. The JAXM client that wants to be implemented as a servlet within the Web-services container can implement the JAXMServlet, and it also must choose to implement either the `OnewayListener` or the `ReqRespListner` interface to indicate the messaging style.

The javax.xml.soap package

The `javax.xml.soap` package is a primary abstraction for the SOAP 1.1 and SOAP with attachments specifications. The `javax.xml.soap` package consists of the following interfaces:

- Detail
- DetailEntry
- Name
- Node
- SOAPBody
- SOAPBodyElement
- SOAPConstants
- SOAPElement
- SOAPEnvelope
- SOAPFault
- SOAPFaultElement
- SOAPHeader
- SOAPHeaderElement
- Text

The `javax.xml.soap` package consists of the following classes:

- AttachmentPart
- MessageFactory
- MimeHeader
- MimeHeaders
- SOAPConnection

- `SOAPConnectionFactory`

- `SOAPElementFactory`

- `SOAPMessage`

- `SOAPPart`

The `javax.xml.soap` package also contains the `SOAPException` exception.

THE MESSAGEFACTORY, SOAPMESSAGE, SOAPPART, AND ATTACHMENTPART OBJECTS

In the section, "The ProviderConnectionFactory and ProviderConnection objects," you learn to create a `ProviderConnection` object for a given JAXM provider. After you obtain a connection, you are responsible for sending messages to the provider.

A `SOAPMessage` object encapsulates the abstraction of a message. The `SOAPMessage` class is actually the root class for all the SOAP messages. To obtain the `SOAPMessage` object, you first need to obtain a `MessageFactory` object. Following are the two ways to obtain `MessageFactory`:

- If you are planning to create a `SOAPMessage` object that takes part in an asynchronous messaging model, you need to obtain the `MessageFactory` object through the `ProviderConnection` object. You call the `ProviderConnection.createMessageFactory()` method to obtain `MessageFactory` for asynchronous messaging.

- If you want to participate within a synchronous-style messaging model, you need to obtain a `MessageFactory` object by calling the `MessageFactory.newInstance()` method because no messaging provider is likely to become available for a standalone client. Even if a message provider is available, you should avoid using the JAXM provider for synchronous calls.

After you obtain a `MessageFactory` object, you need to invoke the `MessageFactory.createMessage()` method to eventually create a `SOAPMessage` object. The `SOAPMessage` object contains the `SOAPPart` object and may also contain the `AttachmentPart` object. If a `SOAPMessage` contains any attachment (the `AttachmentPart` object), the `SOAPMessage` object is encoded as a MIME message. You use the `SOAPMessage.getSOAPPart()` method to obtain a `SOAPPart` object.

THE SOAPELEMENT, SOAPENVELOPE, SOAPBODY, AND SOAPHEADER OBJECTS

The `SOAPElement` object denotes the base class for SOAP objects within the SOAP 1.1 specification. According to the specification, you use the `SOAPElement` to represent the content of the `SOAPBody`, `SOAPHeader`, `SOAPEnvelope`, and `SOAPFault` objects.

You use the SOAPEnvelope object to encapsulate the SOAPHeader and the SOAPBody object that is contained within a SOAPPart object. The SOAPHeader object is optional and can contain a SOAPHeaderElement object as its immediate child.

You create the SOAPEnvelope object by calling the SOAPPart.getEnvelope() method. You create the SOAPBody object by calling the SOAPEnvelope.getBody() method. You create the SOAPHeader object by calling the SOAPEnvelope. addHeader() method. The SOAPHeader.addHeaderElement() method creates a new SOAPHeaderElement object.

THE SOAPCONNECTIONFACTORY AND SOAPCONNECTION OBJECTS

Whenever you want to communicate by using a synchronous point-to-point messaging style, you use a direct connection to a Web-service endpoint rather than going through a messaging provider. Typically, for an asynchronous call, you must obtain a connection to a JAXM provider object.

In the synchronous messaging scenario, you avoid the JAXM provider and try to get a direct connection to the other endpoint. You obtain a SOAPConnection object for a synchronous message just as you do the ProviderConnection object. You obtain the SOAPConnection object through the SOAPConnectionFactory object. You can obtain the SOAPConnection object by calling the SOAPConnectionFactory. createConnection() method.

After you obtain a SOAPConnection object, you can send a SOAPMessage to a remote endpoint by invoking the call() method on the SOAPConnection. The SOAPConnection takes the SOAPMessage and the URLEndpoint objects as arguments.

The call remains blocked until a response SOAPMessage object is received. After the SOAPMessage response is received, the call eventually gets unblocked. For a one-way synchronous message call, you still need to obtain a SOAPMessage object.

JAXM Examples

In this section, you look at some examples that provide you different scenarios of messaging. I begin with a simple producer-consumer example that does not require a JAXM provider.

Before executing these examples, make sure that you have set the following JAR files on the CLASSPATH:

- ◆ jaxm-api.jar
- ◆ jaxm-client.jar
- ◆ log4j.jar
- ◆ dom4j.jar

Refer to Appendix E for information about how to download and set up JWSDP.

The following code is an example of a standalone JAXM client implementation:

```
// Import the appropriate packages for creating a SOAP message
import java.util.*;
import javax.xml.soap.*;
import javax.xml.messaging.*;

// Create a class JAXMStandAloneClient that represents a Stand Alone
client.
public class JAXMStandAloneClient {
  public static void main(String[] args) {
    try {
      // The URLEndpoint indicates the endpoint to which the message
is being //sent
      URLEndpoint endpoint = new
URLEndpoint("http://www.conceptuniv.com/bookdetails");

      // A SOAPConnection is used to send the messages. A
SOAPConnectionFactory is a //factory class that facilitates in
obtaining the connection.
      SOAPConnectionFactory soapConFact =
SOAPConnectionFactory.newInstance();
      SOAPConnection connection = soapConFact.createConnection();

      // A MessageFactory is a factory class that facilitates in
obtaining a //SOAPMessage.
      MessageFactory msgFact = MessageFactory.newInstance();
      SOAPMessage message = msgFact.createMessage();

      // After the SOAPMessage is created, a SOAPPart object is
created, which is a container for the SOAP envelope.
      SOAPPart soapPart=message.getSOAPPart();

      // A SOAP envelope is created using the SOAP part
      SOAPEnvelope envelope = soapPart.getEnvelope();

      // The SOAP envelope facilitates the creation of SOAP header
(optional) and //SOAP body
```

```
      SOAPBody body = envelope.getBody();

        // The Name object contains a local name, a namespace prefix,
  and a namespace //URI. This represents the fully qualified name for
  the SOAP body. A fully qualified //name space is necessary for the
  body element.

      Name gbdName = envelope.createName("GetBookDetails" , "wsns",
  "http://www.conceptuniv.com/wsns/");
      SOAPBodyElement gbd = body.addBodyElement(gbdName);

        // The child elements added to the SOAP body may have Name
  objects with only //the local name.
      Name isbnName = envelope.createName("ISBN");
      SOAPElement isbn = gbd.addChildElement(isbnName);
      isbn.addTextNode("0-7645-8045-8");

        // The SOAPMessage.saveChanges() call, updates this
  SOAPMessage //object with all the changes that have been made to it.
      message.saveChanges();

        // Prints the endpoint to which the message is sent.
      System.out.println("Sending message to URL: " +
  endpoint.getURL());

        // Invokes the call. This call will send the SOAP message to
  the endpoint. //This call will also return a SOAP message that
  contains the response object.
      SOAPMessage response = connection.call(message, endpoint);
      message.writeTo(System.out);

      // Obtain the SOAP part, envelope and body from the response
  object
      SOAPPart resSoapPart = response.getSOAPPart();
      SOAPEnvelope soapEnv = resSoapPart.getEnvelope();
      SOAPBody soapBody = soapEnv.getBody();

        // Prepare an Iterator to iterate through the child elements
  within the //response message
      Iterator it = soapBody.getChildElements(gbdName);

      // Obtain the SOAP body and the value held.
      SOAPBodyElement bodyElement = (SOAPBodyElement)it.next()
      String title = bodyElement.getValue();

      bodyElement = (SOAPBodyElement)it.next();
```

```
        String author = bodyElement.getValue();

bodyElement = (SOAPBodyElement)it.next();
        String price = bodyElement.getValue();

        // Print the values obtained on the console
        System.out.print("Title : ");
        System.out.println(title);

        System.out.print("Author : ");
        System.out.println(author);

        System.out.print("Price : ");
        System.out.println(price);

        connection.close();

    } catch(Throwable e) {
        e.printStackTrace();
    }
  }
}
```

Compile the code. Assuming that you have a Web-services application running on the other end of the application that responds to the request, you can execute this application. I present a dummy receiver later in this section.

In the preceding example, you start by importing the appropriate packages, as follows:

```
import java.util.*;
import javax.xml.soap.*;
import javax.xml.messaging.*;
```

The javax.xml.soap package provides the necessary SOAP implementation while the javax.xml.messaging provides access to MessageFactory.

Then, within the JAXMStandAloneClient class, you denote a URLEndpoint to a Web-services URL that may have an application listening for SOAP messages. You also create the SOAPConnection to the end point by using the SOAPFactory, as follows:

```
public class JAXMStandAloneClient {
  public static void main(String[] args) {
    try {
      URLEndpoint endpoint = new
URLEndpoint("http://www.conceptuniv.com/bookdetails");
```

```
SOAPConnectionFactory soapConFact =
SOAPConnectionFactory.newInstance();
    SOAPConnection connection = soapConFact.createConnection();
```

Then you obtain the SOAPMessage object by creating the MessageFactory object. After you obtain the SOAPMessage, you can build the necessary elements, such as the Envelope, Body, Node, and Text elements, as follows:

```
MessageFactory msgFact = MessageFactory.newInstance();
    SOAPMessage message = msgFact.createMessage();

    SOAPPart soapPart=message.getSOAPPart();
    SOAPEnvelope envelope = soapPart.getEnvelope();

    SOAPBody body = envelope.getBody();
    Name gbdName = envelope.createName("GetBookDetails" , "wsns",
"http://www.conceptuniv.com/wsns/");
    SOAPBodyElement gbd = body.addBodyElement(gbdName);

    Name isbnName = envelope.createName("ISBN");
    SOAPElement isbn = gbd.addChildElement(isbnName);
    isbn.addTextNode("0-7645-8045-8");

    message.saveChanges();
```

In the preceding code, the outcome of the SOAPBody object at runtime is an XML file. The content of SOAPXML file is similar to that of the following code:

```
. . .
. . .
. . .

        <soapenv:Body>
                <wsns:GetBookDetails
xmlns:wsns="http://www.conceptuniv.com/wsns/">
                        <ISBN
xsi:type="xsd:string">0-7645-8045-8</ISBN>
                </wsns:GetBookDetails>
        </soapenv:Body>
. . .
. . .
. . .
```

Eventually, you make the call to the SOAP endpoint and obtain the reply. Assuming that you receive author, title, and price as a book-details response message, you write the following code to call and query the details:

```
    System.out.println("Sending message to URL: " +
endpoint.getURL());

    SOAPMessage response = connection.call(message, endpoint);

    message.writeTo(System.out);

    SOAPPart resSoapPart = response.getSOAPPart();
    SOAPEnvelope soapEnv = resSoapPart.getEnvelope();
    SOAPBody soapBody = soapEnv.getBody();

    Iterator it = soapBody.getChildElements(gbdName);

    SOAPBodyElement bodyElement = (SOAPBodyElement)it.next()
    String title = bodyElement.getValue();

bodyElement = (SOAPBodyElement)it.next();
String author = bodyElement.getValue();

bodyElement = (SOAPBodyElement)it.next();
    String price = bodyElement.getValue();

    System.out.print("Title : ");
    System.out.println(title);

    System.out.print("Author : ");
    System.out.println(author);

    System.out.print("Price : ");
    System.out.println(price);
```

The entire SOAP message that is finally created after the preceding code executes is as follows:

```
POST /bookdetails HTTP/1.1
Host: www.conceptuniv.com
Content-Type: text/xml; charset="utf-8"
Content-Length: n
SOAPAction: "http://www.conceptuniv.com/GetBookDetails"

<?xml version="1.0" encoding="UTF-8"?>
<soapenv:Envelope
xmlns:soapenv="http://schemas.xmlsoap.org/soap/envelope/"
soapenv:encodingStyle="http://schemas.xmlsoap.org/soap/encoding/"
xmlns:xsi="http://www.w3.org/1999/XMLSchema-instance"
```

```
xmlns:xsd="http://www.w3.org/1999/XMLSchema">
        <soapenv:Body>
                <wsns:GetBookDetails
xmlns:wsns="http://www.conceptuniv.com/wsns/">
                        <ISBN
xsi:type="xsd:string">0-7645-8045-8</ISBN>
                </wsns:GetBookDetails>
        </soapenv:Body>
</soapenv:Envelope>
```

The preceding XML-based SOAP document is the outcome of the Java code that you wrote. The XML-based SOAP document traverses across the Web and reaches the receiving end. The receiver bears the responsibility for decapsulating the message. The receiver processes the document and sends an appropriate response message to the request. Throughout the processing of the call, the JAXMStandAloneClient object remains in the blocked state and waits for the response.

The following code provides a dummy receiver. You can deploy a Message receiver servlet that participates in a request-response-style operation at the service-provider end in a Web-service architecture. This servlet just receives a SOAPMessage, displays it at the service provider's end, creates a dummy reply, and sends it back to the JAXMClient.

```
import javax.xml.messaging.*;
import javax.xml.soap.*;
import javax.servlet.*;
import javax.servlet.http.*;


// The DummyReceiver is a JAXMServlet. The JAXMServlet represents, a
superclass for //components that live in a servlet container that
receives JAXM messages. //JAXMServlet object is notified of a
message's arrival using the HTTP-SOAP binding. //The ReqRespListener
is a marker interface for components that are intended to be
//consumers of request-response messages.

public class DummyReceiver extends JAXMServlet implements
ReqRespListener {
    private MessageFactory msgFact = null;
    public void init(ServletConfig servletConfig) throws
ServletException {
        super.init(servletConfig);
        try {
            msgFact = MessageFactory.newInstance();
        } catch (Exception ex) {
            ex.printStackTrace();
        }
```

```
        }

// The method onMessage() specifies how to respond to the requests
it receives. The //following implementation displays the received
message on the receiver's console //and will echo the message back
to the sender.

        public SOAPMessage onMessage(SOAPMessage message) {
            try {
                System.out.println("THE MESSAGE : ");
                message.writeTo(System.out);
                SOAPMessage msg = msgFact.createMessage();
                SOAPEnvelope env = msg.getSOAPPart().getEnvelope();

env.getBody().addChildElement(env.createName("Response")).addTextNod
e("Some processing Info");
                return msg;
            } catch(Exception e) {
                System.out.println("Error...);
                return null;
            }
        }
    }
}
```

The following code is similar to the standalone client code but implements as a servlet. This servlet eventually invokes the service at the Web-service provider's end.

```
import java.util.*;
import javax.servlet.http.*;
import javax.servlet.*;
import javax.xml.messaging.*;
import javax.xml.soap.*;

public class SendingServlet extends HttpServlet {
    ServletContext servletContext;
    private SOAPConnection con;

    public void init(ServletConfig servletConfig) throws
ServletException {
        super.init( servletConfig );
        servletContext = servletConfig.getServletContext();
        try {
        // A SOAPConnection is used to send the messages. A
SOAPConnectionFactory is //a factory class that facilitates in
obtaining the connection.
```

```
        SOAPConnectionFactory scf =
SOAPConnectionFactory.newInstance();
        con = scf.createConnection();
      } catch(Exception e) {
        System.out.println("Error");
      }
    }


    public void doGet(HttpServletRequest req, HttpServletResponse
resp) throws ServletException {
      try {
      // The URLEndpoint indicates the endpoint to which the
message is being sent        URLEndpoint endpoint = new
URLEndpoint("http://www.conceptuniv.com/bookdetails");

      // A MessageFactory is a factory class that facilitates in
obtaining a //SOAPMessage.

        MessageFactory msgFact = MessageFactory.newInstance();
        SOAPMessage message = msgFact.createMessage();

      // After the SOAPMessage is created, a SOAPPart object is
created , which //is a container for the SOAP envelope.

        SOAPPart soapPart=message.getSOAPPart();

      // A SOAP envelope is created using the SOAP part

        SOAPEnvelope envelope = soapPart.getEnvelope();

      // The SOAP envelope facilitates the creation of SOAP header
(optional) and //SOAP body
        SOAPBody body = envelope.getBody();

      // The Name object contains a local name, a namespace prefix,
and a namespace //URI. This represents the fully qualified name for
the SOAP body. A fully qualified name space is necessary for the
body element.

        Name gbdName = envelope.createName("GetBookDetails" ,
"wsns", "http://www.conceptuniv.com/wsns/");
        SOAPBodyElement gbd = body.addBodyElement(gbdName);

      // The child elements added to the SOAP body may have Name
objects with only //the local name.
```

```
        Name isbnName = envelope.createName("ISBN");
        SOAPElement isbn = gbd.addChildElement(isbnName);
        isbn.addTextNode("0-7645-8045-8");

    // The SOAPMessage.saveChanges() call, updates this
SOAPMessage object with //all the changes that have been made to it.

        message.saveChanges();

        System.out.println("Sending message to URL: " +
endpoint.getURL());

    // Invokes the call. This call will send the SOAP message to
the endpoint. //This call will also return a SOAP message that
contains the response object.

        SOAPMessage response = connection.call(message,
endpoint);

        message.writeTo(System.out);

    // Obtain the SOAP part, envelope and body from the response
object and print //the values to the console

        SOAPPart resSoapPart = response.getSOAPPart();
        SOAPEnvelope soapEnv = resSoapPart.getEnvelope();
        SOAPBody soapBody = soapEnv.getBody();

        Iterator it = soapBody.getChildElements(gbdName);

        SOAPBodyElement bodyElement = (SOAPBodyElement)it.next()
        String title = bodyElement.getValue();

        bodyElement = (SOAPBodyElement)it.next();
        String author = bodyElement.getValue();

        bodyElement = (SOAPBodyElement)it.next();
        String price = bodyElement.getValue();

        System.out.print("Title : ");
        System.out.println(title);

        System.out.print("Author : ");
        System.out.println(author);

        System.out.print("Price : ");
```

```
                System.out.println(price);

                connection.close();

                } catch(Throwable e) {
                e.printStackTrace();
                }


        try {
            OutputStream os = resp.getOutputStream();
            os.write("Service Invoked".getBytes());
            os.flush();
            os.close();
        } catch (Exception e) {
            e.printStackTrace();
            System.out.println("Error in servlet response");
        }
    }
}
```

The following code is a client code that uses a JAXM provider for sending the SOAPMessage object. This servlet eventually invokes the service at the Web-service provider's end. The messaging style of invocation in this particular case is asynchronous. Notice that the following code is using a SOAP-RP Profile to execute a Web service:

```
        // Import the appropriate packages for creating a SOAP
message
import java.util.*;
import java.naming.*;
import javax.servlet.http.*;
import javax.servlet.*;
import javax.xml.messaging.*;
import javax.xml.soap.*;
import com.sun.xml.messaging.soaprp.*;

public class SendingServlet extends HttpServlet {
    ServletContext servletContext;

        // The ProviderConnectionFactory facilitates the creation
of a //ProviderConnection. The ProviderConnection is used in sending
SOAP messages using //an asynchronous message model.

    private ProviderConnectionFactory providerFactory;
```

```
    private ProviderConnection pCon;
    private MessageFactory msgFact;


    public void init(ServletConfig servletConfig) throws
ServletException {
        super.init( servletConfig );
        servletContext = servletConfig.getServletContext();
        try {

        // Create an initial context for a JNDI root.
Context ctx = new InitialContext();

        // Obtain a vendor specific messaging provider.
      providerFactory =
(ProviderConnectionFactory)ctx.lookup("Vendor.SomeProviderFactory");

        // Prepare a connection to the messaging provider.
         pCon = providerFactory.createConnection();
        } catch(Exception e) {
           System.out.println("Error");
        }
    }


    public void doGet(HttpServletRequest req, HttpServletResponse
resp) throws ServletException {
        try {
        // Obtain the provider metadata that contains vendor
specific information about the provider.
           ProviderMetaData metaData = pCon.getMetaData();

        // Obtain the information about the supported Profiles.
           String[] supportedProfiles =
metaData.getSupportedProfiles();
           String profile = null;

        // Iterate through the profiles to obtain the SOAP-RP
profile
           for(int i=0; i < supportedProfiles.length; i++) {
           if(supportedProfiles[i].equals("soaprp")) {
                 profile = supportedProfiles[i];
              break;
              }
            }
```

```
            // prepare a SOAPRPmessage using the Profile obtained.
            MessageFactory msgFact =
pCon.createMessageFactory(profile);
            SOAPRPMessageImpl message = (SOAPRPMessageImpl)
msgFact.createMessage();

            // set the senders endpoint (from where the message is
originating).
            message.setFrom(new
Endpoint("http://www.someuri.com/soaprp/sender"));

            // set the receivers endpoint (to which the message is
targeted).
            message.setTo(new
Endpoint("http://www.conceptuniv.com/bookdetails"));

            // Prepare the SOAP Message using the SOAP part, SOAP
envelope and SOAP //Body elements.
            SOAPPart soapPart=message.getSOAPPart();
            SOAPEnvelope envelope = soapPart.getEnvelope();

            SOAPBody body = envelope.getBody();
            Name gbdName = envelope.createName("GetBookDetails" ,
"wsns", "http://www.conceptuniv.com/wsns/");
            SOAPBodyElement gbd = body.addBodyElement(gbdName);

            Name isbnName = envelope.createName("ISBN");
            SOAPElement isbn = gbd.addChildElement(isbnName);
            isbn.addTextNode("0-7645-8045-8");

            // After the message is prepared, send the message using
the provider                      //connection.
            pCon.send(message);
            pCon.close();

            } catch(Throwable e) {
            e.printStackTrace();
            }


        try {
            OutputStream os = resp.getOutputStream();
            os.write("Service Invoked".getBytes());
            os.flush();
            os.close();
```

```
        } catch (Exception e) {
            e.printStackTrace();
            System.out.println("Error in servlet response");
        }
    }
}
```

Summary

JAXM is a standard Java-based API for SOAP-based messaging in the Web-services architecture. The JAXM specification is based on SOAP 1.1 and SOAP with attachments specifications. This chapter explains the requirement of a messaging protocol in Web services. The chapter also elaborates on J2EE messaging architecture. It discusses the similarities and differences between JMS, JavaMail, and JAXM. The chapter provides a detailed explanation of the JAXM architecture. Finally, the chapter provides some useful examples for the JAXM architecture.

Chapter 11

JAX–RPC

IN THIS CHAPTER

- ◆ An Overview of JAX-RPC
- ◆ JAX-RPC mappings
- ◆ JAX-RPC programming model

WEB SERVICES ARE BUILT ON THE DISTRIBUTED CLIENT–SERVER MODEL. The distributed client-server model provides a mechanism that enables a Web-service client to call procedures of a Web-service provider residing on a remote system. Such a mechanism is known as a *remote-procedure call (RPC)*. In the Java-based Web-services framework, the Java API for XML-based Remote Procedure Call (JAX-RPC) provides the RPC mechanism to enable a client to call a remote Web-service procedure by using XML.

The Java API for XML-based Remote Procedure Call (JAX-RPC) is a standard API for invoking remote procedures available at the service endpoint. A *service endpoint* represents a Web-service that other Web-service clients use. In Java Web services, an XML-based protocol such as the Simple Object Access Protocol (SOAP) represents the remote-procedure calls. The JAX-RPC API enables a Java developer to very easily make RPC calls from applications without needing to worry about the complexities of the underlying protocols and the mechanisms that enable such remote-procedure invocations. The JAX-RPC APIs expose easy logic for the programmers to create a simple, yet powerful distributed model to remotely invoke services available in a Web-services framework.

JAX-RPC utilizes the age-old concept of stubs, ties, and configuration files to smoothly integrate the SOAP RPC-style messaging framework to perform Web-service operations.

You need a JAX-RPC implementation to create a client application that uses the JAX-RPC API to invoke a remote method on a service endpoint. Sun Microsystems provides the JAX-RPC reference implementation in the Java Web Services Developer Pack. The JAX-RPC reference implementation includes an `xrpcc` tool that you can use to translate a WSDL file to a Java service and vice versa.

JAX-RPC is an effort from the Java Community Process (JCP), and as of this writing, the JAX-RPC is at proposed final-draft version 0.8. The Java Specification Requests (JSRs) for JAX-RPC is JSR101 and is available at `http://jcp.org/jsr/detail/101.jsp`.

An Overview of JAX-RPC

Java Web-services operations can either be document-oriented or method-oriented. In the document-oriented scenario, messages that are basically XML documents are interchanged between the client and service endpoints. In such a scenario, the application using the JAXM API defines the semantics of the messages. In a method-oriented scenario, client and service endpoint messages (which are XML documents) work correspondingly to perform a remote-procedure call. Parts of the semantics of such messages are predefined. In a method-oriented scenario, the client message contains the information necessary to invoke a remote method that may be written in some other programming language. Similarly, the service endpoint messages contain information of the invoked method and the result of the invocation. The JAX-RPC API facilitates such types of method-oriented Web-services scenarios.

In the Java Web-services framework, JAX-RPC enables you to create Java applications to invoke Web services by using a SOAP-based XML-RPC messaging framework. SOAP-RPC is actually based on the XML-RPC messaging framework that existed before SOAP. JAX-RPC utilizes a lot of ideas of the pre-existing distributed computing world, such as RMI and CORBA. JAX-RPC is a combination of concepts from RMI, CORBA, SOAP, and XML RPC. The JAX-RPC model has a client-side and a server-side for a service. The client can be a JAX-RPC client trying to invoke a procedure exposed by a SOAP-based Web service that may be written in a completely different language. By using JAX-RPC, you can also implement a service on the server-side that any SOAP-enabled client can invoke. In effect, JAX-RPC is a full-fledged distributed model that enables remote procedure calls just as RMI does.

The current JAX-RPC implementation is based on the SOAP 1.1 protocol and HTTP 1.1 network transport. The conventions and the syntax defined within the SOAP 1.1 specification are the guiding rules for the invocation semantics of the JAX-RPC framework.

JAX-RPC not only defines the base-level protocol bindings for SOAP services, but also serves as a flexible architecture, which can support other protocol bindings created in the future. JAX-RPC is also created with simplicity in mind. In the service endpoint of the JAX-RPC architecture, you provide an interface that exposes the service methods, which a remote client can invoke. You also implement the service methods of the interface in the service endpoint. For that, you can use a J2SE-based implementation, a servlet container-based implementation, or a J2EE-based implementation.

One of the main design goals of JAX-RPC is to support the concept of interoperability while maintaining platform neutrality. As the JAX-RPC framework uses SOAP and is based on the Java platform, it eventually becomes the better choice for building modular and flexible Web-services frameworks.

Figure 11-1 provides a high-level overview of a JAX-RPC service framework.

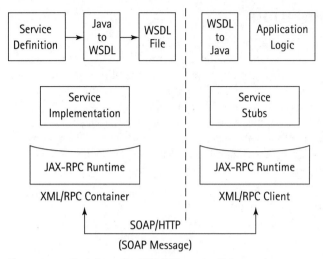

Figure 11-1: Overview of a JAX-RPC service framework

Service endpoint definition

In the JAX-RPC framework, the JAX-RPC service definition is a Java native defin- ition that provides a Java interface known as the *service-endpoint interface*. The service-endpoint interface that you need to implement within the J2SE or the J2EE framework follows certain rules. The service-endpoint interface must extend the java.rmi.Remote interface, and all its exposed methods must throw the java. rmi.RemoteException exception or one of its subclasses. Moreover, the exposed methods must have parameter types and return types that JAX-RPC supports. Usually, the service definition exposes the operations that are available to the con- sumers of the service.

The service definition makes no underlying assumptions about the implementa- tion of the endpoint on the client side. Instead, the definition just relies on a stan- dard assumption that the remote endpoint can understand SOAP-based RPC messages. Following is a simple example of a Java interface that illustrates a ser- vice definition:

```
public interface BookDetailsProvider extends java.rmi.Remote {
    public string getAuthor(String isbn) throws
java.rmi.RemoteException;
...
...
...
}
```

Service implementation

The *service implementation* of a JAX-RPC service definition is a Java-based implementation. In other words, it is an implementation of the service definition within the J2SE or the J2EE framework. You can achieve the implementation of the service definition by using a Java class within the J2SE platform or by using EJB components to implement the service within the J2EE framework.

Usually, vendor-based wizards and tools guide the implementation of the service. Manual coding for implementing the service definition is also possible. In implementing a service definition, you can either implement it as a container-based service in which the container manages the life cycle of the service or you can explicitly code the complete invocation and event-management semantics of the service from scratch. The former is a better approach, as there are several standardized containers that handle different services such as transaction service and messaging service for you.

Service deployment

After you choose to create a service definition in Java and provide a service implementation for the definition, you can deploy the service. You deploy the service on the provider side of the Web services and the client on the consumer side. You also deploy the service within a JAX-RPC-based container.

The JAX-RPC container can be either a J2EE container for the EJB components or a J2SE container for Java classes. Either way, you use a deployment tool to deploy the service. The deployment tool enables you to deploy the components into the appropriate container. Usually the deployment tool is vendor-specific. In case of Sun-based tools, you use an xrpcc tool that comes bundled with the JWSD-pack. The deployment tool provides the protocol bindings for the service endpoints. The protocol binding actually ties an abstract service endpoint definition such as SOAP 1.1 to a specific transport protocol such as HTTP, FTP, or SMTP.

The deployment tool also generates a deployment configuration based on an associated binding for the service endpoint. You also use the deployment tool to export the service definition as a WSDL file. The consumers of the service use the WSDL file to identify the service methods that the service provider makes available. The consumers can then use the deployment tool to create a Java definition from the WSDL file. In other words, the deployment tool helps you in obtaining the Java-to-WSDL and WSDL-to-Java binding of the service definition.

Service invocation

The service invocation happens from the client endpoint. Usually, a client looks up a service definition on a central registry. More specifically, the client of the service looks up a WSDL file within a centralized registry such as UDDI. After the consumer finds the WSDL document, the consumer uses the deployment tool to generate a Java definition, known as the *stub* of the WSDL document. You can consider stub as a proxy representation of the remote Web-service implementation on the client side. The consumer can then use the stubs to invoke the remote service.

The consumer uses the appropriate vendor-based tool to generate the proxy on the client side. Any client program can use the proxy or the stub as a native Java object. As an alternative, the client is also free to choose a *Dynamic Invocation Interface (DII)* to invoke the services on the provider side. The DII enables a client to bind to the operations of the provider side without using the stubs. So the client can avoid the generation of stubs.

Service description

As stated in the previous sections, you can use the deployment tool to generate a WSDL file from a service definition. For all future sections, I refer to the following WSDL description:

```xml
<?xml version="1.0"?>

<definitions name="BookDetails"
targetNamespace="http://www.conceptuniv.com/bookdetails.wsdl"
xmlns:tns="http://www.conceptuniv.com/bookdetails.wsdl"
xmlns:xsd1="http://www.conceptuniv.com/bookdetails.xsd"
xmlns:soap="http://schemas.xmlsoap.org/wsdl/soap/"
xmlns="http://schemas.xmlsoap.org/wsdl/">

    <types>
        <schema
targetNamespace="http://www.conceptuniv.com/bookdetails.xsd"
            xmlns="http://www.w3.org/2000/10/XMLSchema">
          <element name="BookDetailsRequest">
            <complexType>
                <all>
                    <element name="ISBN" type="string"/>
                </all>
            </complexType>
          </element>
          <element name="BookDetails">
            <complexType>
                <all>
                        <element name="title" type="string"/>
                        <element name="author" type="string"/>
                        <element name="price" type="float"/>
                </all>
            </complexType>
          </element>
        </schema>
    </types>
```

```
<message name="GetBookDetailsInput">
    <part name="body" element="xsd1:BookDetailsRequest"/>
</message>

<message name="GetBookDetailsOutput">
    <part name="body" element="xsd1:BookDetails"/>
</message>

<portType name="BookDetailsPortType">
    <operation name="GetBookDetails">
        <input message="tns:GetBookDetailsInput"/>
        <output message="tns:GetBookDetailsOutput"/>
    </operation>
</portType>

    <binding name="BookDetailsSoapBinding"
type="tns:BookDetailsPortType">
    <soap:binding style="document"
transport="http://schemas.xmlsoap.org/soap/http"/>
    <operation name="GetBookDetails">
        <soap:operation
soapAction="http://www.conceptuniv.com/GetBookDetails"/>
        <input>
            <soap:body use="literal"/>
        </input>
        <output>
            <soap:body use="literal"/>
        </output>
    </operation>
</binding>

<service name="BookDetailsService">
    <documentation>My first service</documentation>
    <port name="BookDetailsPort"
binding="tns:BookDetailsSoapBinding">
        <soap:address
location="http://www.conceptuniv.com/bookdetails"/>
    </port>
</service>

</definitions>
```

JAX-RPC Mappings

The JAX-RPC specification suggests the mapping between the following types:

- ◆ XML to Java mapping

- ◆ WSDL to Java mapping

   The mapping helps in understanding how the XML types are represented in Java and vice versa. The mapping is also helpful in understanding the translation and conversion processes of different data types from XML to Java and also the conversion of other semantics such as the port type, operation, or fault from the WSDL file.

XML to Java mapping

This section specifies the mapping between the XML data types to the Java types. The serialization format for the XML data types are based on the SOAP encoding style as provided in the SOAP 1.1 specification.

   Table 11-1 specifies the simple XML types to Java types mapping as stated in the JAX-RPC specification.

TABLE 11-1 XML SIMPLE TYPES

XML simple type	Java data type
xsd:Boolean	boolean
xsd:byte	byte
xsd:short	short
xsd:int	int
xsd:long	long
xsd:float	float
xsd:double	double
xsd:string	java.lang.String
xsd:decimal	java.math.BigDecimal
xsd:integer	java.math.BigInteger
xsd:Qname	javax.xml.rpc.namespace.Qname
xsd:hexBinary	byte[]
xsd:base64binary	byte[]
xsd:dateTime	java.util.Calendar

Table 11-2 specifies the mapping from simple XML types to Java wrapper types. To achieve this mapping, the JAX-RPC specification states that the `nillable` attribute should be set to `true`, as shown in the following code:

```
<xsd:element name="code" type="xsd:int" nillable="true"/>
// Schema instance
<code xsi:nil="true"></code>
```

TABLE 11-2 XML TO JAVA WRAPPER TYPES

XML Simple type	Java wrapper types
xsd:boolean	java.lang.Boolean
xsd:byte	java.lang.Byte
xsd:short	java.lang.Short
xsd:int	java.lang.Integer
xsd:long	java.lang.Long
xsd:float	java.lang.Float
xsd:double	java.lang.Double

The SOAP-encoded types appropriately map to the Java wrapper types. As an example, if you have `soapenc:int` as a XML type, it relevantly maps to the `java.lang.Integer` type. The array types of the XML types with `soapenc` encoding or from the XSD schema appropriately map to the Java array types with the [] operator.

Following is an example illustrates how an XML array is mapped to a Java array:

```
<element name="colors" type="soapenc:Array"/>
<colors soapenc:arrayType="xsd:string[4]">
      <color>Black</color>
      <color>Blue</color>
      <color>Green</color>
      <color>Red</color>
</colors>
```

In the preceding code, an array maps to the `java.lang.Object` array type because the type of the array members is determinable only after inspecting the `soapenc:arrayType` attribute in the schema. Although the schema states that the `soapenc:arrayType` is `xsd:string`, the elements or the members do not determine the necessary type. In other words, the members are just described as `<color></color>` without explicitly determining the type.

The following array specifically creates a `String[]` array:

```
<complexType name="ColorsArray">
        <complexContent>
                <restriction base="soapenc:Array">
                        <sequence>
                                <element name="color"
                                type="xsd:string"
maxOccurs="unbounded"/>
                        </sequence>
                </restriction>
        </complexContent>
</complexType>
```

WSDL to Java mapping

A WSDL file provides the description and the definition for a service in the Web-services framework. The WSDL file is quite important within the service framework for publishing the services that the provider endpoint exposes. You need a vendor-specific tool such as the `xrpcc` tool to convert the WSDL file to a Java interface. This section provides the mapping between the WSDL elements and the appropriate Java syntax.

To begin, the `WSDL` `portType` and operation element is defined as follows:

```
<message name="GetBookDetailsInput">
        <part name="body" element="xsd1:BookDetailsRequest"/>
</message>

<message name="GetBookDetailsOutput">
        <part name="body" element="xsd1:BookDetails"/>
</message>

<portType name="BookDetailsPortType">
        <operation name="GetBookDetails">
                <input message="tns:GetBookDetailsInput"/>
                <output message="tns:GetBookDetailsOutput"/>
        </operation>
</portType>
```

The Java interface that is generated for the preceding WSDL file is as follows:

```
public interface BookDetailsPortType extends java.rmi.Remote {
```

```
        BookDetails GetBookDetails(BookDetailsRequest isbn) throws
java.rmi.RemoteException;
}
```

As you can see in the preceding code, the wsdl:portType element maps to a Java interface while the wsdl:operation element maps as methods within the service interface.

If the WSDL document defines a fault element within the operation, the mapping for the wsdl:fault element is as follows:

```
<message name="GetBookDetailsInput">
        <part name="body" element="xsdl:BookDetailsRequest"/>
</message>

<message name="GetBookDetailsOutput">
        <part name="body" element="xsdl:BookDetails"/>
</message>

<message name="BookDetailsException">
        <part name="body" type="xsd:string"/>
</message>

<portType name="BookDetailsPortType">
        <operation name="GetBookDetails">
                <input message="tns:GetBookDetailsInput"/>
                <output message="tns:GetBookDetailsOutput"/>
                <fault name="BookDetailsException"
message="tns:BookDetailsException"/>
        </operation>
</portType>
```

The relevant Java code for the preceding fault element is as follows:

```
public interface BookDetailsPortType extends java.rmi.Remote {
        BookDetails GetBookDetails(BookDetailsRequest isbn) throws
java.rmi.RemoteException, BookDetailsException;
}
```

The preceding code declares how to throw an exception of type BookDetailsException. BookDetailsException is a direct descendant of the java.lang.Exception type.

JAX-RPC does not provide any mapping for the wsdl:binding element. The wsdl:service element actually maps to the javax.xml.rpc.Service class. Consider the following mapping example:

```
<service name="BookDetailsService">
       <documentation>My first service</documentation>
       <port name="BookDetailsPort"
binding="tns:BookDetailsSoapBinding">
              <soap:address
location="http://www.conceptuniv.com/bookdetails"/>
       </port>
</service>
```

The generated service interface in Java is based on the following design pattern:

```
public interface <ServiceName> extends javax.xml.rpc.Service {
       <serviceEndpointInterface> get<Name_of_wsdl:port>()
       throws ServiceException;
// ... Additional getter methods
}
```

The WSDL file code generates the following service interface in Java:

```
public interface BookDetailsService extends javax.xml.rpc.Service {
       BookDetailsPortType getBookDetailsPort() throws
ServiceException;
}
```

The XML to Java mapping is similar to Java to XML mapping. The same holds true for WSDL to Java mapping.

The SOAP bindings and the SOAP with attachments binding I is discussed in Chapter 10. JAX-RPC uses the same set of APIs as recommended in the JAXM specification to produce the SOAP and SOAP-related messages that need to be sent.

JAX-RPC Programming Model

JAX-RPC is a set of API specifications that enables the Java programmer to make use of the underlying implementation of the RPC-style messaging provider. JAX-RPC specifies the following client-side APIs:

- `javax.xml.rpc.Service interface`
- `javax.xml.rpc.Stub interface`
- `javax.xml.rpc.Call interface`
- `javax.xml.rpc.ServiceFactory` class
- `javax.xml.rpc.JAXRPCException` class

The stated interfaces, classes, and exceptions make up the JAX-RPC client-side programming specification. Either a J2SE runtime container or a J2EE runtime service container provides a JAX-RPC runtime system implementation for these API specifications.

The client–programming model

According to the JAX-RPC specification, a client-programming model requires you to take care of certain considerations. The JAX-RPC requires that a client-programming model is transparent of the implementation details of the service endpoint. In other words, you can program a JAX-RPC client irrespective of the implementation on the server-side. The JAX-RPC client invokes any other Java-based service implementation or non-Java-based service implementation in a similar manner. The service client should also be capable of providing necessary conversion utilities to translate a WSDL definition available at the client's end. In other words, the client should be capable of generating the WSDL-to-Java bindings in the form of stubs and tie objects to expose the provider service as a native Java interface for the client-programming model. The JAX-RPC specification also states that the client-programming model should not provide any specific details about the bindings or the transportation semantics of the underlying network. In other words, the application that plans to use the JAX-RPC client interface should be unaware of how the JAX-RPC invocation takes place, what binding it uses to carry the message, and what kind of transport it provides to marshal the messages across the network.

The J2SE-based service client model uses the following approach to invoke a JAX-RPC service endpoint:

1. The service client first generates the necessary stub classes. To obtain the stub classes, the programmer may first need to run a conversion tool or a WSDL-to-Java compiler on the WSDL file.

2. After generating the stub classes, the service client uses the service interface within the javax.xml.rpc package to obtain a dynamic proxy for the provider endpoint.

3. After creating the Service object, the client can use the Service object to create a Call object that enables the service client to invoke the service at the provider's endpoint.

You're probably ready to see some examples based on the JAX-RPC specifications. To begin, you can actually consider the following two different approaches to code your JAX-RPC application:

◆ Java-centric: You start with a Java service interface and generate the appropriate WSDL file by using a Java-to-WSDL compiler. This approach is best suited for creating a WSDL model at the service provider end, where you may want to create service endpoints for other clients to access.

◆ **WSDL-centric:** In this approach, you start with a WSDL file and run a WSDL-to-Java compiler to obtain the necessary stubs. You can then use the stubs to invoke the implemented service on the provider end. Normally, you use this approach at the client end of a service.

Before you begin programming, you need to make sure that you download the JWSD pack and install it appropriately as discussed in Appendix E.

A simple echo example

This section illustrates how you can implement a simple echo service that echoes back the message that is sent to the service endpoint. The first thing that you do is to implement the service on the provider side. Because you are coding the service definition on the provider side first, you should use the Java-centric approach, as I discuss in the preceding section.

Following is the service definition code for the echo service:

```
package echo;
import java.rmi.Remote;
import java.rmi.RemoteException;

public interface EchoIF extends Remote {
    public String echo(String str) throws RemoteException;
}
```

Notice that you import the `rmi` package because the JAX-RPC messaging model is based on Java's RMI method invocation syntax. Notice, too, that the methods that you are declaring are throwing a `RemoteException` exception, in compliance with the JAX-RPC specification. The JAX_RPC specification states that all mappings of the `wsdl:operation` to the Java type should throw the `RemoteException` exception and any other application-specific exception.

The following class provides an implementation for the service definition that the `EchoIF` interface provides:

```
package echo;

public class EchoImpl implements EchoIF {
    public String echo(String str) {
        System.out.println("Echoing " + str + " back to the
client...");
        return new String("Echoing... " + str);
    }
}
```

After you create these files, you need to compile them under the same directory. For that, you can use the Ant build tool that comes with the JWSDP. The Ant built tool from Apache makes building and maintaining Java code easy. Ant is widely used in most of the enterprise-system development boxes. To execute Ant on the preceding Java files, you need to make sure that you create a build script. Following is a sample build script that you can use for the current example:

```xml
<!DOCTYPE project>

<project name="JAX-RPC: echo" default="setdir" basedir=".">

  <property environment="env" />
  <property file="build.properties"/>

  <target name="setdir"
     description="Creates build directory" >
     <echo message="Creating the directories..." />
     <mkdir dir="${build.dir}/${example-dir}" />
  </target>


  <target name="compile-server" depends="setdir"
      description="Compiles server-side code">
      <echo message="Compiling server-side code..."/>
      <javac
         srcdir="."
         destdir="${build.dir}"
         includes="*.java"
         excludes="*Client.java"
      />
  </target>

  <target name="xrpcc" depends="setdir"
      description="Runs the xrpcc tool for the example.">
      <echo message="Running xrpcc:"/>
      <echo message="${xrpcc} -classpath ${build.dir} -both -keep -d
${build.dir} config.xml"/>
      <echo message="xrpcc is running..."/>
      <exec executable="${xrpcc}">
         <arg line="-classpath ${build.dir}" />
         <arg line="-both" />
         <arg line="-keep" />
         <arg line="-d ${build.dir}" />
         <arg line="config.xml" />
      </exec>
  </target>
```

```xml
    <target name="compile-client" depends="setdir"
        description="Compiles client-side code"  >
        <echo message="Compiling client code..."/>
         <javac
           srcdir="."
           destdir="${build.dir}"
           classpath="${cpath}"
           includes="*Client.java"
        />
    </target>

    <target name="packagewar" depends="setdir"
        description="Builds WAR file">
        <echo message="Building war file..."/>
        <war warfile="${war-file}" webxml="web.xml">
            <classes dir="${build.dir}"
                     includes="${example-dir}/**" />
            <webinf dir="${build.dir}"
                     includes="${webinf-config}" />
        </war>
    </target>

    <target name="deploy"
        description="Copies WAR file to Catalina">
        <echo message="Copying war file to webapps..."/>
        <copy
           file="${war-file}"
           todir="${CATALINA_HOME}/webapps"
           overwrite="yes"
        />
    </target>

    <target name="run"
       description="Runs client">
       <echo message="Running the client..." />
<echo message=" " />
        <java
             fork="on"
             classpath="${cpath}"
             classname="${client-class}" >
            <arg value="${endpoint}" />
            <!-- <classpath  refid="jaxpack-classpath" /> -->
        </java>
   </target>
</project>
```

The preceding code provides you with the build script. Make sure that you save this code as a build.xml file within the same directory as the Java files that you create. In addition, ensure that you have the following build.properties file in the same directory:

```
# This file is referenced by the build.xml file.

release-version=Java(tm) Web Services Developer Pack EA1

script-suffix=bat
PACK_HOME=${env.JWSDP_HOME}
CATALINA_HOME=${env.JWSDP_HOME}
build.dir=build
webinf-config=MyEcho_Config.properties
xrpcc=${PACK_HOME}/bin/xrpcc.${script-suffix}
clib=${PACK_HOME}/common/lib
jwsdp-jars=${clib}/jaxrpc-ri.jar:${clib}/jaxrpc-
api.jar:${clib}/activation.jar:${clib}/dom4j.jar:${clib}/jaxm-api.ja
r:${clib}/jaxm-
client.jar:${clib}/log4j.jar:${clib}/mail.jar:${clib}/xalan.jar:${cl
ib}/xerces.jar
cpath=${jwsdp-jars}:${build.dir}

example-dir=echo
client-class=EchoClient
endpoint=http://localhost:8080/jaxrpc-echo/jaxrpc/EchoIF
webapps-subdir=jaxrpc-echo
war-file=${webapps-subdir}.war
```

You also must make sure that you set the JWSDP_HOME environment variable within the operating system. JWSDP_HOME points to the home directory where you installed the JWSD Pack. Ensure that the PATH environment variable is set to point to the %JWSDP_HOME%\bin directory.

After you set these variables, you need to compile the Java files by using the Ant tool. Type the following command at the command prompt. Make sure that you are within the same directory where you saved the Java files, the build.properties file and the build.xml file as you type this command:

```
Ant compile-server
```

After you execute the preceding code, the output is similar to that shown in Figure 11-2.

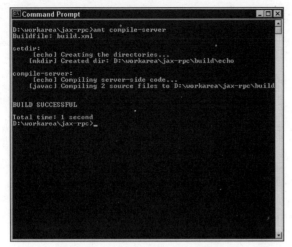

Figure 11-2: Output of the ant compile-server command

You should also locate two class files by the names `EchoIF.class` and `EchoImpl.class` under the `\build\echo` directory. If you can locate these files, you successfully created the service-side classes. Now you need to create a configuration file that enables you to create a WSDL definition of your class file.

Following is a basic syntax for a configuration file:

```xml
<?xml version="1.0" encoding="UTF-8"?>
<configuration
xmlns="http://java.sun.com/jax-rpc-ri/xrpcc-config">
  <rmi name="Model name"
      targetNamespace="Target Namespace for WSDL"
      typeNamespace="Target Namespace for the schema">
    <service name="Service Name"
      packageName="package name">
      <interface name=" Fully qualified name of the interface"
            servantName="Fully qualified name of the Impl"
            soapAction="Optional SoapAction string"
            soapActionBase="Optional prefix for SoapAction"/>
    </service>
  <typeMappingRegistry>
  Optional type mapping information
  </typeMappingRegistry>
  </rmi>
</configuration>
```

The following code provides the configuration file for the echo classes based on the preceding pattern. Make sure that you save the following file as `config.xml`:

```
<?xml version="1.0" encoding="UTF-8"?>
<configuration
   xmlns="http://java.sun.com/jax-rpc-ri/xrpcc-config">
   <rmi name="EchoService"
      targetNamespace="http://someuri.com/wsdl"
      typeNamespace="http://someuri.com/types">
      <service name="MyEcho" packageName="echo">
      <interface name="echo.EchoIF"
         servantName="echo.EchoImpl"/>
      </service>
   </rmi>
</configuration>
```

After you save the `config.xml` file, you need to generate the stubs and ties of the server-side classes that you created. For that, use the `xrpcc` tool that comes bundled with the JWSD Pack. By using the `xrpcc` tool, you can create the stubs and ties that you need to perform the remote-procedure call. You can relate these stubs with the concepts of RMI stubs.

You use the following code to execute the `xrpcc` tool and create the appropriate classes and properties file:

```
xrpcc.bat -classpath build -both -d build config.xml
```

Table 11-3 provides an explanation of the options in the `xrpcc` tool's syntax.

TABLE 11-3 XRPCC SYNTAX

Options	Description
-classpath classpath	Sets the CLASSPATH for the xrpcc tool.
-both	Generates both the client- and the server-side files.
-d directory	Outputs the generated files in the specified directory.
-client	Generates client-side files such as the remote interface, stubs, implementation classes, and service interface.
-server	Generates server-side files such as the service-definition interface, WSDL file, ties, and server configuration file.
-keep	Keeps the generated source files (*.java) after they generate.
-version	Shows the version number of JAX-RPC.

After you execute the `xrpcc` tool, the tool creates the following artifacts.
The classes that the tool creates under the `echo` directory are as follows:

- `Echo_RequestStruct.class`

- `Echo_RequestStruct_SOAPSerializer.class`

- `Echo_ResponseStruct.class`

- `Echo_ResponseStruct_SOAPSerializer.class`

- `EchoIF.class`

- `EchoIF_Stub.class`

- `EchoIF_Tie.class`

- `EchoImpl.class`

- `MyEcho.class`

- `MyEcho_SerializerRegistry.class`

- `MyEchoImpl.class`

The files that the tool creates under the `build` directory are as follows:

- `MyEcho_Config.properties`

- `EchoService.wsdl`

Figure 11-3 provides an overview of the execution process of the `xrpcc` tool.

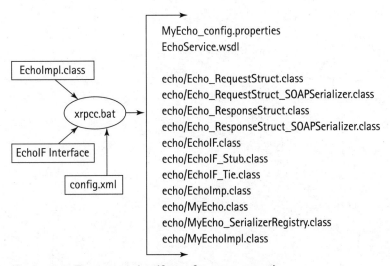

Figure 11-3: The generated artifacts after xrpcc execution

The output of the `Echo_Config.properties` file is similar to that of the following code:

```
# This file is generated by xrpcc.

port0.tie=echo.EchoIF_Tie
port0.servant=echo.EchoImpl
port0.name=EchoIF
port0.wsdl.targetNamespace=http://someuri.com/wsdl
port0.wsdl.serviceName=MyEcho
port0.wsdl.portName=EchoIFPort
portcount=1
```

The output of the `EchoService.wsdl` file is similar that of to the following code:

```
<?xml version="1.0" encoding="UTF-8"?>

<definitions name="EchoService"
targetNamespace="http://someuri.com/wsdl"
xmlns:tns="http://someuri.com/wsdl"
xmlns="http://schemas.xmlsoap.org/wsdl/"
xmlns:soap="http://schemas.xmlsoap.org/wsdl/soap/"
xmlns:xsd="http://www.w3.org/2001/XMLSchema">
  <types/>
  <message name="echo">
    <part name="String_1" type="xsd:string"/>
  </message>
  <message name="echoResponse">
    <part name="result" type="xsd:string"/>
  </message>
  <portType name="EchoIFPortType">
    <operation name="echo">
      <input message="tns:echo"/>
      <output message="tns:echoResponse"/>
    </operation>
  </portType>
  <binding name="EchoIFBinding" type="tns:EchoIFPortType">
    <operation name="echo">
      <input>
        <soap:body
encodingStyle="http://schemas.xmlsoap.org/soap/encoding/"
use="encoded" namespace="http://someuri.com/wsdl"/>
      </input>
      <output>
        <soap:body
encodingStyle="http://schemas.xmlsoap.org/soap/encoding/"
```

```
use="encoded" namespace="http://someuri.com/wsdl"/>
      </output>
      <soap:operation soapAction=""/></operation>
   <soap:binding transport="http://schemas.xmlsoap.org/soap/http" ⏎
style="rpc"/>
   </binding>
  <service name="MyEcho">
   <port name="EchoIFPort" binding="tns:EchoIFBinding">
     <soap:address location="REPLACE_WITH_ACTUAL_URL"/>
   </port>
  </service>
</definitions>
```

After you finish generating the appropriate stubs, ties, and configuration files, the next step is to prepare a deployment descriptor for the Apache Tomcat 4.1-dev Container (Catalina server) that comes bundled with the JWSD-pack.

Refer to Appendix E for more information regarding the Java Web Service Developer Pack and the Tomcat container (Catalina server) setup.

The following code describes the web.xml file, which is nothing but the deployment descriptor for the Catalina server:

```
<?xml version="1.0" encoding="UTF-8"?>

<!DOCTYPE web-app
    PUBLIC "-//Sun Microsystems, Inc.//DTD Web Application 2.3//EN"
    "http://java.sun.com/j2ee/dtds/web-app_2_3.dtd">

<web-app>
  <display-name>
      EchoApplication
  </display-name>
  <description>
     Echo Application
  </description>
  <servlet>
    <servlet-name>
           JAXRPCEndpoint
    </servlet-name>
    <display-name>
           JAXRPCEndpoint
```

```
            </display-name>
            <description>
                    Endpoint for Echo Application
        </description>
        <servlet-class>
                    com.sun.xml.rpc.server.http.JAXRPCServlet
          </servlet-class>
          <init-param>
               <param-name>
                        configuration.file
          </param-name>
               <param-value>
                        /WEB-INF/MyEcho_Config.properties
          </param-value>
          </init-param>
          <load-on-startup>
                     0
          </load-on-startup>
      </servlet>
      <servlet-mapping>
         <servlet-name>
                  JAXRPCEndpoint
          </servlet-name>
          <url-pattern>
                  /jaxrpc/*
          </url-pattern>
      </servlet-mapping>
      <session-config>
         <session-timeout>
                  60
            </session-timeout>
      </session-config>
</web-app>
```

In the preceding deployment descriptor, you specify the servlet mappings to the servlet com.sun.xml.rpc.server.http.JAXRPCServlet. This servlet obtains the configuration details from the Echo_Config.properties file, which you must copy under the /WEB-INF directory of the webapps\root directory of your Catalina server. Notice that you save the web.xml file (the deployment descriptor) under the WEB-INF directory. If you do not want to manually move these files to the appropriate directories, you can package the contents into a WAR file and deploy them on the server by using the Ant tool.

To package the service definition into a WAR file, you need to execute the following command:

```
ant packagewar
```

After you execute the preceding command, a `jaxrpc-echo.war` file is created under the current directory.

The output of this command is similar to that shown in Figure 11-4.

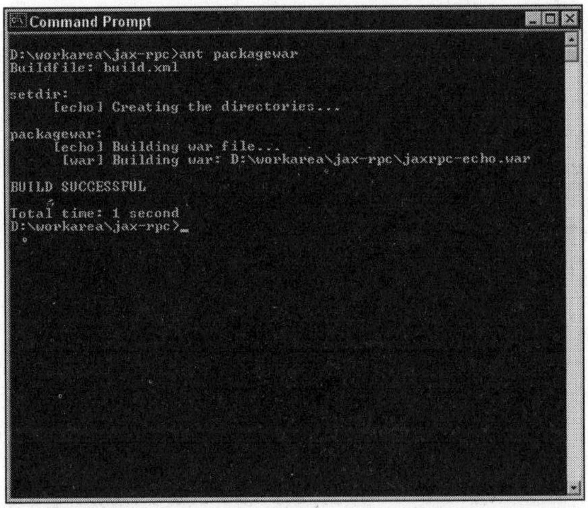

Figure 11-4: The output of the ant packagewar command

The contents of the WAR files are as follows:

◆ One or more service definition interfaces

◆ One or more service definition classes that implement the interfaces

◆ The `xrpcc` generated files such as `tie`, `helper`, `servlet`, and `Echo_Config.properties`

◆ Classes for pluggable serializers and deserializers

◆ Other files required by the service-implementation classes

◆ A deployment descriptor

◆ An optional WSDL file that describes the service

After creating the WAR package, you can deploy the package into the Catalina server. If you have started the server, shut it down before deployment.

To deploy the package, execute the following command on the command prompt:

```
ant deploy
```

After you execute the preceding code, you see output similar to that shown in Figure 11-5.

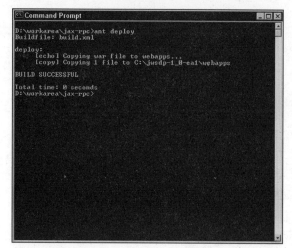

Figure 11-5: Output of the ant deploy command

You should also find the `jaxrpc-echo.war` file under the `%JWSDP_HOME%\` `webapps` directory. The contents in the `jaxrpc-echo.war` file look similar to the one shown in Figure 11-6.

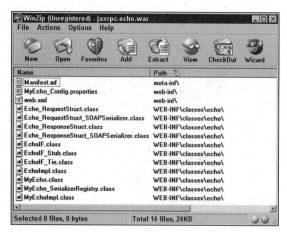

Figure 11-6: Contents within the jaxrpc-echo.war file

To verify the deployment, follow these steps:

1. Start the Catalina server by executing the following command:

   ```
   startup
   ```

   The output on the console is similar to that shown in Figure 11-7.

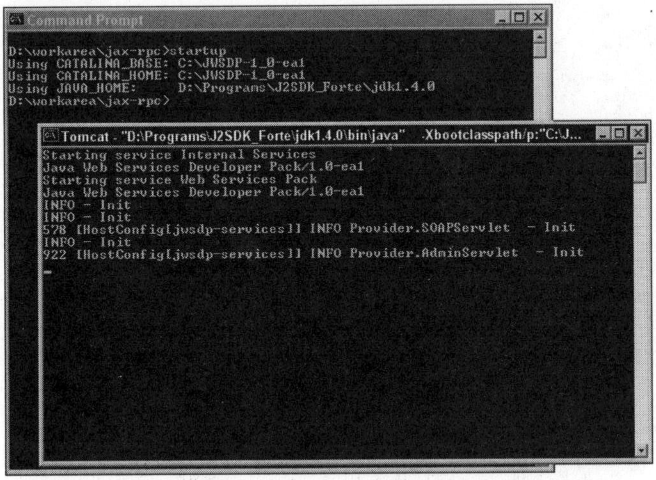

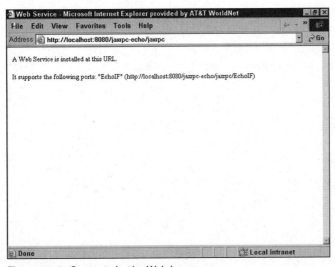

Figure 11-7: Output after starting the Catalina server

2. To make sure that the service is accessible, open a browser window and type the following URL in the browser's address bar:

```
http://localhost:8080/jaxrpc-echo/jaxrpc
```

After you execute the preceding step, you should find that you can view the page that displays a message indicating that your service has been deployed in the Web browser, as shown in Figure 11-8.

Figure 11-8: Contents in the Web browser

After successfully implementing a service at the endpoint, you can create a client to execute the service.

Following is the code for the EchoClient program:

```
package echo;

public class EchoClient {
    public static void main(String[] args) {
        try {
            EchoIF_Stub stub = (EchoIF_Stub)(new
MyEchoImpl().getEchoIF());
            System.out.println("Obtained the stub object...");
            System.out.println("Setting the target endpoint to " +
args[0]);
            stub._setTargetEndpoint(args[0]);
            System.out.println("Invoking the echo method on the
stub...");
            System.out.println(stub.echo("Say something..."));
        } catch (Exception ex) {
            ex.printStackTrace();
        }
    }
}
```

EchoClient is a standalone program that calls the echo operation from the provider service's endpoint. You need to compile the service before executing the service. Compile the service by using the following command:

```
ant compile-client
```

The output of the preceding command is as shown in Figure 11-9.
Finally, use the following command to execute the program:

```
ant run
```

The output of the program is similar to that shown in Figure 11-10.

Figure 11-9: Output of the ant compile-client command

Figure 11-10: Output of the client program

Summary

JAX-RPC is the most important component within the Web-services framework. This chapter explains that JAX-RPC is a service-oriented architecture, which enables Java-based execution of the Web-services framework.

This chapter covers the service definition of a JAX-RPC framework. It provides a brief overview of the implementation and deployment scenarios of the JAX-RPC framework. Then the chapter provides details on JAX-RPC mapping with XML, WSDL, and Java perspectives. Finally, the chapter discusses the JAX-RPC programming model and provides a simple example to invoke a Web service from within a standalone Java client.

Chapter 12

JAXR

IN THIS CHAPTER

- ◆ Overview of JAXR
- ◆ The JAXR programming model
- ◆ JAXR examples

IN THE CURRENT WEB-SERVICES SCENARIO, a business registry plays an important role in facilitating business transactions on the Web. Web-service providers typically use the business registry to publish their services. They advertise the business information that clients need to know to use their services in the business registry. Web-service clients use the business registries to look for various published services and the information associated with them. Currently, you can find various specifications for business registries, such as OASIS, eCo Framework, ebXML, and UDDI. These registries are also known as *XML-based registries*. The *Java API for XML Registries (JAXR)* is a general-purpose Java API that you use to access these XML-based business registries. JAXR specifies a pluggable architecture to support the diverse registry specifications and standards available in the industry.

 JAXR, like other Java APIs for XML, is an initiative of the JCP organization. As of this writing, the JAXR specification is at Version 0.9, which is a proposed final draft. The JSR for the specification is JSR-93 and is available at `http://jcp.org/jsr/detail/93.jsp`.

Overview of JAXR

The JAXR API is an open and interoperable standard for accessing disparate registry standards in the industry. These registries are predominantly based on XML standards and are, therefore, known as *XML registries*. XML registries form the base infrastructure of Web-services architecture and provide the necessary functionality to bind, deploy, and discover the services within a Web-services framework. In other words, an XML registry sits between a service provider and a service

343

client to provide a standard for communicating XML-based messages between them. But the question of interoperability arises as the different registry specifications follow different communication standards.

As an example, you can consider OASIS or ebXML as open-standards organizations defining distributed registry specifications. UDDI is another registry standard. The industry leaders have formed a consortium (UDDI community) that controls the current direction of the UDDI specification.

JAXR is a uniform API standard that enables access to information across all these registry standards. By using the JAXR API, Java applications can easily access information across disparate registries. The JAXR API works along with its related APIs, such as the Java API for XML Processing (JAXP), Java API for XML Binding (JAXB), Java API for XML-based RPC (JAX-RPC), and Java API for XML Messaging (JAXM), to provide robust, interoperable Java-enabled Web services. The JAXR specification takes advantage of different prevalent industry standards such as OASIS, ISO 11179, UDDI, and the ebXML registry working group.

A key difference between JAXR and the XML-based business registries is that, JAXR is an API specification that defines Java interfaces to access and work on the XML-based business registries, while the XML registries are based on industry standards that hold information about a Web service inside the registry in the form of objects.

JSR-93 defines the JAXR specification. It states that the JSR is aimed only at defining the standard Java APIs that enable convenient access to the XML registries from within the Java application.

Any Java-based client can access different registry sources by using the JAXR API. Figure 12-1 provides an overview of JAXR clients accessing disparate registries by using the JAXR API.

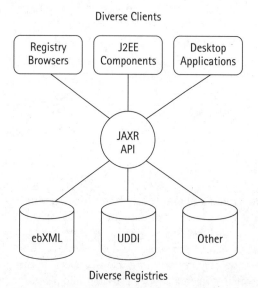

Figure 12-1: Interoperability between Java-based clients and disparate registry standards

XML registries

A *registry* is a service broker that helps in the collaborative process between multiple business-to-business endpoints. Enterprises can use the concept of shared registries as a standard infrastructure to enable B2B operations across the Web. A registry enables clients to look up and discover Web-services components that businesses bind and deploy on such registries. Registries integrate disparate Web services so that they can interoperate by using a common standard. In other words, registries enable the dynamic discovery and integration of Web-services components across the Internet.

XML registries are based on the XML standards. The collaborative processes between disparate endpoints are based on XML messaging. XML registries incorporate the use of the XML schema standards and XML data-encoding standards. Such XML-based standards help in providing smooth interoperability among systems built on different architectures. An XML registry is the key technology used to promote the concept of loose coupling over a huge, distributed environment such as the Internet.

Figure 12-2 provides an overview of the collaborative process between different enterprises participating in the B2B interchange.

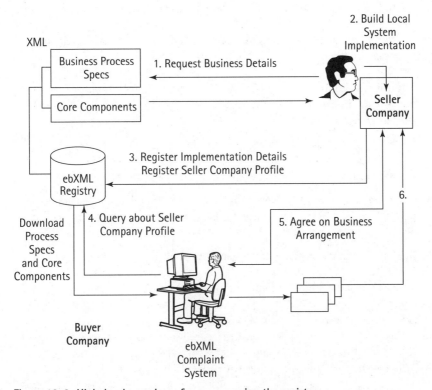

Figure 12-2: High-level overview of a process using the registry

The steps involved in the process are pretty simple. The seller company initiates a query to the registry and obtains from the XML registry a specifications document based on XML standards. The specifications that the seller company obtains define the collaborative business process for a B2B interchange. The seller company uses the definitions in the collaborative business specifications to implement a business system that conforms to the collaborative standards. (The collaborative standards are actually provided by a standards organization such as OASIS or eCo Framework.) After the seller company implements a business system, the company registers information about its services and products to the XML registry. A buyer company uses such registered information to obtain details of the products and services that a potential seller offers. Initially, the buyer company looks up or browses the shared XML registry. The buyer can also query the registry based on various criteria, such as the name of a seller company, geographical preferences, or specific services. After identifying a potential seller, the buyer company can download the published information and relevant conformance documents from the registry. The buyer can implement a buyer-side integration framework conforming to the technical specifications of the seller's systems. After the buyer implements such a system (probably dynamically) that conforms to the specifications promulgated by the seller, the buyer can start negotiating with the seller on a business agreement about the collaborative processes that the seller offers. On successful conclusion of the agreement, the buyer and seller interchange business-specific documents and other core Web-services components across the Internet.

The collaborative process involves different roles of operation. The following list summarizes these roles:

- **Submitting organization (SO):** The *submitting organization,* or the SO, is a business enterprise that submits business-specific collaborative information to a shared registry.

- **Content submitter:** A *content submitter* is a person who is authorized to submit the contents of a business or business-specific collaborative information to the registry. The content submitter acts on the behalf of the SO.

- **Registry operator:** The *registry operator* is an organization that controls and administers the registry. The registry operator is responsible for managing the runtime processes of a registry.

- **Registry Guest:** A *registry guest* is a nonprivileged casual user of the registry. The guest can only browse the registry, without altering the contents. The guest cannot submit or delete any content from the registry.

The registry acts as electronic yellow pages, where enterprises publish their specifications and in which other business entities can look up and discover the registry. The UDDI specification provides a detailed perspective about such registry services such as *White Pages, Yellow Pages,* and *Green Pages.*

You can find more details about UDDI registry services in Chapter 5.

In fact, almost all the registries provide a classification mechanism similar to UDDI. The XML registries provide classification mechanisms to segment the information published in the registry. This classification is based on criteria such as organization name, geographical location, industry classification, product classification, or services that a given organization offers. A registry also acts as a *content store* (similar to a database) in which the published content of different enterprises is stored. The content is actually stored in a *repository*. A registry and a repository are commonly confused terms in the industry. A repository is a container that can hold content and is a component of a registry. In other words, the registry manages the repository. The registry manages access to the content stored in the repository. The JAXR specification does not enable direct access to a repository. The only way to add contents to a repository is through the registry.

The JAXR specification supports the concept of a JAXR provider and a JAXR client. The JAXR provider is an implementation of the JAXR API. Different vendors can provide such implementation. A JAXR client is an application that uses the JAXR API to talk to the JAXR provider. As stated in the preceding section, the JAXR specification supports the usage of multiple registry standards such as UDDI and ebXML.

Capability profiles

The JAXR specification classifies its API into a number of *capability profiles*. A capability profile specifies and documents the capability of a JAXR component. As of this writing, only two such profiles are available. They are *level-0 profile* and *level-1 profile*. The capability level within the JAXR specification is assigned to the following components of the specification:

◆ **Methods in the JAXR API:** The methods in the JAXR API are assigned a capability level. The methods that are assigned the level-0 capability profile provide the most basic registry features, while the methods that are assigned the level-1 capability profile provide advanced registry features. The Javadoc for the JAXR API lists the capability level for all the methods.

◆ **JAXR providers:** The JAXR provider is an implementation of the JAXR API. The provider should implement all the methods within the JAXR API conforming to a specific profile. In other words, if a JAXR provider claims to support the level-0 profile, the provider must implement all methods marked as level-0 profile in the JAXR API. For all the other methods, which are marked as level 1, the JAXR provider must implement them to throw an `UnsupportedCapabilityException` exception. If a JAXR provider is level-1 compliant, the provider should not only implement level-1 methods from the JAXR API, but should also implement level-0 methods. In other words, a JAXR provider that is level-1 compliant is essentially level-0 compliant as well.

◆ **Registry standards:** According to the JAXR specification, JAXR providers that support UDDI should be level-0 compliant, while JAXR providers that support ebXML should be level-1 compliant.

The classes and interfaces within a JAXR API do not have a capability level. Only methods are marked for their levels. In addition, the JAXR clients by definition do not have a capability level. The clients can be built to support only the level-0 profile. In such a case, a level-0 compliant client can access all the JAXR providers and registries available in the industry because the level-0 capability profile is a default profile that all providers and registries in the industry must support. The clients written for the level-1 profile can access only level-1-compliant JAXR providers.

The JAXR Programming Model

The JAXR programming model enables developers to write simple application logic that takes advantage of the underlying JAXR API. The JAXR provider further implements the JAXR API. The JAXR provider is a component that sits between the JAXR API and the registry. Virtually, the provider sits between the JAXR client and the XML registry. The advantage of using the JAXR API is that the Java client can take advantage of the portability standards of the Java language so that it can run on different platforms while still leveraging the interoperability standards of the JAXR API to access any registries.

The JAXR programming model consists of a multitude of components within the architecture of the model. A very high-level overview of the JAXR architecture consists of the JAXR client and the JAXR provider. The client uses the JAXR API to access a registry. The JAXR provider sits in between the JAXR API and the registry, so access to the registry should follow the implementation of the JAXR provider.

Figure 12-3 provides a high-level overview of all the components involved in JAXR architecture.

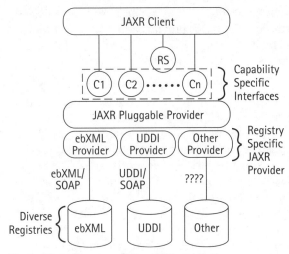

Figure 12-3: Overview of the JAXR architecture

Following are the components within the JAXR architecture:

◆ **JAXR client:** The *JAXR client* is a Java-based application that uses the JAXR API to access the JAXR-provider implementation. You can program the JAXR client as a standalone Java client or a J2EE-based application.

◆ **Connection interface:** The `Connection` *interface* is an object that represents an active session between the JAXR client and the XML registry (via the JAXR provider). The `Connection` object maintains the conversational state between the JAXR client and the XML registry. The JAXR client uses the `ConnectionFactory` to obtain the `Connection` object.

◆ **RegistryService:** `RegistryService` is an interface that the JAXR provider implements. The client obtains reference to a `RegistryService` by using the `Connection` object. The client can use `RegistryService` to obtain information about the capability profile of the JAXR provider. After gaining the knowledge of the capability profile, the client can appropriately access the interfaces that the JAXR provider implements.

◆ **Capability Specific interfaces:** The *Capability Specific interfaces* that a JAXR provider implements enable a client to access capabilities such as life-cycle management or query management.

◆ **JAXR provider:** The *JAXR provider* is a component that sits between the JAXR client and the XML registry. The JAXR provider implements the JAXR API and exposes the implementation to the JAXR client. The three main types of JAXR providers are as follows:

- **JAXR pluggable provider:** The *JAXR pluggable provider* is an abstraction of multiple registry-specific JAXR providers. In other words, the JAXR pluggable provider implements only those features of the JAXR API that are not specific to any particular registry.

- **Registry-specific JAXR provider:** The *registry-specific provider* implements the features of the JAXR API that are specific to a given registry. The JAXR registry-specific provider first receives a JAXR request from a client. The JAXR registry-specific provider then transforms the client's request to a registry-specific request according to the specification of the particular registry on which the request is based. The JAXR registry-specific provider then delegates the registry-specific request to the registry provider by using a protocol that's specific to the registry. The registry provider processes the request and returns a registry-specific response to the registry-specific provider. The registry-specific provider then transforms the registry-specific response into a general JAXR response and sends the response to the client.

- **JAXR bridge provider:** A *bridge provider* is an implementation for accessing a specific class of registries. A *registry class* is a group of all the registries compliant to a specific registry protocol. For example, all the registries compliant to UDDI specifications belong to the class of UDDI registry, while all the registries compliant to ebXML specifications belong to the class of ebXML registry. The *JAXR bridge provider* acts as a bridge between a JAXR client and such classes of registries. For example, a *UDDI bridge provider* acts as a bridge so that a client can access all the registries that conform to the specifications of the UDDI.

- ◆ **Registry provider:** The *registry provider* is a specific implementation of a registry standard such as UDDI and ebXML.

JAXR API

The *JAXR API* is the crucial standards-based interface between the JAXR client and the JAXR provider component. This section explains the JAXR API defined in the specification.

The JAXR API is divided into the following sections:

- ◆ **The `javax.xml.registry` API:** This package bundles the classes and interfaces that enable access to a registry. The API defines the access to the objects within the registry.

- ◆ **The `javax.xml.registry.infomodel` API:** This package bundles the interfaces that define the JAXR information model. The API defines the objects that are contained within the registry.

Following is a list of some of the important interfaces with brief descriptions, as defined by the `javax.xml.registry` API:

◆ **BulkResponse:** The `BulkResponse` interface contains the response of many methods of the API that return a response comprising a collection of objects.

◆ **BusinessLifeCycleManager:** The `BusinessLifeCycleManager` provides the capability to manage the life cycle of the instances of some important interfaces such as the `Organization`, `Service`, `ServiceBinding`, and `Concept` interfaces.

◆ **BusinessQueryManager:** The `BusinessQueryManager` provides the capability to query most of the important high-level interfaces of the information model.

◆ **CapabilityProfile:** The `CapabilityProfile` interface contains the `getCapabilityLevel()` and `getCapabilityVersion()` methods to provide the capability information of a JAXR provider.

◆ **Connection:** The `Connection` interface represents and maintains the state information of a connection between a JAXR client and a JAXR provider.

◆ **DeclarativeQueryManager:** The `DeclarativeQueryManager` interface provides the `createQuery(int queryType, String queryString)` and `executeQuery(Query query)` methods to perform queries by using a declarative query-language syntax. Currently, it supports only SQL-92 declarative syntax.

◆ **Federation:** The `Federation` interface is a subinterface of the `Connection` interface. The `Federation` interface represents a single logical connection to multiple registry providers.

◆ **JAXRResponse:** The `JAXRResponse` interface represents a response to a JAXR request.

◆ **LifeCycleManager:** The `LifeCycleManager` interface provides methods to support life-cycle management needs of objects defined by the information model.

◆ **Query:** The `Query` interface represents a query in a declarative query language. Currently, only SQL query is supported.

◆ **QueryManager:** The `QueryManager` interface acts as the base interface for the `DeclarativeQueryManager` and the `BusinessQueryManager` interfaces.

◆ **RegistryService:** The `RegistryService` interface is the main interface that the JAXR provider implements. A client uses the methods of the `RegistryService` interface to access various capability-specific interfaces that the JAXR provider implements.

Following is a list of exceptions defined by the `javax.xml.registry` API:

- **DeleteException:** This exception is thrown if a partial commit occurs at the time of any `delete***` operations within the `LifeCycleManager` or `BusinessLifeCycleManager` interfaces. The `***` represents a wildcard.

- **FindException:** This exception is thrown if a partial commit occurs at the time of any `find***` operations within the `BusinessQueryManager` interface.

- **InvalidRequestException:** If a JAXR client tries to invoke an API method that is not valid for some reason, this exception occurs.

- **JAXRException:** This exception is the base for other exceptions such as `DeleteException` and `FindException`.

- **SaveException:** This exception is thrown if a partial commit occurs at the time of any `save***` operations within the `LifeCycleManager` or `BusinessLifeCycleManager` interfaces.

- **UnexpectedObjectException:** This exception is thrown if the JAXR provider finds an object of the wrong type within the context of a user request.

- **UnsupportedCapabilityException:** This exception is thrown if a JAXR client tries to invoke an API method that is not supported by the capability profile that the JAXR provider supports.

In addition to the aforementioned interfaces and exceptions, the `javax.xml.registry` API also defines the `ConnectionFactory` class, which is discussed in the section "The ConnectionFactory and Connection objects."

Following is a list of interfaces defined by the `javax.xml.registry.infomodel` API:

- `Association`

- `AuditableEvent`

- `Classification`

- `ClassificationScheme`

- `Concept`

- `EmailAddress`

- `ExtensibleObject`

- `ExternalIdentifier`

- `ExternalLink`

- `ExtrinsicObject`

- ◆ InternationalString

- ◆ Key

- ◆ LocalizedString

- ◆ Organization

- ◆ PersonName

- ◆ PostalAddress

- ◆ RegistryEntry

- ◆ RegistryObject

- ◆ RegistryPackage

- ◆ Service

- ◆ ServiceBinding

- ◆ Slot

- ◆ SpecificationLink

- ◆ TelephoneNumber

- ◆ User

- ◆ Versionable

The following section provides brief explanations of some of the important interfaces in the preceding list.

Registry information model

The registry information model specifies a high-level schema for a registry. The information model provides access to the metadata type stored in the registry. It defines the types of objects stored in the registry and the organization of the stored objects. Both ebXML and UDDI support the concepts of such blueprints for the contents stored in the registry. ebXML has an *ebXML Registry Information Model* (*ebRIM*) specification while the UDDI has a *Data Structure* specification to define the types of the contents in the registry.

The JAXR information model is heavily based on the ebRIM specifications rather than on the UDDI data structures, because the ebRIM specification provides a generic model that is flexible and extensible compared to the UDDI data structures.

Figure 12-4 provides a high-level public view of the registry information model. This figure determines the most visible objects in the JAXR registries.

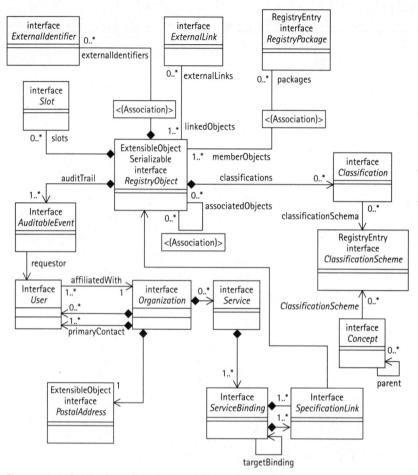

Figure 12-4: Public view of the registry information model

Following are the components in the public view of the information model:

◆ **RegistryObject:** The `RegistryObject` interface provides minimal meta-data for the registry objects. This interface is the base for most of the interfaces in the `javax.xml.registry.infomodel` package.

◆ **Organization:** The `Organization` interface provides information on organizations such as the SO. The `Organization` instance may contain references to the parent organization, contact information, or address of an organization.

◆ **Service:** The `Service` interface provides the details of service provided by a specific organization. The `Service` instance maps to the BusinessService in UDDI.

- **ServiceBinding:** The `ServiceBinding` interface provides technical information about a specific service of a business organization. The `ServiceBinding` instance maps to the `BindingTemplate` in UDDI.

- **SpecificationLink:** The `SpecificationLink` interface provides a reference to the technical specification of `ServiceBinding`. You use the `SpecificationLink` interface like a union of `tModelInstanceInfo` and `instanceDetails` in UDDI.

- **RegistryPackage:** The `RegistryPackage` interface groups logically related `RegistryEntry` interfacestogether. The package can contain many `RegistryObject` objects.

- **ExternalIdentifier:** The `ExternalIdentifier` interface provides additional information about `RegistryObject`. Some examples are social security number and DUNS number.

- **ExternalLink:** The `ExternalLink` interface represents a URI link to the contents that reside outside the registry. An example is a DTD submitted as a `RegistryObject` that contains external links to the home page of a submitting organization.

- **Classification:** You use the `Classification` interface to classify `RegistryObject` in the registry information model. This usage helps in faster access to the registry objects in the registry.

- **ClassificationScheme:** The `ClassificationScheme` interface denotes the taxonomy that you use to categorize the `RegistryObject` instance. The taxonomy can be anything – for example, the eBusiness classification such as the North American Industry Classification System (NAICS) or the United Nations/Standards Products and Services Classification (UN/SPSC).

- **Concept:** The `Concept` interface represents the elements and structural relationship between the elements within the taxonomy. You use the instances of the `Concept` interface to outline tree structures in which the root of the tree is `ClassificationScheme` and each node is a `Concept` instance.

- **Association:** The `Association` interface defines a many-to-many association between different `RegistryObject` objects in the registry information model. An example of an `Association` interface is the association between two `ClassificationScheme` instances.

- **Slot:** The `Slot` interface represents a dynamic mechanism that enables you to add attributes to a `RegistryObject` object. A `Slot` consists of a name, a `slotType` and a collection of values. `RegistryObject` may have 0 or more slots.

- **ExtensibleObject:** The `ExtensibleObject` interface provides a mechanism to add, delete, or look up `Slot` instances within a `RegistryObject` object.

◆ **AuditableEvent:** The `AuditableEvent` interface provides a long-term record of events that occur in the registry. The events are based on client requests. Such events affect the life cycle of `RegistryObject`.

◆ **User:** The `User` interface provides information about the registered users in the registry.

◆ **PostalAddress:** The `PostalAddress` interface defines the attributes of the `PostalAddress` of a `RegistryObject`.

The ConnectionFactory and Connection objects

The `Connection` object denotes the active connection between a JAXR client and a registry provider. It manages the state of the connection. This section provides the details about the JAXR provider managing connections between the JAXR client and the XML registry.

To begin with, a JAXR client should be capable of initiating a connection with the registry. To obtain a `Connection` object, the JAXR client should obtain a reference to `ConnectionFactory`. The preferred way to obtain a `Connection` object is to look up a JNDI tree by name. An alternative way to obtain a `ConnectionFactory` object is to call the `ConnectionFactory.newInstance()` method. This call returns a default `ConnectionFactory` object specified by the JAXR provider. `ConnectionFactory` is always registered in a manner specific to a given provider.

After the JAXR client obtains the `ConnectionFactory` instance, the client can set the properties of the `ConnectionFactory` instance. Table 12-1 specifies different connection properties that a client can set to the `ConnectionFactory` instance.

TABLE 12-1 STANDARD CONNECTION PROPERTIES

Property	Data type	Meaning
Javax.xml.registry. lifeCycleManagerURL	String	This property specifies the URL to the life-cycle manager service within the registry.
Javax.xml.registry. queryManagerURL	String	This property specifies the URL to the query manager service within the registry.
Javax.xml.registry. semanticEquivalence	String	This property specifies the semantic equivalence between two different concepts in the registry.
Javax.xml.registry.uddi. maxRows	Integer	This property specifies the maximum rows to return in a Find operation.
Javax.xml.registry.security. authenticationMethod	String	This property specifies the authentication mechanism to use to authenticate the registry provider.

After the JAXR client sets appropriate properties (by using the `Properties` object) of the `ConnectionFactory`, the client can obtain a `Connection` object by calling the `createConnection()` method of the `ConnectionFactory` instance. The `createConnection()` method checks to determine whether the `Javax.xml.registry.queryManagerURL` property is defined. If the property is not defined, the call raises an `InvalidRequestException` exception.

The JAXR client can choose to denote the type of the `Connection` object. In other words, the client can set the *synchronicity* or the *asynchronicity* of the connection. If the client wants a synchronous use of the `Connection` object, the client can call the `setSynchronous()` method on the `Connection` object by passing a Boolean `true` as a argument. If the client wants an asynchronous connection, the client calls a `setSynchronous()` method by passing a Boolean `false`.

After the JAXR client obtains a `Connection` object, the client can use the connection to obtain different capability-specific interfaces to access the life-cycle manager or the query manager of the registry.

Finally, the client can close a connection by calling the `close()` method of the `Connection` instance.

The following example enables you to obtain a `Connection` object within the client application:

```
import javax.xml.registry.*;
...
...


ConnectionFactory factory =
(ConnectionFactory)ctx.lookup("javax.xml.registry.ConnectionFactory"
);

Properties props = new Properties();
props.put("javax.xml.registry.factoryClass",
"com.sun.xml.registry.uddi.connectionFactoryImpl");
props.put("javax.xml.registry.queryManagerURL",
"http://java.sun.com/uddi/inquiry");
props.put("javax.xml.registry.lifeCycleManagerURL",
"http://java.sun.com/uddi/publish");

factory.setProperties(props);
Connection connection = factory.createConnection();
...
...
connection.setSynchronous(false);

RegistryService rs = connection.getRegistryService();
BusinessLifeCycleManager lcm = rs.getBusinessLifeCycleManager();
```

The LifeCycleManager and BusinessLifeCycleManager interfaces

The life cycle of a `RegistryObject` starts from the creation of the `RegistryObject` and continues until it is deleted. Operations that are performed on the `RegistryObject` are known as the *life-cycle operations*. Some common life-cycle operations that you perform on the `RegistryObject` are as follows:

- Creating the `RegistryObject`
- Updating the `RegistryObject`
- Deleting the `RegistryObject`

The `LifeCycleManager` and the `BusinessLifeCycleManager` interfaces provide a way to manage the life-cycle operations of a `RegistryObject` object. The `LifeCycleManager` interface provides a generic way to access the life cycle of a `RegistryObject` object, while `BusinessLifeCycleManager` provides the common life cycles of key business objects in an explicit API. The use of these interfaces is possible only through a privileged user who is authenticated by a registry's security manager.

The `LifeCycleManager` interface has several factory methods confirming to the naming pattern `create<interface>`. The *`<interface>`* in the naming pattern represents the name of interface within the `javax.xml.registry.infomodel` package. A generic `create()` method, `createObject()`, is also provided.

After you create an object by using the `create<interface>` pattern, you can save it to the registry. To save an object explicitly to the registry, you call the `saveObjects()` method of the `LifeCycleManager` instance by passing a collection of `RegistryObjects`.

You can also use the `deleteObjects()` method of the `LifeCycleManager` instance to delete `RegistryObjects` from the registry. The `deleteObjects()` call also takes a collection of `RegistryObjects` as an argument.

Table 12-2 provides a list of methods available in the `LifeCycleManager` interface:

TABLE 12-2 METHOD SUMMARY OF LIFECYCLEMANAGER

Return Type	Method	Description	Capability Level
Association	createAssociation(RegistryObject targetObject, Concept associationType)	This method uses the specified parameters to create an instance of Association.	0
Classification	createClassification (Classification-Scheme scheme, java.lang.String name, java.lang.String value)	This method creates a Classification instance of an external Classification.	0

Return Type	Method	Description	Capability Level
Classification	createClassification (Concept concept)	This method creates a Classification instance of an internal Classification using the specified Concept.	0
ClassificationScheme	createClassificationScheme (Concept concept)	This method creates a ClassificationScheme using the specified Concept that does not have Classification-Scheme or parent Concept.	0
ClassificationScheme	createClassificationScheme (java.lang.String name, java. lang.String description)	This method is most commonly used to create a ClassificationScheme using the specified parameters.	0
Concept	createConcept(RegistryObject parent, java.lang.String name, java.lang.String value)	This method creates an instance of a Concept.	0
void	createConceptEquivalence (Concept concept1, Concept concept2)	This method uses the two concepts specified as its parameters to create a semantic equivalence. This method does not return anything.	0
EmailAddress	createEmailAddress(java. lang.String address)	This method uses its String parameter to create an EmailAddress instance.	0
EmailAddress	createEmailAddress(java. lang.String address, java. lang.String type)	This method uses its specified parameters to create an EmailAddress instance.	0
ExternalIdentifier	createExternalIdentifier (ClassificationScheme identificationScheme, java. lang.String name, java. lang.String value)	This method uses its specified parameters to create an instance of ExternalIdentifier.	0
ExternalLink	createExternalLink(java.lang. String externalURI, java. lang.String description)	This method uses its specified parameters to create an instanceof ExternalLink.	0

Continued

TABLE 12-2 METHOD SUMMARY OF LIFECYCLEMANAGER *(Continued)*

Return Type	Method	Description	Capability Level
ExtrinsicObject	createExtrinsicObject()	This method uses its specified parameters to create an instance of ExtrinsicObject.	1
InternationalString	createInternationalString()	This method creates an instance of InternationalString.	0
InternationalString	createInternationalString (java.util.Locale l, java.lang. String s)	This method creates an instance of InternationalString using the specified locale and the specified String parameter.	0
InternationalString	createInternationalString (java.lang.String s)	This method creates an instance of InternationalString using the default locale and the specified String parameter.	0
Key	createKey(java.lang. String id)	This method creates a Key instance using the specified parameter.	0
LocalizedString	createLocalizedString(java. util.Locale l, java.lang. String s)	This method uses the specified locale and the String parameters to create an instance of a LocalizedString.	0
java.lang.Object	createObject(java.lang. String className)	This method creates instances of the interfaces of the information model. The createObject(java. lang.String className) method is a factory method.	0
Organization	createOrganization(java. lang.String name)	This method uses the specified String parameter to create an instance of Organization.	0
PersonName	createPersonName(java. lang.String fullName)	This method uses the specified String parameter to create an instance of PersonName.	0
PersonName	createPersonName(java. lang.String firstName, java. lang.String middleName, java.lang.String lastName)	This method uses the specified parameters to create an instance of PersonName.	1

Return Type	Method	Description	Capability Level
PostalAddress	createPostalAddress(java.lang.String streetNumber, java.lang.String street, java.lang.String city, java.lang.String stateOrProvince, java.lang.String country, java.lang.String postalCode, java.lang.String type)	This method uses the specified parameters to create an instance of PostalAddress.	0
RegistryPackage	createRegistryPackage (java.lang.String name)	This method uses the specified parameter to create an instance of RegistryPackage.	1
Service	createService(java.lang.String name)	This method uses the specified parameter to create an instance of Service.	0
ServiceBinding	createServiceBinding()	This method creates an instance of ServiceBinding.	0
Slot	createSlot(java.lang.String name, java.util.Collection values, java.lang.String slotType)	This method uses the specified parameters to create an instance of Slot. The second parameter in this method is of the java.util.Collection type.	0
Slot	createSlot(java.lang.String name, java.lang.String value, java.lang.String slotType)	This method uses the specified parameters to create an instance of Slot. The second parameter in this method is of the java.util.String type.	0
SpecificationLink	createSpecificationLink()	This method creates an instance of SpecificationLink.	0
TelephoneNumber	createTelephoneNumber()	This method creates an instance of TelephoneNumber.	0
User	createUser()	This method creates an instance of User.	0

Continued

TABLE 12-2 METHOD SUMMARY OF LIFECYCLEMANAGER *(Continued)*

Return Type	Method	Description	Capability Level
void	deleteConceptEquivalence (Concept concept1, Concept concept2)	This method takes two Concept parameters and deletes any semantic equivalence that is present between the Concept parameters.	0
BulkResponse	deleteObjects(java.util. Collection keys)	This method deletes objects from the registry, as specified by its parameter.	0
BulkResponse	deprecateObjects(java. util.Collection keys)	This method deprecates objects from the registry, as specified by its parameter.	1
BulkResponse	saveObjects(java.util. Collection objects)	This method saves objects to the registry.	0
BulkResponse	unDeprecateObjects(java. util.Collection keys)	This method undeprecates objects that were deprecated before.	1

Table 12-3 provides a list of methods available in the `BusinessLifeCycleManager` interface:

TABLE 12-3 METHOD SUMMARY OF BUSINESSLIFECYCLEMANAGER

Return Type	Method	Description	Capability Level
BulkResponse	deleteAssociations(java. util.Collection schemeKeys)	This method deletes the Associations as specified by the Keys in its parameter.	0
BulkResponse	deleteClassificationSchemes (java.util.Collection schemeKeys)	This method deletes the ClassificationSchemes as specified by the Keys in its parameter.	0

Return Type	Method	Description	Capability Level
BulkResponse	deleteConcepts(java.util. Collection conceptKeys)	This method deletes the Concepts as specified by the Keys in its parameter.	0
BulkResponse	deleteOrganizations(java. util.Collection organizationKeys)	This method deletes the Organizations as specified by the Keys in its parameter.	0
BulkResponse	deleteServiceBindings(java. util.Collection bindingKeys)	This method deletes the ServiceBindings as specified by the Keys in its parameter.	0
BulkResponse	deleteServices(java.util. Collection serviceKeys)	This method deletes the Services as specified by the Keys in its parameter.	0
BulkResponse	saveAssociations(java.util. Collection associations, boolean replace)	This method saves instances of Associations as specified by its parameters.	0
BulkResponse	saveClassificationSchemes (java.util.Collection schemes)	This method saves instances of ClassificationSchemes as specified by its parameter.	0
BulkResponse	saveConcepts(java.util. Collection concepts)	This method saves Concepts as specified by its parameter.	0
BulkResponse	saveOrganizations(java.util. Collection organizations)	This method saves Organizations as specified by its parameter.	0
BulkResponse	saveServiceBindings(java.util. Collection bindings)	This method saves ServiceBindings as specified by its parameter.	0
BulkResponse	saveServices(java.util. Collection services)	This method saves Services as specified by its parameter.	0

The BusinessQueryManager and DeclarativeQueryManager interfaces

The BusinessQueryManager and the DeclarativeQueryManager interfaces denote access to the query-manager service within the registry. These interfaces provide a mechanism for a client to query the registry for business objects contained in the registry. Nonprivileged users can use these interfaces to browse through the registry to find a specific `RegistryObject`.

The `BusinessQueryManager` interface provides the capability to query important information available in the registry.

Table 12-4 provides a method summary for the `BusinessQueryManager` interface.

TABLE 12-4 METHOD SUMMARY OF BUSINESSQUERYMANAGER

Return Type	Method	Description	Capability Level
BulkResponse	FindAssociations(java.util. Collection findQualifiers, java.util.Collection associationTypes, boolean sourceObjectConfirmed,) boolean targetObject-Confirmed	This method finds Associations that match all the criteria specified in its parameters. It returns a BulkResponse that consists of a Collection of Associations.	0
ClassificationScheme	findClassificationScheme-ByName(java.lang.String namePattern)	This method finds Classification-Schemes based on the specified parameter. It returns a ClassificationScheme that matches the name pattern.	0
BulkResponse	findClassificationSchemes (java.util.Collection findQualifiers, java.util. Collection namePatterns, java.util.Collection classifications, java.util. Collection externalLinks)	This method finds ClassificationSchemes that match all the criteria specified in its parameters. It returns a BulkResponse that consists of a Collection of ClassificationSchemes.	0
Concept	findConceptByPath(java. lang.String path)	This method finds a Concept as specified by the XPath expression path in its parameter.	0
BulkResponse	findConcepts(java.util. Collection findQualifiers, java.util.Collection namePatterns, java.util. Collection classifications, java.util.Collection externalIdentifiers, java.util. Collection externalLinks)	This method finds Concepts that match all the criteria specified in its parameters. It returns a BulkResponse that consists of a Collection of Concepts.	0

Return Type	Method	Description	Capability Level
BulkResponse	findOrganizations(java.util. Collection findQualifiers, java.util.Collection namePatterns, java.util. Collection classifications, java.util.Collection specifications, java.util. Collection externalIdentifiers, java.util.Collection externalLinks)	This method finds Organizations that match all the criteria specified in its parameters. It returns a BulkResponse that consists of a Collection of Organizations.	0
BulkResponse	findRegistryPackages(java. util.Collection findQualifiers, java.util.Collection name-Patterns, java.util.Collection classifications, java.util. Collection externalLinks)	This method finds RegistryPackages that match all the criteria specified in its parameters. This method returns a BulkResponse that consists of a Collection of RegistryPackages.	1
BulkResponse	findServiceBindings(Key serviceKey, java.util. Collection findQualifiers, java.util.Collection classifications, java.util. Collection specifications)	This method finds Service-Bindings that match all the criteria specified in its parameters. This method returns a BulkResponse that consists of a Collection of ServiceBindings.	0
BulkResponse	findServices(Key orgKey, java. util.Collection findQualifiers, java.util.Collection name-Patterns, java.util.Collection classifications, java.util. Collection specifications)	This method finds Services that match all the criteria specified in its parameters. This method returns a BulkResponse that consists of a Collection of Services.	0

The `DeclarativeQueryManager` interface is a more flexible API that provides a generic access to perform ad-hoc queries on the registry. `DeclarativeQueryManager` uses a declarative query syntax for queries. As of this writing, SQL-92 and OASIS ebXML Registry Filter queries are the only declarative query-language syntaxes that are provided by `DeclarativeQueryManager`.

Table 12-5 provides a method summary for the `DeclarativeQueryManager` interface:

TABLE 12-5 METHOD SUMMARY OF DECLARATIVEQUERYMANAGER

Return Type	Method	Description	Capability Level
Query	createQuery(int queryType, java.lang.String queryString)	This method takes a queryType and a String representing a query as parameters. Using the specified parameters, it creates a Query.	0 (optional)
BulkResponse	executeQuery(Query query)	This method creates a Query using the specified parameters.	0 (optional)

JAXR Examples

This section describes the implementation of the JAXR specification. The following example shows how to query a registry by using the JAXR API.

In this example, a standalone JAXR browser looks up the IBM test registry for the name of an organization in the registry. If it finds the name, the example prints details of the organization on the console, in ascending order. For this example, create a `JAXRBrowseHelper` class with an `executeQuery(String query)` method. The `methods` parameter is a string that represents the name of the organization to look up in the registry. You add the necessary business logic necessary to perform the lookup in the `executeQuery(String query)` method. For that, you first create a set of properties to specify the URL of the registry that you want to access and the JAXR RI implementation of the connection factory for the registry. You set the properties to specify the URL of the IBM test query registry that you intend to access and the JAXR RI implementation of the connection factory for the registry, as shown in the following code:

```
Properties properties = new Properties();

properties.setProperty("javax.xml.registry.queryManagerURL",
"http://www-3.ibm.com/services/uddi/testregistry/inquiryapi");
        properties.setProperty("javax.xml.registry.factoryClass",
"com.sun.xml.registry.uddi.ConnectionFactoryImpl");
```

After you set the properties, you need to create a connection. To do so, create an instance of the `ConnectionFactory` class, set the properties of the connection factory and then create the connection. The following code shows how to create the connection:

```
ConnectionFactory factory = ConnectionFactory.newInstance();
    factory.setProperties(properties);
con = factory.createConnection();
```

After you create a connection, obtain a `RegistryService` object by using the connection you created, as shown in the following code:

```
RegistryService regService = con.getRegistryService();
```

As you're to perform simple queries on the registry, obtain a `BusinessQueryManager` object by using the `RegistryService` object, as shown in the following code:

```
BusinessQueryManager busQryMgr = regService.getBusinessQueryManager();
```

Now query the registry for the organization whose name is represented by the parameter of your `executeQuery(String query)` method. For that purpose, use the `findOrganizations()` method of the `BusinessQueryManager` interface. You provide a find qualifier and a name pattern as arguments to the `findOrganizations()` method. For that, define the find qualifiers and the name pattern, as shown in the following code:

```
Collection findQualifiers = new ArrayList();
        findQualifiers.add(FindQualifier.SORT_BY_NAME_ASC);
        Collection namePatterns = new ArrayList();
        namePatterns.add("%" + query + "%");
```

You call the `findOrganizations()` method, passing as arguments the `findQualifiers` and the `namePatterns` objects that you create in the preceding code. The `findOrganizations()` method returns a collection of objects matching the arguments that you specify in the function `FindOrganizations()`, as shown in the following code.

```
BulkResponse response = busQryMgr.findOrganizations(findQualifiers,
namePatterns, null, null, null, null);
```

You use the `BulkResponse` object response to obtain a `Collection`. As you iterate through the `Collection`, locate the `Organization` object. Use the `Organization` object to obtain its information and print it, as shown in the following code:

```
Collection orgs = response.getCollection();

            Iterator oi = orgs.iterator();
            while (oi.hasNext()) {
                Organization org = (Organization) oi.next();
                System.out.println("Organization Name: " +
org.getName().getValue());
                System.out.println("Organization Description: " +
org.getDescription().getValue());
User user = org.getPrimaryContact();
                if (user != null) {
                    PersonName userName = user.getPersonName();
                    System.out.println("\tContact name: " +
userName.getFullName());
                }
```

Now use the Organization object to find the services of the organization as shown in the following code:

```
Collection services = org.getServices();
            Iterator si = services.iterator();
            while (si.hasNext()) {
                Service service = (Service) si.next();
                System.out.println("\tService Name: " +
service.getName().getValue());
                System.out.println("\tService Description: " +
service.getDescription().getValue());
```

You then use the Organization object to find the service bindings associated with the services of the Organization object and print the output, as shown in the following code:

```
ServiceBinding serviceBind = (ServiceBinding) sbi.next();
                    System.out.println("\t\tBinding Description:
" + serviceBind.getDescription().getValue());
                    System.out.println("\t\tAccess URI: " +
serviceBind.getAccessURI());
```

After you create the executeQuery(String query) method of the JAXRBrowseHelper class, call the method, passing an organization name as its parameter. For that, create a JAXRBrowser public class that contains a main() method to accept a user's command-line input of the name of the organization to look up in the registry. In the main() method, create an instance of the JAXRBrowseHelper class and call the executeQuery(String query) method, passing the user input as parameter. The following code shows the JAXRBrowser class:

```
public class JAXRBrowser {
    public static void main(String[] args) {
    if (args.length != 1) {
            System.out.println("Usage: JAXRBrowser <query-string>");
            System.exit(1);
        }
        JAXRBrowseHelper jaxrHelper = new JAXRBrowseHelper();
        jaxrHelper.executeQuery(args[0]);
    }
}
```

Save your application as JAXRBrowser.java. Following is the complete source code of JAXRBrowser.java:

JAXRBrowser.java

```
import javax.xml.registry.*;
import javax.xml.registry.infomodel.*;
import java.net.*;
import java.util.*;

public class JAXRBrowser {
    public static void main(String[] args) {
    if (args.length != 1) {
            System.out.println("Usage: JAXRBrowser <query-string>");
            System.exit(1);
        }
        JAXRBrowseHelper jaxrHelper = new JAXRBrowseHelper();
        jaxrHelper.executeQuery(args[0]);
    }
}

class JAXRBrowseHelper {
    public void executeQuery(String query) {
        Connection con=null;
        try {
            Properties properties = new Properties();

properties.setProperty("javax.xml.registry.queryManagerURL",
"http://www-3.ibm.com/services/uddi/testregistry/inquiryapi");
            properties.setProperty("javax.xml.registry.factoryClass",
"com.sun.xml.registry.uddi.ConnectionFactoryImpl");


            ConnectionFactory factory =
ConnectionFactory.newInstance();
```

```
                    factory.setProperties(properties);
            con = factory.createConnection();

            RegistryService regService = con.getRegistryService();
            BusinessQueryManager busQryMgr =
regService.getBusinessQueryManager();

            Collection findQualifiers = new ArrayList();
            findQualifiers.add(FindQualifier.SORT_BY_NAME_ASC);
            Collection namePatterns = new ArrayList();
            namePatterns.add("%" + query + "%");

            BulkResponse response =
busQryMgr.findOrganizations(findQualifiers, namePatterns, null,
null, null, null);
            Collection orgs = response.getCollection();

            Iterator oi = orgs.iterator();
            while (oi.hasNext()) {
                Organization org = (Organization) oi.next();
                System.out.println("Organization Name: " +
org.getName().getValue());
                System.out.println("Organization Description: " +
org.getDescription().getValue());

                User user = org.getPrimaryContact();
                if (user != null) {
                    PersonName userName = user.getPersonName();
                    System.out.println("\tContact name: " +
userName.getFullName());
                }

                Collection services = org.getServices();
                Iterator si = services.iterator();
                while (si.hasNext()) {
                    Service service = (Service) si.next();
                    System.out.println("\tService Name: " +
service.getName().getValue());
                    System.out.println("\tService Description: " +
service.getDescription().getValue());
                    Collection serviceBindings =
service.getServiceBindings();
                    Iterator sbi = serviceBindings.iterator();
                    while (sbi.hasNext()) {
                        ServiceBinding serviceBind =
```

```
(ServiceBinding) sbi.next();
                        System.out.println("\t\tBinding Description:
" + serviceBind.getDescription().getValue());
                        System.out.println("\t\tAccess URI: " +
serviceBind.getAccessURI());
                    }
                }
            System.out.println();
        }
    } catch (Exception e) {
        e.printStackTrace();
    } finally  {
        if (con != null) {
            try {
                con.close();
            } catch (JAXRException je) {}
        }
    }
  }
}
```

The preceding code prints the information about the organization that you want to query about. Make sure that you are connected to the Internet before running the preceding example.

To compile and execute, the preceding code, use the following build script:

Build.xml

```xml
<project name="JAXR Example" default="build" basedir=".">
  <property name="build" value="build" />
  <property environment="env" />

  <path id="classpath">
    <fileset dir="${env.JWSDP_HOME}/common/lib">
      <include name="*.jar"/>
    </fileset>
  </path>

  <target name="prepare"
   description="Create build directory.">
    <mkdir dir="${build}" />
  </target>

  <target name="build" depends="prepare"
    description="Compile Java files" >
      <javac srcdir="." destdir="${build}">
```

```
        <include name="*.java" />
        <classpath refid="classpath"/>
    </javac>
</target>

<target name="run" depends="build"
    description="Run JAXRBrowser." >
  <java classname="JAXRBrowser" fork="yes">
    <arg line="${commandline}" />
    <classpath refid="classpath" />
    <classpath path="${build}" />
  </java>
</target>
</project>
```

Make sure that you save build.xml and JAXRBrowser.java within the same directory (for example, c:\workarea\jaxr).

After you save both files, execute the following code to compile the JAXR browser:

```
ant build
```

Figure 12-5 shows the output after you use the build command.

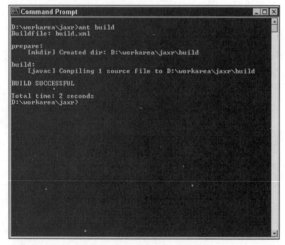

Figure 12-5: Output of the build command

After you build the code, you need to execute it by using the following command:

```
ant -Dcommandline = microsoft run
```

After you execute the preceding code, you should see the output shown in Figure 12-6.

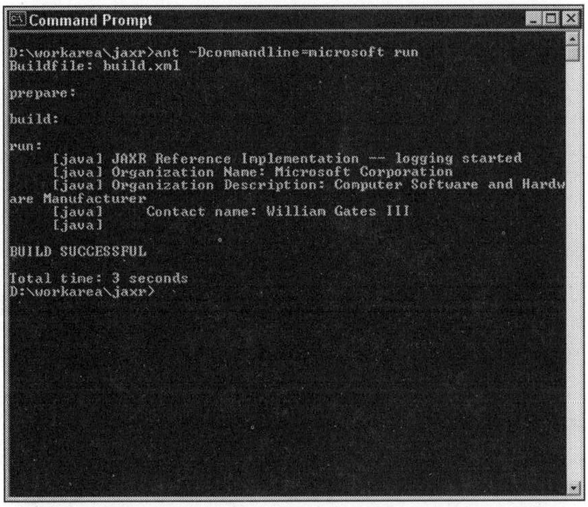

Figure 12–6: Output of the ant run command

Summary

JAXR is a specification that provides a common set of API standards to access disparate registry standards in the industry. The JAXR API is implemented by the JAXR provider to obtain access to an XML registry. This chapter covers the details of the JAXR client, JAXR provider, and XML registries.

The chapter provides information about different levels of capability profiles specified in the JAXR specification. It provides a detailed guideline of the JAXR programming model. The chapter also provides a public view of the JAXR information model and describes the interfaces in the model.

The chapter contains details on connection management, the life cycle, and query management of the registry objects by using different interfaces such as `Connection`, `ConnectionFactory`, `LifeCycleManager`, `BusinessLifeCycleManager`, `BusinessQueryManager`, and `DeclarativeQueryManager`. Finally, the chapter describes a simple standalone registry browser that looks up the registry for an organization by name and displays the information accordingly.

Chapter 13

JSTL

IN THIS CHAPTER

- ◆ Overview of JSTL
- ◆ Expression Language support
- ◆ i18n support
- ◆ Database support
- ◆ XML support

THE JAVASERVER PAGES STANDARD TAG LIBRARIES (JSTL) is an important technology for creating JSP pages in the repertoire of Web developers. The prime goal of JSP is to segregate the role of designer from that of programmer. In addition, JSP encapsulates various repetitive and complex codes with the help of JSP actions and JSP expressions. These goals were achieved with the introduction of the JavaServer Pages Standard Tag Libraries.

Tag libraries have been around in the JSP community for a while, but achieving standardization of a library of tags that dictates compliance across a broad array of vendor tools is a commendable feat indeed.

The JSTL specification defines a library of tags and their respective behaviors. Instead of performing common repetitive tasks across various JSP pages, developers can now use the tags defined in the Standard Tag Library that best correspond to a particular task.

 As of this writing, the JSTL specification is in version 1.0. JSTL is an initiative by the JCP organization and is available as JSR-52 at www.jcp.org/jsr/detail/52.jsp.

Overview of JSTL

In recent years, Java has rapidly matured from a computing language to a complete platform. The J2EE platform is now recognized as a powerful platform for both Web-based and enterprise applications. The J2EE platform provides various components and technologies for developing applications. One such component is the

375

JavaServer Pages (JSP). JavaServer Pages is a server-side scripting language intended to create dynamic content for the Web. A JSP page separates the presentation part from the programming part with the use of various JSP elements and tags. The JSP page developer, however, must code programming logic in scriplets for a JSP page. To work with a database, for example, the JSP developer must code how to set a driver for a database, secure a connection, and query the database. For a data-centric application, the developer must repeatedly code all the JSP pages of the application that interact with the database.

The introduction of *JSP custom tags* has eliminated these repetitive tasks from the development process of a JSP page. Now a developer can create customized tags that perform some common tasks and use them across various pages. In addition to (or instead of) developing their own custom tags, developers can use vendor-supplied custom tags. Many developers in the industry, for example, are currently using the open source Struts JSP tag library of the Jakarta project. But using such tags has certain disadvantages. Vendor specific tags run only on the specific JSP container that supports them. Moreover, different vendors supply different tags to perform the same operation but perhaps with different features. Such nonstandard versions diminish the interoperability feature of the JSP framework.

To overcome this problem, the community felt the need to develop a standardized mechanism to declare a standard set of tags. The result is the JavaServer Pages Standard Tag Libraries (JSTL), developed by the Java Community Process. As the JSTL is packaged within the J2EE bundle, it is available to all those working on the J2EE platform. The main aim of the JSTL is to eliminate scripts in JSP pages by introducing a standard and common set of tags. By using the tags of the JSP Standard Tag Library, a developer can perform various tasks, such as working with databases, processing XML documents, and managing URLs. In addition, the developers need to learn only one set of standardized library tags to become expressive across many scenarios, such as data management. JSP authoring-tool vendors can also use the JSTL to develop powerful JSP applications for the J2EE platform. Moreover, JSP container vendors can fine-tune their containers for the correct implementation of these standardized tags. The introduction of the standard tags not only improved the quality and efficiency of the code, but also contributed to the portability of the framework across disparate system architectures. To understand JSTL, you need a basic understanding of what a JSP custom tag library is. JSP custom tag library is discussed in the following sections.

JSP custom tags

In a JSP page, you use JSP elements and tags to perform various tasks. As I discuss in the preceding section, you may at times need to perform a task repeatedly across various JSP pages in an application. Instead of doing so, you can define your own tags to perform such repeated tasks. Such user-defined tags in a JSP page are known as *JSP custom tags*.

JSP custom tags offer the following benefits:

◆ Custom tags eliminate repetitive tasks.

◆ Custom tags are reusable.

◆ Custom tags have simple syntax.

You define all the custom tags in a file known as the *Tag Library Descriptor (TLD)*. The TLD is an XML file that defines the various characteristics of custom tags, such as the name of the tag, the attributes of the tag, the class file, and the body content.

You also need to define a Java class file to handle the tag. This class file is known as the *tag handler*. The tag handler is usually a JavaBean class.

As I state in the preceding section, a custom tag is an XML-based JSP element defined by the developer. To implement a custom tag, you need to understand the mechanism of how the custom tag works. On a higher level, as a developer, you need to perform the following tasks to implement a custom tag:

◆ Declare the tag library

◆ Create the tag-handler class

◆ Create the TLD

Declaration of a tag library is easy. All you must do is include a `taglib` directive into a JSP page. Following is an example of a `taglib` directive within a JSP page:

```
<%@ taglib uri="/WEB-INF/sometagtemplate.tld" prefix="pre" %>
```

A `taglib` directive declares the usage of a custom tag that you make available to the Web application. The `uri` attribute of the `taglib` directive provides a reference to a template. The template is also referred to as a *Tag Library Descriptor (TLD)*. A TLD is an XML-based document that provides a description of the tags in the tag library. The TLD describes each tag in the tag library so that the Web server or the development tools can use the TLD to validate the usage of the tags within the JSP documents. All TLD files are saved with a `.tld` extension. Almost always, you save the TLD files in the `/WEB-INF` folder. The `prefix` attribute in the `taglib` declaration syntax suggests the name of the prefix that you use in referring to a tag from the specific TLD.

To provide the tag-library reference to the application, you must first implement a tag-handler interface. Then you can package the classes that implement the tag handlers in a JAR file and place the JAR under the `/WEB-INF/lib` folder.

Following is a simple example of a JSP custom tag. This example displays a Hello Custom tag world . . . string on the browser. First, you need to create the following tag-handler class:

SimpleTag.java

```
import javax.servlet.jsp.*;
import javax.servlet.jsp.tagext.*;
import java.io.*;

public class SimpleTag extends TagSupport {
public int doStartTag() {
try {
JspWriter out = pageContext.getOut();
out.print("Hello Custom tag world...");
} catch(IOException e) {
System.out.println(e);
}
return(SKIP_BODY);
}
}
```

Then you need to create the TLD, as follows:

Simple.tld

```
<? xml version="1.0" encoding="ISO-8859-1" ?>
<!DOCTYPE taglib
PUBLIC "-//Sun Microsystems, Inc.//DTD JSP Tag Library 1.1//EN"
"http://java.sun.com/j2ee/dtds/web-jsptaglibrary_1_1.dtd">

<taglib>

<tlibversion>1.0</tlibversion>
<jspversion>1.1</jspversion>

<shortname>simple</shortname>
<urn></urn>
<info>
Simple tag library
</info>

<tag>
<name>simple</name>
<tagclass>SimpleTag</tagclass>
<info>Simple example</info>
<bodycontent>EMPTY</bodycontent>
</tag>

</taglib>
```

Following is a JSP code that uses that simple tag library:

```
Simple.jsp
<HTML>
<HEAD>
<%@ taglib uri="simple.tld" prefix="pre" %>
<TITLE>A simple example</TITLE>
</HEAD>
<BODY>
<H1><pre:simple/></H1>
</BODY>
</HTML>
```

After you execute the preceding JSP code, you see "Hello Custom tag world
. . ." as output on your client browser.

Using custom tags offers many benefits. You can customize your custom tags by
using tag attributes. A custom tag can modify the response of a JSP page. A custom
tag can access the `request` object of the JSP page and can perform queries on the
`request` objects. It can also access other objects on the JSP page. Custom tags can
communicate with other custom tags. Nesting support is also possible, wherein you
can nest a tag inside another tag to provide complex functionality.

Goals of JSTL

The basic goal of a JSTL specification is to provide a standardized set of tag
libraries. This standardization gives you freedom of expression while retaining code
portability across different vendors. Such standardization also benefits the developer by simplifying the page-authoring process.

In authoring a JSP page, you may need to use numerous beans and classes
within the code. You may also find yourself tempted to mix a lot of scripting elements, such as JavaScript and VBScript, within the code. Such a mixture of different scripts eventually messes up your code or makes it unreadable. (Many page
authors are not fluent in all the scripts anyway.)

According to the JSTL 1.0 specification, following are the key aspects of JSTL:

◆ JSTL provides Expression-Language support so that the developer can use
expressions within the code.

◆ JSTL provides flow-control structures such as iterators and conditional
branching.

◆ The JSTL specification includes the concept of *Tag Library Validators
(TLVs)*. The TLVs validate the JSP code to see whether it conforms to a
certain coding style.

◆ JSTL provides URL-based resource access.

◆ JSTL supports internationalization.

◆ JSTL supports access to RDBMS.

◆ JSTL, most importantly, supports XML processing.

Multiple TLDs

JSTL follows the same pattern of implementation that a custom tag library does. In fact, JSTL defines many tag-library descriptors within its framework. JSTL supports these TLDs so that it can neatly separate the discrete functionality that each library provides. Such separation of functionality also provides a sense of *namespace* for the libraries.

Table 13-1 shows the functionalities and the prefixes that you use for the functionalities in the JSP code.

TABLE 13-1 JSTL LIBRARIES AND PREFIXES

Functional Area	URI	Prefix	Example	Description
Core	http://java.sun. com/jstl/ea/core	c	<c:tagname ... >	Provides core tags for expressions, flow controls, and tags for managing URLs.
I18N-capable formatting	http://java.sun. com/jstl/ea/fmt	fmt	<fmt:tagname ...>	Provides tags to support i18n and localized formatting.
Database access (SQL)	http://java.sun. com/jstl/ea/sql	sql	<sql:tagname ...>	Provides tags for working with database.
XML processing	http://java.sun. com/jstl/ea/xml	x	<x:tagname ...>	Provides tags for parsing XML documents and for transforming XML documents according to a XSLT stylesheet.

Table 13-2 provides an outline of different tags available within the TLDs:

Table 13-2 JSTL TAGS

Area	Function	Tags	TLD	Prefix
Core	Expression Language Support	<out>,<set>,<remove> <catch>	/jstl-c	c
	Flow Control	<forEach>,<forTokens>,<if>, <choose>,<when> <otherwise>		
	Import	<import>,<param>,<url>,<redirect>		
i18n	Locale	<locale>	/jstl-fmt	fmt
	Message formatting	<bundle>,<message>,<param>, <requestEncoding>		
	Number and date formatting	<formatNumber>,<parseNumber>, <timeZone>,<formatDate>,<parseDate>		
Database	SQL	<driver>,<transaction>,<query>, <update>,<param>	/jstl-sql	sql
XML	Core	<parse>,<out>,<set>	/jstl-x	x
	Flow Control	<forEach>,<if>,<choose>, <when>, <otherwise>		
	Transformation	<transform>,<param>		

The preceding table describes the JSTL tags and the TLDs in which they are available. You would notice that several tags are available in each TLD. For example, the ⟨parse⟩, ⟨out⟩, ⟨set⟩, ⟨forEach⟩, ⟨if⟩, ⟨choose⟩, ⟨when⟩, ⟨otherwise⟩, ⟨transform⟩, and ⟨param⟩ tags are available within the /jstl-x TLD.

Expression Language Support

Expression-language support in JSTL enables a developer to easily work with application data without using JSP scriplets and expressions. Expression language enables the concept of *scoped attributes* within the JSP to communicate information between the JSP pages and the business logic. "Scoped attributes" refers to those attributes that have a session, a page, or an application scope. As of this writing, the JSTL specification is still not in the community review stage, which means that the people writing the JSTL specification have not chosen a specific expression language. The JCP is still reviewing different expression languages to tie with JSTL, but presently ECMAScript is JSTL's default scripting language.

To stipulate how to use expressions in a JSP page, JSTL currently supports two tag libraries, also known as the *twin libraries*. They are the *Request-Time tag library (JSTL-RT)* and the *Expression Language tag libraries (JSTL-EL)*. In JSTL-RT, you specify expressions in the scripting language of the JSP page, while in JSTL-EL, you specify expressions in the expression language (that would be chosen in the future) that JSTL supports. Attributes support expressions in the JSTL-RT library as rtexprvalues and in the JSTL-EL tag library as elexprvalues. You can access the twin libraries from a JSP page by typing the following lines in the program:

```
<%@ taglib uri="http://java.sun.com/jstl/ea/core" prefix="c" %>
```

(For the JSTL-ER tag library.)

```
<%@ taglib uri="http://java.sun.com/jstl/ea/core-rt" prefix="c-rt" %>
```

(For the JSTL-RT tag library.)

The Java Community Process (JCP) community is considering the following candidates as a possible fit for the expression language:

- ◆ Simplest Possible Expression Language (SPEL)
- ◆ ECMAScript standard
- ◆ JPath
- ◆ JXPath

You use an expression with JSP code by using the following syntax:

```
${expr}
```

This pattern exclusively invokes the expression language that you specify. The following code an example shows the use of an expression language that prints the value from one to ten:

```
<c:forEach var="count" begin="1" end="10">
<c:out value="${count}"/>
</c:forEach>
```

You can use application-specific data within an EL. A JSP-scoped variable is referred by a identifier in the EL by invoking findAttribute(identifier) on the PageContext instance. The PageContext instance can be referred by the implicit object page. If you are interested in accessing the request parameters of an HTTP request for your JSP page, you can use other implicit objects, such as param or params. The following code illustrates the usage of scoped variables in the EL:

```
<c:forEach var="someparam" items="${params}">
Name of the parameter: <c:out value="${someparam.key}"/>
Contents within the parameter list:
<c:forEach var="paramvalue" items="${someparam.value}">
```

```
<c:out value="${paramvalue}"/>
</c:forEach>
</c:forEach>
```

Expression language provides access to Map objects so that you can use such Map objects to store and retrieve data as a key-value pair. The EL syntax uses the .operator and the [] operators to obtain the values in a nested property or collection object, respectively.

The following example shows the usage of the . operator:

```
To email: <c:out value="${user.email}"/>
From email: <c:out value="${myobject.email}"/>,
Subject: Hello there
```

The following code shows the usage of the [] operators:

```
Shopping cart for user:
<c:out value="${carts[user.userId]}"/>
Payment type:
<c:out value="${user.preferences["payment"]}"/>
```

EL support tags

The expression language contains a standard set of core tag libraries that enables the developer to express different behavior within the JSP code. The following sections provide a brief summary of the tags from the core library of all expression languages.

THE <C:OUT> TAG

The <c:out> tag helps the developer to output the result of an evaluated expression to the JSPWriter object within the JSP PageContext.

Following is the syntax for using the stand-alone tag, <c:out> tag. A stand-alone tag is a tag without a body. :

```
<c:out value="value" [escapeXml="{true|false}"]>
[default="defaultValue"] />
```

Following is the syntax for using the <c:out> tag with a body. A tag that has a start and an end tag is referred to as a tag with a body.

```
<c:out value="value" [escapeXml="{true|false}"]>
default value
</c:out>
```

The following code shows the use of the <c:out> tag. The code repeatedly outputs the ID of the books of the collection specified in the items attribute. If a book does not have an ID, the default value appears as specified in the `default` attribute of the `<c:out>` tag.

```
<c:forEach var="books" items="$books">
<c:out value="${books.id} default="No specific ID"/>
</c:forEach>
```

THE <C:SET> TAG

The `<c:set>` tag helps the developer set the value of a JSP-scoped variable.

Following is the syntax for using the `<c:set>` tag without a body:

```
<c:set value="value"
var="varName" [scope="{page|request|session|application}"]/>
```

Following is the syntax for using the `<c:set>` tag with a body:

```
<c:set var="varName" [scope="{page|request|session|application}"]>
body content
</c:set>
```

The following code shows the use of the `<c:set>` tag to set the value of a scoped variable. You specify the name of the scoped variable in the `var` attribute, the scope of the `var` attribute as `session` in the `scope` attribute, and the `action` to be evaluated in the `value` attribute of the `<c:set>`.

```
<c:set var="myVal" scope="session" value="action">
```

 The `<c:set>` tag is supported only by the JSTL-ER library.

THE <C:REMOVE> TAG

The `<c:remove>` tag helps the developer remove a JSP-scoped variable. Following is the syntax for the `<c:remove>` tag:

```
<c:remove var="varName"
[scope="{page|request|session|application}"]/>
```

You use the `<c:remove>` tag to remove the variable `myVal` that you set in the code in the preceding section. You specify the `name` of the scoped variable that you wan to remove in the `var` attribute of the `<c:remove>` tag. You also specify the `scope` of the variable that you want to remove in the `scope` attribute. The following code shows how to use the `<c:remove>` tag:

```
<c:remove var="myVal" scope="session">
```

THE <C:CATCH> TAG

The <c:catch> tag helps the developer trap a exception thrown by any of the code within the <c:catch> nest. Following is the syntax for the <c:catch> tag:

```
<c:catch [var="varName"]>
nested actions
</c:catch>
```

EL flow control

The expression language contains a standard set of core tag libraries to support flow-control structures such as *conditional branching* and *iterations*. The following section provides a brief summary of the tags from the EL core library that support flow control.

THE <C:IF> TAG

The <c:if> tag helps a developer to provide conditional branching based on the truth or falseness of the evaluated expression in the tag. Following is the syntax for the <c:if> tag without a body:

```
<c:if test="testCondition"
var="varName" [scope="{page|request|session|application}"]/>
```

Following is the syntax for the <c:if> tag with a body:

```
<c:if test="testCondition"
[var="varName"] [scope="{page|request|session|application}"]>
body content
</c:if>
```

The following code shows the use of the <c:if> tag to output a result to a user if the language that the user selects matches the test condition. You specify the test condition in the test attribute of the <c:if> tag, as follows:

```
<c:if test="$user.choice == 'English'">
<c:out value="${output.English}"/>
</c:if>
```

THE <C:WHEN> TAG

You use the <c:when> tag within a <c:choose> tag. The <c:when> subtag helps the developer provide an exclusive alternative (similar to, the case keyword) within the < c:choose> tag. The syntax for the <c:when> tag is as follows:

```
<c:when test="testCondition">
body content
</c:when>
```

The following code shows the use of the `<c:when>` tag:

```
<c:when test="$user.choice=='French'">
     <c:out value="${output.French}"/>
</c:when>
```

In the preceding code, you specify a test condition in the `test` attribute of the `<c:when>` tag to determine whether a user has selected `French` as his choice of language. If the test expression is evaluated as `true`, the body of the `<c:when>` tag is processed and a output in French appears.

THE <C:OTHERWISE> TAG

You use the `<c:otherwise>` tag as the last subtag within a `<c:choose>` tag. The `<c:otherwise>` tag helps the developer provide a general alternative (similar to, the default keyword) within the `<c:choose>` tag. Following is the syntax for the `<c:otherwise>` tag:

```
<c:otherwise>
conditional block
</c:otherwise>
```

THE <C:CHOOSE> TAG

The `<c:choose>` tag helps a developer provide a switch case such as syntax that provides a mutually exclusive structure. The syntax for the `<c:choose>` tag is as follows:

```
<c:choose>
<c:when test=... ....>
............
</c:when>
<c:otherwise>

</c:otherwise>
</c:choose>
```

The following code shows the `<c:choose>` tag working along with the `<c:when>` and the `<c:otherwise>` tag to output a result based on a user's choice of language:

```
<c:choose>
   <c:when test="$user.choice=='French'">
```

```
    <c:out value="${output.French}"/>
  </c:when>
  <c:when test="$ user.choice=='German'">
    <c:out value="${output.German}"/>
  </c:when>
  <c:otherwise>
    <c:out value="${output.English}"/>
  </c:otherwise>
</c:choose>
```

In the code, the test condition of each <c:when> tag is evaluated. If the test condition of a <c:when> tag evaluates to true, its corresponding body is processed. If none of the test conditions of the <c:when> tags evaluates to true, the body of the <c:otherwise> tag is processed.

 The <choose> tag does not have attributes.

THE <C:FOREACH> TAG

You use the <c:foreach> tag to iterate through a list. The list is a collection of objects or a general condition that can provide a sequence of numbers. Following is the syntax for the <c:foreach> tag, used to iterate a collection of objects:

```
<c:forEach [var="varName"] items="collection"
[varStatus="varStatusName"]
[begin="begin"] [end="end"] [step="step"]>
body content
</c:forEach>
```

Following is the syntax for the <c:foreach> tag, used to iterate a fixed number of times:

```
<c:forEach [var="varName"]
[varStatus="varStatusName"]
begin="begin" end="end" [step="step"]>
body content
</c:forEach>
```

The following code shows the use of the <c:foreach> tag:

```
<c:forEach var="books" items="$books">
    <c:out value="${books}"/>
```

```
</c:forEach>
```

The code repeatedly outputs the value of the books item of the collection specified in the items attribute.

THE <C:FORTOKENS> TAG

You use the <c:forTokens> tag to iterate a sequence of tokens separated by a specified delimiter. The syntax for the <c:forTokens> tag is as follows:

```
<c:forTokens items="stringOfTokens" delims="delimiters"
[var="varName"]
[varStatus="varStatusName"]
[begin="begin"] [end="end"] [step="step"]>
body content
</c:forEach>
```

You specify the name of the scoped variable for the current item in the var
attribute. You specify the string of tokens in the items attribute. You then specify
the characters that separate the string of tokens in the delims attribute. For each
iteration of the string of tokens, the output of the tokens, separated by the . character, appears. The following code shows the use of the <c:forTokens> tag:

```
<c:forTokens var="myToken" items="red, blue| blue, green, violet"
delims="|,">
  <c:out value="${myToken}"/> .
</c:forTokens>
```

EL URL-related actions

The expression language contains a standard set of core tag libraries to support
URL-related actions within the JSP code. The following sections discuss the URL-
related actions, such as linking, importing, and redirecting URL resources, which
the JSTL specifications provide.

THE <C:IMPORT> TAG

You use the <c:import> tag to import the contents of a URL resource referred by
the <c:import> tag within the JSP page. Following is the syntax of the
<c:import> tag if the resource content is inlined or exported as a String object:

```
<c:import url="url" [context="context"]
[var="varName"] [scope="{page|request|session|application}"]
[charEncoding="charEncoding"]>
optional body content for <c:param> subtags
</c:import>
```

Following is the syntax of the <c:import> tag if the resource content is exported as a Reader object:

```
<c:import url="url" [context="context"]
varReader="varReaderName"
[charEncoding="charEncoding"]>
body content where varReader is consumed by another action
</c:import>
```

If you want to include a resource from the Web and process it in your JSP page, for example; you typically use the <c:import> tag with the url attribute specifying the resource in your JSP page, as follows:

```
<c:import url="ftp://myresource.com/resource.html"/>
```

THE<C:URL> TAG

The <c:url> tag helps the developer refer to a URL specified within the <c:url> tag. The tag provides a reference to a URL after applying the necessary URL-rewriting rules. The syntax for the <c:url> tag without a body content is as follows:

```
<c:url url="value"
[var="varName"] [scope= "{page|request|session|application}"]/>
```

The syntax for the <c:url> tag with a body content to specify query string parameters is as follows:

```
<c:url url="value"
[var="varName"] [scope="{page|request|session|application}"]>
<c:param> subtags
</c:url>
```

You can use the <c:url> tag to rewrite URLs returned from a JSP page. The url used here is a relative URL. The param tag is used to provide the value of an ISBN for a particular book that is appended to the URL. The following code illustrate the use of the <c:url> tag:

```
<c:url var="url"
   value="${pageContext.request.contextPath}/bookdetails" >
   <c:param name="getbookdetails" value="${ISBN}" />
</c:url>
<p><strong><a href="<c:out value='${url}'/>">
```

THE <C:PARAM> TAG

You use the <c:param> tag to add request parameters to other tags such as <c:import>, <c:url>, and <c:redirect> tags. The <c:param> tag is added as a nested subtag within the specified tags. The syntax for the `<c:param>` tag with the `value` parameter specified in the `value` attribute is as follows:

```
<c:param name="name" value="value"/>
```

The syntax for the `<c:param>` tag with `parameter value` specified in the body content is as follows:

```
<c:param name="name">
parameter value
</c:param>
```

The following code shows how you can provide your `name` and `password` parameters by using the `<c:param>` tag along with the `<c:import>` tag to include a resource in your JSP page. You use the `name` and the `value` attribute of `<c:param>` to specify the name of the parameter and the parameter value, respectively, as follows:

```
<c:import url="/Login/login">
   <c:param name="name" value="Robert"/>
    <c:param name="password" value="password"/>
</c:import>
```

THE <C:REDIRECT> TAG

You use the `<c:redirect>` tag to embed a redirection logic within the JSP code. The `<c:redirect>` tag sends an HTTP redirect to the Web client (browser). The syntax for the `<c:redirect>` tag without body content is as follows:

```
<c:redirect url="value"/>
```

Following is the syntax for the `<c:redirect>` tag with a body content to specify query-string parameters:

```
<c:redirect url="value">
<c:param> subtags
</c:redirect>
```

```
The following code shows the redirection logic for a current JSP
page. If an application error occurs while processing a JSP, you can
redirect the flow of the JSP to a new page. You can also add some
parameters to the relative URL to which you redirect the page, as
follows:<c:redirect url"/error.jsp">
      <c:param name="erorid" value="500"/>
</c:redirect>
```

i18n Support

i18n, or *internationalization*, is the most prominent feature that visitors to many sites are increasingly expecting today. i18n is a specification that enables developers to code the Web process in a language independent manner (such as English or French). To achieve such a language-independent Web process, the i18n specification takes advantage of another specification known as *localization*.

i18n locale

Localization is a process whereby a language-independent i18n application is customized for a specific locality. In other words, localization specifies a locale for the i18n process. A *locale* represents a specific cultural, geographical, or political preference for the application. The locale is based on a resource bundle that specifies locale-specific messages. The `<fmt:locale>` tag helps the developer specify the locale that a specific resource bundle is using. Following is the syntax of the `<fmt:locale>` tag:

```
<fmt:locale value="locale"
[variant="variant"]
[scope="{page|request|session|application}"]/>
```

To specify a particular locale, you use the `value` attribute of the `<fmt:locale>` tag and specify the language code in it. The language code is a lowercase, two-letter code defined by ISO-639. You specify a German locale, for example, as follows:

```
<fmt:locale value="de"/>
```

You can visit `www-old.ics.uci.edu/pub/ietf/http/related/iso639.txt` to access the ISO-639-defined language codes.

i18n message formatting

The locale-specific information of an i18n application is actually held in a resource bundle. The resource bundle holds messages associated with that i18n application. Every message in the resource bundle has a key associated with the message. To understand the use of the resource bundle, consider the following example.

If the user of an i18n application is interested in using a resource bundle by the name of `signin` for two different languages such as English and French, you need to provide two resource bundles with the names `signin_en` and `signin_fr`. The suggested names are a combination of the base name of the resource bundle (signin) and the locale for the i18n localization (en or fr). Now, depending on the specific localization that the user of an i18n application prefers, a given key (such as greeting) can either be mapped to en (Hello) or fr (Bonjour).

The following sections provide the necessary tags to format an i18n message.

THE <FMT:BUNDLE> TAG

A resource bundle contains set of objects that you can localize. You use the <fmt:bundle> tag to load a specific resource bundle. Following is the syntax for the <fmt:bundle> tag:

```
<fmt:bundle basename="basename"
[prefix="prefix"]
[var="varName"]
[scope="{page|request|session|application}"]>
body content
</fmt:bundle>
```

The following code shows the use of the <fmt:bundle> tag:

```
<fmt:locale value="de"/>
<fmt:bundle basename="resourcename">
</fmt:bundle>
```

In the preceding code, you specify the fully qualified resource name of the bundle in the basename attribute. The basename attribute, along with the value attribute of the <fmt:locale> tag, uniquely identifies the resource bundle.

THE <FMT:MESSAGE> TAG

You use the <fmt:message> tag to look up a specific localized message within a loaded resource bundle. Following is the syntax of the <fmt:message> tag without a body content:

```
<fmt:message key="messageKey"
[bundle="resourceBundle"]
[var="varName"]
[scope="{page|request|session|application}"]/>
```

Following is the syntax of the <fmt:message> tag with a body to specify message parameters:

```
<fmt:message key="messageKey"
[bundle="resourceBundle"]
[var="varName"]
[scope="{page|request|session|application}"]>
<fmt:param> subtags
```

```
</fmt:message>
```

Following is the syntax of the <fmt:message> tag with a body to specify key and optional message parameters:

```
<fmt:message [bundle="resourceBundle"]
[var="varName"]
[scope="{page|request|session|application}"]>
key
optional <fmt:param> subtags
</fmt:message>
```

In the <fmt:message> tag, you specify the message key that needs to be lookd up in the key attribute. You specify the localization context in the bundle attribute of the <fmt:message> tag. In this code, the Hello message appears in German, as it specifies the German language code in the <fmt:locale> tag. The following code illustrates the use of the <fmt:message> tag:

```
<fmt:locale value="de"/>
<fmt:bundle basename="resourcename" var="testBundle" />
<fmt:message key="Hello" bundle="${testBundle}"/>
```

THE <FMT:PARAM> TAG

You use the <fmt:param> tag to provide a parameter as a parametric replacement within a <fmt:message> tag. Following is the syntax of the <fmt:param> tag with a value specified via the value attribute:

```
<fmt:param value="messageParameter"/>
```

Following is the syntax of the <fmt:param> tag with a value specified via body content:

```
<fmt:param>
body content
</fmt:param>
```

The following code shows the use of the <fmt:param> tag:

```
<fmt:message key="date" bundle="${testBundle}"/>
<fmt:param><fmt:formatDate type="both"/>
</fmt:param>
</fmt:message>
```

In the preceding code, you specify the key attribute to look up the localized message. You then use the <fmt:param> tag to supply a single parameter to format the date and time. According to the language code that you specify in the `<fmt:locale>` tag, a localized message corresponding to the `key` value appears along with the formatted date and time.

THE <FMT:REQUESTENCODING> TAG

You use the `<fmt:requestEncoding>` tag to set the character-encoding rules for the JSP `Request` object. Following is the syntax for the `<fmt:requestEncoding>` tag:

```
<fmt:requestEncoding [value="charsetName"]/>
```

This tag is specifically used to interpret the user request. You can interpret the character set of the incoming request in the current page that processes the request. As an example, if someone submits a form in the Russian character set, you can place the `<fmt:requestEncoding>` at the top of the current page, as follows:

```
<fmt:requestEncoding value=" KOI8-R"/>
```

i18n number and date formatting

The i18n application also provides formatting rules for numbers and dates. The JSTL specification provides the actions for formatting the numbers, dates, and times of an i18n application in a locale-specific manner. The following sections provide brief summaries of the different tags that you use in formatting the date, time, and numbers of an i18n application.

THE <FMT:TIMEZONE> TAG

You use the `<fmt:timeZone>` tag to specify the time zone for which you need to format the time information. The syntax for the `<fmt:timeZone>` tag is as follows:

```
<fmt:timeZone value="timeZone"
[var="varName"]
[scope="{page|request|session|application}"]>
body content
</fmt:timeZone>
```

The following code shows how to use the `<fmt:timeZone>` tag to specify the time zone for which you format or parse time information. You specify the time zone in the `value` attribute of the `<fmt:timeZone>` tag, as follows:

```
<fmt:timeZone value="GMT">
 </fmt:timeZone>
```

THE <FMT:FORMATNUMBER> TAG

You use the `<fmt:formatNumber>` tag to specify the locale-specific formatting for numbers, currencies, and percentages for the i18n application. The syntax for the `<fmt:formatNumber>` tag without a body is as follows:

```
<fmt:formatNumber value="numericValue"
[type="{number|currency|percent}"]
[pattern="customPattern"]
[currencyCode="currencyCode"]
[currencySymbol="currencySymbol"]
[groupingUsed="{true|false}"]
[maxIntegerDigits="maxIntegerDigits"]
[minIntegerDigits="minIntegerDigits"]
[maxFractionDigits="maxFractionDigits"]
[minFractionDigits="minFractionDigits"]
[var="varName"]
[scope="{page|request|session|application}"]/>
```

Following is the syntax for the <fmt:formatNumber> tag with a body to specify the numeric value to be formatted:

```
<fmt:formatNumber [type="{number|currency|percent}"]
[pattern="customPattern"]
[currencyCode="currencyCode"]
[currencySymbol="currencySymbol"]
[groupingUsed="{true|false}"]
[maxIntegerDigits="maxIntegerDigits"]
[minIntegerDigits="minIntegerDigits"]
[maxFractionDigits="maxFractionDigits"]
[minFractionDigits="minFractionDigits"]
[var="varName"]
[scope="{page|request|session|application}"]>
numeric value to be formatted
</fmt:formatNumber>
```

The following code shows the use of the <fmt:formatNumber> tag to format a numeric value to a number in a locale-specific manner. You specify the numeric value to be formatted in the value attribute of the <fmt:formatting> tag, as follows:

```
<fmt:formatNumber value="123456789"/>
```

The following code shows how to use the <fmt:formatNumber> tag to format a numeric value to a currency in a locale-specific manner. You specify the numeric value to be formatted in the value attribute of the <fmt:formatting> tag and specify the type attribute as currency, as follows:

```
<fmt:formatNumber value="123456789" type="currency"/>
```

THE <FMT:PARSENUMBER> TAG

You use the `<fmt:parseNumber>` tag to parse a string that may contain a number, currency, or percentage in a locale-specific manner. Following is the syntax for the `<fmt:parseNumber>` tag without a body:

```
<fmt:parseNumber value="numericValue"
[type="{number|currency|percent}"]
[pattern="customPattern"]
[parseLocale="parseLocale"]
[integerOnly="{true|false}"]
[var="varName"]
[scope="{page|request|session|application}"]/>
```

Following is the syntax for the `<fmt:parseNumber>` tag with a body to specify the numeric value to be parsed:

```
<fmt:parseNumber [type="{number|currency|percent}"]
[pattern="customPattern"]
[parseLocale="parseLocale"]
[integerOnly="{true|false}"]
[var="varName"]
[scope="{page|request|session|application}"]>
numeric value to be parsed
</fmt:parseNumber>
```

The following code shows how to use the `<fmt:parseNumber>` tag to parse the string representation of currency that you formatted in a locale-sensitive manner. You specify the string representation of the currency that you want to parse in the `value` attribute of the `<fmt:parseNumber>` tag. In the `type` attribute, you specify that the string specified in the `value` attribute should be parsed as `currency`, as follows:

```
<fmt:formatNumber value="123456789" type="currency" var="cur"/>
<fmt:parseNumber value="${cur}" type="currency"/>
```

THE <FMT:FORMATDATE> TAG

You use the `<fmt:formatDate>` tag to format the date or time in a locale-specific manner. Following is the syntax for the `<fmt:formatDate>` tag without a body:

```
<fmt:formatDate [value="date"]
[type="{time|date|both}"]
[dateStyle="{default|short|medium|long|full}"]
[timeStyle="{default|short|medium|long|full}"]
[pattern="customPattern"]
[timeZone="timeZone"]
```

```
[var="varName"]
[scope="{page|request|session|application}"]/>
```

Following is the syntax for the <fmt:formatDate> tag with a body to specify the date to be formatted:

```
<fmt:formatDate [type="{time|date|both}"]
[dateStyle="{default|short|medium|long|full}"]
[timeStyle="{default|short|medium|long|full}"]
[pattern="customPattern"]
[timeZone="timeZone"]
[var="varName"]
[scope="{page|request|session|application}"]>
date value to be formatted
</fmt:formatDate>
```

The following code shows how to use the <fmt:format> tag to format a date and time in a locale-specific manner. You specify the format of the current date as GMT in the value attribute of the <fmt:timeZone> tag. You specify both the date and time to be formatted in the type attribute of the <fmt:formatDate> tag. You also specify the full formatting style to use to format the date and time by using the dateStyle and the timeStyle attributes, as follows:

```
<fmt:timeZone value="GMT">
   <fmt:formatDate type="both" dateStyle="full" timeStyle="full"/>
   </fmt:timeZone>
```

THE <FMT:PARSEDATE> TAG
You use the <fmt:parseDate> tag to parse a formatted date or a time represented within a string in a locale-specific manner. Following is the syntax for the <fmt:parseDate> tag without a body:

```
<fmt:parseDate value="dateString"
[type="{time|date|both}"]
[dateStyle="{default|short|medium|long|full}"]
[timeStyle="{default|short|medium|long|full}"]
[pattern="customPattern"]
[timeZone="timeZone"]
[parseLocale="parseLocale"]
[var="varName"]
[scope="{page|request|session|application}"]/>
```

Following is the syntax for the <fmt:parseDate> tag, with a body to specify the date value to be parsed:

```
<fmt:parseDate [type="{time|date|both}"]
[dateStyle="{default|short|medium|long|full}"]
[timeStyle="{default|short|medium|long|full}"]
[pattern="customPattern"]
[timeZone="timeZone"]
[parseLocale="parseLocale"]
[var="varName"]
[scope="{page|request|session|application}"]>
date value to be parsed
</fmt:parseDate>
```

The following code shows how to parse a string representation of a formatted date and time. You specify the string representation of the formatted date that you want to parse in the `value` attribute of the `<fmt:parseDate>` tag. You specify that the string representation in the `value` attribute contains both time and date in the `type` attribute. You specify that you're parsing the full version of the `date` component of the string representation in the `dateStyle` attribute. You also specify that you're parsing a short version of the `time` component of the string representation in the `timeStyle` attribute. You use the `timeZone` attribute to specify the time zone against which information in the string representation is interpreted. The following example shows the use of the `<fmt: parseDate>` tag:

```
<fmt:timeZone value="GMT">
    <fmt:formatDate type="both" dateStyle="full" timeStyle="full"
var="formatdate"/>
<fmt:parseDate value="${formatdate}" type="both" dateStyle="full"
timeStyle="short" timeZone="GMT" />
 </fmt:timeZone>
```

Database Support

In any given Web-services framework, you need to make sure that the messages that traverse to and from an endpoint are actually processed correctly and stored in an appropriate container such as a Relational Data Base Management System (RDBMS) for later retrieval. In addition, the most prominent action of any front-end logic is to communicate with the business logic, which in turn talks to a datastore at the backend. Sometimes, the presentation logic needs to interact directly with the datastore to process a message. In such cases, a mechanism should be available within the JSP pages to access the datastore in a flexible, yet simple, manner.

The following sections provide a brief summary of the tags that you use in the core SQL library of the JSTL specification.

The core SQL tag-support library in the JSTL specification enables the developer to take advantage of the data-storage and retrieval mechanisms that are based on SQL. The JSTL SQL tags enable the developer to perform queries on the database, obtain the query results, perform updates, and incite transactions on a group of databases.

The <sql:query> tag

You use the `<sql:query>` tag to perform queries on a datastore. Following is the syntax for the `<sql:query>` tag without body content:

```
<sql:query sql="sqlQuery"
var="varName" [scope="{page|request|session|application}"]
[dataSource="dataSource"]
[maxRows="maxRows"]
[startRow="startRow"]/>
```

Following is the syntax for the `<sql:query>` tag, with a body to specify query arguments:

```
<sql:query sql="sqlQuery"
var="varName" [scope="{page|request|session|application}"]
[dataSource="dataSource"]
[maxRows="maxRows"]
[startRow="startRow"]>
<sql:param> actions
</sql:query>
```

Following is the syntax for the `<sql:query>` tag with a body to specify query and optional query parameters:

```
<sql:query var="varName"
[scope="{page|request|session|application}"]
[dataSource="dataSource"]
[maxRows="maxRows"]
[startRow="startRow"]>
query
optional <sql:param> actions
</sql:query>
```

The following code shows the use of the `<sql:query>` tag for retrieving data from the `books` table of a database. You specify the name of the exported scope variable in the `var` attribute as `books`. You specify the datasource `myDS` associated to the database that you intend to query in the `datasource` attribute. You then specify the query for retrieving all the rows from the `books` table in the body of the `<sql:query>` tag, as follows:

```
<sql:query var="books" dataSource="${myDS}">
```

```
SELECT * FROM PUBLIC.books
</sql:query>
```

The <sql:update> tag

You use the `<sql:update>` tag to perform SQL updates such as add, update, and delete on a datastore. Following is the syntax for the `<sql:update>` tag without body content:

```
<sql:update sql="sqlUpdate"
[dataSource="dataSource"]
[var="varName"] [scope="{page|request|session|application}"]/>
```

Following is the syntax for the `<sql:update>` tag with a body to specify update parameters:

```
<sql:update sql="sqlUpdate"
[dataSource="dataSource"]
[var="varName"] [scope="{page|request|session|application}"]>
<sql:param> actions
</sql:update>
```

Following is the syntax for the `<sql:update>` tag with a body to specify update statements and optional update parameters:

```
<sql:update [dataSource="dataSource"]
[var="varName"] [scope="{page|request|session|application}"]>
update statement
optional <sql:param> actions
</sql:update>
```

The following code shows the use of the `<sql:update>` tag. You use the `<sql:update>` tag to delete a book from the `books` table with a `bookid` of 3. You specify the name of the exported `scope` variable for the update result in the `var` attribute. You also specify the datasource `myDS` associated to the database, which you update in the `datasource` attribute. You specify the `update` statement in the body of the `<sql:update>` tag, as follows:

```
<sql:update var="update" dataSource="${myDS}">
   DELETE FROM books WHERE bookid=3
 </sql:update>
```

The <sql:transaction> tag

You use the `<sql:transaction>` tag to perform transactions on a group of databases. The `<sql:transaction>` tag helps in establishing a transactional context for a database query and update tags. Following is the syntax for the `<sql:transaction>` tag:

```
<sql:transaction [dataSource="dataSource"]
[isolation=isolationLevel]
<sql:query> and <sql:update> statements
</sql:transaction>
```

The isolation level can be specified as shown in the following code:

```
isolationLevel ::= "read_committed"
| "read_uncommitted"
| "repeatable_read"
| "serializable"
```

The following code shows the usage of the `<sql:transaction>` tag to establish a transaction context for performing updates and querying a database:

```
<sql:transaction dataSource="${myDS}">
  <sql:update var="books">
    create table books (
      bookid int primary key,
      bookTitle varchar(40)
    )
  </sql:update>
  <sql:update var="update">
    INSERT INTO books VALUES (1,'Learning Java')
  </sql:update>
  <sql:update var="update">
    INSERT INTO books VALUES (2,'Learning XML')
  </sql:update>
  <sql:query var="deejays">
    select * from PUBLIC.books where bookTitle=?
<sql:param value="${title}" />
  </sql:query>
</sql:transaction>
```

In the preceding code, you specify the datasource in the `datasource` attribute of the `<sql:transaction>` tag. You can also specify the isolation level of your transaction in the `isolationLevel` attribute of the `<sql:transaction>` tag. If you do not specify the isolation level in the `isolationLevel` attribute, the isolation level in which you configure your datasource is taken into account. You use the `<sql:update>` tags to create the table `books` and insert data in it. You then query the `books` table for a particular `bookTitle`. The `<sql:transaction>` tag groups the nested `<sql:update>` and the `<sql:query>` tags into a transaction. You do not specify the `datasource` attribute in the `<sql:update>` and `<sql:query>` tags while using them with the `<sql:transaction>` tag.

The <sql:driver> tag

You use the `<sql:driver>` tag to create a `DataSource` object based on the `DriverManager` type of JDBC. `DataSource` is a wrapper around the `DriverManager` instance. Following is the syntax for the `<sql:driver>` tag:

```
<sql:driver var="varName"
[scope="{page|request|session|application}"]
[driver="driverClassName"]
[url="jdbcUrl"]
[user="userName"]/>
```

This tags helps in setting an application-wide datasource. You can set a `DataSource` object based on the JDBC driver `sun.jdbc.odbc.JdbcOdbcDriver` as follows:

```
<sql:driver var="myds" driver="sun.jdbc.odbc.JdbcOdbcDriver"
url="jdbc:mysql://www.conceptuniv.com/datasource"/>
```

The <sql:param> tag

The `<sql:param>` tag is a subtag that you use to set the values of the parameters of a query or a update tag. Following is the syntax of the `<sql:param>` tag with the parameter `value` specified in the `value` attribute:

```
<sql:param value= "value"/>
```

Following is the syntax of the `<sql:param>` tag with parameter `value` specified in the body content:

```
<sql:param>
parameter value
</sql:param>
```

The following code shows the use of the `<sql:param>` tag to set the parameter of a `<sql:query tag>`. In this code, you query the `books` table based on the author whose name passes as a parameter. You specify the name of the exported `scope` variable in the `var` attribute as `books`. You specify your datasource `myDS` in the `datasource` attribute. You then specify the query string for retrieving the rows from the `books` table based on a particular author's name. You pass the author's name in the `value` attribute of the `<sql:param>` tag, as follows:

```
<sql:query var="books" dataSource="${myDS}">
```

```
select * from PUBLIC.books where author=?
<sql:param value="${name}" />
</sql:query>
```

XML Support

The concept of Web-services is heavily based on the XML message structures. All the messages that traverse through the messaging channels are either XML documents or XML RPC invocations based on the SOAP messaging protocols. To support such increasing use of XML-based structures, supporting XML core tag libraries within the JSTL specification becomes almost mandatory.

The JSTL specification provides the basic XML-based tags categorized into basic, flow-control, and transformation syntaxes.

The following sections provide a brief summary of the different tags supported within the core XML tag library of the JSTL specification.

XML core tags

The XML core tags actually support the XML expression language based on the XPath framework. As a result, most of the tags are very similar to the basic support tags of the EL syntax.

THE <X:PARSE> TAG

You use the `<x:parse>` tag to parse a XML document. Following is the syntax for the `<x:parse>` tag in which you specify an XML document via a `String` or `Reader` object:

```
<x:parse {xmlUrl="URLforXMLDocument"|xmlText="XMLDocument"}
[filter="filter"]
[{var="varName"|varDom="varName"}]
[{scope="{page|request|session|application}" |
scopeDom="{page|request|session|application}"}]/>
```

Following is the syntax for the `<x:parse>` tag in which you specify an XML document via the body content:

```
<x:parse [filter="filter"]
[{var="varName"|varDom="varName"}]
[{scope="{page|request|session|application}" |
scopeDom="{page|request|session|application}"}]>
XML Document to parse
</x:parse>
```

The following code shows how to parse an XML document and store the resulting object tree by using the `<x:parse>` tag. You specify in the `var` attribute the JSP-scoped attribute where your object tree is to be stored. You also provide the XML document to be parsed in the body of the `<x:parse>` tag, as follows:

```
<x:parse var="book">
  <books>
    <author>
      <name>John Alex</name>
      <title>Learning Java</title>
    </author>
    <author>
      <name>Andrew Johnes</name>
      <title>Learning XML</title>
    </author>
  </books>
</x:parse>
```

THE <X:OUT> TAG

You use the `<x:out>` tag to display the resulting evaluated expression of the XPath into a `JSPWriter` object. The syntax for the `<x:out>` tag is as follows:

```
<x:out select="XPathExpression" [escapeXml="{true|false}"]/>
```

The `<x:out>` tag is similar to `<c:out>` tag defined in the expression-language syntax. The following code illustrates the use of the `<x:out>` tag:

```
<x:parse var="book">
  <books>
    <author>
      <name>John Alex</name>
      <title>Learning Java</title>
    </author>
  </books>
</x:parse>
<x:out select="$book/books/author/title[string(.)]"/>
```

This code selects the `<title>` tag and outputs the `name` to the page. The output displays `Learning Java`. The variable `$book` specifies a context for the XPath.

THE <X:SET> TAG

You use the `<x:set>` tag to set the resulting value of a evaluated XPath expression with a JSP-scoped variable. Following is the syntax for the `<x:set>` tag without a body:

```
<x:set select="XPathExpression"
var="varName" [scope="{page|request|session|application}"]/>
```

Following is the syntax for the `<x:set>` tag with a body:

```
<x:set var="varName" [scope="{page|request|session|application}"]>
value
```

`</x:set>`The following code shows how to store a list of titles of an author in the JSP-scoped attribute, as specified by the attribute `var`, by using the `<x:set>` tag:

```
<x:set select="$book/title[author=$request:author]"  var="titles"/>
```

XML flow control

Apart from having the capability to perform some basic actions such as displaying the results or setting the value of a scoped variable, controlling the flow of the structure of an XPath expression within the JSTL specification is also important. The XML flow-control tags within the JSTL specification provide a means to control the flow of an expression by using syntax similar to that of the EL expressions. The XML control-flow tags support conditional branching and iterations.

THE <X:IF> TAG

You use the <x:if> tag to conditionally branch within the XPath expression, based on the evaluated result of the `<x:if>` tag. Following is the syntax of the `<x:if>` tag:

```
<x:if select= "PathExpression"
[var= "varName"] [scope= "{page|request|session|application}"]>
body content
</x:if>
```

The following code evaluates the XPath expression specified by the `select` attribute:

```
<x:if select="$book/[author='James']">
James Book
</x:if>
```

In the preceding code, if the expression evaluates to true, the body of the <x:if> tag is processed.

THE <X:WHEN> TAG

The `<x:when>` tag is a subtag within the `<x:choose>` tag. It enables the developer to provide a exclusive case of logic within a `<x:choose>` tag. Following is the syntax for the `<x:when>` tag:

```
<x:when select="XPathExpression">
body content
</x:when>
```

THE <X:OTHERWISE> TAG

The `<x:otherwise>` tag is also a subtag within the `<x:choose>` tag. It enables the developer to provide a general case of logic within a `<x:choose>` tag. Following is the syntax for the `<x:otherwise>` tag:

```
<x:otherwise>
conditional block
</x:otherwise>
```

THE <X:CHOOSE> TAG

You use the `<x:choose>` tag to provide a switchcase-like syntax that provides mutually exclusive branching within the code. Following is the syntax for the `<x:choose>` tag:

```
<x:choose>
  <x:when select="...">
    ...
  </x:when>
  <x:when select="...">
    ...
  </x:when>
  ...
  <x:otherwise>
    ...
  </x:otherwise>
</x:choose>
```

The following code shows an `<x:choose>` tag:

```
<x:choose>
  <x:when select="$user/ID">
    Hello Your ID is <x:out select="$user/ID[string(.)]"/>
  </x:when>
  <x:when select="$user/name">
    Hello Your name is <x:out select="$user/name[string(.)]"/>
  </x:when>
  <x:otherwise>
    Hello
  </x:otherwise>
</x:choose>
```

In the preceding code, there is an <x:choose> tag: that contains two <x:when> tags and a <x:otherwise> tag. The attribute of each of the <x:when> tags specifies an XPath expression that gets evaluated to a boolean value. If the XPath expression is evaluated to true, the body of the corresponding <x:when> tag is rendered. Otherwise, the body of the <x:otherwise> tag is rendered.

THE <X:FOREACH> TAG

You use the <x:forEach> tag to provide iterations based on a collection of objects or a static sequence of elements within the JSP code. Following is the syntax for the <x:forEach> tag:

```
<x:forEach [var= "varName"] select= "XPathExpression">
body content
```

The following code illustrates the usage of the <x:forEach> tag:

```
<x:parse var="book">
  <books>
    <author>
      <name>John Alex</name>
      <title>Learning Java</title>
    </author>
</books>
</x:parse>
<x:forEach select="$book//author/*">
    <x:out select="string(.)"/>
</x:forEach>
```

It displays the author's name and the book title for all authors in the XML document.

XML transformation support

XML transformation is the capability to transform the semantic structure of a given XML document into that of a different structure, such as a Word document, a PDF file, a WML file, or another XML document. The XSL specification details the elements of such a transformation in the W3C document specific to XSL. You use the XSLT parsers to practically transform the structure of an XML document. Such transformations are transparent to the user of the JSTL specification. The developer just needs to use the XML-transformation tag library available within the JSTL specification, and the rest of the process is taken care of by the transform engine. The following sections describe the XML-transformation tags.

THE <X:TRANSFORM> TAG

The <x:transform> tag enables the developer to apply a specific transformation to a given XML document. The developer needs to provide a specific XSLT stylesheet or a transformer object for the transformation to occur. Following is the syntax for the <x:transform> tag with an XML document specified via a String or Reader object:

```
<x:transform
{xmlUrl= "URLforXMLDocument"|xmlText="XMLDocument"}
{xsltUrl= "URLforXSLTStylesheet"|xsltText="XSLTStylesheet"}
[{var= "varName"|result= "resultObject"}]
[scope= "{page|request|session|application}"] />
```

Following is the syntax for the <x:transform> tag with an XML document specified via the body content:

```
<x:transform
{xsltUrl= "URLforXSLTStylesheet"|xsltText="XSLTStylesheet"}
[{var= "varName"|result= "resultObject"}]
[scope= "{page|request|session|application}"]>
XML Document to parse
</x:parse>
```

The following code shows how to transform an XML document by using the <x:transform> tag in your JSP page:

```
<c:import url="http://myresource.com/resource" var="xmldoc"/>
<c:import url="/WEB-INF/xslt/resource.xsl" var="xsltstylesheet"/>
<x:transform source="$xmldoc" xslt="$xsltstylesheet"/>
```

In the preceding code, you include an XML document from the Web by using the <c:import> tag. You then transform the document by using an XSLT stylesheet present in the /WEB-INF/xslt directory of your Web application. You specify the document to transform and the stylesheet to use in the source and the xslt attributes of the <x:transform> tag.

THE <X:PARAM> TAG

You use the <x:param> tag to set the transformation parameters within the <x:transform> tag. Following is the syntax of the <x:param> tag with the parameter value specified in the value attribute:

```
<x:param name="name" value="value"/>
```

Following is the syntax of the `<x:param>` tag with the `parameter value` specified in the body content:

```
<x:param name="name">
parameter value
</x:param>
```

The following code shows the use of the `<x:param>` tag to set parameters for the transformation of an XML document:

```
<c:import url="http://myresource.com/resource" var="xmldoc"/>
<c:import url="/WEB-INF/xslt/resource.xsl" var="xsltstylesheet"/>
  <x:transform source="$xmldoc" xslt="$xsltstylesheet">
<x:param name="para" value="value"/>
  </x:transform>
```

Summary

This chapter discusses a preview of the JSP custom-tag facility. It then discusses the goals of the JSTL specification. The chapter details the expression-language syntax and then provides brief summaries of different EL syntaxes such as those of the basic tags, the control-flow tags, and the URL-related tags. The chapter explains the i18n support provided within the JSTL specification and briefs you about the locale tags, the message-formatting tags, and the number-formatting tags of the i18n core tag libraries. It also provides details about database support within the JSTL specification. Finally, the chapter briefs you on XML support as well, including the core tags, the flow-control tags, and the transformation tags within the XML core tag library of the JSTL specification.

Part IV

Appendixes

APPENDIX A
WSDL Basics

APPENDIX B
SOAP Fundamentals

APPENDIX C
Fundamentals of UDDI Version 2.0
Programmer's API

APPENDIX D
XML Primer

APPENDIX E
Java WSDP

Appendix A

WSDL Basics

WSDL IS A STANDARD consolidated from existing standards such as NASSL, SCL, and SDL. WSDL defines an XML grammar that describes service abstraction as a set of communication endpoints. These communication endpoints (on both ends of the messaging channel) can be considered as message ports.

An Overview of WSDL

In a WSDL document, services are defined as a set or collection of communication endpoints that, in the case of a wire protocol, can be considered *ports*. A *message* is data that is exchanged on the message channel. *Port types* are collections of operations. *Binding* is a reusable protocol and data-format specification for a given port type. On the basis of this definition, the WSDL specification documents the following elements in the definition of Web services:

- ◆ **Type:** Refers to a container for data-type definitions by using a type system.
- ◆ **Message:** Refers to an abstract typed definition of data being transmitted.
- ◆ **Operation:** Refers to an abstract description of an action supported by the service.
- ◆ **Port type:** Refers to an abstract set of operations supported by a single or multiple endpoints.
- ◆ **Binding:** Refers to a specific protocol and data-format specification for a specific port type.
- ◆ **Port:** Refers to an endpoint, which is a combination of a network and a binding address.
- ◆ **Service:** Refers to a collection of related endpoints.

A WSDL document comprises a set of definitions. The grammar of these definitions is as follows:

```
<wsdl:definitions name="nmtoken"? targetNamespace="uri"?>
    <import namespace="uri" location="uri"/>*

    <wsdl:documentation .... /> ?
```

```
<wsdl:types> ?
    <wsdl:documentation .... />?
    <xsd:schema .... />*
    <-- extensibility element --> *
</wsdl:types>

<wsdl:message name="nmtoken"> *
    <wsdl:documentation .... />?
    <part name="nmtoken" element="qname"? type="qname"?/> *
</wsdl:message>

<wsdl:portType name="nmtoken">*
    <wsdl:documentation .... />?
    <wsdl:operation name="nmtoken">*
        <wsdl:documentation .... /> ?
        <wsdl:input name="nmtoken"? message="qname">?
            <wsdl:documentation .... /> ?
        </wsdl:input>
        <wsdl:output name="nmtoken"? message="qname">?
            <wsdl:documentation .... /> ?
        </wsdl:output>
        <wsdl:fault name="nmtoken" message="qname"> *
            <wsdl:documentation .... /> ?
        </wsdl:fault>
    </wsdl:operation>
</wsdl:portType>

<wsdl:binding name="nmtoken" type="qname">*
    <wsdl:documentation .... />?
    <-- extensibility element --> *
    <wsdl:operation name="nmtoken">*
        <wsdl:documentation .... /> ?
        <-- extensibility element --> *
        <wsdl:input> ?
            <wsdl:documentation .... /> ?
            <-- extensibility element -->
        </wsdl:input>
        <wsdl:output> ?
            <wsdl:documentation .... /> ?
            <-- extensibility element --> *
        </wsdl:output>
        <wsdl:fault name="nmtoken"> *
            <wsdl:documentation .... /> ?
            <-- extensibility element --> *
        </wsdl:fault>
    </wsdl:operation>
```

```
</wsdl:binding>

<wsdl:service name="nmtoken"> *
    <wsdl:documentation .... />?
    <wsdl:port name="nmtoken" binding="qname"> *
        <wsdl:documentation .... /> ?
        <-- extensibility element -->
    </wsdl:port>
    <-- extensibility element -->
</wsdl:service>

<-- extensibility element --> *

</wsdl:definitions>
```

Certain rules should be kept in mind when referencing document definitions, naming documents, and adding contextual documentation. The following a list gives some of these rules, as introduced by WSDL:

◆ You can associate a namespace with a document location by using the import element. The import element enables you to separate different elements of service definitions into independent documents that you can import, if necessary.

◆ You can reference definitions of a WSDL document, such as port, message, service, portType, or binding.

◆ You can assign an optional `name` attribute of the type NCNAME for WSDL documents to provide a lightweight form of documentation. Alternatively, you can specify a `targetNamespace` attribute of type URI, but the specified URI should not be a relative URI.

◆ You can place the documentation element inside any WSDL language element. The optional `wsdl:document` element is used as a container for readable documentation.

Now that you know the rules introduced by WSDL, I can discuss the elements that constitute a *service*. A service is defined by using the following six elements:

◆ types

◆ message

◆ portType

◆ binding

◆ port

◆ service

To know more about the preceding elements, refer to Chapter 3.

Binding Extensions

In addition to the service elements in the preceding section, the Web Services Description Language (WSDL) 1.1 specifications define binding extensions for the SOAP 1.1 and HTTP GET/POST protocols and the MIME format. The following sections discuss these binding extensions.

SOAP 1.1

WSDL provides binding for SOAP 1.1 endpoints. The following sections describe the binding extension elements used for SOAP bindings.

SOAP:BINDING

The `soap:binding` element specifies that a binding is bound to the SOAP format. The `soap:binding` element must be present whenever you're using SOAP binding. It has the following signature:

```
<definitions .... >
    <binding .... >
        <soap:binding transport="uri"? style="rpc|document"?>
    </binding>
</definitions>
```

The `transport` attribute specifies the URI that identifies the transport of SOAP corresponding to the binding. The SOAP specification stipulates that, for HTTP binding, the following URI must be specified in the transport attribute:

```
http://schemas.xmlsoap.org/soap/http
```

The `style` attribute specifies whether the operation is RPC-oriented or document-oriented.

SOAP:OPERATION

The `soap:operation` element provides overall information about the binding operation. It has the following signature:

```
<definitions .... >
    <binding .... >
```

```
        <operation .... >
            <soap:operation soapAction="uri"? style="rpc|document"?>?
        </operation>
    </binding>
</definitions>
```

The `style` attribute specifies whether the operation is RPC-oriented or document-oriented. If the `style` attribute is not specified, the `style` attribute of the `soap:binding` element is taken into consideration. If the `style` attribute is not specified even in the `soap:binding` element, assume that the operation is document-oriented.

The `soapAction` attribute specifies the URI of the `soapAction` header. This value is necessary for HTTP protocol binding of SOAP. This value must not be specified for other bindings.

SOAP:BODY

The `soap:body` element indicates how the message parts are contained in the Body element of the SOAP message. The `soap:body` element has the following signature:

```
<definitions .... >
    <binding .... >
        <operation .... >
            <input>
                <soap:body parts="nmtokens"? use="literal|encoded"?
                            encodingStyle="uri-list"?
namespace="uri"?>
            </input>
            <output>
                <soap:body parts="nmtokens"? use="literal|encoded"?
                            encodingStyle="uri-list"?
namespace="uri"?>
            </output>
        </operation>
    </binding>
</definitions>
```

The `parts` attribute specifies which message part should be included in the SOAP Body element. The `use` attribute specifies whether the message part is encoded or the message part refers to a concrete schema definition.

SOAP:FAULT

The contents of the SOAP Fault Details element is specified by the `soap:fault` element. It has the following signature.

```
<definitions .... >
    <binding .... >
```

```
            <operation .... >
               <fault>*
                  <soap:fault name="nmtoken" use="literal|encoded"
                                 encodingStyle="uri-list"?
namespace="uri"?>
               </fault>
            </operation>
      </binding>
</definitions>
```

The `name` attribute relates the `soap:fault` element to the `wsdl:fault` element that is defined for the operation.

SOAP:HEADER AND SOAP:HEADERFAULT

The `soap:header` and the `soap:headerfault` elements define the headers inside the Header element. The `soap:header` and `soap:headerfault` elements have the following signatures.

```
<definitions .... >
   <binding .... >
      <operation .... >
         <input>
            <soap:header message="qname" part="nmtoken"
use="literal|encoded"
                              encodingStyle="uri-list"?
namespace="uri"?>*
               <soap:headerfault message="qname" part="nmtoken"
use="literal|encoded"
                                 encodingStyle="uri-list"?
namespace="uri"?/>*
            <soap:header>
         </input>
         <output>
            <soap:header message="qname" part="nmtoken"
use="literal|encoded"
                              encodingStyle="uri-list"?
namespace="uri"?>*
               <soap:headerfault message="qname" part="nmtoken"
use="literal|encoded"
                                 encodingStyle="uri-list"?
namespace="uri"?/>*
            <soap:header>
         </output>
      </operation>
   </binding>
</definitions>
```

The `message` attribute of the `soap:header` element is of the type `QName`. The `message` attribute together with the `part` attribute references the message part that specifies the Header type. The `part` attribute is of the type `nmtoken`.

The `soap:headerfault` element appears inside the `soap:header` element. The `soap:headerfault` element specifies the Header used to transmit error information. The `soap:headerfault` element is an optional element.

SOAP:ADDRESS

The `soap:address` element, which provides an address to a port, has the following signature:

```
<definitions .... >
    <port .... >
        <binding .... >
            <soap:address location="nmtoken" />
        </binding>
    </port>
</definitions>
```

HTTP GET/POST

The binding extension elements used for HTTP `GET/POST` binding are described in the following sections.

HTTP:ADDRESS

The `http:address` element specifies the port's base URI with its `location` attribute. It has the following signature:

```
<definitions .... >
    <port .... >
        <http:address location=="uri" />
    </port>
</definitions>
```

HTTP:BINDING

The `http:binding` element specifies that the HTTP protocol is used. It has the following signature:

```
<definitions .... >
    <binding .... >
        <http:binding verb="nmtoken"/>
    </binding>
</definitions>
```

The `verb` attribute specifies common HTTP actions such as `GET` and `POST`.

HTTP:OPERATION

The `http:operation` element specifies the relative URI that, along with the URI specified in the `http:address` element, constitutes the URI of the request. The `http:operation` element specifies the relative URI using the `location` attribute. The `http:operation` element has the following signature:

```
<definitions .... >
    <binding .... >
        <operation .... >
            <http:operation location="uri"/>
        </operation>
    </binding>
</definitions>
```

HTTP:URLENCODED

The `http:urlEncoded` element `<http:urlEncoded/>` specifies that all the message parts are encoded following the standard URI-encoding rules.

HTTP:URLREPLACEMENT

The `http:urlReplacement` element `<http:urlReplacement/>` specifies that all the message parts are encoded using a replacement algorithm.

Besides the preceding protocols, the Web Services Description Language (WSDL) 1.1 specifications also define binding extensions for the MIME message format — specifically, the following MIME type bindings:

◆ `Multipart/Related`

◆ `text/xml`

◆ `application/x-www-form-urlencoded`

◆ Others (if the MIME type strings completely define the contents)

The binding extension elements for MIME are as follows:

◆ The `mime:content` element

◆ The `mime:multipartRelated` element

◆ The `mime:mimeXml` element

WSDL in UDDI Registry

WSDL serves as an XML language for describing protocol bindings, interfaces, and the deployment details of network services. It complements the UDDI standard by offering a uniform way to describe protocol bindings and abstract interfaces of arbitrary network services. The following process shows how WSDL supports the creation of UDDI businessService entries:

1. Create the WSDL service-interface definition. This definition includes protocol bindings and service interfaces.

2. Implement the service interface to build services conforming to the industry-standard service definitions.

3. Deploy and register the new service in the UDDI repository to make it publicly available.

Appendix B

SOAP Fundamentals

SIMPLE OBJECT ACCESS PROTOCOL *(SOAP)* 1.1 defines a packaging model and an encoding mechanism to exchange information between entities in a distributed environment. This information is exchanged by using XML. SOAP comprises the following components:

- ◆ **The SOAP Envelope construct:** An enclosing construct that contains zero or more SOAP Headers. However, it contains only one SOAP body. Because the SOAP envelope is the top element of an XML document, it defines a framework to specify the details of a message.

- ◆ **The SOAP encoding rules:** Define the rules that you need to follow in exchanging application-specific data types.

- ◆ **The SOAP RPC representation:** Enables you to invoke an RPC-style request that provides access to the remote procedures exposed by a service interface.

SOAP messages always route through a message path. A *message path* consists of one or more nodes for processing the SOAP message, in addition to the final destination of the message. These SOAP processing nodes are also known as *endpoints*. The message path is a chain of processing nodes that provide message-filtering capabilities for the SOAP messages routing through it.

 For more information on SOAP messages, refer to Chapter 4.

The following sections discuss the various rules that SOAP messages follow.

Rules Followed by SOAP Messages

All SOAP messages must have a *SOAP Envelope* and a *SOAP Body*. Optionally, they may also have a *SOAP Header*. The following sections discuss the rules defined by the SOAP specifications for the SOAP Envelope, Header, and Body elements.

The SOAP Envelope element

The SOAP Envelope element represents the SOAP message. According to the SOAP specifications, the SOAP Envelope element should follow these rules:

◆ The element name must be *Envelope*.

◆ The element can contain namespace declarations, additional attributes, and additional subelements.

◆ If the element contains additional attributes, they should be namespace-qualified.

◆ If the element contains additional subelements, they should be namespace-qualified and should precede the SOAP Body element.

The Envelope element should be associated with the `http://schemas.xml.soap/soap/envelop/namespace` namespace. If a SOAP message containing a SOAP Envelope element that's associated with a different namespace is received, the message is discarded. If a SOAP application receives a SOAP message through a request/response protocol, the SOAP application must return a SOAP VersionMismatch faultcode message.

The SOAP Header element

The SOAP Header element is used to provide additional features such as application-specific information that a SOAP processor may require, to process a SOAP message. SOAP provides some attributes in the Header element that specify whether the features should be processed. The attributes also specify who should use these features and for what purpose. The SOAP Header element should follow these rules:

◆ The element name must be *Header*.

◆ The Header element being an optional element may be present in a SOAP message.

◆ If present, the Header element must appear as the topmost child element of the Envelope element.

◆ The Header element can contain child elements, also known as *header entries*.

◆ All header entries must be the immediate child elements of the Header element.

◆ All child elements of the Header element must be namespace-qualified.

◆ A Header entry should be identified by its fully qualified element name. A fully qualified name consists of the namespace URI and a local name.

- The SOAP `encodingStyle` attribute can be used to specify the encoding styles of the header entries.

- The SOAP `mustUnderstand` attribute can be used to specify how to process the header entries.

- The SOAP `actor` attribute can be used to specify who should process the header entries.

The SOAP Body element

The SOAP Body element is a mandatory element of a SOAP message. It contains the necessary information that the recipient of the SOAP message requires. The SOAP Body element should follow these rules:

- The element name must be *Body*.

- The Body element must be present in a SOAP message.

- If a Header element is present, the Body element should follow it.

- If a Header element is not present, the Body element must be the first immediate child element of the Envelope element.

- The Body element can contain child elements that are known as *body entries*.

- The child elements of a Body element must be namespace-qualified.

- Body entries should be identified by their fully qualified element name. A fully qualified name consists of the namespace URI and a local name.

- The SOAP `encodingStyle` attribute can be used to specify the encoding style of the body entries.

The SOAP Fault element

In addition to the Envelope, Header, and Body elements, a SOAP message also contains a SOAP Fault element. The SOAP Fault element contains error messages for the enclosing SOAP message. The SOAP Fault element can appear only once as a body entry inside the SOAP Body element. The subelements of the SOAP Fault element are as follows:

- `faultcode`: The `faultcode` element must be present in a SOAP Fault element. SOAP defines the following basic faultcode values:

  - `VersionMismatch`

  - `MustUnderstand`

  - `Client`

  - `Server`

- ◆ `faultstring`: The `faultstring` element must be present in a SOAP Fault element. The `faultstring` element should provide human-readable information describing the error if any error occurs during processing the SOAP message.

- ◆ `faultactor`: The `faultactor` element indicates the URI that is responsible for the fault. All intermediaries must include the `faultactor` element in the SOAP Fault element. The final destination application can specify the `faultactor` element to indicate that it generated the fault.

- ◆ `detail`: The `detail` element provides error information relating to the Body element. A Body element must contain the `detail` element if its content is not processable.

SOAP Encoding Rules

The Soap encoding rules are listed as follows:

- ◆ A *value* is a string that represents the name of a measurement or several primitive values. Values can be either simple or complex. Strings and integers are examples of simple values, whereas an array is an example of compound value. Values are represented as element content. Individual element content must represent multireference value. Multi-reference values can be referenced by more than one accessor.

- ◆ All elements that contain a value must represent the type of the value. They can do so by satisfying one of the following conditions:

  - ■ The instance of the element that contains a value also contains a `xsi:type` attribute.

  - ■ The parent element of the instance of the element contains a `SOAP-ENC:arrayType` attribute.

  - ■ The element name that contains a value has a relationship with the type of the value.

- ◆ Character data represents simple value. A simple value should have a type that is specified in the XML Schemas Specification, Part 2: Datatypes, or whose source type is declared. You can find the XML Schemas Specification, Part 2: Datatypes at `http://www.w3.org/TR/xmlschema-2/`.

- ◆ Compound values are encoded as a sequence of elements.

- ◆ A multireference simple or compound value is encoded as an element that contains an attribute `id` of type `ID`.

- ◆ Strings and byte arrays are represented as multireference simple values.

◆ SOAP arrays can be either single-reference or multireference values. Embedded or independent element's content can represent the SOAP array values. They have a type of `SOAP-ENC:Array` or its derived type. SOAP arrays must contain a `SOAP-ENC:arrayType` attribute.

SOAP RPC Representation

SOAP is used to make remote procedure calls and responses. The SOAP Body element contains the RPC method calls and responses with the following representation:

◆ Method invocations are modeled as `struct`.

◆ The name and the type of the `struct` are identical to its corresponding method name.

◆ Each `struct` contains an accessor for each `[in]` or `[in/out]` parameter.

◆ The accessor's name and type correspond to the name and type of the parameters.

◆ Method responses are modeled as `structs`.

◆ The `struct` contains an accessor for the return value and for each `[out]` and `[in/out]` parameter.

◆ The accessor's name and type corresponds to the name and type of the parameters.

◆ The SOAP Fault element encodes method faults.

Rules for SOAP Messages with Attachments

A SOAP message packet contains a SOAP message and some entities that are related to the SOAP message in some manner. These entities are often referred to as *attachments*. Predefined rules for the creation of a SOAP message package are as follows:

◆ The `root` part of the Multipart/Related structure should carry the primary SOAP message.

◆ The additional MIME parts must either contain a `Content-ID` MIME header or `Content-Location` MIME header.

◆ The `Content-ID` and `Content-Location` MIME headers should always be structured as defined in RFC 2045 and RFC 2557, respectively.

◆ The `type` parameter of the Multipart/Related media is always equal to the `Content-Type` header for the primary SOAP 1.1 message.

 You can refer to RFC 2045 at `www.ietf.org/rfc/rfc2045.txt` and RFC 2557 at `www.ietf.org/rfc/rfc2557.txt`.

Besides these rules, the SOAP Messages with Attachments specification also recommends that a SOAP message package should have a `start` parameter in addition to the required parameters for the Multipart/Related media type.

At times, you may need to transmit a SOAP message with attachments, such as documents or image files. This data is usually in binary format.

Rules Followed by SOAP Attributes

This section describes some of the important SOAP attributes and the rules followed by them. These attributes are as follows:

◆ **The SOAP `encodingStyle` attribute:** The `encodingStyle` attribute defines the serialization rules of a SOAP message. The `encodingStyle` attribute can be present in any SOAP element. It is a global attribute, and therefore its scope extends from the element that contains it to the enclosed child elements. The value of this attribute represents URIs that identify the serialization rules. SOAP serialization rules are identified by URIs such as `http://schemas.xmlsoap.org/soap/encoding`. Messages that follow the serialization rules identified by this URI should specify the URI in the `encodingStyle` attribute.

◆ **The SOAP `actor` attribute:** SOAP messages always travel through a message path. In addition to the final destination of the message, a message path consists of one or more processing nodes or SOAP intermediaries for processing the SOAP message. The intermediaries and the final destination are identified by a URI. A SOAP message's Header element may be sent to an intermediary. The intermediary that receives a Header element must not send the Header element farther in the message path. To indicate who should receive the Header element, the SOAP `actor` attribute is called. The SOAP `actor` attribute is a global attribute. If you do not specify the SOAP `actor` attribute, the final destination is considered to be the only recipient of the SOAP message.

◆ **The SOAP `mustUnderstand` attribute:** As I discuss in the preceding paragraph, the SOAP `actor` attribute specifies the recipient of the Header element of a SOAP message. To indicate whether the recipient should process the header entries of a Header element, you use the `mostUnderstand` attribute. The value of the SOAP `mostUnderstand` attribute is either 1 or 0. The value 1 implies that the recipient should process the header entries of the Header element according to the semantics specified by the fully qualified name of the Header element.

Rules for Using SOAP in HTTP

If SOAP is used over HTTP, the SOAP semantics map to the underlying HTTP semantics. SOAP messages may be used together with the *HTTP Extension framework*. Clients can enforce the use of the HTTP Extension framework by using a mandatory extension declaration and the M-HTTP method name prefix such as `M-Post`. Servers can enforce the use of HTTP Extension framework by using the `510 Not Extended` status code.

If used with HTTP, SOAP provides the SOAP request parameters in an HTTP request and the SOAP response parameters in an HTTP response.

If an HTTP application includes SOAP entity bodies, it must use the `text/xml` content type.

The `SOAPAction` HTTP-request header field specifies a URI that identifies the purpose of the request. All HTTP clients that send a SOAP HTTP request must specify the URI value in the `SOAPAction` HTTP header field.

SOAP HTTP uses status codes to provide status information on processing a request. If an error occurs during processing, the SOAP HTTP server must issue an HTTP `500 Internal Server Error` response, along with a SOAP Fault element.

Appendix C

Fundamentals of UDDI Version 2.0 Programmer's API

IN THE CURRENT E-BUSINESS SCENARIO, Web services are considered indispensable for carrying out business on the Web. Web services enable companies or individuals to publish their services that other clients, companies, individuals, or Web services can use. But the main challenge lies in the adoption of a standard mechanism that facilitates business description and business transaction on the Web in a global manner. This is where the role of *Universal Description, Discovery, and Integration (UDDI)* comes into picture. It provides a framework that enables potential business partners to discover each other on the Web. UDDI also defines how business partners perform business transactions on the Web.

The UDDI framework was initiated by a group of industrial leaders such as IBM, Microsoft Corp, and Ariba, Inc. Currently, more than 200 frontline companies are members of the UDDI community. The UDDI framework is based on the World Wide Web Consortium (W3C) and Internet Engineering Task Force (IETF) standards, such as XML, HTTP, and Domain Name Systems (DNS) protocols. It also relies on the Simple Object Access Protocol (SOAP) as its message-passing protocol. UDDI itself is a group of Web-based e-commerce directories, where registered companies can advertise their businesses. Businesses that host these directories are known as *Operator Sites*. Web services can register in these directories (also known as *registries*) and provide information regarding their services. Information can range from basic information, such as name of the service, business identifiers, and contact information, to descriptions of business and transaction procedures. Individual clients, business houses, and other Web services can access the directories and obtain the required information of the published registered service.

Following are some of the benefits that the UDDI projects provide:

- ◆ Companies can register with a service provider and make their services available to clients as well as reach out for additional prospective clients.

- ◆ Registered companies get wider market coverage.

- ◆ Companies can describe their services programmatically in a single, open, and secure environment.

431

- ◆ Companies can provide value-added services.

- ◆ Clients seeking services get access to a large number of registered service providers.

- ◆ Clients can view the service information, service details, and transaction procedures of various registered service providers and choose accordingly.

 You can register your company's products and services in UDDI's Business Registry at www.uddi.org/register.html.

The UDDI Community is developing a set of open specifications for implementing a standard service registry. The various UDDI Version 2.0 specifications are as follows:

- ◆ UDDI Version 2.0 Programmer's API Specification

- ◆ UDDI Version 2.0 Data Structure Specification

- ◆ UDDI Version 2.0 XML Schema

- ◆ UDDI Version 2.0 Replication Specification

- ◆ UDDI Version 2.0 XML Replication Schema

- ◆ UDDI Version 2.0 XML Custody Schema

- ◆ UDDI Version 2.0 Operator's Specification

Of the preceding UDDI specifications, the UDDI Version 2.0 Programmer's API Specification provides various messages to work with UDDI registries. As a programmer, you would use this API the most. Therefore, in this appendix, I would discuss the UDDI Version 2.0 Programmer's API Specification and the messages provided by the APIs of the specification.

The UDDI Version 2.0 Programmer's API Specification enables you to develop programs to discover Web services. You can also use this specification to build UDDI-compatible registries. The UDDI community designed the UDDI Version 2.0 Programmer's API Specification in accordance with the following design principles:

- ◆ **Security:** The UDDI community center provides the following two types of API to work with UDDI:

  - ■ **Inquiry API:** This API enables programs to access registries for information about services. You do not require any authentication to use this API.

- **Publishing API:** This API enables programs to store and change information or business data in the registries. To use this API's functions, you must register with an Operator Site and provide your credentials. The Publisher API functions are called over HTTPS (SSL3.0).

◆ **Versioning:** The programmer API is version-stamped to cope with the API versioning upgrade. A version attribute called the `generic` is provided, which accompanies all SOAP messages.

◆ **SOAP Messaging:** UDDI uses SOAP messages.

◆ **XML convention:** UDDI is based on the eXtensible Markup Language (XML) and uses specific XML constructs for the specification.

◆ **Error handling:** If some error occurs during the API calls, error codes return as per the SOAP specification.

The UDDI Version 2.0 Programmer's API comprises the inquiry API and the publishing API. You use the inquiry API messages of the programmers API to inquire a UDDI registry for published Web services. The publishing API provides various messages that you use to publish services on a UDDI registry.

The Inquiry API

The *Inquiry API* is used by programs to access registries for services. You use the various messages of the inquiry API in your program to access services in UDDI registries. The UDDI Version 2.0 Programmer's API Specification specifies This API provides three types of query patterns that are used by the programs to access the registries.

The Inquiry Patterns

The following three sections describe the query patterns that are used by registry specific programs to query a UDDI registry.

THE BROWSE PATTERN

Programs that typically explore hierarchical data follow this pattern. The program first browses for more general information and gradually narrows the query for more specific information.

You can use this pattern to first enquire whether the business you are looking up is registered in the registry. For this, you use the `find_business` call. After you locate your business, you can perform queries on more specific information that you require by using the `find_service` call.

THE DRILL-DOWN PATTERN

To understand the drill-down pattern, you need to know the concept of *access keys*. The UDDI project provides the following four data types:

- `businessEntity`
- `businessService`
- `bindingTemplate`
- `tModel`

You require an access key to obtain details of these data types. All data elements define the required access key. You acquire an access key by using one of the find_xx calls. After you acquire the access key, you can use it to access business details by passing its value as an argument in the `get_businessDetail` call.

THE INVOCATION PATTERN

A program that wants to access a registered service obtains the details of a business instance and the location at which business transactions should start. These details are obtained from the `bindingTemplate` data. The program caches the information and uses it whenever required. But if the service moves to a different location, the program needs to query the UDDI registry again for the new `bindingTemplate` information. A program can call the `get_bindingDetails()` method, passing the original `bindingKey` value as a parameter. After the program gets the required information, it replaces the cached information with the newly acquired data.

The following sections discuss various messages provided by the Inquiry API.

The Inquiry API messages

You can use the messages of the Inquiry API in your program to inquire UDDI registries. Some of the important messages are discussed in this section.

THE FIND_BINDING MESSAGE

You call this message to look up specific bindings within a registered service. The following example displays the syntax of the find_binding message:

```
<find_binding serviceKey="uuid_key" [maxRows="nn"] generic="2.0"
         xmlns="urn:uddi-org:api_v2" >
                    [<findQualifiers/>]
                    <tModelBag/>
</find_binding>
```

The following list elaborates on the various elements of this example:

- `serviceKey`: Identifies a `businessService` element in the registry.
- `maxRows`: Specifies the number of results that should return to you.

- ◆ findQualifiers: Changes the behavior of the search functionality.

- ◆ tModelBag: Specifies tModel keys. Binding templates that contain all the tModel keys specified in this arguments are returned.

The find_binding call returns a bindingDetail message. If you do not provide the required arguments the call returns an empty bindingDetail structure.

If an error occurs, a dispositionReport element returns with the following information:

- ◆ E_invalidKeyPassed: Appears if the uuid_key value passed in the serviceKey attribute does not match with any of the serviceKey values.

- ◆ E_unsupported: Appears if the value of the findQualifier attribute is invalid.

THE FIND_BUSINESS MESSAGE

You call this message to access information about the business and the services that the business offers. Following is the syntax of the find_business message:

```
<find_business [maxRows="nn"] generic="2.0" xmlns="urn:uddi-org:
api_v2" >
        [<findQualifiers/>]
        [<name/> [<name/>]...1]
[<discoveryURLs/>]
[<identifierBag/>]
[<categoryBag/>]
[<tModelBag/>]
</find_business>
```

The following list describes the elements of this message:

- ◆ maxRows: Used to specify the number of results that should return.

- ◆ findQualifiers: Used to change the behavior of the search functionality.

- ◆ name: Used to specify the name of the business that you want to access in this argument. You can specify up to five values.

- ◆ IdentifierBag: Used to provide a business-identifier references list in this argument.

- ◆ categoryBag: Used to provide a list of category references in this argument.

- ◆ discoveryURLs: Used to specify a list of URLs, which is matched with the discoveryURL data associated with any registered information.

After you call `find_business`, it returns a `businessList` that provides information regarding each matching business and the services that it provides. If no matches are found, a `businessList` structure with zero `businessInfo` structure is returned.

If any error occurs in the call, a `dispositionReport` structure returns with the following information:

♦ `E_nameTooLong`: Appears if the value passed in the `name` argument exceeds the maximum value specified in the UDDI data structure reference.

♦ `E_unsupported`: Appears if you pass an invalid `findQualifier` value.

♦ `E_tooManyOptions`: Appears if you specify more than five `name` values.

THE FIND_RELATEDBUSINESSES MESSAGE

The `find_relatedBusinesses` message returns a `relatedBusinessList` message. You call this message to access the information of the `relatedBusinessesList` message. The syntax of the `find_relatedBusinesses` message is as follows:

```
<find_relatedBusinesses generic="2.0" xmlns="urn:uddi-org:api_v2" >
[<findQualifiers/>]
<businessKey/>
[<keyedReference/>]
</find_relatedBusinesses>
```

The following list describes the individual elements of this message:

♦ `findQualifiers`: Used to change the behavior of the search functionality.

♦ `businessKey`: Used to specify the `businessEntity` object to use as the entry point of your search. This attribute takes the `uuid_key` as a value.

♦ `keyedReference`: Used to specify that the `find_Related` method result should include businesses that are specifically tied to your `businessEntity` object.

After you call the `find_relatedBusinesses` message, it returns a `related-BusinessesList`. If no matches are found, it returns a `relatedBusinessesList` containing an empty `relatedBusinessInfos` element.

A `dispositionReport` structure with the following information returns if any error occurs in the call:

♦ `E_invalidKeyPassed`: Appears if the `uuid_key` or `tModel` key value passed in the `serviceKey` attribute does not match with any of the `businessKey` or `tModel` key values.

♦ `E_unsupported`: Appears if you specify an invalid `findQualifier` value.

THE FIND_SERVICE MESSAGE

The `find_service` method returns a `serviceList` message. You call this method to access the information about the `serviceList` message. The syntax of the `find_service` message is as follows:

```
<find_service businessKey="uuid_key" " [maxRows="nn"] generic="2.0
        xmlns="urn:uddi-org:api_v2" >
        [<findQualifiers/>]
        [<name/> [<name/>]...2]
[<categoryBag/>]
[<tModelBag/>]
</find_service>
```

The preceding syntax has the following arguments:

- ◆ `businessKey`: Specify the `uuid_key` of a registered businessEntity instance in this argument to access its information.

- ◆ `maxRows`: Use this argument to specify the number of results that should return to you.

- ◆ `findQualifiers`: Specify this argument to change the behavior of the search functionality.

- ◆ `name`: Specify the name of the business that you want to access in this argument. You can specify up to five values.

- ◆ `categoryBag`: Provide a list of category references in this argument.

- ◆ `tModelBag`: Specify a list of `tModel uuid_key` values in this argument.

After you call the `find_relatedBusinesses` message, a `relatedBusinessesList` returns. If no match is found, the returned `serviceList` message contains an empty `businessServices` element.

If any error occurs in the call, a `dispositionReport` structure returns with the following information:

- ◆ `E_invalidKeyPassed`: Appears if the `uuid_key` or `tModel` key value passed in the `serviceKey` attribute does not match with any `businessKey` or `tModel` key values.

- ◆ `E_nameTooLong`: Appears if the value in the `name` argument exceeds the maximum value specified in the UDDI data structure reference.

- ◆ `E_unsupported`: Appears if you specify an invalid `findQualifier` value or if you do not specify a `name` value.

THE FIND_TMODEL MESSAGE

You call this message to locate a list of tModel entries that match the arguments that you specify. The syntax of the find_tModel message is as follows:

```
<find_tModel [maxRows="nn"] generic="2.0" xmlns="urn:uddi-org:
api_v2" >
          [<findQualifiers/>]
          [<name/>]
[<identifierBag/>]
[<categoryBag/>]
</find_tModel>
```

The preceding syntax has the following arguments:

- ◆ maxRows: Use this argument to specify the number of results that should be returned.

- ◆ findQualifiers: Specify this argument to change the behavior of the search functionality.

- ◆ name: Specify the name of the business that you want to access in this argument. You can specify up to five values.

- ◆ identifierBag: Specify a list of business-identifier references in this argument to retrieve the matching tModelInfo elements.

- ◆ categoryBag: Provide a list of category references in this argument to retrieve the matching tModelInfo elements.

After you call find_tModel, a tModelList message returns. If no match is found, the returned tModelList message contains an empty tModelInfos element.

If any error occurs in the call, a dispositionReport element returns with the following information:

- ◆ E_nameTooLong: Appears if the value passed in the name argument exceeds the maximum value specified in the UDDI data structure reference.

- ◆ E_unsupported: Appears if you specify an invalid findQualifier value or if you do not specify a name value.

THE GET_BINDINGDETAIL MESSAGE

To communicate with a registered business, you require the run-time bindingTemplate information, which you can access by calling the get_bindingDetail message. The syntax of the get_bindingDetail message is as follows:

```
<get_bindingDetail generic="2.0" xmlns="urn:uddi-org:api_v2" >
        <bindingKey/> [<bindingKey/> ...]
</get_bindingDetail>
```

The preceding syntax takes the bindingKey argument. You specify one or more uuid_key values in this argument. The uuid_key value should match with the key of the registered bindingTemplate data instance.

After you call the get_bindingDetail message, a bindingDetail message returns.

If any error occurs in your call, a dispositionReport structure returns. The E_invalidKeyPassed error appears if even one of the values passed in the bindingKey argument does not match with any known bindingKey values.

THE GET_BUSINESSDETAIL MESSAGE

You call the get_businessDetail API to access registered businessEntity information. The syntax of the get_businessDetail message is as follows:

```
<get_businessDetail generic="2.0" xmlns="urn:uddi-org:api_v2" >
        <businessKey/> [<businessKey/> ...]
</get_businessDetail>
```

The preceding syntax takes the businessKey argument. You specify one or more uuid_key values corresponding to registered businessEntity data instances in this argument.

After you call the get_businessDetail message, a businessDetail message returns.

If any error occurs in the call, a dispositionReport structure returns. The E_invalidKeyPassed error appears if one of the values passed in the businessKey argument does not match with any known businessKey values.

THE GET_ BUSINESSDETAILEXT MESSAGE

You call the get_businessDetailExt message to access registered business-Entity information. The syntax of the message is as follows:

```
<get_businessDetailExt generic="2.0" xmlns="urn:uddi-org:api_v2" >
        <businessKey/> [<businessKey/> ...]
</get_businessDetailExt>
```

The preceding syntax takes the businessKey argument. You specify one or more uuid_key values corresponding to registered businessEntity data instances.

After you call the get_businessDetailExt message, a businessDetailExt message returns.

If any errors occur in your call, a dispositionReport structure returns with the following information:

- ◆ E_invalidKeyPassed: Appears if one of the values you passed in the businessKey argument does not match with any known businessKey values.

- ◆ E_unsupported: Appears if the Operator Site does not support this message.

THE GET_SERVICEDETAIL MESSAGE

You call the get_serviceDetail message to access the registered businessService structure information. The syntax of the message is as follows:

```
<get_serviceDetail generic="2.0" xmlns="urn:uddi-org:api_v2" >
        <serviceKey/> [<serviceKey/> ...]
</get_serviceDetail>
```

The preceding syntax takes the ServiceKey argument. You specify one or more uuid_key values in this argument corresponding to registered businessService data instances.

After you call the get_serviceDetail message, a serviceDetail message returns.

A dispositionReport element returns if any error occurs in the call. The E_invalidKeyPassed appears if one of the values passed in the bindingKey argument does not match with any known serviceKey values.

THE GET_TMODELDETAIL MESSAGE

You call the get_tModelDetail message to access registered tModel data. The syntax of the message is as follows:

```
<get_tModelDetail generic="2.0" xmlns="urn:uddi-org:api_v2" >
        <tModelKey/>
        [<tModelKey/> ...]
</get_tModelDetail>
```

The preceding syntax takes the tModelKey argument. You specify one or more uuid_key values in this argument corresponding to tModelKey values of registered tModel data instances.

After you call the get_tModelDetail message, a tModelDetail message returns.

A dispositionReport structure returns if any error occurs in the call. The E_invalidKeyPassed error returns if one of the values passed in the tModelKey argument does not match with any known tModelKey values.

The UDDI Publishing API

You use the Publishing API calls to publish and update your business in a registry of an Operator Site. The following sections discuss the various calls of the UDDI Publishing API.

The add_publisherAssertions call

You use the `add_publisherAssertions` API call to add one or more instances of `publisherAssertion` into your assertion collection. The syntax is as follows:

```
<add_publisherAssertions generic="2.0" xmlns="urn:uddi-org:api_v2" >
      <authInfo/>
<publisherAssertion>
<fromKey/>
<toKey/>
<keyedReference/>
</publisherAssertion>
      [<publisherAssertion/> ...]
</add_publisherAssertions>
```

This syntax takes the following arguments:

◆ `authInfo`: Specify an authentication token element in this argument. You obtain an authentication token element by calling the `get_authToken` API.

An *authentication token element* provides the necessary authentication information. The authentication token values are required for calling all the publishers API. You can obtain the authentication token by calling `get_authToken`, which I discuss in the section "The get_authToken call," later in this appendix.

◆ `publisherAssertion`: Specify one or more relationship assertions in this argument.

After you call `add_publisherAssertions`, a `dispositionReport` message returns.

If any error occurs in the call, a `dispositionReport` structure returns with the following information:

◆ `E_invalidKeyPassed`: Returns if one of the `uuid_key` values does not match any known business key or `tModelKey` values.

◆ `E_authTokenExpired`: Returns if the authentication token passed in the `authInfo` call has expired.

◆ `E_authTokenRequired`: Returns if the authentication token passed in the `authInfo` call is invalid or if an authentication token is not passed in the `authInfo` call.

The delete_binding call

You use this API call to delete one or more instances of the `bindingTemplate` data. The syntax is as follows:

```
<delete_binding generic="2.0" xmlns="urn:uddi-org:api_v2" >
        <authInfo/>
        <bindingKey/> [<bindingKey/> ...]
</delete_binding>
```

The preceding syntax takes the following arguments:

◆ `authInfo`: Specify an authentication token element in this argument. You obtain an authentication token element by calling `get_authToken`.

◆ `bindingKey`: Specify one or more `uuid_key` values in this argument, corresponding to registered `bindingTemplate` data instances.

After you call `add_publisherAssertions`, a `dispositionReport` message returns if the call is successful.

If any error occurs in the call, a `dispositionReport` structure returns with the following information:

◆ `E_invalidKeyPassed`: Returns if one of the `uuid_key` values does not match with any known business key or `tModelKey` values.

◆ `E_authTokenExpired`: Returns if the authentication token passed in the `authInfo` call has expired.

◆ `E_authTokenRequired`: Returns if the authentication token passed in the `authInfo` call is invalid or if an authentication token is not passed in the `authInfo` call.

◆ `E_userMismatch`: Returns if a `bindingKey` value passed in the `bindingKey` argument corresponds to a `bindingTemplate` that is not controlled by the individual associated with the authentication token.

The delete_business call

You use the `delete_business` API call to delete one or more instances of the `businessEntity` data. The syntax of the call is as follows:

```
<delete_business generic="2.0" xmlns="urn:uddi-org:api_v2" >
        <authInfo/>
        <businessKey/>
        [<businessKey/> ...]
</delete_business>
```

The preceding syntax takes the following arguments:

- ◆ `authInfo`: Specify an authentication token element in this argument.

- ◆ `businessKey`: Specify one or more `uuid_key` values in this argument, corresponding to registered `businessEntity` data instances.

After you call `delete_business`, a `dispositionReport` message returns if the call is successful.

If any error occurs in the call, a `dispositionReport` element returns with the following information:

- ◆ `E_invalidKeyPassed`: Returns if one of the `uuid_key` values does not match with any known business key values.

- ◆ `E_authTokenExpired`: Returns if the authentication token passed in the `authInfo` call has expired.

- ◆ `E_authTokenRequired`: Returns if the authentication token passed in the `authInfo` call is invalid or an authentication token is not passed in the `authInfo` call.

- ◆ `E_userMismatch`: Returns if a `bindingKey` value passed in the `bindingKey` argument corresponds to a `bindingTemplate` that is not controlled by the individual associated with the authentication token.

The delete_publisherAssertions call

You call `delete_publisherAssertions` to delete one or more `publisherAssertion` elements from your assertion collection. The syntax of the call is as follows:

```
<delete_publisherAssertions generic="2.0" xmlns="urn:uddi-org:
api_v2" >
        <authInfo/>
<publisherAssertion>
<fromKey/>
<toKey/>
<keyedReference/>
</publisherAssertion>
        [<publisherAssertion/> ...]
</delete_publisherAssertions>
```

The preceding syntax takes the following arguments:

- ◆ `authInfo`: Specify an authentication token element in this argument.

- ◆ `publisherAssertion`: Specify one or more publisher assertion structures in this argument, corresponding to an exiting assertion.

After you call `delete_business`, a `dispositionReport` message returns if the call is successful.

If any error occurs in your call, a `dispositionReport` element returns with the following information:

- ◆ `E_assertionNotFound`: Returns if the passed assertion structure does not correspond to a structure in the assertion collection.

- ◆ `E_authTokenExpired`: Returns if the authentication token passed in the `authInfo` call has expired.

- ◆ `E_authTokenRequired`: Returns if the authentication token passed in the `authInfo` call is invalid or if an authentication token is not passed in the `authInfo` call.

The delete_service call

You use the `delete_service` call to delete one or more `businessService` elements from the registry. The syntax is as follows:

```
<delete_service generic="2.0" xmlns="urn:uddi-org:api_v2" >
        <authInfo/>
        <serviceKey/>
        [<serviceKey/> ...]
</delete_service>
```

The syntax takes the following arguments:

- ◆ `authInfo`: Specify an authentication token element in this argument.

- ◆ `serviceKey`: Specify one or more `uuid_key` values in this argument, corresponding to registered `businessService` data instances.

After you call `delete_service`, a `dispositionReport` message returns if the call is successful.

If any error occurs in your call, a `dispositionReport` structure returns with the following information:

- ◆ `E_invalidKeyPassed`: Returns if any one of the `uuid_key` values does not match with any known business key values.

- ◆ `E_authTokenExpired`: Returns if the authentication token passed in the `authInfo` call has expired.

- ◆ `E_authTokenRequired`: Returns if the authentication token passed in the `authInfo` call is invalid or an authentication token is not supplied in the `authInfo` call.

- ◆ E_userMismatch: Returns if a bindingKey value passed in the bindingKey argument corresponds to a bindingTemplate that is not controlled by the individual associated with the authentication token.

The delete_tModel call

You call delete_tModel to delete one or more tModel structures. The syntax of the call is as follows:

```
<delete_tModel generic="2.0" xmlns="urn:uddi-org:api_v2" >
        <authInfo/>
        <tModelKey/> [<tModelKey/> ...]
</delete_tModel>
```

The syntax takes the following arguments:

- ◆ authInfo: Specify an authentication token element in this argument.

- ◆ tModelKey: Specify one or more uuid_key values, corresponding to registered tModel data instances, in this argument.

After you call delete_tModel, a dispositionReport message returns if the call is successful.

If any error occurs in the call, a dispositionReport element returns with the following information:

- ◆ E_invalidKeyPassed: Returns if any one of the specified uuid_key values does not match with any known business key values.

- ◆ E_authTokenExpired: Returns if the authentication token passed in the authInfo call has expired.

- ◆ E_authTokenRequired: Returns if the authentication token passed in the authInfo call is invalid or an authentication token is not specified in the authInfo call.

- ◆ E_userMismatch: Returns if a bindingKey value passed in the bindingKey argument corresponds to a bindingTemplate that is not controlled by the individual associated with the authentication token.

The discard_authToken call

You use the discard_authToken call to inform the operator site to discard the authentication token. The syntax of the discard_authToken call is as follows:

```
<discard_authToken generic="2.0" xmlns="urn:uddi-org:api_v2" >
        <authInfo/>
</discard_authToken>
```

The syntax takes the `authInfo` argument. You specify an authentication token element in this argument. This authentication token element is obtained by using the `get_authToken` API call.

After you call `discard_authToken`, a `dispositionReport` message returns if the call is successful.

A `dispositionReport` element returns if any error occurs in the call. The `E_authTokenRequired` error returns if the authentication token passed in the `authInfo` call is invalid or no authentication token is provided while using the `authInfo` call.

The get_assertionStatusReport call

The `get_assertionStatusReport` call is used to view the status of publisher assertions. The syntax of the get_assertionStatusReport call is as follows:

```
<get_assertionStatusReport generic="2.0" xmlns="urn:uddi-org:
api_v2" >
        <authInfo/>
[<completionStatus/>]
</get_assertionStatusReport>
```

The preceding syntax takes the following arguments:

- ◆ `authInfo`: Specify an authentication token element in this argument. The authentication token element is obtained by calling `get_authToken`.

- ◆ `completionStatus`: In this argument, specify the completion status. This argument can take any of the following values: `status:complete`, `status:toKey_incomplete`, or `status:fromKey_incomplete`.

After you call `get_assertionStatusReport`, an `assertionStatusReport` message returns.

If any error occurs in the call, a `dispositionReport` element returns with the following information:

- ◆ `E_invalidCompletionStatus`: Returns if the specified `completionStatus` value is invalid.

- ◆ `E_authTokenExpired`: Returns if the authentication token specified in the `authInfo` call has expired.

- ◆ `E_authTokenRequired`: Returns if the authentication token passed in the `authInfo` call is invalid or no authentication token is specified in the `authInfo` call.

The get_authToken call

The `get_authToken` call is used to obtain the authentication token that is required for calling all the Publishing API calls. The syntax of the `get_authToken` call is as follows:

```
<get_authToken generic="2.0" xmlns="urn:uddi-org:api_v2"
        userID="yourAssignedLoginName"
        cred="yourCredential" />
```

The preceding syntax takes the following arguments:

- `userID`: Specify your user identifier in this argument.

- `cred`: Specify your password in this argument.

After you call `get_authToken`, an `authToken` message returns. The `authToken` message contains the `authInfo` element that you use for calling all the Publishing API call.

If any error occurs in the call, a `dispositionReport` element returns. The `E_unknownUser` error returns if the specified `userID` or password is not valid.

The get_publisherAssertions call

The `get_publisherAssertions` call is used to obtain the full set of publisher assertions. The syntax of the call is as follows:

```
<get_publisherAssertions generic="2.0" xmlns="urn:uddi-org:api_v2" >
        <authInfo/>
</get_publisherAssertions
```

The preceding syntax takes the `authInfo` argument. You specify an authentication token element in this argument.

After you call `get_publisherAssertions`, a `publisherAssertions` message returns. The `publisherAssertions` message contains a `publisherAssertion` element for each registered `publisherAssertion`.

If any error occurs in the call, a `dispositionReport` element returns with the following information:

- `E_authTokenExpired`: Returns if the authentication token specified in the `authInfo` call has expired.

- `E_authTokenRequired`: Returns if the authentication token specified in the `authInfo` call is invalid or no authentication token is specified in the `authInfo` call.

The get_registeredInfo call

You use the get_registeredInfo API call to obtain your businessEntity or tModel data. The syntax of this call is as follows:

```
<get_registeredInfo generic="2.0" xmlns="urn:uddi-org:api_v2" >
        <authInfo/>
</get_registeredInfo>
```

The preceding syntax takes the authInfo argument.

After you call get_registeredInfo, a registeredInfo message returns. The registeredInfo message contains one or more businessInfo elements or tModel elements.

If any error occurs in the call, a dispositionReport element returns with the following information:

◆ E_authTokenExpired: Returns if the authentication token passed in the authInfo call has expired.

◆ E_authTokenRequired: Returns if the authentication token specified in the authInfo call is invalid or no authentication token is specified in the authInfo call.

The save_binding call

You use the save_binding API call to save the bindingTemplate element. The syntax of the call is as follows:

```
<save_binding generic="2.0" xmlns="urn:uddi-org:api_v2" >
        <authInfo/>
        <bindingTemplate/> [<bindingTemplate/>...]
</save_binding>
```

The preceding syntax takes the following arguments:

◆ authInfo: Specify an authentication token element in this argument.

◆ bindingTemplate: Specify one or more bindingTemplate elements in this argument.

After you call save_binding, a bindingDetail message returns.

If any error occurs, a dispositionReport element returns with the following information:

◆ E_invalidKeyPassed: Returns if the specified uuid_key values do not match with the known business key values.

- ◆ E_authTokenExpired: Returns if the authentication token specified in the authInfo call has expired.

- ◆ E_authTokenRequired: Returns if the authentication token specified in the authInfo call is invalid or no authentication token is specified in the authInfo argument.

- ◆ E_userMismatch: Returns if a bindingKey value specified in the bindingKey argument corresponds to a bindingTemplate that is not controlled by the individual associated with the authentication token.

- ◆ E_accountLimitExceeded: Returns if the limit of the user account is exceeded.

The save_business call

You use the save_business call to save your businessEntity element. The syntax of the call is as follows:

```
<save_business generic="2.0" xmlns="urn:uddi-org:api_v2" >
        <authInfo/>
        <businessEntity/> [<businessEntity/>...]
</save_business>
```

The preceding syntax takes the following arguments:

- ◆ authInfo: Specify an authentication token element in this argument.

- ◆ businessEntity: Specify one or more businessEntity elements in this argument.

After you call save_business, a businessDetail message returns.

If any error occurs, a dispositionReport element returns with the following information:

- ◆ E_authTokenExpired: Returns if the authentication token specified in the authInfo call has expired.

- ◆ E_authTokenRequired: Returns if the authentication token passed in the authInfo call is invalid or you do not pass an authentication token in the authInfo call.

- ◆ E_userMismatch: Returns if a bindingKey value passed in the bindingKey argument corresponds to a bindingTemplate that is not controlled by the individual associated with the authentication token.

- ◆ E_invalidKeyPassed: Returns if any of the specified uuid_key values do not match with any known business key values.

◆ E_invalidValue: Returns if the specified keyValue is invalid.

◆ E_accountLimitExceeded: Returns if the limit of the user's account is exceeded.

The save_service call

The save_service API call is used to save or update one or more of your business-Service elements. The syntax is as follows:

```
<save_service generic="2.0" xmlns="urn:uddi-org:api_v2" >
        <authInfo/>
        <businessService/> [<businessService/>...]
</save_service>
```

The preceding syntax takes the following arguments:

◆ authInfo: Specify an authentication token element in this argument.

◆ businessService: Specify one or more businessService elements in this argument.

After you call save_service, a serviceDetail message returns. The serviceDetail message contains information about the businessService elements.

If any error occurs, a dispositionReport element returns in with the following information:

◆ E_authTokenExpired: Returns if the authentication token specified in the authInfo call has expired.

◆ E_authTokenRequired: Returns if the authentication token passed in the authInfo call is invalid or you do not specify an authentication token in the authInfo call.

◆ E_userMismatch: Returns if a bindingKey value passed in the bindingKey argument corresponds to a bindingTemplate that is not controlled by the individual associated with the authentication token.

◆ E_invalidKeyPassed: Returns if any of the specified uuid_key values do not match with any known business key values.

◆ E_invalidValue: Returns if the specified keyValue is invalid.

◆ E_valueNotAllowed: Returns if the Operator Site rejects the specified businessService data.

◆ E_accountLimitExceeded: Returns if the limit of the user's account is exceeded.

The save_tModel call

The `save_tModel` API call is used to save or update one or more of your `tModel` elements. The syntax of the call is as follows:

```
<save_tModel generic="2.0" xmlns="urn:uddi-org:api_v2" >
        <authInfo/>
        <tModel/> [<tModel/>...]
</save_tModel>
```

The preceding syntax takes the following arguments:

- `authInfo`: Specify an authentication token element in this argument.

- `tModel`: Specify one or more `tModel` elements in this argument.

After you call `save_tModel`, a `tModelDetail` message returns. This message contains information about the `tModel` elements.

If any error occurs, a `dispositionReport` element returns in with the following information:

- `E_authTokenExpired`: Returns if the authentication token specified in the `authInfo` call has expired.

- `E_authTokenRequired`: Returns if the authentication token passed in the `authInfo` call is invalid or you do not specify an authentication token in the `authInfo` call.

- `E_userMismatch`: Returns if a `bindingKey` value passed in the `bindingKey` argument corresponds to a `bindingTemplate` that is not controlled by the individual associated with the authentication token.

- `E_invalidKeyPassed`: Returns if any of the specified `uuid_key` values does not match with any known business key values.

- `E_invalidValue:` Returns if the specified `keyValue` is invalid.

- `E_valueNotAllowed:` Returns if the Operator Site rejects the specified `businessService` data.

- `E_accountLimitExceeded`: Returns if the limit of the user's account is exceeded.

The set_publisherAssertions call

The `set_publisherAssertions` call is used to manage the tracked relationship assertions of a publisher's account. The syntax of the call is as follows:

```
<set_publisherAssertions generic="2.0" xmlns="urn:uddi-org:api_v2" >
     <authInfo/>
<publisherAssertion>
<fromKey/>
<toKey/>
<keyedReference/>
</publisherAssertion> [<publisherAssertion>...]
</set_publisherAssertions>
```

The preceding syntax takes the following arguments:

♦ authInfo: Specify an authentication token element in this argument.

♦ publisherAssertion: Specify one or more relationship assertions in this argument.

After you call set_publisherAssertions, a publisherAssertions message returns.

If any error occurs, a dispositionReport element returns in with the following information:

♦ E_authTokenExpired: Returns if the authentication token specified in the authInfo call has expired.

♦ E_authTokenRequired: Returns if the authentication token passed in the authInfo call is invalid or you do not specify an authentication token in the authInfo call.

♦ E_userMismatch: Returns if a bindingKey value passed in the bindingKey argument corresponds to a bindingTemplate that is not controlled by the individual associated with the authentication token.

♦ E_invalidKeyPassed: Returns if any of the specified uuid_key values do not match any known business key values.

Appendix D

XML Primer

IN THE CURRENT SCENARIO, XML is becoming the preferred technology for exchanging data over the Internet. A knowledge of XML, therefore, is important to conveniently understanding other technologies, such as WSDL and SOAP, in the stack of Web services.

This appendix briefly covers the specifications of the eXtensible Markup Language (XML), eXtensible Stylesheet Language (XSL), XSL Transformations (XSLT), XML Path Language (XPath), XML Schema, and XML Namespaces, formulated per the W3C recommendations.

The eXtensible Markup Language (XML) 1.0

XML was developed by an XML Working Group, formed under the auspices of the World Wide Web Consortium (W3C), with the following design goals:

◆ XML should be simple and easy to use across the Internet.

◆ XML should support variety of applications.

◆ XML should conform to SGML documents.

◆ XML should have minimum optional features.

◆ XML documents should be easy to create and easy to comprehend.

◆ Programs processing XML documents should be easy to develop.

 You can view the specifications of the *eXtensible Markup Language (XML)* 1.0 (second edition) per the W3C recommendation at www.w3.org/ TR/REC-xml.

XML documents

An XML document consists of entities. Entities contain content and can contain either parsed or unparsed data. An XML document contains a document entity that acts as the root of the document. A well-formed document should meet the following constraints:

- ◆ It should contain one or more elements between a start tag and an end tag. An empty element that does not have a start-tag and an end-tags should have an empty-element tag. The syntax of an empty-element tag is < ...element name---/>
- ◆ All tags should be nested correctly.
- ◆ All parsed entities referred to (directly or indirectly) should be well-formed.
- ◆ It should have a `root` or `document` element. This `root` element should not appear in the content of any other element.

Characters

A *parsed entity* contains a sequence of characters that represent either *markup* or *character data*. An XML processor must accept all characters in the following range:

```
Char ::= #x9 | #xA | #xD | [#x20-#xD7FF] | [#xE000-#xFFFD] |
[#x10000-#x10FFFF]
```

Character data

All text that is not markup text constitutes the character data of a document. Character data has the following grammar:

```
CharData ::=   [^<&]* - ([^<&]* ']]>' [^<&]*)
```

Comments

Comments in an XML documents should conform to the following specifications:

- ◆ Comments can appear outside markup anywhere in a document.
- ◆ Comments are not recognized as character data.
- ◆ The double-hyphen that you use to represent strings should not appear inside comments.
- ◆ Parameter reference entities should not appear inside comments.

Comments have the following grammar:

```
Comment ::= '<!--' ((Char - '-') | ('-' ((Char - '-')))* '‡'
```

Processing Instructions

Processing instructions in an XML document should follow these specifications:

◆ Processing instructions are not considered character data.

◆ Processing instructions begin with a `PITarget`.

◆ Parameter reference entities of processing instructions should not appear inside comments.

◆ You can use the XML notation mechanism, which is a syntax to declare `PITargets`, as shown in the following code:

```
PITarget ::=  Name - (('X' | 'x') ('M' | 'm') ('L' | 'l'))
```

Processing instructions have the following grammar:

```
PI ::=  '<?' PITarget (S (Char* - (Char* '?>' Char*)))? '?>'
```

PITarget ::= Name – (('X' | 'x') ('M' | 'm') ('L' | 'l'))CDATA section

You use the CDATA sections in XML documents to prevent blocks of text containing characters from being recognized as markup by XML parsers. The specifications for CDATA sections are as follows:

◆ CDATA sections can appear anywhere that character data can appear.

◆ CDATA sections begin with '! [CDATA['.

◆ CDATA section ends with ']]>'.

◆ CDATA sections cannot nest.

CDATA sections have the following grammar:

```
CDSect ::=CDStart Cdata CDEnd
CDStart ::= '<![CDATA['
CDATA ::= (Char* - (Char* ']]>' Char*))
CDEnd ::= ']]>'
```

Prolog and document type declaration

Document type declarations define the constraints of the structure of an XML document. A well-formed XML document is not considered a valid document, if it does not have a corresponding document type declaration. The markup declarations that the document declaration points to or contains provide a grammar known as *document tType definition (DTD)* for a class of documents. The document type declaration has the following grammar:

```
doctypedecl::= '!DOCTYPE' S Name (S ExternalID) ? S? ('('(markupdecl
| DeclSep)*')' S?)? '>')
DeclSep ::= PEReference | S
Markupdecl ::= elementdecl |
                        AttlistDecl |
                        EntityDecl |
                    NotationDecl |
                                    PI |
                Comment
```

The document type declaration should follow these constraints:

◆ The document type declaration should appear before the first element of the XML document.

◆ The document type declaration can refer to an external subset that contains markup declarations or can contain the markup declarations.

◆ In markup declaration, parameter-entity replacement text should be nested correctly.

◆ A well-formed document must have a `doctypedecl` declaration, which neither points to an external subset nor contains an internal subset.

◆ In a Document Type Definition (DTD) parameter entity, references cannot appear in literals, processing instructions, comments, and the content of ignored conditional sections.

◆ The `Name` in the document type declaration and the element type of the root element should match.

◆ Parameter-entity replacement text must nest correctly within markup declarations.

◆ In an internal DTD subset, parameter-entity references can occur only where markup declarations can occur.

◆ An external subset must match the production for `extsubsetDecl`. The grammar of `extsubsetDecl` is as follows:

```
ExtSubset ::= TextDecl? ExtSubsetDecl
ExtSubsetDecl ::=( markupdecl | conditionalSect | DeclSep)*
```

Standalone document declaration

Standalone declarations appear as a component of the XML declarations to provide information about whether any declarations appear external to the document entity or in parameter entities. The standalone document declaration has the following grammar:

```
SDDecl ::= S 'standalone' Eq (("'"
                ('yes' | 'no') "'") | ('"'
                ('yes' | 'no') '"'))
```

The value 'yes' in a standalone declaration signifies that no external markup declarations affect the information passing from an XML processor to the application. However, a standalone document declaration has no meaning in the absence of an external markup declaration. In the absence of a standalone document declaration, the value is assumed to be 'no'.

Logical structures of an XML document

Each XML document contains one or more elements. Each element has a name and may have a set of attribute specifications consisting of a name and a value. Element of an XML document has the following grammar:

```
Element ::= EmptyElementTag | STag content Etag
```

The name in an element's end tag must match with the start-tag element type. The start tag has the following grammar:

```
Stag ::= '<' Name (S Attribute)* S? '>'
Attribute ::= Name Eq AttValue
```

The attributes must not appear more than once in the same start tag or empty-element tag, and attribute values must be of the declared type. The attribute value cannot contain direct or indirect entity references to external entities.

All start tags must be accompanied by an end tag. The end tag has the following grammar:

```
Etag ::= '</' Name S? '>'
```

Text between start tags and end tags is known as *content*. The content has the following grammar:

```
content ::=  CharData? ((element | Reference | CDSect
                | PI | Comment) CharData?)*
```

You use empty-element tags for elements that do not contain any content. They have the following grammar:

```
EmptyElemTag ::= '<' Name (S Attribute)* S? '/>'
```

You use an element-type declaration to constraint element content. You can declare an element type more than once, and it has the following grammar:

```
elementdecl ::= '<!ELEMENT' S Name S
                  contentspec S? '>'
contentspec ::= 'EMPTY' | 'ANY' |
                Mixed | children
```

Mixed content

An element type is said to have *mixed content* if elements of that type contain character data, which may be interspersed with a child element. Mixed content has the following declaration:

```
Mixed ::= '(' S? '#PCDATA' (S? '|' S? Name)* S? ')*'
        | '(' S? '#PCDATA' S? ')'
```

In the preceding declaration, Name specifies the types of elements that may appear as children. A Name must appear only once in a mixed-content declaration.

Attribute-list declaration

An attribute associates name-value pairs with elements. It appears within start tags and emptyelement tags. You use an *attribute-list declaration* for the following purposes:

◆ An attribute-list declaration defines a set of attributes.

◆ An attribute-list declaration establishes type constraints for the defined attributes.

◆ The Name in the AttlistDecl is the type of an element.

◆ The Name in the AttlistDef is the name of the element.

An attribute-list declaration provides default values for attributes, as follows:

```
AttlistDecl ::= '<!ATTLIST' S Name AttDef* S? '>'
AttDef ::= S Name S AttType S DefaultDecl
```

Attribute types

Attribute types can be of the following three types:

- ◆ String type

- ◆ Set of tokenized type

- ◆ Enumerated type

The grammar of an attribute type is as follows:

```
AttType   ::=   StringType |
        TokenizedType |
        EnumeratedType
StringType ::= 'CDATA'
TokenizedType ::= 'ID'|
          'IDREF'| 'IDREFS'|
       'ENTITY'| 'ENTITIES'|
       'NMTOKEN'| 'NMTOKENS'
EnumeratedType ::= NotationType | Enumeration
NotationType ::= 'NOTATION' S '(' S?
                 Name (S? '|' S? Name)* S? ')'
Enumeration ::= '(' S? Nmtoken (S? '|' S? Nmtoken)* S? ')'
```

The rules followed by attribute types are as follows:

- ◆ Values of type ID must match Name production.

- ◆ Element types can have only one ID attribute specified.

- ◆ An ID attribute must be declared either #IMPLIED or #REQUIRED.

- ◆ IDREF values must match the values of some ID attributes.

- ◆ ENTITY values must match Name production.

- ◆ ENTITIES value must match Names.

- ◆ NMTOKEN must match Nmtoken production.

- ◆ NMTOKENS must match Nmtokens.

- ◆ For Enumerated types, an element type can have only one NOTATION attribute specified.

- ◆ An element declared EMPTY must not declare a NOTATION attribute.

Attribute defaults

An *attribute declaration* mainly defines how an XML processor should handle a declared attribute that is absent in a document. The grammar for an attribute declaration is as follows:

```
DefaultDecl ::= '#REQUIRED' | '#IMPLIED'
            | (('#FIXED' S)? AttValue)
```

The keyword #REQUIRED in an attribute declaration specifies that the attribute must be provided. The keyword #IMPLIED in an attribute declaration specifies that no default value is provided.

Conditional sections

Conditional sections are part of the external subset of the document type declaration. Conditional sections have the following grammar:

```
conditionalSect ::= includeSect | ignoreSect
includeSect ::= '<![' S? 'INCLUDE'
                S? '[' extSubsetDecl
                            ']]>'
ignoreSect ::= '<![' S? 'IGNORE' S?
            '[' ignoreSectContents*
                            ']]>'
```

Some of the rules for the conditional sections are as follows:

◆ The keyword INCLUDE makes the content of the conditional section part of DTD.

◆ The keyword IGNORE specifies that the content of the conditional section is not a logical part of DTD.

eXtensible Stylesheet Language (XSL)

This section discusses some of the important specifications of eXtensible Stylesheet Language *(XSL)* Version 1.0, per the W3C recommendations.

To view the detailed specification, you can visit www.w3.org/TR/xsl/.

XSL is a language for expressing stylesheets. You use XSL stylesheets to dictate how to present an XML document in a presentation medium. A stylesheet processor requires an XML document and a stylesheet to produce a presentation of the XML content, as specified by the stylesheet. The presentation process consists of the following two subprocesses:

- **Tree transformation:** During this process, a *result tree* is constructed from the XML source tree. The structure of the result tree can vary significantly from the structure of the source tree. For example, source data can be sorted and rearranged into a tabular presentation in the result tree. Formatting information can also be added during the process. In XSL, the result tree is known as the *element and attribute tree.*

- **Formatting:** During this process, the result tree is interpreted by a formatter to produce the presentation. For this formatting, semantics are included in the result tree as *formatting objects.* Formatting objects constitute the nodes of the result tree. For the finer aspects of presentation, a set of *formatting properties* is also used.

The following sections discuss formatting objects and formatting properties defined in the specification.

Formatting objects

Formatting objects can be classified into the following three types.

- Formatting objects that generate areas.
- Formatting objects that return areas but do not generate areas.
- Formatting objects that you use in the generation of areas.

Some of the important formatting objects, grouped according to their functionality per the W3C specifications, I describe in the following sections.

FORMATTING OBJECTS FOR DECLARATIONS, PAGINATION, AND LAYOUT

The following sections describe the formatting objects for declarations, pagination, and layout:

THE FO:ROOT FORMATTING OBJECT   The `fo:root` formatting object is the top root of the formatting object tree. The `fo:root` formatting object has the following children:

- A `fo:layout-master-set` object
- An optional `fo:declarations` object
- One or more `fo:page-sequence` objects

The `fo:root` object does not generate areas. Its child `fo:page-sequence` object returns `page-viewport` areas.

The `fo:root` formatting object has the following grammar:

```
(layout-master-set,declarations?,page-sequence+)
```

The property `media-usage` applies to the `fo:root` formatting object.

THE FO:DECLARATION FORMATTING OBJECT   The `fo:declaration` formatting object you use to group global declarations for a stylesheet. The `fo:declaration` object does not generate or return any areas. It has the following grammar:

```
(color-profile)+
```

THE FO:COLOR-PROFILE FORMATTING OBJECT   The `fo:color-profile` formatting object you use to declare an ICC color profile for a stylesheet. The `fo:color-profile` object does not generate or return any areas. The following properties apply to the fo:color-profile object:

- `src`
- `color-profile-name`
- `rendering-intent`

THE FO:PAGE-SEQUENCE FORMATTING OBJECT   The `fo:page-sequence` formatting object specifies how to create a sequence of pages in a document. The `fo:page-sequence` formatting object generates a sequence of viewport/reference pairs and returns the `page-viewport` areas. The `fo:page-sequence` formatting object has the following contents:

```
(title?,static-content*,flow)
```

The following properties apply to the `fo:page-sequence` object:

- `country`
- `format`

- language

- letter-value

- grouping-separator

- grouping-size

- id

- initial-page-number

- force-page-count

- master-reference

THE FO:FLOW FORMATTING OBJECT   The `fo:flow` formatting object contains a sequence of flow objects that provide the flowing text content distributed into pages. The `fo:flow` formatting object does not generate any areas. It returns a concatenated sequence of areas that is returned by its children. The `fo:flow` formatting object has the following content:

```
(%block;)+
```

The `flow-name` property applies to the `fo:flow` object.

THE FO:LAYOUT-MASTER-SET FORMATTING OBJECT   The `fo:layout-master-set` formatting object acts as a wrapper for all masters used in the document. The `fo:layout-master-set` formatting object generates no area directly. The `fo:layout-master-set` object has the following contents:

```
(simple-page-master|page-sequence-master)+
```

THE FO:SIMPLE-PAGE-MASTER FORMATTING OBJECT   The `fo:simple-page-master` formatting object you use to generate a page and specify its geometry. The `fo:simple-page-master` formatting object does not generate areas directly. The `fo:simple-page-master` object has the following grammar:

```
(region-body,region-before?,region-after?,region-start?,region-end?)
```

The following properties apply to the `fo:simple-page-master` object:

- master-name

- page-height

- page-width

- reference-orientation

- writing-mode

THE FO:PAGE-SEQUENCE-MASTER FORMATTING OBJECT   The `fo:page-sequence-master` formatting object specifies sequences of page-masters that you use in generating a sequence of pages. The `fo:page-sequence-master` formatting object does not generate any areas directly. The `fo:page-sequence` formatting object uses the `fo:page-sequence-master` object to generate pages. The `fo:page-sequence-master` object has the following contents:

```
(single-page-master-reference|repeatable-page-master-reference|repeatable-page-master-alternatives)+
```

The `master-name` property applies to the fo:page-sequence-master object.

BLOCK-LEVEL FORMATTING OBJECT
The block-level formatting object I describe in the following section.

THE FO:BLOCK FORMATTING OBJECT   The `fo:block` formatting object you use for formatting paragraphs, titles, headlines, and figures. The `fo:block` formatting object generates one or more normal block-areas. The `fo:block` returns the `generated` areas, `page-level-out-of-line` areas, and `reference-level-out-of-line` areas that its children return. The `fo-block` object has the following grammar:

```
(#PCDATA|%inline;|%block;)*
```

Some important properties that apply to the `fo-block` object are as follows:

- ◆ `break-after`
- ◆ `break-before`
- ◆ `color`
- ◆ `text`
- ◆ `id`

THE FO:BLOCK-CONTAINER FORMATTING OBJECT   The `fo:block-container` formatting object is used to generate block-level reference area. The `fo:block-container` formatting object generates one or more reference pairs and `page-level-out-of-line` areas that its children return. The `fo-block-container` object has the following grammar:

```
(%block;)+
```

Some important properties that apply to the fo:block-container object are as follows:

- ◆ `break-before`

- ◆ `clip`

- ◆ `height`

- ◆ `id`

- ◆ `display-align`

INLINE-LEVEL FORMATTING OBJECTS

The inline-level formatting objects are as I describe in the following sections.

THE FO:CHARACTER FORMATTING OBJECT   The `fo:character` formatting object you use to represent a character mapped to a glyph (a representation of a character). It generates one or more normal `inline-areas`. It also returns one or more normal `inline-areas`. Some important properties that apply to the `fo-character` formatting object are as follows:

- ◆ `alignment-adjust`

- ◆ `alignment-baseline`

- ◆ `character`

- ◆ `color`

- ◆ `text-depth`

THE FO:INITIAL-PROPERTY-SET FORMATTING OBJECT The `fo:initial-property-set` formatting object you use to specify the formatting properties of the first line of a `fo:block` object. The `fo:initial-property-set` formatting object does not generate or return any areas. Some important properties that apply to the `fo:initial-property-set` formatting object are as follows:

- ◆ `color`

- ◆ `id`

- ◆ `letter-spacing`

- ◆ `line-height`

- ◆ `word-spacing`

THE FO:EXTERNAL-GRAPHIC FORMATTING OBJECT   The `fo:external-graphic` formatting object you use for graphics, where the graphics data is outside the `fo` element. The `fo:external-graphic` formatting object generates and returns one `inline-level` viewport area and one `reference-area` containing the external graphic. Some important properties that apply to the `fo:external-graphic` formatting object are as follows:

- ◆ alignment-adjust
- ◆ clip
- ◆ content-type
- ◆ height
- ◆ line-height
- ◆ scaling

THE FO:INLINE FORMATTING OBJECT   The fo:inline formatting object you use to format a text portion with a background or to format a border-enclosed text portion. The fo:inline formatting object generates one or more normal inline-areas. The fo:inline object returns the generated areas, any page-level-out-of-line areas, and any reference-level-out-of-line areas that its children return. The fo:inline formatting object has the following grammar:

(#PCDATA|%inline;|%block;)*

Some important properties that apply to the fo:inline formatting object are as follows:

- ◆ alignment-adjust
- ◆ color
- ◆ height
- ◆ id
- ◆ visibility
- ◆ width

THE FO:LEADER FORMATTING OBJECT   The fo:leader formatting object you commonly use to generate glyph sequences in tables of contents. You also use it to create horizontal rules for use as separators. The fo:leader formatting object generates and returns a single normal inline-area. The fo:leader formatting object has the following grammar:

(#PCDATA|%inline;)*

Some important properties that apply to the fo:leader formatting object are as follows:

- ◆ alignment-adjust
- ◆ color

- text-depth
- id
- rule-style
- letter-spacing

THE FO:PAGE-NUMBER FORMATTING OBJECT   The fo:page-number formatting object you use to provide an inline-area. The content of the inline-area is the page-number where the inline-area is placed. The fo:page-number formatting object generates a single normal inline-area. It also returns a single normal inline-area. Some important properties that apply to the fo:page-number formatting object are as follows:

- alignment-adjust
- color
- text-decoration
- id
- visibility
- word-spacing

FORMATTING OBJECTS FOR TABLES

The following sections describe the formatting objects for tables:

THE FO:TABLE-AND-CAPTION FORMATTING OBJECT The fo:table-and-caption formatting object you use to format a table along with its caption. The fo:table-and-caption formatting object generates one or more normal block-areas. The fo:table-and-caption object returns the generated areas, page-level-out-of-line areas, and reference-level-out-of-line areas, as returned by its children. The fo:table-and-caption object has the following grammar:

(table-caption?,table)

Some important properties that apply to the fo:table-and-caption object are as follows:

- break-after
- break-before
- id
- intrusion-displace
- text-align

THE FO:TABLE-CAPTION FORMATTING OBJECT The `fo:table-caption` formatting object you use to contain block-level formatting objects and contains the table caption. The `fo:table-caption` formatting object you use only while using the `fo:table-and-caption` object. It generates one or more normal `reference-areas`. In addition to these areas, a `fo:table-caption` object returns any `page-level-out-of-line` areas returned by its children. The `fo:table-caption` object has the following content:

```
(%block;)+
```

Some important properties that apply to the `fo:table-caption` object are as follows:

- ◆ `block-progression-dimension`
- ◆ `height`
- ◆ `id`
- ◆ `inline-progression-dimension`
- ◆ `intrusion-displace`
- ◆ `keep-together`
- ◆ `width`

THE FO:TABLE FORMATTING OBJECT The `fo:table` formatting object you use to format the tabular material of a table. It generates one or more normal `block-areas`. It returns one or more normal `block-areas`, any `page-level-out-of-line` areas, and any `reference-level-out-of-line` areas returned by its children. The `fo:table` object has the following content:

```
(table-column*,table-header?,table-footer?,table-body+)
```

Some important properties that apply to the `fo:table` object are as follows:

- ◆ `border-progression-dimension`
- ◆ `border-separation`
- ◆ `break-after`
- ◆ `break-before`
- ◆ `id`
- ◆ `table-layout`

THE FO:TABLE-HEADER FORMATTING OBJECT   The `fo:table-header` formatting object you use to contain the table header content. The `fo:table-header` formatting object does not generate any areas. It returns a concatenated sequence of areas returned by its children. The `fo:table-header` object has the following content:

```
(table-row+|table-cell+)
```

Some important properties that apply to the `fo:table-header` object are as follows:

- `border-after-precedence`
- `border-before-precedence`
- `border-end-precedence`
- `border-start-precedence`
- `id`
- `visibility`

THE FO:TABLE-FOOTER FORMATTING OBJECT   The `fo:table-footer` formatting object you use to contain the table footer content. The `fo:table-footer` formatting object does not generate any areas. It returns a concatenated sequence of areas returned by its children. The `fo:table-footer` object has the following contents:

```
(table-row+|table-cell+)
```

Some important properties that apply to the `fo:table-footer` object are as follows:

- `border-after-precedence`
- `border-before-precedence`
- `border-end-precedence`
- `border-start-precedence`
- `id`
- `visibility`

THE FO:TABLE-BODY FORMATTING OBJECT   The `fo:table-body` formatting object contains the table body content. The `fo:table-body` formatting object does not generate any areas. Each child of the `fo:table-body` formatting object returns a sequence of area. This formatting object just concatenates these sequences and returns a concatenated sequence of areas. The `fo:table-body` object has the following contents:

```
(table-row+|table-cell+)
```

Some important properties that apply to the fo:table-body object are as follows:

- ◆ border-after-precedence
- ◆ border-before-precedence
- ◆ border-end-precedence
- ◆ border-start-precedence
- ◆ id
- ◆ visibility

THE FO:TABLE-ROW FORMATTING OBJECT The `fo:table-row` formatting object you use to group table cells into rows. The `fo:table-row` formatting object does not generate any areas. Each child of the `fo:table-row` formatting object returns a sequence of area. This formatting object just concatenates these sequences and returns a concatenated sequence of areas. The `fo:table-row` object has the following contents:

```
(table-cell+)
```

Some important properties that apply to the `fo:table-row` object are as follows:

- ◆ border-after-precedence
- ◆ border-before-precedence
- ◆ border-end-precedence
- ◆ border-start-precedence
- ◆ break-after
- ◆ break-before
- ◆ id
- ◆ height
- ◆ visibility

FORMATTING OBJECTS FOR LISTS

The formatting objects for lists are as I describe in the following sections.

THE FO:LIST-BLOCK FORMATTING OBJECT The `fo:list-block` formatting object you use to format a list. The `fo:list-block` formatting object generates one or more normal block-areas. In addition to normal block-areas, the `fo:list-block` object returns any `page-level-out-of-line` areas and any `reference-level-out-of-line` areas returned by its children. The `fo:list-block` object has the following content:

```
(list-item+)
```

Some important properties that apply to the `fo:list-block` object are as follows:

- ◆ `break-after`
- ◆ `break-before`
- ◆ `id`
- ◆ `intrusion-displace`
- ◆ `keep-together`
- ◆ `keep-with-next`
- ◆ `keep-with-previous`
- ◆ `provisional-distance-between-starts`
- ◆ `provisional-label-separation`

THE FO:LIST-ITEM FORMATTING OBJECT The `fo:list-item` formatting object you use to provide the label and the body of a list item. The `fo:list-item` formatting object generates one or more normal block-areas. In addition to normal block-areas, the `fo:list-item` object returns any `page-level-out-of-line` areas and any `reference-level-out-of-line` areas returned by its children. The `fo:list-item` object has the following contents:

```
(list-item-label,list-item-body)
```

Some important properties that apply to the `fo:list-item` object are as follows:

- ◆ `break-after`
- ◆ `break-before`
- ◆ `id`
- ◆ `intrusion-displace`
- ◆ `keep-together`
- ◆ `keep-with-next`

♦ keep-with-previous

♦ relative-align

THE FO:LIST-ITEM-BODY FORMATTING OBJECT The fo:list-item-body formatting object you use to provide the contents of a list item body. The fo:list-item-body formatting object does not generate any areas. Each child of the fo:list-item-body formatting object returns a sequence of area. This formatting object just concatenates these sequences and returns a concatenated sequence of areas. The fo:list-item-body object has the following contents:

(%block;)+

Some important properties that apply to the fo:list-item-body object are as follows:

♦ id

♦ keep-together

THE FO:LIST-ITEM-LABEL FORMATTING OBJECT The fo:list-item-label formatting object you use to provide the contents of a list item label. The fo:list-item-label formatting object does not generate any areas. Each child of the fo:list-item-label formatting object returns a sequence of area. This formatting object just concatenates these sequences and returns a concatenated sequence of areas. The fo:list-item-label object has the following content:

(%block;)+

Some important properties that apply to the fo:list-item-label object are as follows:

♦ id

♦ keep-together

LINK AND MULTIFORMATTING OBJECTS
The following sections discuss the link and multiformatting objects.

THE FO:BASIC-LINK FORMATTING OBJECT The fo:basic-link object you use to represent the start resource of a simple link that has a single target. The fo:basic-link formatting object generates one or more normal inline-areas. In addition to normal inline-areas, the fo:basic-link returns any page-level-out-of-line areas and any reference-level-out-of-line areas returned by its children. The fo:basic-link object has the following content:

(#PCDATA|%inline;|%block;)*

Some important properties that apply to the `fo:basic-link` object are as follows:

- `alignment-adjust`
- `baseline-shift`
- `external-destination`
- `id`
- `indicate-destination`
- `show-destination`
- `target-processing-context`
- `target-stylesheet`

THE FO:MULTI-SWITCH FORMATTING OBJECT   The `fo:multi-switch` formatting object you use to provide specifications for alternative subtrees of formatting objects and to control the switching from one alternative sub-trees to another. The `fo:multi-switch` formatting object does not generate any areas. It returns the sequence of areas as returned by the current `fo:multi-case` object. The `fo:multi-switch` object has the following content:

```
(multi-case+)
```

Some important properties that apply to the `fo:multi-switch` object are as follows:

- `auto-restore`
- `id`

THE FO:MULTI-CASE FORMATTING OBJECT   The `fo:multi-case` formatting object you use to contains each alternative subtree of formatting objects. The `fo:multi-case` formatting object does not generate any areas. Each child of the `fo:multi-case` formatting object returns a sequence of area. This formatting object just concatenates these sequences and returns a concatenated sequence of areas. The `fo:multi-case` object has the following content:

```
(#PCDATA|%inline;|%block;)*
```

Some important properties that apply to the `fo:multi-case` object are as follows:

- `id`
- `starting-state`

◆ case-name

◆ case-title

THE FO:MULTI-PROPERTIES FORMATTING OBJECT   The fo:multi-properties formatting object you use to switch from one property set to another that associate with a given content portion. The fo:multi-properties formatting object does not generate any areas. Each child of the fo:multi-properties formatting object returns a sequence of area. This formatting object just concatenates these sequences and returns a concatenated sequence of areas. The fo:multi-properties object has the following contents:

(multi-property-set+,wrapper)

The id property applies to the fo:multi-properties object.

OUT–OF–LINE FORMATTING OBJECTS
The following sections discuss the out-of-line formatting objects:

THE FO:FLOAT FORMATTING OBJECT   The fo:float formatting object you use to control the positioning of an image. The fo:float generates an optional single area and one or more block-areas. The fo:float object has the following content:

(%block;)+

Some important properties that apply to the fo:float object are as follows:

◆ float

◆ clear

THE FO:FOOTNOTE FORMATTING OBJECT   The fo:footnote formatting object you use to produce footnote citations. The fo:footnote formatting object does not generate any areas. It returns the areas returned by its child. The fo:footnote object has the following content:

(inline,footnote-body)

The common accessibility properties applies to the fo:footnote object.

Formatting properties
XML is the standard data format for Java-based Web services. XML data carried across the Web enables Java-based Web services to operate. But sometimes, XML

data must be presented – say, on the browser – for a Web service to operate. With the help of XSL, a stylesheet writer can write an *XSLT transformation* of the XML source file that needs to be formatted and rendered for multiple media – and especially for the Web. Now designers can indicate how an XML document is styled, laid out, and paginated to a presentation medium such as a browser. To format and render such XML documents, XSL1.0 provides both formatting objects and properties.

The preceding section on Formatting objects lists XSL's formatting objects. In this section, I discuss some of the formatting properties of XSL objects, grouped into sets of properties according to functionality, per the W3C specifications.

COMMON ACCESSIBILITY PROPERTIES

The following are some common accessibility properties:

◆ The `source-document` property acts as a pointer to the XML document that you use for the object tree. This property applies to all the formatting object that are contained in the `fo:flow` or `fo:static-content` object. The `source-document` property has the following grammar:

   <uri-specification> [*<uri-specification>*]* | none | inherit

◆ The `role` property applies to all the formatting objects that are contained in the `fo:flow` or `fo:static-content` object. The `role` property has the following grammar:

   <string> | *<uri-specification>* | none | inherit

COMMON ABSOLUTE-POSITION PROPERTIES

Following are some common `absolute-position` properties:

◆ The `absolute-position` property applies to the `fo:block-container` formatting object. It has the following value:

   auto | absolute | fixed | inherit

◆ The `top` property applies to positioned elements. It has the following value:

   <length> | *<percentage>* | auto | inherit

In addition to the aforementioned properties, the common absolute-position properties set also consists of the following properties:

◆ right

◆ bottom

◆ left

COMMON AURAL PROPERTIES

Following are some common `aural` properties:

- ◆ The `azimuth` property applies to all elements. It has the following value:

  ```
  <angle> | [[ left-side | far-left | left | center-left |
  center | center-right | right | far-right | right-side ] ||
  behind ] | leftwards | rightwards | inherit
  ```

- ◆ The `cue-after` property applies to all elements. It has the following value:

  ```
  <uri-specification> | none | inherit
  ```

- ◆ The `elevation` property applies to all elements. It has the following value:

  ```
  <angle> | below | level | above | higher | lower | inherit
  ```

- ◆ The `pitch` property applies to all elements. It has the following value:

  ```
  <frequency> | x-low | low | medium | high | x-high | inherit
  ```

- ◆ The `play-during` property applies to all elements. It has the following value:

  ```
  <uri-specification> mix? repeat? | auto | none | inherit
  ```

- ◆ The `pause-after` property applies to all elements. It has the following value:

  ```
  <time> | <percentage> | inherit
  ```

- ◆ The `speak` property applies to all elements. It has the following value:

  ```
  normal | none | spell-out | inherit
  ```

- ◆ The `volume` property applies to all elements. It has the following value:

  ```
  <number> | <percentage> | silent | x-soft | soft | medium |
  loud | x-loud | inherit
  ```

In addition to the aforementioned properties, the common `aural` properties set also consists of the following properties:

- ◆ cue-before
- ◆ pause-before
- ◆ pitch-range
- ◆ richness
- ◆ speak-header
- ◆ speak-numeral
- ◆ speak-punctuation

- ◆ speech-rate

- ◆ stress

- ◆ voice-family

COMMON BORDER, PADDING, AND BACKGROUND PROPERTIES

Some common border, padding, and background properties are as follows:

- ◆ The `background-attachment` property applies to all elements. It has the following value:

  `scroll | fixed | inherit`

- ◆ The `background-color` property applies to all elements. It has the following value:

  `<color> | transparent | inherit`

- ◆ The `background-image` property applies to all elements. It has the following value:

  `<uri-specification> | none | inherit`

- ◆ The `background-position-vertical` property applies to all formatting objects to which background applies. It has the following value:

  `<percentage> | <length> | top | center | bottom | inherit`

- ◆ The `border-before-color` property specifies the border color on the before edge of a `block-area` or `inline-area` area. It has the following value:

  `<color> | inherit`

- ◆ The `border-before-style` property specifies the `border-style` for the `before-edge`. It has the following value:

  `<border-style> | inherit`

- ◆ The `border-before-width` property specifies the `border-width` for the `before-edge`. It has the following value:

  `<border-width> | <length-conditional> | inherit`

- ◆ The `padding-before` property specifies the padding width on the `before-edge` of a `block-area` or `inline-area`. It has the following value:

  `<padding-width> | <length-conditional> | inherit`

- ◆ The `padding-after` property specifies the padding width on the `after-edge` of a `block-area` or `inline-area`. It has the following value:

  `<padding-width> | <length-conditional> | inherit`

In addition to the preceding properties, the common border, padding, and background properties set also contains the following properties:

- `background-repeat`

- `background-position-horizontal`

- `border-after-color`

- `border-after-style`

- `border-after-width`

- `border-start-color`

- `border-start-style`

- `border-start-width`

- `border-end-color`

- `border-end-style`

- `border-end-width`

- `border-top-color`

- `border-top-style`

- `border-top-width`

- `border-bottom-color`

- `border-bottom-style`

- `border-bottom-width`

- `border-left-color`

- `border-left-style`

- `border-left-width`

- `border-right-color`

- `border-right-style`

- `border-right-width`

- `padding-start`

- `padding-end`

- `padding-top`

- `padding-bottom`

- `padding-left`

- `padding-right`

COMMON FONT PROPERTIES

Following are the common font properties:

◆ The `font-family` property applies to all elements. It has the following value:

```
[[ <family-name> | <generic-family> ],]* [<family-name>
| <generic-family>] | inherit
```

◆ The `font-selection-strategy` property applies to all elements. It has the following value:

```
auto | character-by-character | inherit
```

◆ The `font-size` property applies to all elements. It has the following value:

```
<absolute-size> | <relative-size> | <length> | <percentage>
| inherit
```

◆ The `font-style` property applies to all elements. It has the following value:

```
normal | italic | oblique | backslant | inherit
```

In addition to the preceding properties, the common font properties set also contains the following properties:

◆ `font-stretch`

◆ `font-size-adjust`

◆ `font-variant`

◆ `font-weight`

COMMON HYPHENATION PROPERTIES

Following are the common hyphenation properties:

◆ The `country` property applies to the `fo:block`, `fo:character`, and `fo:page-sequence` formatting objects. It has the following value:

```
none | <country> | inherit
```

◆ The `language` property applies to the `fo:block`, `fo:character`, and `fo:page-sequence` formatting objects. It has the following value:

```
none | <language> | inherit
```

◆ The `script` property applies to the `fo:block`, `fo:character`, and `fo:page-sequence` formatting objects. It has the following value:

```
none | auto | <script> | inherit
```

◆ The hyphenate property applies to the fo:block and the fo:character formatting objects. It has the following value:

false | true | inherit

In addition to the preceding properties, the common hyphenation properties set also contains the following properties:

◆ language

◆ hyphenation-character

◆ hyphenation-push-character-count

◆ hyphenation-remain-character-count

COMMON MARGIN PROPERTIES

Following are the common margin properties:

◆ The margin-top property applies to all elements. It has the following value:

<margin-width> | inherit

◆ The space-before property applies to all block-level formatting objects. It has the following value:

<space> | inherit

◆ The start-indent property applies to all block-level formatting objects. It has the following value:

<length> | <percentage> | inherit

In addition to the preceding properties, the common margin properties set also consists of the following properties:

◆ margin-bottom

◆ margin-left

◆ margin-right

◆ space-after

◆ end-indent

AREAALIGNMENT PROPERTIES

Following are the areaalignment properties:

◆ The alignment-adjust property applies to all inline formatting objects. It has the following value:

```
auto | baseline | before-edge | text-before-edge | middle
| central | after-edge | text-after-edge | ideographic |
alphabetic | hanging | mathematical | <percentage> | <length>
| inherit
```

◆ The `baseline-shift` property applies to all `inline` formatting objects. It has the following value:

```
baseline | sub | super | <percentage> | <length> | inherit
```

◆ The `display-align` property applies to the `fo:table-cell`, `fo:region-body`, `fo:region-before`, `fo:region-after`, `fo:region-start`, `fo:region-end`, `fo:block-container`, `fo:inline-container`, `fo:external-graphic`, and `fo:instream-foreign-object` formatting objects. It has the following value:

```
auto | before | center | after | inherit
```

In addition to the preceding properties, the `area-alignment` properties set also consists of the following properties:

◆ `alignment-baseline`

◆ `dominant-baseline`

◆ `relative-align`

AREADIMENSION PROPERTIES

Following are the areadimension properties:

◆ The `content-height` property applies to the `fo:external-graphic` and `fo:instream-foreign-object` formatting objects. It has the following value:

```
auto | scale-to-fit | <length> | <percentage> | inherit
```

◆ The `height` property applies to all elements except non-replaced inline elements, table columns, and column groups. It has the following value:

```
<length> | <percentage> | auto | inherit
```

◆ The `scaling` property applies to the `fo:external-graphic` and `fo:instream-foreign-object` formatting objects. It has the following value:

```
uniform | non-uniform | inherit
```

In addition to the preceding properties, the area-dimension properties set also consists the following properties:

◆ `block-progression-dimension`

◆ `content-width`

- ◆ inline-progression-dimension
- ◆ max-height
- ◆ max-width
- ◆ min-height
- ◆ min-width
- ◆ scaling-method
- ◆ width

BLOCKANDLINERELATED PROPERTIES

Following are the blockandlinerelated properties:

- ◆ The hyphenation-keep property applies to the fo:block formatting object. It has the following value:

  auto | column | page | inherit

- ◆ The hyphenation-ladder-count property applies to the fo:block formatting object. It has the following value:

  no-limit | <number> | inherit

- ◆ The last-line-end-indent property applies to the fo:block formatting object. It has the following value:

  <length> | <percentage> | inherit

- ◆ The line-height property applies to all elements. It has the following value:

  normal | <length> | <number> | <percentage> | <space>
  | inherit

- ◆ The text-align property applies to all block-level elements. It has the following value:

  start | center | end | justify | inside | outside | left
  | right | <string> | inherit

In addition to the preceding properties, the block-and-line-related properties set also consists of the following properties:

- ◆ line-height-shift-adjustment
- ◆ line-stacking-strategy
- ◆ linefeed-treatment
- ◆ white-space-treatment

- ◆ `text-align-last`
- ◆ `text-indent`
- ◆ white-**space-collapse**
- ◆ wrap-**option**

CHARACTER PROPERTIES

Following are the character properties:

- ◆ The `character` property applies to the `fo:character` formatting object. It has the following value:

  `<character>`

- ◆ The `letter-spacing` property applies to all elements. It has the following value:

  `normal | <length> | <space> | inherit`

- ◆ The `text-decoration` property applies to all elements. It has the following value:

  `none | [ [ underline | no-underline] || [ overline | no-overline ] || [ line-through | no-line-through ] || [ blink | no-blink ] ] | inherit`

- ◆ The `text-shadow` property applies to all elements. It has the following value:

  `none | [<color> || <length> <length> <length>? ,]* [<color> || <length> <length> <length>?] | inherit`

- ◆ The `word-spacing` property applies to all elements. It has the following value:

  `normal | <length> | <space> | inherit`

COLORRELATED PROPERTIES

The color property applies to all elements. It has the following value:

`<color> | inherit`

FLOATRELATED PROPERTIES

Following are the floatrelated properties:

- ◆ The `clear` property applies to `block-level` elements. It has the following value:

  `start | end | left | right | both | none | inherit`

♦ The `float` property applies to all except the positioned elements and generated content. It has the following value:

```
before | start | end | left | right | none | inherit
```

KEEPS AND BREAKS PROPERTIES
Following are the keeps and breaks properties:

♦ The `break-after` property applies to all block-level formatting objects, `fo:list-item`, and `fo:table-row`. It has the following value:

```
auto | column | page | even-page | odd-page | inherit
```

♦ The `keep-together` property applies to all block-level formatting objects, inline formatting objects, `fo:table-caption`, `fo:table-row`, `fo:list-item`, `fo:list-item-label`, and `fo:list-item-body`. It has the following value:

```
<keep> | inherit
```

♦ The `orphans` property applies to all block-level elements. It has the following value:

```
<integer> | inherit
```

In addition to the preceding properties, the keeps and breaks properties set also consists of the following properties:

♦ `break-before`

♦ `keep-with-next`

♦ `keep-with-previous`

♦ `widows`

LAYOUT-RELATED PROPERTIES
Following are the `layout-related` properties:

♦ The `clip` property applies to all block-level and replaced elements. It has the following value:

```
<shape> | auto | inherit
```

♦ The `overflow` property applies to all block-level and replaced elements. It has the following value:

```
visible | hidden | scroll | error-if-overflow | auto | inherit
```

In addition to the preceding properties, the `layout-related` properties set also contains the following properties:

- ◆ `reference-orientation`
- ◆ `span`

LEADER AND RULE PROPERTIES

Following are the leader and rule properties:

- ◆ The `leader-alignment` property applies to the `fo:leader` formatting object. It has the following value:

  `none | reference-area | page | inherit`

- ◆ The `leader-pattern` property applies to the `fo:leader` formatting object. It has the following value:

  `space | rule | dots | use-content | inherit`

In addition to the preceding properties, the leader and rule properties set also consists of the following properties:

- ◆ `leader-pattern-width`
- ◆ `leader-length`
- ◆ `rule-style`
- ◆ `rule-thickness`

PROPERTIES FOR DYNAMIC-EFFECTS FORMATTING OBJECTS

Following are the properties for dynamic-effects formatting objects:

- ◆ The `active-state` property applies to the `fo:multi-property-set` formatting object. It has the following value:

  `link | visited | active | hover | focus`

- ◆ The `auto-restore` property applies to the `fo:multi-switch` formatting object. It has the following value:

  `true | false`

- ◆ The `external-destination` property applies to the `fo:basic-link` formatting object. It has the following value:

  `<uri-specification>`

- The `starting-state` property applies to the `fo:multi-case` formatting object. It has the following value:

  ```
  show | hide
  ```

In addition to the preceding properties, the `dynamic-effects` property set also consists the following properties:

- `case-name`

- `case-title`

- `destination-placement-offset`

- `indicate-destination`

- `internal-destination`

- `show-destination`

- `switch-to`

- `target-presentation-context`

- `target-processing-context`

- `target-stylesheet`

PROPERTIES FOR MARKERS
Following are the properties for markers:

- The `marker-class-name` property applies to the `fo:marker` formatting object. It has the following value:

  ```
  <name>
  ```

- The `retrieve-position` property applies to the `fo:retrieve-marker` formatting object. It has the following value:

  ```
  first-starting-within-page | first-including-carryover
  | last-starting-within-page | last-ending-within-page
  ```

In addition to the preceding properties, the properties for markers set also consists the following properties:

- `retrieve-class-name`

- `retrieve-boundary`

PAGINATION AND LAYOUT PROPERTIES
Following are the pagination and layout properties:

◆ The `blank-or-not-blank` property applies to the `fo:conditional-page-master-reference` formatting object. It has the following value:

`blank | not-blank | any | inherit`

◆ The `column-count` property applies to the `fo:region-body` formatting object. It has the following value:

`<number> | inherit`

◆ The `flow-name` property applies to the `fo:flow` and the `fo:static-content` formatting objects. It has the following value:

`<name>`

In addition to the preceding properties, the pagination and layout properties set also consists of the following properties:

◆ `column-gap`

◆ `extent`

◆ `force-page-count`

◆ `initial-page-number`

◆ `master-name`

◆ `master-reference`

◆ `maximum-repeats`

◆ `media-usage`

◆ `odd-or-even`

◆ `page-height`

◆ `page-position`

◆ `page-width`

◆ `precedence`

◆ `region-name`

TABLE PROPERTIES

Following are the `table` properties:

◆ The `border-after-precedence` property applies to the `fo:table`, `fo:table-body`, `fo:table-header`, `fo:table-footer`, `fo:table-column`, `fo:table-row`, and `fo:table-cell` formatting objects. It has the following value:

`force | <integer> | inherit`

♦ The `caption-side` property applies to the `fo:table-and-caption` formatting object. It has the following value:

`before | after | start | end | top | bottom | left | right | inherit`

♦ The `column-number` property applies to the `fo:table-column` and the `fo:table-cell` formatting objects. It has the following value:

`<number>`

In addition to the preceding properties, the `table` properties set also consists of the following properties:

♦ `border-before-precedence`

♦ `border-collapse`

♦ `border-end-precedence`

♦ `border-separation`

♦ `border-start-precedence`

♦ `column-width`

♦ `empty-cells`

♦ `ends-row`

♦ `number-columns-repeated`

♦ `number-columns-spanned`

♦ `number-rows-spanned`

♦ `starts-row`

♦ `table-layout`

♦ `table-omit-footer-at-break`

♦ `table-omit-header-at-break`

WRITING-MODE-RELATED PROPERTIES
Following are the writing-mode-related properties:

♦ The `glyph-orientation-horizontal` property applies to the `fo:character` formatting object. It has the following value:

`<angle> | inherit`

- The `text-altitude` property applies to the `fo:block`, `fo:character`, `fo:leader`, `fo:page-number`, and `fo:page-number-citation` formatting objects. It has the following value:

  `use-font-metrics | <length> | <percentage> | inherit`

In addition to the preceding properties, the writing-mode-related properties set also consists of the following properties:

- `direction`
- `glyph-orientation-vertical`
- `text-depth`
- `unicode-bidi`
- `writing-mode`

MISCELLANEOUS PROPERTIES

Following are the miscellaneous properties:

- The `content-type` property applies to the `fo:external-graphic` and `fo:instream-foreign-object` formatting objects. It has the following value:

  `<string> | auto`

- The `id` property applies to most of the formatting objects. It has the following value:

  `<id>`

- The `ref-id` property applies to the `fo:page-number-citation` formatting object. It has the following value:

  `<idref> | inherit`

In addition to the preceding properties, the miscellaneous properties set also contains the following properties:

- `provisional-label-separation`
- `provisional-distance-between-starts`
- `score-spaces`
- `src`
- `visibility`
- `z-index`

SHORTHAND PROPERTIES
Following are the shorthand properties:

- The `background` property applies to all elements. It has the following value:

  `[<background-color> || <background-image> || <background-repeat> || <background-attachment> || <background-position> ]] | inherit`

- The `border` property applies to all elements. It has the following value:

  `[ <border-width> || <border-style> || <color> ] | inherit`

- The `cue` property applies to all elements. It has the following value:

  `<cue-before> || <cue-after> | inherit`

- The `font` property applies to all elements. It has the following value:

  `[ [ <font-style> || <font-variant> || <font-weight> ]? <font-size> [ / <line-height>]? <font-family> ] | caption | icon | menu | message-box | small-caption | status-bar | inherit`

In addition to the preceding properties, the shorthand properties set also consists of the following properties:

- `background-position`
- `border-bottom`
- `border-color`
- `border-left`
- `border-right`
- `border-style`
- `border-spacing`
- `border-top`
- `border-width`
- `margin`
- `padding`
- `page-break-after`
- `page-break-before`
- `page-break-inside`

- ◆ pause
- ◆ position
- ◆ size
- ◆ vertical-align
- ◆ white-space
- ◆ xml:lang

XSL Transformations

XSLT, a part of XSL, is a language that you use to transform XML documents into other XML documents. Transformations expressed in XSLT are known as *stylesheets*. Transformations define rules to use to transform a source tree into a result tree. Transformations occur by matching a pattern to the elements of a source tree and relating it to a template. The template is then instantiated to create a part of the result tree.

 To view the detailed XSLT specification, you can visit www.w3.org/TR/xslt.

A stylesheet consists of a set of template rules that you can classify as a *pattern* and a *template*. The following sections discuss the various structures of a stylesheet.

XSLT namespace

The XML processor recognizes elements and attributes for this namespace by using the namespace mechanism. Some specifications of the XSLT namespace are as follows:

- ◆ Elements from the XSLT namespace are recognized only in the stylesheet.
- ◆ Any extension made by vendors must be in a separate namespace.
- ◆ XSLT stylesheets are free to use any prefix for referring elements in a namespace but must have a namespace declaration that binds the prefix to the URI of the XSLT namespace.
- ◆ An XSLT processor must ignore any unrecognized attributes without giving an error.

For more information on the XSLT namespace, visit www.w3.org/1999/XSL/Transform.

Stylesheet element

A stylesheet is represented by an xsl:stylesheet element in an XML document. The xsl:transform element can also be used in place of xsl:stylesheet.

The xsl:stylesheet element may contain the following types of elements:

- xsl:import
- xsl:include
- xsl:strip-space
- xsl:preserve-space
- xsl:output
- xsl:key
- xsl:decimal-format
- xsl:namespace-alias
- xsl:attribute-set
- xsl:variable
- xsl:param
- xsl:template

Forward-compatible processing

An element can be processed in the forward-compatible mode if any of the following conditions are met:

- If the element is an xsl:stylesheet element with a version attribute that's not equal to 1.0.
- If the element is a literal-result element that has an xsl:version attribute with a value that's not equal to 1.0.
- If the element is a literal-result element and it does not have an xsl:version attribute.

Combining stylesheets

You use the following two mechanisms to combine stylesheets:

- **The inclusion mechanism:** The *inclusion mechanism* does not change the semantics of the stylesheets that you're combining. In the inclusion mechanism, the stylesheet uses the `xsl:include` element. The `xsl:include` element has an `href` attribute with a value that's a URI reference identifying the stylesheet to include. The `xsl:include` element must be a top-level element. The `xsl:include` element appears as follows:

  ```
  <xsl:include
  href = uri-reference />
  ```

- **The import mechanism:** The `import mechanism` enables stylesheets to override each other. In the inclusion mechanism, the stylesheet uses the `xsl:import` element. The `xsl:import` element has an `href` attribute with a value that's a URI reference identifying the stylesheet to import. As must the `xsl:include` element, the `xsl:include` element must be a top-level element. The `xsl:import` element appears as follows:

  ```
  <xsl:import
  href = uri-reference />
  ```

Embedding stylesheets

You can embed an XSLT stylesheet in another non-XML resource by using the following two embedding forms:

- The XSLT stylesheet can be *textually* included in an another non-XML resource.

- The `xsl:stylesheet` element may occur in an XML document other than as the document element.The xsl:stylesheet element in such embedding uses its `ID` attribute to specify a unique identifier.

Data models

Following are some of the rules specified for stylesheet data models:

- The result tree may have any sequence of nodes as children that would be possible for an element node.

- A result tree need not be a well-formed XML document if written out by using the XML output method.

- Every node has a base URI.

- The base URI of the document node is the URI of the document entity.

♦ The base URI for other nodes, such as a text node or a comment node, is
the base URI of the parent of the node.

♦ The root node provides a mapping that specifies the URI for each
unparsed entity declared in the document's DTD.

♦ Text nodes are removed from the tree if the text node has only whitespace
characters.

Expressions

XSLT uses expressions for the following purposes:

♦ To select nodes for processing.

♦ To specify conditions for different ways of processing a node.

♦ To generate text to insert in the result tree.

An expression must match the XPath production Expr expression.

Template rules

Template rules are instructions that you use for processing nodes. Template rules uses
a pattern to identify the node to which the template applies. A *pattern* specifies a
set of conditions on a node. A template rule is specified by using the xsl:template
element, as follows:

```
<xsl:template
     match = pattern
     name = qname
     priority = number
      mode = qname>
</xsl:template>
```

The match attribute is a pattern that identifies the nodes to which the template
rule applies.
A pattern has the following grammar:

```
Pattern ::= LocationPathPattern | Pattern '|' LocationPathPattern
LocationPathPattern ::= / ' RelativePathPattern?' |
IdKeyPattern (('/' | '//') RelativePathPattern)? |
'//'? RelativePathPattern
IdKeyPattern ::=  'id' '(' Literal ')' |
 'key' '(' Literal ',' Literal ')'
```

```
RelativePathPattern ::= StepPattern | RelativePathPattern '/'
StepPattern | RelativePathPattern '//' StepPattern

StepPattern ::= ChildOrAttributeAxisSpecifier NodeTest Predicate*

ChildOrAttributeAxisSpecifie ::= AbbreviatedAxisSpecifier |
('child' | 'attribute') '::'
```

XSL elements

Some of the important XSL elements that you use to create the result tree I discuss in the following sections.

THE XSL:NAMESPACE-ALIAS ELEMENT

The `xsl:namespace-alias` element declares that a namespace URI is an alias of another namespace URI. The `xsl:namespace-alias` element has the following form:

```
<xsl:namespace-alias
stylesheet-prefix = prefix | "#default"
result-prefix = prefix | "#default"/>
```

The value of the `stylesheet-prefix` attribute specifies the namespace URI that appears in the stylesheet. The value of the `result-prefix` attribute specifies the namespace URI that appears in the result tree.

THE XSL:ELEMENT ELEMENT

The `xsl:element` element you use to create an element with an expanded name is specified by the `name` attribute. The `xsl:element` element contains a template for the attributes and the children for the element that are created. The `xsl:element` element has the following form:

```
<xsl:element
  name = { qname }
  namespace = { uri-reference }
  use-attribute-sets = qnames>
</xsl:element>
```

THE XSL:ATTRIBUTE ELEMENT

The `xsl:attribute` element you use to add attributes to elements. The extended name of the added attribute is specified by the value of the `name` attribute or the value of the optional `namespace` attribute. The `xsl:attribute` element has the following form:

```
<xsl:attribute
  name = { qname }
  namespace = { uri-reference }>
  </xsl:attribute>
```

THE XSL:ATTRIBUTE-SET ELEMENT

The xsl:attribute-set element you use to define a named set of attributes. The xsl:attribute-set element can consist zero or more xsl:attribute elements. The value of the name attribute that is a QName specifies the name of the attribute set. The xsl:attribute-set element has the following form:

```
<xsl:attribute-set
  name = qname
  use-attribute-sets = qnames>
</xsl:attribute-set>
```

THE XSL:PROCESSING-INSTRUCTION ELEMENT

The xsl:processing-instruction element you use to create a processing-instruction node. It contains a template for the string value of the processing-instruction node. The xsl:processing-instruction node has the following form:

```
<xsl:processing-instruction
  name = { ncname }>
</xsl:processing-instruction>
```

THE XSL:COMMENT ELEMENT

The xsl:comment element you use to create a command node in the result tree. It contains a template for the string value of the comment node. It has the following form:

```
<xsl:comment>
</xsl:comment>
```

THE XSL:COPY ELEMENT

The xsl:copy element is to copy the current node. The xsl:copy element contains a template for the attributes and children of the created node. The xsl:copy element has the following form:

```
<xsl:copy
  use-attribute-sets = qnames>
</xsl:copy>
```

THE XSL:VALUE-OF ELEMENT

The xsl:value-of element you use to create a text node in the result tree. The select attribute is an expression. This expression is evaluated and converted to a string that specifies the string value of the created-text node. The xsl:value-of element has the following form:

```
<xsl:value-of
  select = string-expression
disable-output-escaping = "yes" | "no"/>
```

THE XSL:NUMBER ELEMENT

The xsl:number element you use to insert a formatted number into a result tree. The number is specified by an expression in the value attribute. This expression is evaluated and converted to a number. The number is then rounded to an integer and converted to a string. The xsl:number element has the following form:

```
<xsl:number
  level = "single" | "multiple" | "any"
  count = pattern
  from = pattern
  value = number-expression
  format = { string }
  lang = { nmtoken }
  letter-value = { "alphabetic" | "traditional" }
  grouping-separator = { char }
  grouping-size = { number } />
```

THE XSL:FOR-EACH ELEMENT

The xsl:for-each element you use to specify the template for selected node. The select attribute of the xsl:for-each element is an expression. This expression is evaluated to a node set.

The xsl:for-each element contains a template that is instantiated for the node specified by the select attribute. The xsl:for-each element has the following form:

```
<xsl:for-each
  select = node-set-expression>
  </xsl:for-each>
```

THE XSL:IF ELEMENT

The xsl:if element you use for conditional processing. The xsl:if element contains a template. The test atrribute of the xsl:if element is an expression. The expression is evaluated to a boolean. If the Boolean value is true, the template is instantiated. The xsl:if element has the following form:

```
<xsl:if
  test = boolean-expression>
</xsl:if>
```

THE XSL:CHOOSE ELEMENT

The xsl:choose element you also use for conditional processing. The xsl:choose element contains a sequence of xsl:when elements. The xsl:choose element can also contain an xsl:otherwise element. Both the xsl:when element and the xsl:otherwise element contain a template. The test attribute of the xsl:when element is an expression. This expression is evaluated to a boolean. As the xsl:choose element is processed, all the xsl:when elements are tested. The template of the first xsl:when element with a test that returns as true is instantiated. If none of the xsl:when elements test true, the template of the xsl:otherwise element is instantiated. The xsl:choose element has the following form:

```
<xsl:choose>
<!-- Content: (xsl:when+, xsl:otherwise?) -->
</xsl:choose>

<xsl:when
test = boolean-expression>
</xsl:when>

<xsl:otherwise>
</xsl:otherwise>
```

THE XSL:SORT ELEMENT

The xsl:sort element you use as a child of an xsl:apply-templates or xsl:for-each element to process a sorted node. The select attribute of the xsl:sort element is an expression. This expression is evaluated with that node as the current node to a string that serves as a sort key for the node. The order attribute of the xsl:sort element specifies whether the string is sorted in ascending or descending order. The language of the sort key is specified by the lang attribute. The data-type attribute specifies the data type of the string, which can be a text, a number, or a QName. The case-order attribute specifies the sorting of uppercase and lowercase letters. The xsl:sort element has the following form:

```
<xsl:sort
  select = string-expression
  lang = { nmtoken }
  data-type = { "text" | "number" | qname }
  order = { "ascending" | "descending" }
  case-order = { "upper-first" | "lower-first" } />
```

THE XSL:VARIABLE ELEMENT

The xsl:variable element, along with the xsl:param element, you use to bind variables to values. Both xsl:variable and xsl:param elements have a name attribute that is a QName, which specifies the name of the variable. The select attribute is an expression that is evaluated to return the value to which the variable binds. The `xsl:variable` and the `xsl:param` elements have the following form:

```
<xsl:variable
  name = qname
  select = expression>
</xsl:variable>

<xsl:param
  name = qname
  select = expression>
</xsl:param>
```

THE XSL:COPY-OF ELEMENT

The `xsl:copy-of` element you use to insert a result-tree fragment into the result tree. The `select` attribute of the `xsl:copy-of` element is an expression. If the expression is evaluated, it can be a result-tree fragment or a `nodeset` or neither of the two. In the first case, the result-tree fragment is copied into the result tree. If the expression evaluates to a `node-set`, all the nodes are copied in the node tree in document order. If the expression evaluates to neither a result-tree fragment nor a `node-set`, the result is converted to a string and copied to the result tree. The `xsl:copy-of` element has the following form:

```
<xsl:copy-of
select= expression />
```

Refer to the XML path language section for the node-set object.

THE XSL:WITH-PARAM ELEMENT

The `xsl:with-param` element you use to pass parameters to templates. The `name` attribute of the `xsl:with-param` element is a `QName` that specifies the name of the parameter. The `xsl:with-param` element can appear within both `xsl:call-template` and `xsl:apply-template` elements. The `xsl:with-param` element has the following form:

```
<xsl:with-param
  name = qname
  select = expression>
</xsl:with-param>
```

XSLT-specific additional functions and elements

Some of the important XSLT-specific functions and elements added to the XSLT core library are as follows:

◆ The `document` function enables access to XML documents other than the main source document. The `document` function is of the following form:

```
node-set document(object, node-set?)
```

◆ The `xsl:key` element you use to declare keys. A key contains the node, the key name, and the key value. The `name` attribute of the `xsl:key` element is a QName that specifies the name of the key. The `match` attribute of the `xsl:key` element is a `pattern`. Key information is provided for only those nodes that match the `pattern` of the `match` attribute. The `use` attribute is an expression that specifies the value of the key. The `xsl:key` element has the following form:

```
<xsl:key
  name = qname
  match = pattern
  use = expression />
```

◆ The `format-number` function converts a number to a string. The number to format is specified by the first argument of the function. To format a number, the `format-number` function uses the format-pattern string specified by its second argument and the decimal format specified by the optional third argument. The `format-number` function has the following form:

```
string format-number(number, string, string?)
```

◆ The `xsl:decimal-format` element you use to control the interpretation of a formal pattern used by the `format-number` function. The `name` attribute of the `xsl:decimal-format` is a QName that specifies a decimal format. The `decimal-separator` attribute specifies the character used for the decimal sign. The `grouping-separator` attribute specifies the character used for grouping separators. The `percent` attribute specifies the character used for the percent sign. The `per-mille` attribute specifies the character used for the per-mille sign. The `zero-digit` attribute specifies the character used for the digit zero. The `digit` attribute specifies the character used for a digit. The `infinity` attribute specifies the string used to represent infinity The `xsl:decimal-format` element has the following form:

```
<xsl:decimal-format
  name = qname
  decimal-separator = char
  grouping-separator = char
  infinity = string
  minus-sign = char
  NaN = string
  percent = char
  per-mille = char
```

```
zero-digit = char
digit = char
pattern-separator = char />
```

◆ The `current` function returns a `node-set` that has the current node as its only function. The `current` function has the following form:

```
node-set current()
```

◆ The `unparsed-entity-uri` function returns an URI of an unparsed entity with the specified name. The `unparsed-entity-uri` function has the following form:

```
string unparsed-entity-uri(string)
```

◆ The `generate-id` function returns a string that represents the first node of the specified `node-set`. The `generate-id` has the following form:

```
string generate-id(node-set?)
```

XML Path Language

This section discusses some important specifications stipulated in the XML Path Language (XPath) Version 1.0 W3C Recommendation and XML Path Language (XPath) 2.0 W3C Working Draft.

To view the detailed specification you can visit `www.w3.org/TR/xpath` and `www.w3.org/TR/xpath20/`.

XPath is a language that you use to address a part of XML documents for providing functionality shared between XSL Transformations (XSLT) and XPointers (XPointer).

XPath models an XML document as a tree of nodes, such as element nodes, attribute nodes, and text nodes. XPath consists of expressions. The expressions are evaluated to yield an object. The objects can be of the following types:

◆ `node-set`

◆ `boolean`

◆ `number`

◆ `string`

Expression evaluations occur corresponding to a context specified by XSLT and XPointer. The context consists of the following:

♦ A node.

♦ A pair of nonzero positive integers.

♦ A set of variable bindings.

♦ A function library.

♦ The set of namespace declaration in scope for the expression.

Location paths

A *location path* is an expression that selects a set of nodes relative to the context node. If the location path expression is evaluated, the result comprises node-sets containing the nodes selected by the location path.

Some examples of location path are as follows:

♦ The location path child::para selects the para element children of the context node.

♦ The location path child::* selects all element children of the context node.

♦ The location path child::text() selects all text-node children of the context node.

♦ The location path child::node() selects all the children of the context node, irrespective of their node types.

♦ The location path attribute::name selects the name attribute of the context node.

♦ The location path child::para[position()=1] selects the first para child of the context node.

♦ The location path child::para[position()=last()] selects the last para child of the context node.

♦ The location path child::para[position()=last()-1] selects the last but one para child of the context node.

♦ The location path child::para[position()>1] selects all the para children of the context node other than the first para child of the context node.

The LocationPath grammar is as follows:

```
LocationPath::= RelativelocationPath|
                        AbsoluteLocationpath
AbsoluteLocationPath ::= '/' RelativeLocationPath? |

AbbreviatedAbsoluteLocationPath
RelativeLocationPath ::= Step |
                   |RelativeLocationPath '/' Step|
              AbbreviatedAbsoluteLocationPath
```

Location step

A *location step* consists of the following three parts:

- ◆ An axis
- ◆ A node test
- ◆ Zero or more predicates

The location step's grammar is as follows:

```
Step ::= AxisSpecifier NodeTest Predicate*|
              Abbreviatedstep
AxisSpecifier ::= AxisName '::'
                        | AbbreviatedAxisSpecifier
```

Axes

Some of the axes defined by the specification are as follows:

- ◆ The `child` axis contains the children of the context node.
- ◆ The `descendent` axis contains the descendants of the context node.
- ◆ The `parent` axis contains the parent of the context node, if one exists.
- ◆ The `ancestor` axis contains the ancestors of the context node.
- ◆ The `following-sibling` axis contains all the following siblings of the context node.
- ◆ The `preceding-sibling` axis contains all the preceding siblings of the context node.
- ◆ The `attribute` axis contains the attributes of the context node.
- ◆ The `namespace` axis contains the namespace nodes of the context node.

◆ The `self` axis contains just the context node.

◆ The `descendent-or-self` axis contains the context node and the descendants of the context node.

◆ The `ancestor-or-self` axis contains the context node and the ancestors of the context node.

Axes have the following grammar:

```
AxisName ::= 'ancestor'| 'ancestor-or-self' |
             'attribute' | 'child' |
             'descendant' | 'descendant-or-self' |
             'following' | 'following-sibling' |
             'namespace' | 'parent' |
               'preceding' | 'preceding-sibling' |
             'self'
```

Node tests

Every axis has a principal node type that can be any of the following:

◆ The principal node type is element if an axis contains elements.

◆ The principal node type is attribute for attribute axis.

◆ The principal node type is namespace for namespace axis.

A node test is a `Qname` that is true if the following conditions are true:

◆ If the type of the node is the principal node type.

◆ If the expanded-name of the node is equal to the expanded-name specified by the `Qname`.

A node test has the following grammar:

```
NodeTest::= NameTest | NodeType '(' ')' | 'processing-instruction'
'(' Literal')'
```

Predicates

A `Predicate` filters a `node-set` with respect to an axis to produce a new `node-set`. A predicate has the following grammar:

```
Predicate ::= '[' PredicateExpr ']'
PredicateExpr ::= Expr
```

Expressions

The XPath language provides various types of expressions that act as the building blocks of the language. XPath expressions have the following grammar:

```
Expr ::= OrExpr | AndExpr | ForExpr | QuantifiedExpr | IfExpr
| GeneralComp | ValueComp | NodeComp | OrderComp
| InstanceofExpr | RangeExpr | AdditiveExpr | MultiplicativeExpr
| UnionExpr | IntersectExceptExpr | UnaryExpr | CastExpr |
PathExpr
```

Some of the XPath expressions, along with their grammar, are as follows:

◆ A *primary* expression has the following grammar:

```
PrimaryExpr ::= Variable| Literal
                        | FunctionCall | ParenthesizedExpr
```

◆ A *path* expression locates nodes and returns a sequence of nodes from a tree. The path expression has the following grammar:

```
PathExpr ::= AbsolutePathExpr | RelativePathExpr
AbsolutePathExpr ::= ("/" RelativePathExpr?) | ("//"
RelativePathExpr)
RelativePathExpr ::= StepExpr (("/" | "//") StepExpr)*
StepExpr ::= AxisStep | GeneralStep
```

◆ A *sequence* is an ordered collection of values or nodes. A sequence is constructed by using ParenthesizedExpr with the following grammar:

```
ParenthesizedExpr ::= " (" ExprSequence? ")"
ExprSequence ::= Expr ("," Expr)*
RangeExpr ::= Expr  "to" Expr
```

◆ *Arithmetic* expressions are what you use to perform arithmetic operations. Following is the grammar to use for arithmetic expressions:

```
AdditiveExpr ::= Expr ("+" | "-") Expr
MultiplicativeExpr ::= Expr ("*" | "div" | "mod") Expr
UnaryExpr ::= ("-" | "+") Expr
```

◆ You use *comparison* expressions to compare two values. Comparison expressions have the following grammar:

```
ValueComp ::= Expr ("eq" | "ne" | "lt" | "le" | "gt" |
"ge") Expr
GeneralComp ::= Expr ("=" | "!=" | "<" | "<=" | ">" |
">=") Expr
```

```
NodeComp ::=  Expr  ("==" |  "!==")  Expr
OrderComp ::= Expr  ("<<" |  ">>" |  "precedes" |  "follows")
Expr
```

◆ *Logical* expressions you use to provide either a boolean true or a boolean false value. The logical expression has the following grammar:

```
OrExpr ::= Expr  "or"  Expr
AndExpr ::=  Expr  "and"  Expr
```

◆ *For* expressions you used for iteration. The for expression has the following grammar:

```
ForExpr ::=  ForClause "return"  Expr
ForClause ::= "for" "$" QName "in" Expr ("," Variable "in"
Expr)*
```

◆ Conditional expressions you use for conditional processing. Conditional expressions have the following grammar:

```
IfExpr ::= "if" "(" Expr ")" "then" Expr "else"  Expr
```

◆ *Quantified* expressions support universal quantifications. Quantified expressions have the following grammar:

```
QuantifiedExpr ::= ("some" "$" |  "every" "$") QName "in"
Expr "satisfies"  Expr
```

Core function library

The *core function library* contains functions that you use to evaluate expressions. XPath implementations should also include these functions in the function library. Some of these functions are as follows:

◆ number last()

◆ number position()

◆ number count(node-set)

◆ string local-name(node-set?)

◆ string namespace-uri(node-set?)

◆ string string(object?)

◆ boolean starts-with(string, string)

◆ string translate(string, string, string)

◆ boolean boolean(object)

◆ number number(object?)

◆ `number round(number)`

◆ `number sum(node-set)`

XML Schema

The W3C XML schema specifications consist of the following three parts:

◆ XML Schema Part 0: Primer

◆ XML Schema Part 1: Structures

◆ XML Schema Part 2: Datatypes

 To view the detailed specification, you can visit `www.w3.org/TR/ xmlschema-0/`, `www.w3.org/TR/xmlschema-1/`, and `www.w3.org/TR/ xmlschema-2/`.

The following sections discuss these parts.

XML Schema Part 0: Primer

The XML Schema Part 0: Primer basically defines the descriptions, purposes, and use of schemas. It also provides the descriptions and use of the schema definition language.

XML Schema Part 1: Structures

The XML Schema Part 1: Structures defines the natures of XML schemas along with their component parts. It also specifies the XML markup constructs to use to represent schemas and specifies how schemas apply to XML documents.

In the specification, XML schemas are described in terms of a conceptual abstract-data model that consists of the following:

◆ Type definition components

◆ Declaration components

◆ Model group components

◆ Identity-constraint definition components

◆ Group definition components

◆ Annotation components

XML schemas consist of *schema components*. The schema components are grouped as *primary* components, *secondary* components, and *helper* components. The primary-component group consists of the following schema components:

- ◆ Simple type definitions
- ◆ Complex type definitions
- ◆ Attribute declarations
- ◆ Element declarations

The secondary-component group consists of the following schema components:

- ◆ Attribute group definitions
- ◆ Identity-constraint definitions
- ◆ Model group definitions
- ◆ Notation declarations

The helper-component group consists of the following schema components:

- ◆ Annotations
- ◆ Model groups
- ◆ Particles
- ◆ Wildcards
- ◆ Attribute uses

A schema is represented by one or more `schema` documents. A `schema` document contains a representation of schema components. A `schema` document has the following grammar:

```
<schema
  attributeFormDefault = (qualified | unqualified) : unqualified
  blockDefault = (#all | List of (extension | restriction |
substitution))  : "
  elementFormDefault = (qualified | unqualified) : unqualified
  finalDefault = (#all | List of (extension | restriction))  : "
  id = ID
  targetNamespace = anyURI
  version = token
  xml:lang = language
>
```

```
  Content: ((include | import | redefine | annotation)*,
(((simpleType | complexType | group | attributeGroup) | element |
attribute | notation), annotation*)*)
</schema>
```

The following sections discuss some of the schema components.

ATTRIBUTE DECLARATIONS

Attribute declarations provide local validation of attribute information-item values and specifies default values for attribute information items. The attribute-declaration schema component has the following properties:

- ◆ {name}

- ◆ {target namespace}

- ◆ {type definition}

- ◆ {scope}

- ◆ {value constraint}

- ◆ {annotation}

The `<attribute>` element is the XML representation of an attribute-declaration schema component. You have the following four built-in attribute declarations:

- ◆ Attribute declaration for the `type` attribute.

- ◆ Attribute declaration for the `nil` attribute.

- ◆ Attribute declaration for the `schemaLocation` attribute.

- ◆ Attribute declaration for the `noNamespaceSchemaLocation` attribute.

ELEMENT DECLARATIONS

Element declarations mainly provide local validation of element information-item values and specify default values for element information items.

The element-declaration schema component has the following properties:

- ◆ {name}

- ◆ {target namespace}

- ◆ {type definition}

- ◆ {scope}

- ◆ {value constraint}

- {nillable}

- {identity-constraint definitions}

- {substitution group affiliation}

- {substitution group exclusions}

- {disallowed substitutions}

- {abstract}

- {annotation}

ATTRIBUTE GROUP DEFINITIONS

Attribute group definitions are primarily used for reference from the XML representation of schema components. Attribute group definitions have the following properties:

- {name}

- {target namespace}

- {attribute uses}

- {attribute wildcard}

- {annotation}

NOTATION DECLARATIONS

Notation declarations are referenced during the validation of strings. Notation declarations have the following properties:

- {name}

- {target namespace}

- {system identifier}

- {public identifier }

- {annotation}

XML Schema Part 2: Datatypes

The XML Schema Part 2: Datatype specifies facilities for defining datatypes to associate with XML element types and attributes in XML schemas, as well as in other XML specifications. The datatypes defined in the specification can be classified into either *primitive datatypes* or *derived datatypes*. The primitive datatypes are datatypes that are not defined in terms of other datatypes. The simple datatypes defined by the specification are as follows:

- string

- boolean

- decimal

- float

- double

- duration

- dateTime

- time

- date

- gYearMonth

- gYear

- gMonthDay

- gDay

- gMonth

- hexBinary

- base64Binary

- anyURI

- QName

- NOTATION

Derived datatypes are datatypes that are defined in terms of other datatypes. The simple datatypes defined by the specification are as follows:

- language

- NMTOKEN

- NMTOKENS

- Name

- NCName

- ID

- IDREF

- IDREFS

- ENTITY

- ◆ ENTITIES

- ◆ integer

- ◆ nonPositiveInteger

- ◆ negativeInteger

- ◆ long

- ◆ int

- ◆ short

- ◆ byte

- ◆ nonNegativeInteger

- ◆ unsignedLong

- ◆ unsignedInt

- ◆ unsignedShort

- ◆ unsignedByte

- ◆ positiveInteger

XML Namespaces

An *XML namespace* is a collection of names that you use in XML documents as element types and attribute names, identified by a URI reference. This section discusses some important specifications of the XML namespaces per the W3C recommendation.

 To view the detailed specification, you can visit www.w3.org/TR/1998/ PR-xml-names-19981117.

You declare a namespace by using some reserved attributes. Some of the grammars and rules laid down in the specification are as follows:

- ◆ The grammar of some of the attributes that you use for declaring namespace appears as follows:

```
NSAttName    ::= PrefixedAttName | DefaultAttName
PrefixedAttName ::= 'xmlns:' NCName
DefaultAttName  ::= 'xmlns'
```

```
NCName ::= (Letter | '_') (NCNameChar)*
NCNameChar ::= Letter |Digit | '.' | '-' | '_' |
CombiningChar | Extender
```

◆ Some XML document names may be given as qualified names according to the following grammar:

```
QName ::= (Prefix ':')? LocalPart
Prefix ::= NCName
LocalPart ::= NCName
```

◆ Element types of XML documents are given as qualified names according to the following grammar:

```
Stag ::= '<' QName (S Attribute)* S? '>'
Etag ::= '</' QName S? '>'
EmptyElemTag ::= '<' QName (S Attribute)* S? '/>'
```

◆ Attribute names of XML documents are given as qualified names according to the following grammar:

```
Attribute ::= NSAttName Eq AttValue |
              QName Eg AttValue
```

◆ Element names and attribute types are given as qualified names if they appear in DTD declarations. The grammar for qualified names in DTD declarations is as follows:

```
Doctypedecl ::= '<!DOCTYPE' S QName (S ExternalID)? S? ('['
(markupdecl
                | PEReference | S)* ']' S?)? '>'
elementdecl ::= '<!ELEMENT' S QName S contentspec S? '>'
cp ::= (QName | choice | seq) ('?' | '*' | '+')?
Mixed ::= '(' S? '#PCDATA' (S? '|' S? QName)* S? ')*'
              | '(' S? '#PCDATA' S? ')'
AttlistDecl ::= '<!ATTLIST' S QName AttDef* S? '>'
AttDef ::= S (QName | NSAttName) S AttType S DefaultDecl
```

◆ XML document tags cannot contain attributes that have identical names. Tags also cannot have attributes that have the same name and structure and that have prefixes bound to identical namespace names.

Appendix E

Java WSDP

WEB SERVICES ARE SELF-CONTAINED applications that work as a single system to provide Web-based services. Web services enable companies or individuals to publish their services so that other clients or Web services can use them. Similarly, companies or individuals can use other Web services published on the Web. Web services essentially comprise the following technologies:

◆ **Universal Description, Discovery, and Integration (UDDI):** A standard that describes available Web services. This standard enables service providers to advertise their services on the Web. Service requesters can look up the service providers by using SOAP messaging and invoke the required service.

◆ **Simple Object Access Protocol (SOAP):** A standard that enables a service requestor to look up services on the Web by using XML documents.

◆ **Web Services Description Language (WSDL):** An XML-based *interface definition language* (*IDL*) used for describing Web services. WSDL defines the interface, semantics, and implementation characteristics of a service.

◆ **Electronic Business eXtensible Markup Language (ebXML):** A suite of XML specifications necessary for B2B transactions. It defines the core components, message-exchange capabilities, business processes, transaction mechanism, registry and repository, trading partner agreement, and security of transactions.

 Refer to Chapter 1 of this book for more information on Web services.

Java Web Services Developer Pack

Because of its robust and portable features, the J2EE architecture has established itself as the primary platform for developing enterprise applications. With the rising demand for Web services, the Java platform is integrating and providing the necessary technologies necessary to develop Web services. The Java platform thus enables existing J2EE applications to migrate to a Web-services system easily. Moreover,

J2EE's compatibility with XML, the platform-independent data format, makes it an obvious choice for developing Web services. Many middleware-supplier companies such as IBM, Oracle, and BEA have adopted J2EE as their platform.

To build XML-based Web services by using the Java 2 platform, Sun Microsystems, Inc., offers the *Java Web Services Developer Pack (Java WSDP)*. You can download the Java Web Services Developer Pack, Early Access 2, from `http://java.sun.com/webservices/downloads/webservicespack.html`. This pack consists of the following technologies:

- Java API for XML Messaging (JAXM) 1.0.1 EA2 (Early Access 2)
- Java API for XML Processing (JAXP) 1.2 EA2 (Early Access 2)
- Java API for XML Registries (JAXR) 1.0 EA2 (Early Access 2)
- Java API for XML-based RPC (JAX-RPC) 1.0 EA2 (Early Access 2)
- Java Server Pages Standard Tag Library (JSTL) 1.0 Beta 1
- Apache Tomcat 4.1-dev Container
- Ant Build Tool 1.4.1
- Java WSDP Registry Server 1.0 EA2
- deploytool (Web Application Deployment Tool)

 The JWSDP pack was tested on Windows 2000, Windows XP, Solaris 2.8, and the RedHat Linux 7.2. To install the Java Web Services Developer Pack, Early Access 2, you need a Java 2 Platform Standard Edition (J2SE) SDK 1.3.1 or higher.

The following sections give you a brief overview of all the technologies that make up the Web Services Developer Pack.

Java Server Pages Standard Tag Library (JSTL)

A *tag library* defines tags that provide common functionality necessary in a JSP application. According to the J2EE specification, you use a JSP page in the presentation layer of n-tier architecture. You mainly use JSP for content generation in a Web application. In a JSP application, you typically use Java scriplets to provide dynamic content. Instead of using scriplets, you can also define your own custom tags or use tags from different vendors that provide the same functionality. To simplify things further, Sun Microsystems provides the Java Server Pages such as processing XML documents, working with databases, and managing URLs. By using the JSTL, you can concentrate on the content generation of a JSP page without needing to worry about its programming part. To augment JSP's goal of separating the role of a programmer and a content developer, JSTL supports an expression language (EL). In a JSP application, you typically use expressions or scriplets to call a JavaBean component or else to work with application data. Instead of using programming-language-specific codes in your JSP page, you can use the standard tags, which use the default expression language (ECMAScript) that JSTL currently supports.

The following code shows an expression that accesses data from a JavaBean component:

```
<%= myData.getData()>
```

You can use a more simple syntax of the expression language to perform the same operation, as shown in the following code:

```
<x:stdTag att="${myData.getData}">
```

The Java Server Pages Standard Tag Library consists of two libraries:

- **The JSTL-RT tag library:** Contains expressions specified in the JSP scripting language.

- **JSTL-EL tag library:** Contains expression specified in the expression language.

Table E-1 lists some important tags and their brief description:

TABLE E-1 SOME CORE TAGS AND THEIR DESCRIPTIONS

Tags	Descriptions
<out>	Similar to JSP expressions. You use this tag to evaluate an expression and display the result.
<set>	Used to set an attribute's value to a JSP scope.
<remove>	Used to remove a scoped attribute.

Refer to Chapter 13 for more information on JSTL.

Java API for XML Messaging (JAXM)

JAXM supports XML messaging by using the Java platform. JAXM conforms to the Simple Object Access Protocol (SOAP) 1.1 and SOAP with attachments specifications. SOAP messages can be of two types: messages with attachments and messages without attachments. You can send any files by using a SOAP message with an attachment. The JWSDP consists of the following JAXM components:

◆ The API specification (Javadoc documentation) for JAXM

◆ The JAXM Reference Implementation (RI)

◆ Various documents about the RI

◆ Sample applications

Refer to Chapter 10 for more information on JAXM.

Java API for XML Processing (JAXP)

JAXP is a specification that you use to process XML-related documents from within Java applications. It enables you to parse XML documents as a stream of events or as an object tree. It also enables you to convert data into other data formats. JAXP performs this parsing by providing an abstraction layer to plug-in SAX parsers, DOM parsers, and XSL processors. To provide such functionality, JAXP endorses the following set of standards:

◆ W3C XML 1.0 Recommendation (Second Edition)

◆ W3C XML Namespaces 1.0 Recommendation

◆ Simple API for XML (SAX) 2.0

◆ Document Object Model (DOM) Level 2

◆ XSLT 1.0

Refer to Chapter 8 of this book for more information on JAXP.

Java API for XML Registries (JAXR)

JAXR is a Java API that you use to access various XML registries. JAXR consists of the following two parts:

♦ **JAXR clients:** Applications that use the JAXR API to access the registries through the JAXR provider.

♦ **JAXR providers:** Applications that use the JAXR API to provide the JAXR client access to the XML registries.

The JAXR API provides the following two packages to work with XML registries:

♦ `javax.xml.registry`

♦ `javax.xml.registry.infomodel`

The Web Services Developer Pack consists of the following JAXR components:

♦ The JAXR 1.0 Early Access 2 (EA2) Reference Implementation (RI)

♦ A registry browser

♦ API documentation

♦ Sample programs

Refer to Chapter 12 for more information on JAXR.

Java API for XML-based RPC (JAX-RPC)

JAX-RPC is an API that you use to build Web services. You also use JAX-RPC to create clients that uses remote-procedure calls (RPC) and XML. You can use JAX-RPC to develop your Web-service applications that call remote computer resources according to SOAP 1.1 specifications. You make these calls by using the XML-based SOAP protocol. After a JAX-RPC service is implemented, the service is deployed on a server-side JAX-RPC implementation.

Refer to Chapter 11 for more information on JAX-RPC.

Tomcat 4.0 Servlet/JSP Container

The Java Web Service Developer Pack (JWSDP) download contains the Apache Tomcat 4.1-dev Container Container. The Tomcat container of the JWSDP implements the Servlet 2.3 and JSP 1.2 specifications. A Web container basically provides the environment necessary for Java servlets and Java Server Pages to run. The Tomcat container was developed in an open environment and is released under the Apache Software license. You can use a Tomcat Web server as a standalone server or integrate it with other Web servers, such as Apache version 1.3 or later and Microsoft Internet Information Server version 4.0 or later. If you want to integrate it with other Web servers, you need to install a Web-server adapter. Table E-2 discusses the directories of the Tomcat container.

TABLE E-2 DIRECTORIES OF THE TOMCAT CONTAINER

Directory Name	Description
Bin	Contains scripts such as those to start and shut down the container.
Config	Contains Tomcat's configuration file, server.xml. It also contains other configuration files such as the web.xml file that provide the default value of the Web application as its loaded in the container. The tomcat-users.xml file contains information such as the username and password that it provides during the installation.
Lib	Contains the JAR files of the common classes.
Log	Contains the log file of the server.
Shared	Contains classes that are shared by all applications.
Temp	Used by the Java Virtual Machine for storing temporary files.
Webapps	Contains your Web Applications.

To start the Tomcat server for deploying or running your application, type the following command at the command prompt:

```
startup
```

To stop the Tomcat server, type the following command on the command line:

```
shutdown
```

Ant build tool

The Ant build tool is meant for building Java applications. As a platform-independent tool, Ant enjoys many benefits over other operating-system-specific tools such as `make` and `gnumake`. The Ant tool performs the building process in an object-oriented manner. Tasks relating to building an application are represented by objects. These objects constitute a target tree. During the building process, the Ant tool uses an XML-based configuration file that calls the target tree to perform the building tasks.

You run the Ant tool to build your application by typing the following command at the command prompt.

```
ant build
```

On running, Ant first looks for a build file, `build.xml`, in the current directory. The `build.xml` file contains information necessary for building your application. You can also save the build file in the parent directory. If you save the build file in the parent directory, you must use the `-find` option while running the Ant tool. Upon your specifying the `-find` option, the Ant tool moves up the directory hierarchy, searching for the build file. Instead of using the `build.xml` file, you can use another build file by using the `buildfile` option. The syntax for specifying a file as a build file is as follows:

```
ant build -buildfile myfile.xml
```

In the preceding code, `myfile.xml` is the file that you want to use as the build file.

The build file that you specify represents your project. A build file can represent only one project at a time. A project defines at least one or more targets or tasks that you want to perform – for example, compiling your application or deleting directory trees. You generally specify what target to use while running the Ant tool. If you do not specify the target, Ant uses the project's default target.

A *task* is a Java code that you can execute. You can use Ant's built-in tasks or define your own tasks. The following list describes some of the built-in tasks that Ant provides:

- ◆ `Ant`: Starts the Ant tool that uses a build file in the current directory.

- ◆ `AntStructure`: Creates a DTD of the build file that Ant uses.

- ◆ `Copy`: Copies a file to a new file.

- ◆ `Mkdir`: Creates a new directory.

- ◆ `Move`: Moves a file or a set of files to a new directory.

- ◆ `Delete`: Deletes files.

- ◆ Fail: Leaves the current build, throwing a BuildException.

- ◆ Get: Gets a file from a URL.

- ◆ Mail: Sends mail by using SMTP.

- ◆ Jar: Creates a JAR file for a set of files.

- ◆ Javac: Compiles Java source files.

- ◆ Java: Executes Java files, using the Ant JVM or any other JVM.

- ◆ Property: Sets a project's property.

- ◆ Record: Records the current build process to a file.

- ◆ Sql: Executes SQL statements.

- ◆ Zip: Creates a zip file.

- ◆ Unzip: Unzips a zip file.

In this appendix, you use the build tool to basically compile and create your applications directory structure.

deploytool

You use deploytool to deploy Web applications on the Tomcat server. You also use deploytool to package your Web application into a WAR file. You can also modify the web.xml file to configure your application by using deploytool.

Registry Server

After you develop your Web services, you need to advertise your service. You advertise Web services in a registry. Clients and other Webs services look up the registry to locate the Web service and use it.

The Java Web Services Developer Pack (Java WSDP) Registry Server provides a registry for the testing purposes. You can use the registry server that comes along with the WSDP to test your Web services application. The Java Web Services Developer Pack (Java WSDP) Registry Server contains the following components:

- ◆ The Java WSDP Registry Server 1.0 Early Access 2 (EA2) release.

- ◆ A database, based on the native XML database Xindice, to persist registry data.

- ◆ A graphical user interface (GUI) tool, Indri. You use this GUI to create and inspect your database data.

To work with the registry server, follow these steps:

1. To start Tomcat, navigate to the `<JWSDP_HOME>\bin` directory and type the following command at the command prompt:

   ```
   startup
   ```

2. To start the `Xindice` database, navigate to the `<JWSDP_HOME>\bin` directory and type the following command at the command prompt:

   ```
   xindice-start
   ```

3. To access the Registry Server database, use the graphical user interface (GUI) tool `Indri`. To start the `Indri` tool, go to the `<JWSDP_HOME>\samples\registry-server` directory and type the following command:

   ```
   registry-server-test.bat run-indri
   ```

   This command launches the `Indri` GUI, as shown in Figure E-1.

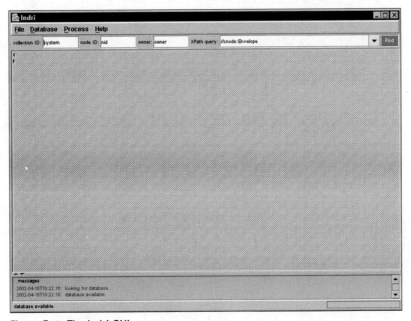

Figure E-1: The Indri GUI

Using the Registry Server, you can save a business to the registry server, locate a business in the registry server, and delete a business from the registry server. To save a business in the Registry Server, you work with the SaveBusiness.xml file in your <JWSDP_HOME>\samples\registry-server\xml directory. To save a business, perform the following steps:

1. Choose File → Open. Go to the xml directory and open SaveBusiness.xml.

   The SaveBusiness.xml file opens in the text area of the GUI, as shown in Figure E-2.

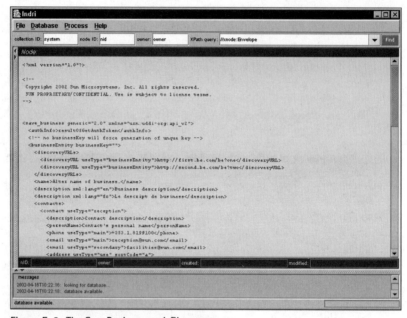

Figure E-2: The SaveBusiness.xml file opens.

 You can check the validity of the XML file through the GUI by choosing Processes → Check Content from the menu bar. If the XML document is valid, the message document is well formed appears in the status bar.

2. In the Collection ID text box, enter **uddi**. In the Owner text box enter **testowner** and press Enter.

3. Choose Database → Create Node from the menu bar. This action saves your business in the registry server.

To check whether your business is stored, choose Database → Clear Text Area from the menu bar.

Now choose Database → Get Node from the menu bar. The content of your business appears in the text area of the GUI, as shown in Figure E-3.

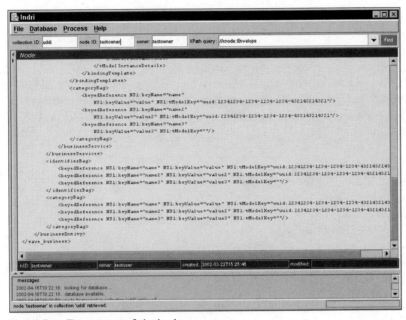

Figure E-3: The content of the business appears.

You can also locate a business by its name in the Indri GUI. You can delete a business by choosing Database → Delete Node from the menu bar. To close the GUI, choose File → Exit from the menu bar.

Working with the Java Web Services Developer Pack

This section discusses the various steps involved in developing a Web application by using the JWSDP. In this section, I demonstrate how you can develop a Web component that uses a Java bean to generate a welcome message based on the name a user provides. You compile this JavaBean component by using the Ant tool. I then discuss how you can deploy the application on the Tomcat server by using deploytool. Before starting to develop this application, you must set the path that points to your Java 2 Platform Standard Edition (J2SE) installation's bin directory and your Java Web Services Developer Pack installation's bin directory. If you have J2sdk1.4.0 and jwsdp-1_0-ea2 installed in your C: drive, set the path as shown:

```
SET PATH=%PATH%; c:\J2sdk1.4.0\bin; c:\ jwsdp-1_0-ea2\bin
```

Set the required environment variables as follows:

```
JAVA_HOME= c:\J2sdk1.4.0
JWSDP_HOME= c:\ jwsdp-1_0-ea2
```

To work with the Ant tool, you must create a `build.properties` file. This file contains authentication information that the Tomcat Manager application (of the Tomcat server) uses. This information is verified against the `tomcat-users.xml` file. The `tomcat-users.xml` file, which is in the `conf` folder of your JAXB installation, contains the username and password that you provide during installation of the Java Web Services Developer Pack. The `tomcat-users.xml` file looks similar to the following example:

```
<?xml version='1.0'?>
<tomcat-users>
  <role rolename="admin"/>
  <role rolename="manager"/>
  <role rolename="provider"/>
  <user username="name" password="password"
roles="admin,manager,provider"/>
</tomcat-users>
```

The username and password that you specify in the `build.properties` file should match the username and password of the `tomcat-users.xml` file. If they do not match, the Tomcat Manager application prevents you from accessing the server.

You create a `build.properties` file and specify the username and password in it as follows:

```
username=name password=password
```

Save this file in your home directory.

 Your home directory is generally `C:/ Documents and Settings/Your login`.

After setting up the environment and creating the `build.properties` file, you can create your Web component. Your Web component basically is a simple JSP page that uses a JavaBean component. The JSP page displays a text box in which a user can enter a name. After the user submits the name, the JSP page displays a welcome message.

To begin creating your Web component, create a folder called `example` in your Java Web Services Developer Pack installation. In the `example` folder, create a folder called `web`. In the `web` folder, create a JSP file by using the following code:

```
<%@ page import="exampleApp.SayHello" %>
<%@ page contentType="text/html; charset=ISO-8859-5" %>

<html>
<head>

 <title>Welcome Application</title>
</head>

<body bgcolor="white">

<jsp:useBean id="welcome" class="exampleApp.SayHello"/>

<jsp:setProperty name="welcome" property="*" />


<h1><FONT FACE="ARIAL" SIZE=8>Welcome To The Test Site</FONT></h1>
<hr>
<p><FONT FACE="ARIAL" SIZE=8>Enter your name:</p></FONT>
<form method="get">
<input type="text" name="name" size="25">
<br>
<p>
<input type="submit" value="Submit">
<input type="reset" value="Reset">
</form>
<%
 String name = request.getParameter("name");

 if (name!=null && name.length() > 0 ){
%>

<p><FONT FACE="ARIAL" SIZE=6>Welcome <%= welcome.getName()%>
<%
}
%>

</body>
</html>
```

After creating the JSP page, your next step is to create a JavaBean component. In the `example` directory, create a directory called `src`. In the `src` directory, create another directory called `exampleApp`. In the `exampleApp` directory, create the JavaBean source file by using the following code:

```
package exampleApp;
public class SayHello{
  private String name;
   public SayHello() {

   }
      public String getName () {
        return name;
      }
public void setName(String name) {
            this.name=name;
        }
      }
```

You now create a build file called `build.xml`. You use this build file to build your application. The Ant tool uses the information in this file to compile your JavaBean component and to create the directory structure necessary for deployment. In the `example` directory, create the `build.xml` file by using the following code:

```
<project name=" example" default="build" basedir=".">
<target name="init">
      <tstamp/>
  </target>
  <property name="example" value="example" />
  <property name="path" value="/${example}"/>
  <property name="build"
value="${jwsdp.home}/example/${example}/build" />
  <property name="url"        value="http://localhost:8080/manager"/>
  <property file="build.properties"/>
  <property file="${user.home}/build.properties"/>
   <path id="classpath">
     <fileset dir="${jwsdp.home}/common/lib">
       <include name="*.jar"/>
     </fileset>
   </path>
   <taskdef name="install"
classname="org.apache.catalina.ant.InstallTask"/>
   <taskdef name="reload"
classname="org.apache.catalina.ant.ReloadTask"/>
```

```xml
    <taskdef name="remove"
classname="org.apache.catalina.ant.RemoveTask"/>
 <target name="prepare" depends="init"
description="Create build directories.">
    <mkdir dir="${build}" />
    <mkdir dir="${build}/WEB-INF" />
    <mkdir dir="${build}/WEB-INF/classes" />
  </target>
 <target name="install" description="Install web application"
          depends="build">
    <install url="${url}" username="${username}"
password="${password}"
          path="${path}" war="file:${build}"/>
  </target>
<target name="reload" description="Reload web application"
          depends="build">
    <reload  url="${url}" username="${username}"
password="${password}"
          path="${path}"/>
  </target>
<target name="remove" description="Remove web application">
    <remove url="${url}" username="${username}"
password="${password}"
          path="${path}"/>
  </target>
<target name="build" depends="prepare"
 description="Compile app Java files and copy HTML and JSP pages" >
    <javac srcdir="src" destdir="${build}/WEB-INF/classes">
    <include name="**/*.java" />
     <classpath refid="classpath"/>
    </javac>
    <copy todir="${build}/WEB-INF">
      <fileset dir="web/WEB-INF"    >
        <include name="web.xml" />
      </fileset>
    </copy>
    <copy todir="${build}">
      <fileset dir="web">
        <include name="*.html" />
        <include name="*.jsp" />
        <include name="*.gif" />
      </fileset>
    </copy>
  </target>
</project>
```

To describe your application, create a web.xml file with the following code:

```
<web-app>
    <display-name>Hello Greetings</display-name>
    <description>
      This is a Hello Greetings example
    </description>
</web-app>
```

You use the web.xml file to configure your application. You can also use deploytool to generate the web.xml file. Create a WEB-INF directory in your web directory. Save web.xml in the WEB-INF directory.

At the command prompt, navigate to the example folder and type the following command:

```
ant build
```

If your application is built successfully, you see an output similar to that shown in Figure E-4.

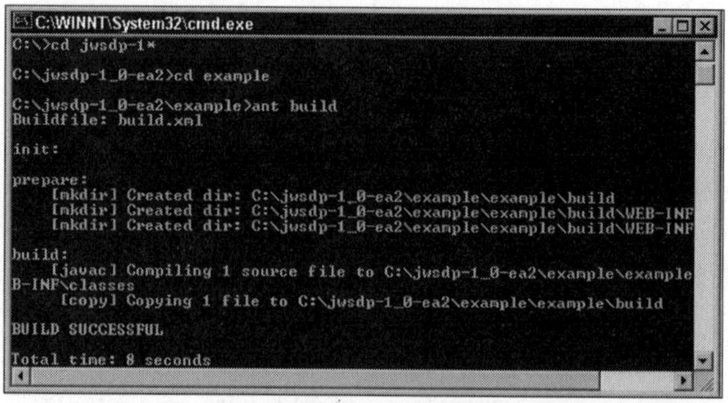

Figure E-4: The output that appears if a file is built successfully

You are now ready to deploy your application on the Tomcat server. To deploy the application, start the Tomcat server by typing the following at the command prompt:

```
startup
```

After your Tomcat server starts, launch deploytool from the command prompt by using the following command:

```
deploytool
```

The deploytool launches, as shown in Figure E-5.

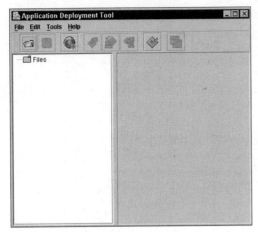

Figure E-5: The deploytool interface

To deploy your application, follow these steps:

1. Choose File → New Web Component from the menu bar. The New Web Component Wizard-Introduction dialog box appears.

2. Click Next. The New Web Component Wizard-WAR File dialog box appears.

3. In the New Web Component Wizard-WAR File dialog box, select the Create New Stand-Alone WAR Module and then click Browse. The Choose Module File dialog box appears.

4. Browse to the `example` folder and specify the filename as **Appwar**.

5. Click Choose Module File.

6. In the New Web Component Wizard-WAR File dialog box, notice that the filename `Appwar.war` appears in the Module File Name text box. Specify **WebApp** in the WAR Display Name text box, as shown in Figure E-6.

7. To add your files to the WAR file, click the Edit button in the Contents area. The Edit Contents Of WebApp dialog box appears. Browse to your JavaBean source file and click Add. Similarly, browse to your JavaBean class file and click Add. The file is added in the Contents of WebApp pane, as shown in Figure E-7.

8. Click OK.

9. In the New Web Component Wizard-WAR File dialog box, click Next. The New Web Component Wizard-Choose Component Type dialog box appears.

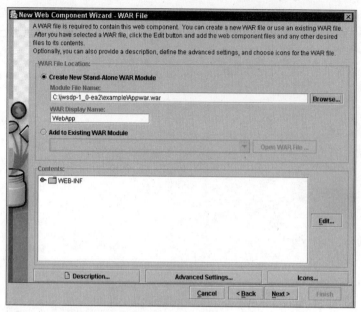

Figure E-6: In WAR Display Name box, specify WebApp.

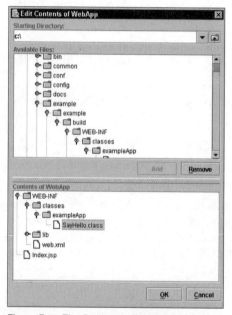

Figure E-7: The Contents of WebApp pane

10. Select JSP in the New Web Component Wizard-Choose Component Type dialog box and click Next. The New Web Component Wizard-Component General Properties dialog box appears.

11. In the JSP Filename drop-down list box, select your JSP file Index.jsp. In the Web Component Name text box, enter **Index,** as shown in Figure E-8.

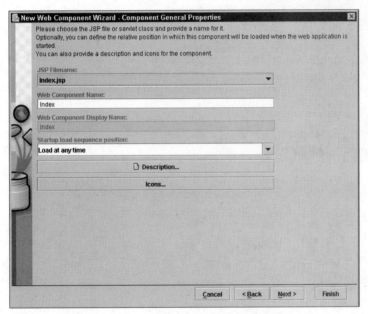

Figure E-8: In the Web Component Name field, enter Index.

12. Click Finish to close the Web Component Wizard-Component General Properties dialog box.

13. In the Application Deployment Tool window, choose Tools → Deploy from the menu bar.

14. In the Text Input Dialog dialog box that appears, specify **/WelcomeApp** in the Enter Web Context text box, as shown in Figure E-9.

Figure E-9: The Text Input Dialog dialog box

15. Click OK. The Specify Server Attributes dialog box appears. Specify the
    username and password that you provided during the installation of the
    Java Web Services Developer Pack, as shown in Figure E-10.

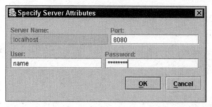

Figure E-10: The Specify Server Attributes dialog box

16. Click OK. The Deployment Console window appears. It displays the status
    of deployment. If the deployment is successful, an output similar to that
    shown in Figure E-11 appears.

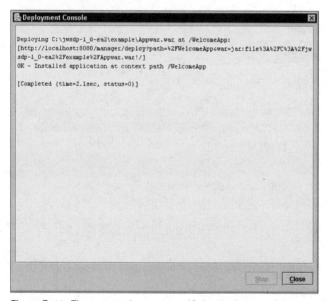

Figure E-11: The output that appears if the deployment is successful

After deploying the application, you can run it. Open a browser window and
type the following address in the address bar:

```
http://localhost:8080/ WelcomeApp
```

In the Enter Your Name text box, as shown in Figure E-12 enter a name.

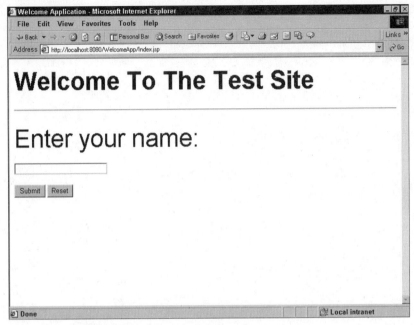

Figure E-12: In the Enter Your Name text box, enter a user name.

The JSP page displays the welcome message, as shown in Figure E-13.

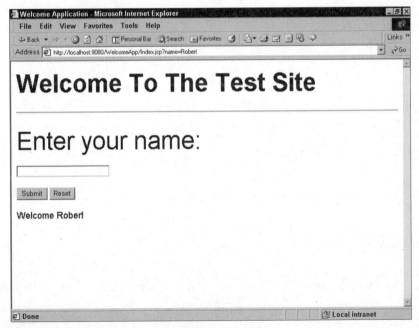

Figure E-13: Sample output of the JSP page

Index

A

absolute-position properties, XSL formatting, 475

abstraction
  JAXM messaging model, 296–297
  partitioning service into, 7
  service-oriented architecture, 4–6

accessibility properties, XSL formatting, 475

actions, JSP directive elements, 180

Active Server Pages. *See* ASP

alias, declaring namespace, 495

alignment, XSL formatting, 480–481

alternate path, EL flow control tags
  exclusive (c:when), 385–386
  general (c:otherwise), 386

Ant build tool, 521–522

ANY content, 42–43

Apache SOAP Toolkit, 109–117

application, error caused by, 95

architecture, system
  JSP, overview of, 175–187
  n-tier model, 154–155
  overview, 151
  servlets, 155–171
  session tracking, 171–175
  three-tier model, 153
  two-tier model (simple client and server), 152

array, 99–100

ASP (Active Server Pages), 156

assertion collections
  accessing and changing information, 141
  adding data structures
    (add_publisherAssertions call),
    138–139
  deleting (delete_publisherAssertion),
    443–444
  depicting relationships between businesses
    (publisherAssertion), 131–132
  full set, getting
    (get_publisherAssertions), 447
  saving complete set
    (set_publisherAssertions call), 142

status of current business registrations
    (get_assertionStatusReport call),
    140–141, 446

tracking relationship
    (set_publisherAssertions),
    451–452

attachments, messages with, 427–428

attribute
  adding to elements, 495–496
  defining named set, 496
  property binding declaration JAXB, 249
  scoped, JSTL expression-language support,
    381–383
  SOAP, rules followed by, 428–429
  XML document, 43–46

attribute, XML
  declarations, 509
  defaults, 460
  group definitions, 510
  list declaration, 458
  types, 459
  values, 35

aural properties, XSL formatting, 476–477

authentication token, UDDI publishing
  discarding, 445–446
  obtaining, 141, 447

axes path language (XPath), 503–504

B

background properties, XSL formatting, 477–478

bindings
  deleting from UDDI publishing API, 442
  finding specific, 136, 434–435
  invoking, 21
  saving, 448–449
  schema JAXB, 242–250
  SOAP message over HTTP, 100–101,
    104–108
  specifying, SOAP 1.1 (soap:binding), 416
  UDDI data structures, 129–130
  variables to values (xsl:variable),
    498–499
  WSDL, 71–80

537

JAXM (Java API for XML Messaging) SOAP
abstraction
content, 299–300
direct connection to Web-service
endpoint, 300
interfaces, listed, 298–299
provider connection, 299
root class, 299
JAXP (Java API for XML Processing)
described, 209–211, 518
DOM, 223–238
SAX, 211–223
JAXR (Java API for XML Registries)
capability profiles, 347–348
described, 343–344, 519
registry, querying with, 366–373
XML registries, 345–347
JAXR (Java API for XML Registries)
programming model
API, 350–353
client and registry provider, active connection
(Connection object), 356–357
described, 348–350
life-cycle operations (LifeCycleManager
and BusinessLifeCycleManager),
358–363
query-manager service interfaces
(BusinessQueryManager and the
DeclarativeQueryManager), 363–366
registry information model, 353–356
JAX-RPC (Java API for XML-based Remote
Procedure Call)
described, 315–317, 519
programming model, 325–341
service deployment, 318
service description, 319–320
service endpoint definition, 317
service implementation, 318
service invocation from client, 318–319
WSDL to Java, mapping, 323–325
XML to Java, mapping, 321–323
JAX-RPC (Java API for XML-based Remote
Procedure Call) programming model
client-programming model, 326–327
client-side APIs, specified, 325–326
echo example, 327–341

JSP (Java Server Pages)
components, 177–180
custom tags, 184–187
described, 175–177, 204–206
information about, 177–178
JavaBean component, implementing with,
180–184
tag handler class, 185–187
variable, setting value (c:set), 384
JSP (Java Server Pages) directive elements
actions, 180
custom tags (taglib), 178
declarations, 179
expressions, 179
implicit objects, 179–180
include file contents, 178
page, information to server about, 178
scriptlets, 179
JSTL (Java Server Pages Standard Tag Library)
custom tags, 376–379
database support, 398–403
described, 184–185, 375–376, 381–383
expression language support tags, 383–385
flow control structures, 385–388
goals, 379–380
internationalization, 391–398
multiple descriptors, support for, 380–381
URL-related activities, 388–390
XML support, 403–409
J2EE (Java Platform 2 Enterprise Edition)
architecture, described, 189–193
JAXM, 292–293
overview, 151
platform, component and insfrastructural
services, 191–193
Web services, 193–204, 206–208
JWSDP. See Java WSDP

K

keeps, XSL formatting, 484

L

layout
objects, 461–464
properties, 484–485, 486–487
leader, formatting, 485

Y